GLOBAL COMMUNICATIONS, INTERNATIONAL AFFAIRS AND THE MEDIA SINCE 1945

Increasingly commercialised news media organisations play an important part in the global flow of modern communications. The impact of the media and their relationship to the international system has scarcely begun to be appreciated. In *Global Communications, International Affairs and the Media since 1945*, Philip Taylor traces the increased involvement of the media in issues of war and peace. The author analyses the nature, role and influence of communications within the international arena in the modern world and its interaction with foreign policy.

Politics, society, culture, the economy and foreign affairs are all now inseparable from the information created and exchanged on an international basis. Mass communication and mass media are comparatively recent phenomena but provide the conditions in which politicians, statesmen and soldiers have been increasingly forced to operate. Using case studies which include the Gulf War and Vietnam, *Global Communications* details contemporary problems of reportage whilst also providing a comprehensive historical context. This book offers a study of media in practice rather than in theory and details the realities of living in an information age.

Global Communications provides an accessible guide to this growing field for students of communications studies, media studies, international relations and international history.

Philip Taylor is Reader in International Communications and Deputy Director, Institute of Communications Studies, University of Leeds.

EXPLAINING AUSCHWITZ AND HIROSHIMA
History Writing and the Second World War, 1945–1990
R.J.B. Bosworth

IDEOLOGY AND INTERNATIONAL RELATIONS
IN THE MODERN WORLD
Alan Cassels

Forthcoming:
WAR AND COLD WAR IN THE MIDDLE EAST
Edward Ingram

NORTH EAST ASIA
An International History
John Stephan

RUSSIA AND THE WORLD IN THE
TWENTIETH CENTURY
Teddy Uldricks

REVOLUTIONARY ARMIES IN THE
MODERN ERA
S.P. MacKenzie

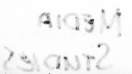

GLOBAL COMMUNICATIONS, INTERNATIONAL AFFAIRS AND THE MEDIA SINCE 1945

Philip M. Taylor

First published 1997
by Routledge
11 New Fetter Lane, London EC4P 4EE

Simultaneously published in the USA and Canada
by Routledge
29 West 35th Street, New York, NY 10001

Typeset in Times by Routledge
Printed and bound in Great Britain by T J International,
Padstow, Cornwall

British Library Cataloguing in Publication Data
A catalogue record for this book is available from the British Library

Library of Congress Cataloguing in Publication Data
Taylor, Philip M.
Global communications, international affairs and the media since 1945 /
Philip M. Taylor
Includes bibliographical references and index.
1. Communication, International. 2. Mass media–Political aspects.
3. World politics–1945–
I. Title. II. Series: New international history series.
P96.I5T39   1997
302.2–dc21   97–930
                                                CIP

ISBN 0–415–11678–3 (hbk)
ISBN 0–415–11679–1 (pbk)

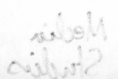

To Debbie,
for still being here

CONTENTS

CONTENTS

SERIES EDITOR'S PREFACE

What we now refer to as 'international' history was the primary concern of those whose work is now recognised as the first attempt by Europeans to conduct a truly 'historical' investigation of the past, and it has remained a central preoccupation of historians ever since. Herodotus, who attempted to explain the Persian Wars, approached the subject quite differently from his successor, Thucydides. Herodotus believed that the answers to the questions that arose from the confrontation between the Persians and the Greeks would be found in the differences between the two cultures; accordingly, he examined the traditions, customs and beliefs of the two civilisations. Critics have long pointed out that he was haphazard in his selection and cavalier in his use of evidence. The same has never been said of Thucydides, who, in attempting to explain the Peloponnesian Wars, went about his task more methodically, and who was meticulous in his use of evidence. Over the next two thousand years, men like Machiavelli, Ranke and Toynbee have added to the tradition, but the underlying dichotomy between the 'anthropological' and the 'archival' approach has remained. Diplomatic historians have been condemned as mere archive-grubbers; diplomatic history as consisting of what one file-clerk said to another. The 'world-historians', the synthesisers, have been attacked for creating structures and patterns that never existed, for offering explanations that can never be tested against the available evidence.

The aim of 'The New International History' is to combine the two traditions, to bring Herodotus and Thucydides together. While drawing upon the enormous wealth of archival research conducted by those historians who continue to work in the political tradition of formal relations between states, the authors in this series will also draw upon other avenues of investigation that have become increasingly fruitful since the Second World War. Ideology and culture, immigration and communications, myths and stereotypes, trade and finance have come to be regarded by contemporary scholars as elements essential to a good understanding of international history, and yet, while these approaches are to be found in detailed monographs and scholarly journals, many of their discoveries have not been presented in a readable and accessible form to students and the public. 'The New International History', by providing books organised along thematic, regional or historiographical lines, hopes to repair this omission.

[Anyone interested in the conduct of international relations in the twentieth century is aware of the significant – perhaps revolutionary – role that the media has come to play. Reportage and commentary in print, on radio and television, and most recently on the internet, have profoundly altered the way in which states conduct business with one another. And the relationship between journalists and officials is fraught with complications because, in spite of their dependence upon one another, they have learned to regard one another with suspicion that borders on hostility. Most students of this phenomenon come from the media world itself, and few bring to their analysis any sense of historical perspective. Their work suffers from this defect. Philip Taylor, with ground-breaking work on propaganda during First World War, between the First and Second World Wars and on the Gulf War behind him, is uniquely qualified to offer an historical synthesis of the role of the media in 'the information age'. Provocative and stimulating, careful and analytical, *Global Communications, International Affairs and the Media since 1945* is an excellent example of 'the new international history'.

Gordon Martel

PREFACE

This book stems from a long-standing interest in the role of news and image management in the context of twentieth-century foreign policy. Like many historians, however, I have always felt slightly nervous about straying away from the past and into more contemporary issues – the cherished domain of social scientists. My favourite foreign country – the USA, that is – has forced a re-think. As the sole remaining superpower, the United States is struggling to come to terms with what its role should be in the post-Cold War era. And, as a society which has always been deeply conscious of its self-image, and one indeed whose very emergence to super-power status has coincided with the communications revolution (phenomena which are not unrelated), the degree to which America is not only agonising about what its future role in the world should be, but also about how that role is *perceived*, is to some extent forcing it to reinvent itself. It is this process of reinvention which arouses, even concerns, the historical curiosity, especially if one suspects that the past is in danger of becoming yet another foreign country.

As a consequence of my first biting this bullet during the Persian Gulf War of 1991, when I was particularly alarmed at both the lack of historical context in much news reporting and with the extent to which journalists were so easily being manipulated by the largely American-led military and political establishments, I suspected that there was indeed a role for the historian in the analysis of contemporary issues. Recent trends towards more open government in democratic societies, combined with the avail-ability of new research resources such as the Internet and the World Wide Web, helped me to overcome some of the traditional obstacles which have hampered British historians especially from doing this, in particular the Thirty Year Rule. But what convinced me more than anything else was the realisation that secrecy has now become extremely difficult to sustain given the plethora of information which today reaches the public domain. To my astonishment, it was possible to glean from public sources a remarkably accurate impression of what was actually going on in the Gulf War, either while it was happening or pretty soon afterwards, in a way, for example, that would have been inconceivable so soon after the Second World War or even the Falklands conflict of 1982.

My suspicion was reinforced by the reaction to the resultant book, *War and the Media: Propaganda and Persuasion during the Gulf War* (Taylor 1992). Even though it was written within six months of the war's end, I was confident about its accuracy – and remain so even after a period of five years (I would put the figure somewhere between 95 and 98 per cent). The so-called post-war sensational 'revelations' – Iraqi soldiers being buried alive, the extent of Iraqi nuclear or chemical capabilities, the accuracy of Patriot missiles or the percentage of 'smart' weaponry used against Iraq – were all known about either during or shortly after the conflict, and had reached the public domain via the media long before they were 'dragged up' as 'fresh information on what really happened' in the subsequent televised anniversary commemorations. Of course, on-going consequences such as Gulf War Syndrome, or the Iraqi version of events while Saddam Hussein remains in power, remind us that gaps in our knowledge still exist. Memoirs by participants reduce the number of those gaps continuously. But the point is that, with careful scrutiny, it was possible to gain a reasonably accurate picture of what really happened in that conflict much sooner than perhaps ever before. In other words, the amount of new information which has emerged since 1991 has done very little to amend the fundamental view of how that conflict was fought which we were given at the time. Modifications have to be made here and there, certainly, but, overall, our picture now is only different to a minuscule degree from that which we were given, or rather had painted for us, by both the military and the media in 1991.

This might appear to be a remarkable testament, at one and the same time, to both the military's openness and the media's performance in covering the war accurately. However, the overwhelming consensus of academic opinion – to which I subscribe – is that the international media had a very poor war in 1991. The judgement is that they became part of the conflict, subjective participants in it rather than objective observers. For the most part, journalists uncritically regurgitated what they were told: they magnified the significance of issues such as the Scud–Patriot duels which were really quite insignificant militarily; they minimised the role of carpet bombing through their concentration on the 'video-game war'; and they became part of the disinformation campaign to dupe Saddam Hussein into believing that the liberation of Kuwait would take place from the sea rather than from the planned knock-out punch by land. Wittingly or unwittingly, the media provided a highly distorted image of the 'real war' in which real people – mainly Iraqi soldiers – died. And, in the process, the illusion was created that this had been a 'smart war' fought largely with 'smart technology' in which casualties were kept to a minimum. At the two key points where the war was militarily fought and won – at the receiving end of six weeks of carpet bombing and during a ferocious 100-hour ground war – the media record during Operation Desert Storm is remarkable by its absence.

After *War and the Media* appeared, I suddenly found myself being invited around the world to address journalistic and military groups, particularly the latter. I still do. After lectures delivered at NATO's military headquarters, SHAPE, and to the US Air Force Special Operations Command School in Florida, as well as at military bases in Britain and Germany, I quickly realised that the military, and the American military in particular, was far more advanced in its thinking than I had ever imagined about operating in the information age – and that professional soldiers were keen to understand the historical dimension of that thinking as it translated into new post-Cold War doctrines. It also went some way to explain their 'success' during the 'information war' in the Gulf. As an aside, it was a sobering position to realise that military personnel who actually waged war were interested in what I had to say about the media images of them doing just that. This was because, in my naïvety, I had failed to appreciate that they had not actually seen those images; they had been far too busy doing other things! But this also led to the realisation that there is far more concerted consideration in military circles about the role of the media in the information age than there ever is amongst journalists about what the military get up to when nations go to war.

So, while the military appeared to be spending a good deal of their time worrying about the media, there emerged a sense that the media really bothered about the military only when political decisions forced the armed forces to go off to war or into other dangerous situations. Military hostility to the media may indeed be a thinly disguised resentment about the whims of political expediency. Professional volunteer soldiers, especially at the officer-career level, are really no more than civil servants who, as such, are subject to the beck and call of politicians whose careers are determined by election cycles of a few years rather than by any long-term consideration for views other than their own political survival. Diplomats suffer likewise. This may well be the price of democracy but, for any public servant whose ethos is to 'serve the public', it is often a bitter pill to swallow: short-term politics in exchange for a sense of long-term service to the national interest. The media, thanks to recent trends of deregulation, competition and commercialism, have also become quite short-termist; journalists and their crews are increasingly freelance or on temporary contracts, and their sense of responsibility therefore is to their next story rather than to the institutions they either serve or report about. Consequently, there is a growing absence of institutional memory, which means that many mistakes of the past are repeated and lessons have constantly to be re-learned.

As a result, the military have been forced to become far better prepared and equipped to handle the media, in situations which attract media attention, than the media seem capable of dealing with military situations – in any other way, that is, than going native. This may well be an Anglo–American phenomenon which does not apply to Europe, given that Britain and the USA have long since abandoned conscription, and, as a result, very few contemporary journalists from those two countries have any direct personal experience of military service. Yet this appeared to be one more explanation why the majority of journalists covering the Gulf War were all too readily and uncritically prepared to accept military claims about such issues as 'collateral damage', 'interdiction', 'bomb damage assessment' and other such jargon-ridden military specialisations. And if this was the case, why therefore were the armed forces of Britain and the United States so sensitive to the media images of what they are paid to do for a living? Moreover, if it had proved to be quite easy to impose the military's agenda upon the media in the Gulf War, why not so, apparently, at other times?

This struck me as all the more interesting because it is too often forgotten – in both official and journalistic circles – that the historical record of military–media, and indeed of government–media, relations is more one of cooperation than of conflict. The demise in recent years of the specialised foreign and defence correspondents and their replacement by all-purpose reporters may well reflect trends in the commercialisation of the news media, but it has coincided with an increased professionalisation of official information management. Non-specialised reporters are therefore increasingly confronted by specialised information officers. I became concerned about how and why many members of the news media no longer seemed able to see through or beyond, or to stand back from, the official lines they were being fed. This consolidated my interest in news management, especially as I began to encounter a similar situation in the realm of diplomacy. Too often I encountered news stories which effectively were reproductions of official press releases. It has always been the case that reporters are only as good as their sources, but if they are increasingly unable to verify and cross-check the information they are being given, due to pressures of time and competition, especially in this era of 'real-time' television coverage, then how different is the media agenda from the official agenda? Moreover, given the sheer volume and variety of information which is now made available by all sorts of sources, official or otherwise, much more rapidly than ever before, something was clearly happening which cried out for further investigation.

We are currently witnessing significant changes, not just in international affairs but also in the realm of communications and the media. Analysis of contemporary news management, therefore, has to be accompanied by an examination of the apparent susceptibility of the media to resort to the kind of cheer-leading we saw during the Gulf War, as distinct from the kind of confused reporting we experienced during the war in former Yugoslavia when Western media management was notable by its absence. Was this conspiracy, or cock-up? Either way, it suggested a serious failure somewhere in the business of international journalism.

Having said that, whether as a participant or as an observer, because the media's role in international affairs is frequently overlooked in academic studies, there is a tendency to take them seriously only when they act as a catalyst of some sort. That, however, happens only infrequently. On a day-to-day basis, the media interact with world events erratically, selectively, and sometimes unpredictably. The aim of this book is to explain some of the historical roots of these and other issues being discussed about our information age. No historian likes rigid cut-off dates, but essentially the book is about the period from 1945. Where necessary, however, I have traced back certain trends before that date. It is hoped that some of the ideas contained here will serve to stimulate both further research and some rethinking about elements of the media's interface with governments in peacetime as well as in times of war. If the book can contribute to the debate about the changing role of the media, and of military and foreign affairs, in the aftermath of the Cold War, then it will have achieved its objectives. I am conscious that it will not sit easily in any disciplinary delin-eation, but it is designed for students of the media and communications, history, war studies and international affairs.

Although it has not been an easy book to write, as my wife Sue can testify, I trust that it will be easy to read. But I am aware that there are many disquieting arguments contained herein, some of which run counter to accepted wisdom in both academic and practical professional circles. I have not tried to be wilfully controversial, although I recognise that these are controversial issues. I hope, therefore, that above all this book will provoke debate, not only about the way the media and communications have been used and abused in the past but how they are likely to be in the future. More than anything, I hope it will prompt some heartfelt re-thinking about the responsibilities of journalists in a free society. I also recognise that, in places, I am generalising massively, especially with a profession as diverse as the news media. But these are issues relevant to the nature of democracy, and to the conduct within that context of interest groups such as those hard-nosed journalists who too often take refuge in a standpoint of 'that's the way the world is', rather than thinking though the consequences of their behaviour in abstract or philosophical terms. The absence of such thinking, one suspects, is why their gut reaction to media studies as an academic subject is invariably hostile. Working professional journalists have precious little time to devote to the conceptual or abstract aspects of their daily, deadline driven, routines. Training, instinct and experience are qualities which they value much higher than any form of academic or philosophical theorising. It might not be so worrying if they confined their venom to the Glasgow Media Group and other 'ivory tower' studies of what they do; but when, occasionally, members of the profession break rank with calls for more 'good news', or for more graphic descriptions of what real wars do to real people, they are also attacked, which marginalises a debate which is central

PREFACE

to what their role in society should be. This book is designed to be a starting point in this debate, especially for those who tend to take for granted the way information about what happens in the world reaches the majority of us and those who are not prepared to accept the brush-off of 'that's just the way it is'.

Crag Bottom Farm, Two Laws
December 1996

ACKNOWLEDGEMENTS

Over the past five years, I have spoken at length to numerous military and diplomatic personnel from the NATO countries about these issues, and I would like to thank them all for their time and cooperation. They would not thank me for naming them individually, and so I am respecting their wish for anonymity as serving officers and diplomats. I quote only from material that is already in the public domain.

Throughout my research, I have encountered scores of journalists who have been willing to share their experiences with me, and I would like to thank Kate Adie, John Simpson and Nik Gowing in particular for their insights. My colleagues at the Institute of Communications Studies at the University of Leeds, some of whom are former journalists, have also provided invaluable information, not least because their research brings them into regular contact with working journalists who have proved remarkably willing to find time to provide access and interviews, on which I have also drawn for this book. In particular, I should like to thank Brent MacGregor, Howard Smith, Judith Stamper, Helen Sissons and Dianne Myers, all of whom have considerable experience of how journalism operates in practice. Other colleagues have also proved amenable to share their varied disciplinary knowledge with me, especially Robin Brown who read parts of this manuscript and provided insights from his background in international relations. Nicholas Pronay, David Morrison, Richard Howells, Steven Lax, Steven Hay, Graham Roberts, David Gauntlett and Paul Statham all helped to broaden my perspective with their insights from sociology, history, media and cultural studies and technology. Nor could I fail to thank my old friend, Professor John Young of Leicester University, for his comments on this manuscript, especially those sections dealing with the Cold War, an area in which he is Britain's leading scholar.

ABBREVIATIONS
AND ACRONYMS

4POG	Fourth Psychological Operations Group
ABC	American Broadcasting Company
AFP	Agence Français Press
AP	Associated Press
BBC	British Broadcasting Corporation
BPA	Battlefield Psychological Activities
C^2W	Command and Control Warfare
CBS	Columbia Broadcasting System
CIA	Central Intelligence Agency
CMA	Civil–Military Affairs
CNN	Cable News Network
CPSU	Communist Party of the Soviet Union
DBS	Direct Broadcasting by Satellite
DoD	Department of Defense
EH	Electra House
ENG	Electronic News Gathering
ESAF	El Salvador Armed Forces
FCC	Federal Communications Commission
FMNL	Faribundo Marti Front for National Liberation
GATT	General Agreement on Tariffs and Trades
GHQ	General Headquarters
GII	Global Information Infrastructure
GLAVIT	Soviet censorship agency
GOSTELRADIO	Soviet broadcasting network
IFOR	Implementation Force (NATO in Bosnia)
INTELSAT	International Telecommunications Satellite Organization
IPS	Inter Press Service
ITN	Independent Television News
ITU	International Telecommunications Union
JUSPAO	Joint United States Public Affairs Office
KGB	Soviet intelligence organisation
LDCs	Less Developed Countries
MACV–SOG	Military Assistance Command, Vietnam–Studies and Observation Group
MIST	Military Information Support Team
MoI	Ministry of Information
MOOTW	Military Operations Other Than War

NAM	Non-Aligned Movement
NANAP	Non-Aligned News Agency Pool
NATO	North Atlantic Treaty Organisation
NBC	National Broadcasting Company
NCEO	Non Combative Evacuation Operation
NGO	Non-Governmental Organisation
NII	National Information Infrastructure
NSC	National Security Council
NVA	North Vietnamese Army
NWICO	New World Information and Communications Order
OOTW	Operations Other Than War
OPINFO	Operational Information
OSS	Office of Strategic Services
OWI	Office of War Information
PAO	Public Affairs Officer (US)
PAT	PSYOP Analyst Terminal
PCA	Psychological Consolidation Activities
PID	Political Intelligence Department
PIO	Public Information Officer (UK)
PKK	Kurdish Workers Party
PoW	Prisoner of War
PSYOP(S)	Psychological Operation(s)
PSYWAR	Psychological Warfare
PWB	Psychological Warfare Branch, SHAEF
PWD	Psychological Warfare Division, SHAEF
PWE	Political Warfare Executive
RAF	Royal Air Force
RFE	Radio Free Europe
RL	Radio Liberty
SDI	Strategic Defense Initiative ('Star Wars')
SHAEF	Supreme Headquarters, Allied Expeditionary Force
SHAPE	Supreme Headquarters, Allied Powers, Europe
SOE	Special Operations Executive
SPA	Strategical Psychological Activities
TASS	Official Soviet news agency
UN	United Nations
UNESCO	United Nations Educational, Scientific and Cultural Organisation
UNITAF	United Nations Task Force
UPI	United Press International
USIA	United States Information Agency
VOA	Voice of America

INTRODUCTION – THE THIRD WAVE AND THE FOURTH DIMENSION
Communications and the media in the information age

⌈Our world is undergoing significant changes and the bland are leading the blind. Politicians speak in sound-bites while newspaper headlines compress the complexities of the world into clichés.⌉ Ours is a world in which television talk-show hosts have replaced political commentators as the principal interlocutors of prime ministerial and presidential aspirations at election time, and a world where sleaze and sophistry have triumphed over sophistication and subtlety in the media. Politics and public information about it is increasingly 'packaged'[2] for ready consumption in a manner more akin to entertainment than instruction or information – hence the advent of a new word: 'infotainment'. Live television brings the dramatic doings of the globe into our living rooms instantaneously. It is a fast world, with fast morals and fast media – and seemingly vast problems.

On the surface, such phenomena as tabloid journalism and 'real-time' television are harmless attempts to explain a complicated world full of complex issues in a manner which helps the public to understand them better, and in an entertaining and exciting way, so that informed decisions can be made about the collective well-being. As such, it could be argued, modern journalism serves the public well as a force for their democratic 'right to know', imparting news and information in ways which serve their democratic 'need to know'. If this has to be done in an entertaining or exciting manner, then surely that says far more about the audience than it does about the journalists who serve that audience?

This is a standard argument from the increasingly commercialised news media organisations which today play such an important part in the global flow of communications. But there is another way of looking at it, especially in so far as international affairs are concerned. World events demand better, fuller and more contextualised reporting than they currently receive. So, too, does an informed citizenship in an increasingly globalised world. Reducing foreign news coverage to an alleged 'lowest common denominator' may well in fact be a recipe for over-simplification to the point of serious distortion and misunderstanding. In reality, does the practice of covering world events in twelve column inches or a three-minute news segment encourage prejudice

1

rather than empathy, national pride rather than international harmony, and emotional rather than rational judgements?

ORDER AND DISORDER IN THE INFORMATION AGE

Since the Cold War was officially declared over in 1990, to be followed by the collapse of the Soviet Union and the announcement by US President Bush of the existence of a 'New World Order', global events now appear to be moving so rapidly and chaotically that *disorder* seems a more appropriate description of what is happening in the international system. It has even been suggested that an 'unparalleled popular interest in international affairs' has taken place as 'a natural reaction to the spectacle of a shrinking globe, a sober reflection on the part of millions of bewildered people who have learned through bitter experience that their own lives and fortunes may be jeopardised by the turn of events in a remote part of the world'.[3] Those who have yet to consult the note might guess that those words were written quite recently – in 1991 perhaps, possibly even as far back as 1989. In fact they were written in 1940, in one of the earliest textbooks specifically dedicated to international relations. Historians often irritate other scholars when they point out that there is rarely anything new under the sun. The phrase 'New World Order', after all, was used by H. G. Wells as long ago as 1944.[4]

From the establishment of the international news agencies in the mid-nineteenth century to the formation of the global digital superhighways of today, the speed at which information flows around the world has revolutionised every aspect of our daily lives in ways no less significant than the agricultural and industrial revolutions did so. This 'communications revolution'[5] had no tangible beginnings, in that it can be traced back variously to the development of the printing press, of writing, even of language, and it is certainly far from finished as we approach the next millennium in anticipation of travelling through 'cyberspace'. But the past one hundred and fifty years, and the past fifty especially, have seen it accelerate at an ever more rapid rate, to the point where it is now almost impossible to understand how our world ever functioned without telephones, television or computers. Indeed, as Hamid Mowlana has pointed out, 'the technologies and institutions of communication that have become so central to world politics and economics over the past couple of decades have fundamentally altered the nature and sources of power and influence, both domestically and internationally'.[6]

We quickly take so much of this change for granted. The fluctuating price of coffee, the postcard from a friend on holiday, the telephone call to an emigrant relative, the news report from South Africa, the televisation of the Olympic Games in Atlanta, the cheap last-minute flight advertised on Teletext, the latest blockbuster feature film from Bombay on video, logging on to the World Wide Web – all these aspects of international communications are now so commonplace that they function almost invisibly in the background of our daily lives. In fact, they are central to the running of what we now call, not wholly appropriately, our global village. Indeed politics, society, culture, the economy and foreign affairs all now operate inseparably from the information created, shared and exchanged on an international basis, while the mass media continue to occupy the most significant place for most people when they access the world beyond their immediate environment. That the mass media are almost entirely twentieth-century phenomena is what, quite simply, has made this millennium fundamentally different from all those that have gone before it. Together, perhaps, with the internal combustion engine, penicillin and the splitting of the atom, they have served to transform the very nature not only of how human beings live their lives but of how they perceive the world around them.

But when we start to think a little more about the messages and images being carried to us from different parts of the globe by the media, those of us who care become less complacent. Wars, famines, floods, terrorist attacks and genocide appear on our television screens almost nightly, prompting cries from the concerned to 'do something'. What, precisely, should be done is rarely clear, but do *something*. In this respect, the Cold War, for all its dangers and crises, at least appeared to provide a degree of order in the form of an East–West superpower rivalry around which world events revolved for almost half a century. Military planners even talk almost nostalgically about 'the good old days' when at least they knew who their friends and enemies were. What has happened since? How much has actually changed? Is the world indeed more chaotic, a safer or a more dangerous place? And besides, how many of us actually care anyway?

If the term 'communications revolution' means anything, it involves the shift from interpersonal to mediated communication – in other words to a form of communication whereby external sources of information to which we would not otherwise have had access are provided for us by others. And this process is happening at an ever-accelerating pace, while the sheer number and variety of such sources is proliferating to the point that we could be forgiven for feeling that we are suffering from an information overload. Jean Baudrillard, that doyen of post-modernist thinking, has put it thus: 'there is more and more information, and less and less meaning'.[7] In order to begin an appreciation of what he means by this, it is necessary that we first understand the processes involved in getting all this information into the public domain, by which more and more sophisticated technologies are employed to mediate what is, after all, essentially one group of people's world-view to the rest of us. And this begs the question of whether the world really is more chaotic and less meaningful, or does it simply appear so because the version we are getting of it via the media is so much more varied and therefore more confusing? Or are the media simply failing to explain world events as clearly as they had once been able to do in the past? How many people, for example, could honestly own up to understanding what was happening in the war in former Yugoslavia, even though it was covered extensively by the media for three and a half years? In other words, as more people have more access to more information, more rapidly than ever before, is this aiding clarity or merely creating confusion? Moreover, now that there is the beginning of a discernible shift from mediated communications back to personal communications, namely the ability, thanks to technology like the Internet, for individuals to by-pass the traditional mass media and to gain direct access to information about world events, is there now a possibility that clarity will displace confusion, that the blind will see and the bland will go away? Apart from the likely consequences for the future of the mass media, will the digital superhighways lead to greater empowerment for individuals who no longer have to rely upon other people's world-views because they now have the capacity to form their own? Furthermore, will these digital highways merely prove eventually to be every bit as congested as their concrete counterparts have become?

Although mass communication and the mass media are comparatively recent phenomena, barely a century old, we have scarcely begun to appreciate their relationship to the international system, whether as contributors to, or merely conveying a sense of, its order and disorder. Historians as a profession, it has to be said, have not served this uniqueness particularly well. Even now, very few general history textbooks mention communications and the media, except possibly in passing, and although a considerable amount of high-quality historical research has been undertaken into specific areas and specific subjects – the two World Wars, the role of cinema and radio, the use of the media as an instrument of propaganda[8] – very little of it has yet to penetrate the 'mainstream' of historical writing and teaching about this mass media century of ours. The Cold War, for example, looks very different when viewed through the films emanating from Hollywood and Peking or the broadcasts of Radio Moscow and the Voice of America than it does from the diplomatic papers of the State Department and the Kremlin. It looks different still if looked at through a combination of these sources. Yet there remains a tendency for history textbooks to rely on traditional sources to tell the story, and it is left to that strange new subspecies, the media historian, to revise how that story was perceived *at the time* by the wider public through the media available to them. Often this history from the middle casts fresh light on events above and below it, as a window, a mirror or a prism, but alas only slowly do mainstream historians take this on board as they continue in their assumption that politicians, statesmen and soldiers make history, not the media. Up to a point, of course, they are right, but to ignore or minimise the conditions in which those statesmen and soldiers increasingly have been forced to operate as the century has unfolded is to miss the fundamental reality of what has been termed our 'information age'.

This is a book about that reality. It is an area which so far has been charted mainly by non-historians: programme-makers on how politicians have used television,[9] journalists writing about their experiences and insights,[10] or scholars working in other academic disciplines, notably sociology, political science, media studies and cultural studies. It is perhaps to be expected that such analysts will concern themselves with current issues, while historians not unnaturally confine themselves to the past. Perhaps, some might think, that is where they should stay. Arthur Schlesinger is one who would disagree. In 1970, when discussing Daniel Bell's sociological notion of a 'post-industrial society',[11] he argued that 'as the nation at the extreme frontier of technological development, America has been the first to experience the unremitting shock and disruptive intensity of accelerated change. The crises we are living through are the crises of modernity. Every nation, as it begins to reach a comparable state of technical development, will have to undergo comparable crises'.[12] The key words here are 'accelerated change'. Because many scholars of contemporary issues are identifying so many areas of change – from globalisation on a wider front to new patterns of work and leisure much closer to home – and because so much of this relates to matters of communication and information, an understanding of the past is essential in order to identify what it is that things are changing *from*, and what really is new. And this is why we are beginning to see the emergence of that other new subspecies of recent evolution, the contemporary historian, who is uniquely equipped to place events like the war in former Yugoslavia in their due historical perspective.

There are, however, so many different approaches to a subject like communications and the media that one can quickly be forgiven for sensing that one is approaching a minefield. Not only do practitioners rarely see eye to eye with the academics who write about what they do, but the huge number of different academic disciplines looking at this field also tends to be divided within and amongst themselves about the best way of going about their research. Of course there are very good reasons for these divisions: historical reasons. Yet the academic diaspora of media scholars has led to a multiplicity of methodological approaches that often serves more to fragment than to unify the field.[13] Hence scholars from departments of English, dealing with the media as popular culture texts, clash with empirical sociologists who assemble data about their reception. Electrical engineers who write about the transformation of telecommunications from analogue to digital formats in terms of graphs and scientific equations tend to be beyond the comprehension of both. Yet while communications and the media constitute interesting subjects in their own right, whether viewed from a sociological or cultural or any other point of view, they simply cannot be separated from the conditions in which they operate. Modern communication is indeed about technology, but it also about human creativity. Because *something* is communicated to *someone*, an *impact* or an *influence* is likely to be the result, which often depends on how *creatively* the *content* of communications is *deployed*.

5

What that impact is and how it is measured, however, has again been the subject of continuing, and often ferocious, debate. Psychologists, for example, who attempt to evaluate the impact of televised violence on children, clash with others who argue that television cannot be blamed because some other sociological factors have to be considered. It is a damning testament to this fragmentation that, after almost forty years of research into television audiences (longer, if one includes similar research into cinema) there is no conclusive evidence either way that satisfies researchers from all the different disciplinary backgrounds. This failure is more serious than it may at first appear, since in fact it undermines all other research into the media and communications in whatever disciplinary branch, since no matter how much scholars talk about the media as cultural 'texts' and how people read them, or the effectiveness of propaganda or advertising campaigns, the question always remains: 'Yes, but does it work?' In other words, because we have not yet developed a satisfactory model to prove a direct causal link between media influence and human behaviour, all the research which scholars do into subjects ranging from pornography to cultural imperialism is undermined by the retort: 'prove it'.

One response to this might be: 'prove it didn't work'. However, the absence of a universally accepted causal link haunts those who, for example, take an unpopular stand in the latest moral panic about television and the violent behaviour of children when they are met by the retort: 'yes, but there must be a link, or else why would advertisers spend so much money persuading us to buy their products?' Of course, there is evidence that some people respond to certain images or messages in a certain way at certain times. And simple common sense tells us that the media must have some influence, not least because it is not just advertisers, but also governments and media corporations, who spend vast amounts of money on persuasion in the belief that it is worth the expense in terms of likely returns. But why certain people respond, or do not respond, to certain messages at certain other times and in certain other circumstances remains an inexact science – rather, as Karl Popper reminded us long ago, like history itself.

Just because a proven causal link has yet to be found, however, does not automatically mean that one does not exist; merely that we have yet to find it. This is because an approach to communications requires not one but a multitude of disciplinary approaches. For this is the ultimate interdisciplinary, or multi-disciplinary, subject. It transcends – or should do – the traditional arts/science/social science divides. To even begin to understand how communications function within the context of our modern world, we need to embrace technology, psychology, sociology, political science, philosophy, law, textual analysis and linguistics, media and communications studies and audience research. We must therefore begin to consider ways of drawing from the sheer variety of disciplinary approaches, theoretical and empirical, and testing findings in the real world, if the necessary intellectual breakthrough needed to take us all forward is to be found. Nor is the historian irrelevant in all this, for his or her experience in evaluating masses of different pieces of evidence, as well as providing some long-term historical context and perspective, is essential if we are to appreciate just what it is about the information age which makes it different from previous periods in human history, and what the consequences of this are.

There can be little doubt that the world's geo-political configuration in the 1990s is fundamentally different from that of the five decades which preceded it. But whether disorder has replaced the order that was the Cold War is open to considerable doubt. International organisations are increasing in number, at political, economic, environmental and all sorts of other levels. Global communications facilitate increased awareness of events throughout a 'shrinking world', even in those diminishing number of places which still erect barriers to inhibit the flow of information. The very buzzword 'globalisation' suggests an unprecedented degree of interconnectedness. This has been going on for some time, although to some extent the Cold War and the erection of 'iron' or 'bamboo' curtains tended to conceal the degree to which the process was taking place. Indeed, ever since the laying of a global cable network in the mid-nineteenth century, the acquisition of ever-increasing quantities of information has required mounting specialisation on the part of 'experts' to make sense of it all. Hence the rise of the international news agencies which specialised in the gathering of global data as a commodity to be sold on to their customers in the media. Without such expertise, or without a framework such as the bi-polar nature of the Cold War through which events can be viewed in simplistic terms, perhaps the world has, and always will, be seen as chaotic or disordered. The question for most people, therefore, is not so much a matter of 'the more you know, the less you understand' but rather one of 'how do I make sense of the world given the masses of information now available?' For the non-specialist, a principal function of the mass media is to help them do this. Media performance thus becomes a matter of vital concern.

REINVENTING WHEELS

As the Cold War drew to a close between 1989 and 1991, there was much talk of 'an end of history', by which its principal proponent, Francis Fukuyama, meant the triumph of liberal democracy over the forces of authoritarianism which had threatened its emergence throughout this century or indeed since the Enlightenment.[14] Among other things, Fukuyama suggested:

> It is frequently asserted that global information technology and instant communications have promoted democratic ideals, as in the case of CNN's world-wide broadcasting of the occupation of Tienanmen Square in 1989, or of the revolutions in Eastern Europe later that year.[15]

7

So indeed it is, but Fukuyama was also correct to point out that 'communications technology itself is value-neutral' because 'the ability of technology to better human life is critically dependent on a parallel moral progress in man'.[16] We would do well to remember these admittedly high-sounding words when next confronted with the inevitable grandiose claims made for the latest technological breakthrough in communications and how they will benefit the human race.

This is because we will in fact have heard it all before. When President Buchanan and Queen Victoria celebrated the laying of the trans-Atlantic telegraph cable by exchanging messages in 1858, one newspaper felt that 'tomorrow the hearts of the civilised world will beat in a single pulse, and from that time forth forevermore the continental divisions of the earth will, in a measure, lose those conditions of time and distance which now mark their relations'.[17] Alexander Graham Bell wrote of his invention of the telephone in 1876 that 'I believe in the future wires will unite the head offices of telephone companies in different cities, and a man in one part of the country may communicate by word of mouth with another in a distant place'.[18] What is now commonplace seemed like science fiction then. Guglielmo Marconi, the inventor of wireless telegraphy, went further, stating that 'communication between peoples widely separated in space and thought is undoubtedly the greatest weapon against the evils of misunderstanding and jealousy'.[19] The development of his invention into radio broadcasting was greeted with even greater euphoria. Radio, it was felt, was particularly well placed to fight these demons by virtue of its inherent point-to-multipoint characteristics which enabled it to transcend literacy, race, creed, culture, class and country. As such it was seen as a great force for national unity on the one hand and for greater international understanding on the other. With the growth of international broadcasting in the 1930s, idealists saw the potential for the 'linking of all the inhabitable parts of the globe with abundant, cheap, significant, true information about the world from day to day'.[20] Hilda Matheson, a senior BBC executive in the 1930s, saw broadcasting as 'a huge agency of standardisation, the greatest the world has ever seen'.[21] In his speech inaugurating the BBC's Empire Service in 1932, Sir John (later Lord) Reith stated: 'it has been our resolve that the great possibilities and influences of the medium should be exploited to the highest human advantage. . . . the service as a whole is dedicated to the best interests of mankind.'[22] A World War later, not to mention the Holocaust, Stalin's purges, and genocide in Bosnia and Rwanda, it is indeed fair to recall such words with a degree of scepticism.

Sometimes this kind of lofty idealism was accompanied by a suspicion that, in the wrong hands, communications could serve precisely the opposite intentions. Reith, the founding Director General of the BBC, worried:

The wireless, one of the great gifts of Providence to mankind, is a trust of which we are humble ministers. Our prayer is that nothing mean or cheap may lessen its value, and that its message may bring happiness and comfort to those who listen.[23]

That prayer fell on the deaf ears of one Josef Paul Goebbels, who realised that 'real broadcasting is true propaganda. Propaganda means fighting on all battlefields of the spirit, generating, multiplying, destroying, exterminating, building and undoing'.[24] In short, the history of communication technologies is a parallel story of high optimism about their potential for good followed by a record of abuse on the part of unscrupulous individuals, organisations and governments exploiting them for their own purposes.

Nonetheless, the belief that communications can serve a positive purpose, empowering individuals, liberating them while uniting them into a global civilisation, continues to permeate the rhetoric of politicians and technocrats alike. When US Vice-President Al Gore called for the creation of a Global Information Infrastructure (GII) at the International Telecommunications Union (ITU) conference at Buenos Aires in March 1994, he argued that it could:

help educate our children and allow us to exchange ideas in and within a community and among nations. It will be a means by which families and friends will transcend the barriers of time and distance. It will make possible a global information marketplace, where consumers can buy or sell products. . . . The development of the GII must be a cooperative effort among governments and peoples. It cannot be dictated or built by a single country. It must be a democratic effort. And the distributed intelligence of the GII will spread participatory democracy.[25]

There is much to address in this – and it has been greeted sceptically by influential sections of the academic community[26] – but the one thing it clearly reveals is that history does not end but merely repeats itself.

That aside, the Fukuyama debate did serve to present 'a challenge to historians to break some of their conventions and patterns of thinking which hardened into orthodoxies at the same time as the Cold War seemed to freeze the world-historical process in the post-war era'.[27] Regardless therefore of the contribution which historians can make to the interdisciplinary study of communications and their impact, one can only hope this will also apply to their own historical studies of our mass media age. However, even after half a century, there is still a remarkable paucity of works on the history of television. Cinema, twice as old and half as important during the past fifty years, has recently fared much better – especially as the centenary of the medium approached[28] – and now scholars from a variety of disciplines recognise the significance of cinema films, whether as texts within their own cultural terms or within the context of mirroring their times. Radio, although served seminally by Asa Briggs in the United Kingdom and Erik Barnow in the United States, still has some way to go and remains something of a poor relation.[29] But television, that most pervasive medium of our generation, has yet to be deemed worthy of serious historical consideration.

Again, there are some understandable explanations for this. Archives and evidence are the lifeblood of the historical profession. A lamentable fact is that there is no archive anywhere in the world where all the broadcast output of a television or radio station has been preserved from its inception. Television programmes are made to be broadcast, not preserved, especially since they are made by commercial organisations whose only incentive to keep them is the possibility of sale to a nostalgic cable channel or retransmission at some later date. Preserving their output for future historical research is simply not within their institutional culture. Tapes are wiped for re-use, their content gone forever with the wind. I have argued elsewhere that this failure to preserve our contemporary communications heritage – even down to electronic forms of communication such as e-mail – is likely to have disastrous effects for future generations of historians who, from the standpoint of 2096, will look back to the one-time uniqueness of the twentieth century only to find that they have no more than a patchwork of randomly preserved media output for their research purposes.[30] But however disposable the media might appear to us to be at the moment, they have become an integral part of our world and are therefore worthy of study as to why this is so, which in turn may tell us something about ourselves, their consumers.

While the mass media remain the principal means through which most people glean their view of the world, communications technologies do provide alternatives in the form of personal communications. The first of these was of course the telephone, although today we must add the fax machine and the modem if we talk of instantaneous communication. Other forms of personal communication that enable us to by-pass the media by 'time-shifting' or recording messages for absorption at a later time include the telephone answer machine, audio and video cassettes and even the photocopier. These technologies empower individuals by virtue of the fact that they potentially decrease dependence on the media of press, radio, film and television as sole providers of information at pre-set times, and we will see how they have been used in recent years as alternative sources, especially in societies where there are state-controlled mass media. This raises some doubts about the continuing validity of the phrase 'mass communication', in that technology is enabling individuals to communicate information on a mass scale, and globally, in ways that have not been possible before. What we are beginning to see emerge is a 'mass of individual communication' that forces us to re-think what we have traditionally understood to be the 'public sphere'. The mass media remain central to that public sphere but no longer enjoy a near-monopolistic role in communicating public information around it. Perhaps that is why they are shifting their emphasis away from traditional methods of reporting world events in order to compete more effectively at the level of infotainment. Hence the surprise which the *Daily Mirror* created in Britain in November 1996 when it ran a foreign news story on its front page – a picture of a starving child from Zaire above the headline: 'PLEASE HELP ME'.[31] So unusual was this exception to the recent norm that it merely served to reinforce how much the mass media have changed their priorities in recent years. Yet for all the alarmist media coverage about an impending crisis in Zaire in late 1996, international humanitarian intervention was not deemed necessary, which begs the question of how well the media understood the issues involved or how capable they were in communicating realistic options to their consumers.

THE THIRD WAVE

The end-of-history debate prompted some, almost philosophical, thinking by historians about the relevance of what they do. It also provided an extremely useful analogy for our purposes here, namely the notion that a single monumental event is like a stone being thrown into the centre of a lake, creating ripples which make their inevitable way to the shoreline. The French Revolution was one such occasion, the events of 1989–91 another. Although we have no single monumental event here, we do have stones – communications technologies – and we do have ripples or rather, to borrow from Alvin Toffler, the waves which they create.

In 1980 Toffler articulated his notion of what he described as the Third Wave, by which he meant that societies evolve from their initial agricultural base (first wave) through the process of industrialisation (second wave) to the more recent post-industrial or 'post-modern' era in which knowledge-based industries are superseding the farm and the factory in economic and societal significance.[32] When these waves collide and overlap, they create tensions or crises. The gathering, processing, evaluation and presentation of information about the world in which we live forms the basis of this third wave now making its way to the shoreline of many countries, and not just in cutting-edge info-societies like the United States but in other countries – developed and developing – as well. Toffler suggested that:

> The Third Wave brings with it a genuinely new way of life based on diversified, renewable energy sources; on methods of production that make most factory assembly lines obsolete; on new, non-nuclear families; on a novel institution that might be called the 'electronic cottage'; and on radically changed schools and corporations of the future. . . . It

11

is a civilization with its own distinctive world outlook, its own ways of dealing with time, space, logic and causality.[33]

Although Toffler's ideas have proved highly influential in the corridors of power, one has to search very hard in the vast academic literature about communications to find even the most passing reference to his work.[34]

In *The Third Wave* (1980) and, more recently, *War and Anti-War* (1993) Toffler postulates some interesting notions about the monumental changes we are undergoing in the information age and how we might understand and respond to what can appear to be the kind of chaotic global developments described in our 1940 international relations textbook. Before we do that, however, we might first consider the nature of chaos itself and borrow from scientific theory. It has been pointed out that 'Chaos has become not just theory but also method, not just a canon of beliefs but also a way of doing science'.[35] It can also be a way of understanding the information age in which we live. One needs to bear in mind, however, that Chaos Theory is the most inappropriate of scientific labels. To the casual observer, for example, international affairs appear to be an unpredictable business conducted by unfathomable people. Likewise, Chaos Theory appears to be a random process whereby seemingly unrelated events affect events elsewhere in the world, popularised by the analogy that the flapping of a butterfly's wings in China can affect weather patterns a month later in New York. Yet Chaos Theory is a highly complicated mathematical process whereby order is given to disorder. Scientists are discovering that there are patterns to ascertain the flapping movements back and forth of a flag in the wind or the rising column of cigarette smoke which breaks into swirls. Similarly with international affairs, most analysts would agree that there is an order masquerading as disorder. This order is aperiodic, in that it consists of trends that never quite find a steady state; events almost repeat their patterns of behaviour from one crisis to another, but never succeed in doing so in quite the same way. Nonetheless, if we analyse those patterns, we can begin to bring ordered analysis to what has previously appeared to be disordered behaviour. Although I would suggest that this is as good a way as any for researching history, I would not offer this model as a means of forecasting, since measurements can never really be perfect and history never repeats itself precisely. But, given a certain set of ingredients, we can have a pretty good idea of what will turn out. All we need thereafter is the courage of our convictions. The problem is that a chain of events in any given crisis can contain a critical point of tension that can magnify small changes ('for want of a nail, the shoe was lost; for want of a shoe, the horse was lost' and so on). In Chaos Theory, such critical points are everywhere, especially when the media are present. Occasionally, the media even create those critical points, as when pictures of a butchered American airman being dragged through a warlord's camp in Somalia prompted a change of direction in

American foreign policy. However, once we understand how news journalism responds to the flapping of a butterfly's wings in some part of the globe, and not to others, we can begin to see why Bosnia and Rwanda received massive media coverage and Ngorno-Karrabach and East Timor did not. On the other hand, this may all be over-elaboration; it may just be a simple matter of practicalities. As Mort Rosenblum of the Associated Press, who was on the spot in Ngorno-Karrabach when war first broke out but who was unable to find any means of physically or technically communicating his copy from the war zone, put it: 'It was a great story and, naturally, there was no way to file it.' [36]

If we accept Toffler's premise that the pace at which things are changing is not only accelerating at a destabilising rate, itself difficult enough for the individual to adapt to, but also that the acceleration itself is having profound effects on every aspect of the 'way we relate to other people, to things, to the entire universe of ideas, art and values',[37] then this can affect the rate of making decisions. All decision-making systems have limits as to how fast they can adjust in order to make complex decisions. It is my contention in this book that this accelerated pace has been progressively affecting the conduct of international affairs since 1945 and that the ripples created by the introduction of new communication technologies are influencing the way decisions about war and peace are not just made but are also perceived through the media. And that perception is not necessarily a picture of the world as it is, but a flawed construct created by the distortion, compression and manipulation, not necessarily of communication technologies themselves (although that happens) but of the increasing amounts of information they carry. Simplification masquerades as complexity, illusions masquerade as reality, texts masquerade as context and quantity masquerades as quality. These developments, I would suggest, actually contribute not only to the appearance of chaos but also to the making of crises. They certainly serve to alter their nature.

In the 1960s, there were great hopes that the computer would somehow solve the problem of this accelerated rate of change, especially because of its ability to handle the vast amounts of information becoming available, and that it would therefore simplify the increasing complexity of life. But a computer, like any other decision-making apparatus, is only as good as the *quality* of information it receives. Today, the speed at which information travels, whether in 'cyberspace' or on what is termed 'real-time' television, does not automatically produce a situation conducive to sensible, considered decision-making. A few years ago, a conference was held with the title: 'It's Live, but is it Real?'[38] Many post-modernist philosophers find this an extremely fertile field for discussion. Here, we will confine ourselves to less ambitious debates, although we will end up in the same territory.

Many writers now agree that information, including misinformation, will change the world politically, militarily and economically. In *The Third Wave*,

Toffler argued that if we look at global power in the broadest sense the most basic division in the world was not between East and West, but between agricultural (first-wave) and industrial (second-wave) powers. Now, a process of 'trisection' is taking place, in other words the world system is splitting into three parts – three different layers or tiers – or rather three different 'civilizations'. First-wave agricultural societies will continue to exist along-side the mass-manufacturing, cheap-labour supplying, societies during this transitional period. But we are now seeing the emergence of information-intensive third-wave powers whose economies depend not on the plough or the assembly-line but on 'brainpower'. Toffler's influence can be identified in Al Gore's speech to the ITU about the GII, when the Vice-President stated:

> Approximately 60 per cent of all US workers are 'knowledge workers' – people whose jobs depend on the information they generate and receive over our information infrastructure. As we create new jobs, 8 out of 10 are in information-intensive sectors of our economy.[39]

In other words, the US is already surfing the third wave and, following the Clinton administration's call to implement a National Information Infrastructure, it intends to keep doing so.

The use of the word 'civilization' is justified not just because the technology is changing but also because all the social institutions designed for the second wave – for a mass production, mass media, mass society – are in crisis, and this includes the health system, the family, the education system, transportation, various ecological systems – as well as our value and epistemological systems. As this happens, the shock waves created by these changes collide with the old. When the first and the second waves collided in the past, there were civil wars, upheavals, political revolutions and forced migrations. Now, as the third wave gains momentum and clashes with the other two, new power structures, new ways of conducting international affairs and new ways of waging war and creating peace are likely to emerge.

Because those riding each wave have different interests and require different resources, they view the world from different perspectives. This creates tension as second-wave powers which have a vested interest in protecting their existing industrial power base fear that they will be swept aside by the global tidal wave of information and communications. Hence Iran bans satellite dishes, China fears the 'disinformation' carried on the Internet, the Pentagon fears 'info-bombers' sending viruses into defence computers, and so on, but the third wave continues to batter on their walls because, no matter how much countries emulate the position of King Canute, the waves are unstoppable.

Even *within* societies these waves are clashing simultaneously, thanks to the relentless internationalisation of communications and information. For example, in Brazil tribal populations are being cleared to make room for agriculture while the cities concurrently explode with factories built along-side office blocks wired to the global economy. India and China provide further examples as they try to balance the relationship between all three waves. Moreover, Toffler suggests that, because mass society was a product of the industrial revolution and, as that revolution and its institutions disintegrate around us, at least in the developed world, a process of 'demassification' is now occurring. For example, once it was necessary to send a roll of film to be processed in a central laboratory for return in a few days, but then came the high street store which could develop it overnight. Then it became a one-hour service. Since the 1960s we have Polaroid technology which places the entire process in our individual hands, there and then. Of course, not everyone has a Polaroid camera, because some people still prefer to use the high street store and many are dissatisfied with the quality of Polaroid photographs. The same analogy could be applied to the media. Likewise, telephone answer machines and video-recorders enable us to re-order the time at which information can be consumed. And 'demassification' also has ramifications for the mass media, as people turn more and more to alternative forms of information, for example via the Internet, and become less dependent on those second-wave technologies, in other words on the mass media. Again, people still buy newspapers and watch television, but the Internet – though much hyped – is in fact proving to be the fastest growing medium of international communications, with more than 50 million users world-wide by the mid 1990s. Within a period of barely five years, thanks to the affordable personal computer and the modem, it has evolved from being a system of linked computers used by academic and military elites into the first truly third-wave global mass medium. But it is not a mass medium in the second-wave sense. Rather, it allows individuals to access the information contained on millions of computers world-wide directly, nearly instantaneously, and individually, when they choose to log-on rather than having that incalculable amount of data mediated to them by a newspaper, radio or television station produced in accordance with pre-set schedules and deadlines.

In *War and Anti-War*, Toffler extended his premise by arguing that the way states make war is similar to the way they make wealth: if the way wealth is made is changed, you inevitably change the way you make war. And if you change the way you make war, there are new ways of thinking to be done about changing the way you make peace. Agricultural societies waged war seasonally, with farmer–soldiers forming small armies to fight battles outside the growing season. With the coming of the industrial revolution, particularly following Napoleon and the French Revolution, mass production was accompanied by mass conscription. The machine society produced machine guns which caused mass destruction – industrialised warfare. And if we are now in the process of transforming the way we create wealth, from the industrial to the informational process, there is a parallel change taking place with warfare, of which the Gulf War of 1991 provided us with our first real insight of the shape of things to come.

Just as the economy has become increasingly dependent on information, so also has the military. Knowledge-based strategies now form the basis of out-thinking military opponents and minimising casualties, while 'smart' weapons are more capable of achieving specific goals with unprecedented accuracy than the old-fashioned, second-wave, 'dumb' variety. Knowledge weapons and information warfare thus assume a position of centrality in third-wave warfare, rather than standing at the periphery as in the second or being virtually non-existent as in the first. Conversely, the ability to sustain peace will depend increasingly on the acquisition, processing, dissemination and control of knowledge, whether it be the satellite surveillance of troop movements, the deployment of targeted information, or neutralising free-lance nuclear scientists and computer hackers to pre-empt and counteract terrorism. And just as the economy demassifies to form third-wave niche markets, so also does warfare change into a form of niche warfare; instead of one giant conflict (the Cold War) we now have a host of small wars, no two of which are alike.

Such thinking logically leads to a need for governments to consider proactive measures in the use of knowledge and information to support national or even supranational objectives with regard to each new crisis or conflict, to ride the wave rather than be drowned by it. Knowledge-based societies, in other words, value knowledge weapons to support their national or international objectives. Internally, they agonise about issues such as the future role of government in some kind of demassified 'electronic democracy', but the conduct of external relations could hardly be allowed to go down the same route. This brings us to propaganda. This much misunderstood word is not used here in the usual popular pejorative sense. To most people, propaganda alas remains a dirty word involving dirty tricks, a process designed to seduce people into believing something they would not otherwise have believed. For many, propaganda equates with falsehoods or, at best, half-truths. It is nasty because it is devious, manipulative and dangerous. In Western culture, moreover, it is associated with totalitarianism and war while its most famous exponents remain Adolf Hitler and Josef Goebbels, and successive communist leaders from Stalin to Mao to Kim Il Sung. Yet there is a delusion in democracies that propaganda is something which only those types of regime go in for and which democracies are forced into only reluctantly when confronted by war against such adversaries.

Most historians who have investigated its increasing deployment during the course of this century agree that, as a process, propaganda is also a value-neutral concept. It is neither a 'good' nor a 'bad' thing; it merely *is*. It is a process of persuasion distinguished by other processes deploying information – such as advertising and even education – by the question of intent.[40] The intentions of those undertaking the process ought to be the object of scrutiny and judgement, not the process itself. The techniques employed are after all frequently common to other persuasive processes, but if the intent is to persuade people to think and behave in a way desired by the source, then it is propaganda. But it might not be 'bad' propaganda, in that the intention might be eminently honourable: because of its historical associations with the excesses and abuses of the Third Reich or the Soviet Union, this should not automatically damn all propaganda, although it has tended to do so in the popular mind. But what about propaganda for peace, for example? Is that automatically a bad thing? It is if you are a warmonger! The intentions of the source and the interests of the recipient may well coincide, which is why practitioners talk about 'consolidation propaganda'. And while, in public, practitioners tend to eschew the word in favour of such euphemisms as 'publicity', 'political advertising', 'public information' and even 'marketing', the archives are resplendent with examples of how they are quite prepared privately to admit that they are indeed in the business of propaganda. Democracies have evolved a tradition of 'propaganda with facts' but, as a Soviet journalist pointed out in the 1960s, 'you can make people believe a fact if you express that fact "without prejudice". And facts can be selected in such a way that of themselves they will make the hearer reach the desired conclusion.' [41]

Propaganda is therefore about much more than the communication of lies. Indeed it has to be, especially when used within the context of democratic societies. But to take our analogy further, the development of modern propaganda from the First World War through to the end of the Cold War can be seen as a second-wave process. We are only just beginning to see third-wave propaganda in the form of 'information warfare' which draws on previous usages in terms of tried and tested techniques, but understanding of which clashes with second-wave thinking about it. Because third-wave propaganda, particularly in the form of psychological operations (PSYOPS), also requires some fundamental re-thinking, it is examined in some detail in this book.

These are admittedly huge issues and it is not possible to do more than introduce them here. It is hoped that the modest ideas contained herein will stimulate further research. However, as with any book, there are limits as to what can be done. The information explosion of the past hundred years has meant that no one individual is capable of consuming all that is available in a lifetime, no matter how large a computer memory one has access to. Instead, most people continue to rely on information processors, or rather information professionals, who process the data for us. For our news of the world, for example, we still rely heavily on journalists, who in turn still rely heavily on the news agencies. Throughout the process of information-gathering and packaging for public use, decisions have to be made about whether one piece of information has higher credence or relevance over another. Not all information has equal significance for every individual, even though the Internet gives the impression that all information has equal

status. In a sense, the fundamental challenge of this demassifying information age is how to train people to evaluate the importance of certain bits (or
bytes) of information over others. But for as long as people still choose to
rely on the mass media, they also need to understand that the very process
of selection and omission, which is by definition part and parcel of the journalistic profession, brings us back into the realm of propaganda. Journalists
working in free societies would be horrified at such an accusation, and when
it has been levelled by academics such as Noam Chomsky, who accuses them
of 'manufacturing consent',[42] they react fiercely. True, it is easy to see
conspiracies where perhaps none exist, but the central role which journalism
continues to play for most people in our society, providing our 'window on
the world' through relaying one piece of information at the expense of
another, certainly brings us back to the question of intent. Most professional journalists intend to be objective in their reporting but, because the
very business of news gathering and presentation is a selective process, the
end product is invariably subjective in effect. Hence the constant self-
agonising over issues of bias. And too frequently do journalists hide under
the second-wave argument that they are serving the public's 'right to know'
when third-wave circumstances are now forcing them more and more into a
position of 'can I get the story out on time, and ahead of the rest – and will
it annoy our sponsors?'

In this 'information age' (or 'age of propaganda'[43]) it has long been fash-
ionable to talk about the information rich (usually meaning the developed
world) and the information poor (namely the 'Third World').[44] But everyone
is affected by the access to, or denial of, global information because information has become the lifeblood of our contemporary world. It has become
the principal commodity by which we measure levels not only of education,
skills and knowledge but also of progress, wealth and development on a
personal, local, national and international scale. Moreover, as the 'world-
wide information landscape' becomes increasingly interconnected
electronically and is now shifting in the direction of interactive visual technology, it has been argued that the existing gap between 'haves' and
'have-nots' will diminish. Irving Goldstein, the head of INTELSAT, a
consortium of more than 135 countries that owns and operates some twenty
satellites providing telecommunications services to virtually the entire world,
has predicted that information 'will be for the twenty-first century what oil
and gas were for the beginning of the twentieth century. It will fuel
economic and political power and give people everywhere more freedom and
momentum than the fastest automobile or supersonic jet. Information is no
longer the province of the privileged few, nations or individuals, or the
economic or power elite. It is the fare of the masses, shaping how they view
their lives, their governments, and the world around them. . . . Information
will be transmitted in every form we've known and in forms we cannot yet
even imagine.'[45]

Only time will tell. History tends to be kind only to the accurate prophets. At the moment, however, there are still considerable gaps between information rich and poor, and not just between the developed and underdeveloped world but even within developed countries themselves.

Having said that, one can see why such claims are being made. For example, if one considers for a moment the amount of money invested in communications in the average Western household, it is amongst the largest of on-going expenditures, possibly even more so than food. From the colour television set in the lounge (and at least one more in the bedroom or kitchen) attached to the video recorder(s) and possibly a cable or satellite system, the hardware alone can amount to £1000 or more. On top of that is the recurrent cost of using them: in Britain, almost £100 for a receiving licence fee (something which doesn't apply in the United States) plus around £25 per month for satellite or cable services, and maybe two or three video rentals a week from the local store at a cost of around £3 per time. Add to that the cost of the blank video tapes for 'time-shifting' or subsequent viewing, at around £2 each. And how many radio sets are in this average home at a cost of between £20 and £60 each, or in the family car? Then there is the telephone, with all its charges and the dreaded quarterly bill (at least local calls are free in the United States), in addition to the ever-ubiquitous mobile phone, answer machine and fax. And we have not yet arrived at the ultra-modern home, with its multimedia computer at around £1000, Internet access at about £10 per month, plus the necessary software and the CD-ROM games (at around £50 per time). Usually there will be a camera, and sometimes a camcorder and other 'peripherals'. In all, the cost of this adds up to a considerable amount of money. It also provides unprecedented opportunities for those information professionals to access individual homes, while at the same time it allows individual members of that household not only to access them but to by-pass them as well.

Herein lies one of the key features of the third wave that is fast approaching the growing numbers of people who decide to spend their income in this way. This is that much communications technology allows a two-way process, or, to use the jargon, is 'interactive'. Whereas in the past individuals had to rely on communication technologies which lay in the hands of the information professionals, now thanks to diminishing costs they are able to become information processors themselves (I am reluctant to repeat the word 'professional' here because mere possession of the technology does not automatically produce those artistic standards we have come to expect from people who make their living using it). Possessing a 35 mm camera does not turn its user into Ansell Adams. But possession of a domestic camcorder is turning increasing numbers of people into potential news-gatherers for television; regularly we see footage shot by private individuals on our nightly news bulletins, with the infamous beating of Rodney King by the Los Angeles police being a most striking example. Such footage may not be of professional standard, but the television company uses it because it is better than having no footage at all. Hence the profession of journalism is demassifying to the point where everyone is a potential journalist. During the abortive Soviet coup in August 1991, the footage of demonstrators throwing Molotov cocktails at tanks outside the Russian parliament was shot by an amateur photographer and sent by courier to CNN's bureau before it was transmitted around the world, including back into Russia itself.[46] Similarly, ordinary drivers with mobile phones alert radio stations to traffic jams, while CIA documents secured by one individual under the American Freedom of Information Act are placed on the World Wide Web for wider distribution. Quite simply, there are now so many varied sources of information available to the interested individual that, on one level, it is now possible to glean a much fuller picture of events than ever before. However, because most people still rely upon the mass media for their window on the world, and because the mass media are highly selective in the way they seize upon some events and not others, a distorted view of the world prevails. For example, surveys reveal that more people are afraid of crime than are statistically likely to fall victim to it. Likewise, fear of flying is disproportionate to the actual risks involved. With foreign affairs, the media usually choose to concentrate on events when there is a fear that a crisis might impact upon ordinary people, which undoubtedly contributes to the feeling that the events of the world are appearing on our TV screens at random, adding to the sense of disorder rather than reassuring us of its equilibrium. Moreover, events with little likely historical significance become magnified to the point that they will undoubtedly arouse curiosity in the future precisely for that reason. This is what makes the media such an important phenomenon of our times, not so much in terms of 'reality' but more in terms of the illusion of reality they create.

THE FOURTH DIMENSION

States continue to deal with one another in many traditional ways and at a variety of different levels, but all of these dealings involve communication of some sort. It is thus misleading to identify communications as a specific and separate element of inter-state relations that also embrace diplomatic, military and economic affairs. However, it is the contention of this book that communications have become so important in the way states perceive and deal with one another that they constitute a fourth dimension worthy of analysis in its own right. It is a dimension frequently overlooked by scholars of international relations and even by international historians. Within it are such phenomena as the role of public and media opinion (frequently quite distinct phenomena), the censorship and the propagandistic manipulation of that opinion for self-serving ends, the dissemination of messages to foreign governments and peoples by whatever communication technologies are

20

available to serve national self-interests, public diplomacy, cultural affairs and psychological warfare (now called psychological operations).

The fourth dimension of international affairs was recognised as important by early scholars of political science and foreign policy in the 1950s. Reflecting the Cold War climate in which he was writing, Harold Lasswell for example saw 'political warfare' as central to inter-state activity, embracing 'more than the means of mass communication':

> Political warfare adds the important idea that all instruments of policy need to be properly correlated. . . . Diplomacy, for example, can be used to keep potential enemies neutral or to detach allies from the enemy. . . . When we speak of diplomacy, we have in mind the making of official comments. Whereas mass communications aims to large audiences, diplomacy proceeds by means of official negotiations. . . . Political warfare also includes the use of economic means.[47]

Hence states deal with other in essentially four ways,[48] or dimensions, in an attempt to secure their national objectives. Of course, numbering a model tends to suggest that one dimension has priority over another, that the first is more important than the fourth. This does not apply here, since each of these dimensions assumes a greater significance in relations between states at different times while also operating simultaneously. But for convenience, let us say that the first dimension is diplomacy, the negotiation of contracts suitable to both (or, in the case of multi-lateral diplomacy, all) sides. The second is the economic dimension, concerning the exchange of resources. The third is the military dimension, the use or threatened use of military resources to achieve national, and now increasingly multi-national, objectives. A further dimension, sometimes labelled the 'hidden dimension', is intelligence activity, namely the gathering of secret information to fuel the activities of the political and military establishments to assist their bargaining positions. But because this type of work feeds all the other dimensions and is generally covert, for our purposes here we are going to subsume this activity into the fourth dimension. This is what may be termed the psychological or informational dimension, which involves the gathering and communication of information, ideas, perceptions and messages. Naturally this also takes place within the other three dimensions, but it has become a distinctive aspect of inter-state relations in its own right. Although we are about to immerse ourselves in this fourth dimension, it is however essential to remember at all times that it does not function separately from the other three but that it always impacts upon them, and vice versa. Communications is about something, and for us to understand its relevance and significance we need to know a little about that something. Hence, in Chapter 1, I outline the major relevant developments and issues defining the fourth dimension since 1945 so that the subsequent issues chosen for discussion can be dealt with thematically. But this is not a history of international relations, nor a history of political economy, nor a history of conflict since the end of the Second World War. Some knowledge of those areas on the reader's part would, however, enhance an appreciation of what is to follow.

At its simplest, all communication involves the active transmission and reception of *something*. The word itself comes from the Latin word to 'share'. That something is invariably a signal or message containing information that can inform, instruct, persuade, educate, propagandise, incite or entertain. The information can take the form of words or sounds or images, or a combination of these, now also presented in other forms such as digital data. International communication is communication between two or more parties (people, governments, organisations) who are located in different geographical regions. Over the past four hundred years we have come to define the principal system for organising society as the nation-state. Communication between nation-states takes place at a variety of levels. Communication between officially appointed representatives of governments is usually referred to as diplomacy, or, when that breaks down, as conflict or war. It is in these areas of inter-state activity that there are long-established procedures and practices for their conduct, and it is here that the equilibrium which on a day-to-day basis most of us don't see tends to exist. For the media, that normality is boring.

Communication between non-governmental actors, such as business corporations or even individual citizens, can manifest itself in a wide variety of exchanges, from trade to travel or any other form of sharing information and experiences. For this reason some scholars prefer the phrase 'world communication' because 'the adjective "international" is too restrictive'.[49] I shall use it here for precisely that reason, not least because world communication is too vast a topic to be embraced here.

So far this is pretty straightforward. Yet international communication is further facilitated by removing the constraints of time and space which have traditionally prevented human beings in different places from communicating with one another. The fundamental aspect of international communication as we understand it today is technology. Not only has technology overcome time and space but it has also made possible instantaneous international mass communication. Not that such communication takes place in an unregulated way. The media of communication are invariably controlled by someone, whether they be news organisations, multi-national corporations or governments. Even in democracies, governments regulate communications, although the past fifteen years have seen massive deregulation in areas like cross-media ownership. However, as one new medium comes along, others have always wondered whether they would be displaced – and it is in this anxiety that the beginnings of inter-media rivalry can be detected. After the invention of telegraphy, for example, telephony was seen as a threat, and telephony itself in turn felt threatened by the invention of radio. Then came television, the enemy of the cinema, and both of these felt threatened once domestic video recorders appeared. Now, new communications technologies are appearing to threaten the established media which by now have also formed established institutional practices creating norms of behaviour not dissimilar from those which have evolved as instruments of state communications. But again, with the third wave approaching, things are likely to change. Indeed, new technologies appear so rapidly that there is barely time to consider their ramifications – and the regulations for dealing with them – before another one appears. My sole reason for mentioning this is to explain why accelerated pace forces us to leave behind the opportunity for considered reflection on the significance of developments as they occur. This book offers my own reflections, and I have confined myself largely to issues and eschewed data and tables except where they illustrate a point of historical significance. Such is the nature of second-wave information processors like the book. For up-to-date specific information – for example about the number of satellites currently in orbit – one should consult the World Wide Web.

The preparation of this book has made me realise that the nature of historical research is also undergoing significant change, in that much of the research for the book was undertaken by searching for information not in traditional archives but across the Internet from the desk in my study. I have also noticed the way my students increasingly rely on this method for their coursework and the extent to which the data they present is so much more current than that contained in the books and articles in libraries that we list for them. 'Virtual worlds', for this generation, are becoming a reality.

TO HAVE OR HAVE NOT

Throughout the world, new information technologies are making it possible for the information 'have-nots' to catch up and plug in to this increasingly globalised and accessible system, whether it be in Thailand, the fastest-growing mobile communications market in the world in 1995, or in places like Hong Kong and Singapore which have joined the top ranks of the world's economic centres. For historical reasons, there is admittedly a lot of catching up to do, but the traffic jams of the Lagos rush hour, the mobile fax units of Somalian nomads and the satellite movie channels available in the hotels of Cairo should serve as a reminder that the new technologies have provided an opportunity for at least some sections of Third World communities to join the information 'haves' much faster than they would otherwise have been able to do. No longer can one divide the developed and developing world simply into 'haves' and 'have-nots'. Within all societies, rich or poor, there are such divisions. Yet, despite the costs involved, and the electrical power needed to drive the technology, expenditure needed for communications is in fact comparatively cheap, or certainly affordable, and is becoming more so. As one scholar has pointed out, this situation may help 'the poor to move beyond being simply a passive audience. Cheaper and more accessible technologies allow individuals and groups to become their own message-makers. . . . Alternative communication networks link together grassroots and policy groups throughout the globe, working on environmental, peace and relief efforts and forging together interests and activists into a new global civil society.'[50]

We are thus clearly undergoing dramatic changes in the way information and communications, or info-communications, are both proliferating and becoming more accessible. In one sense, therefore, I have outlined an old-fashioned framework for an old-fashioned (second-wave) book for, as the Director of MIT's Media Laboratory, Nicholas Negroponte, has written:

> The transition from an industrial age to a post-industrial age has been discussed so much and for so long that we may not have noticed that we are passing into a post-information age.[51]

Echoing elements of the idea about demassification, he then goes on to argue that 'in the information age mass media got bigger and smaller at the same time'. [In other words, as the mass media found themselves having to cater for increasingly specialised niche markets within society (for example as 'broadcasting' shifted to 'narrowcasting') the actual number of mass media outlets has proliferated as new, smaller, niche markets were identified to compete with the traditional larger ones. So, whereas thirty years ago a national broadcasting station in any given weekly programme schedule would include news, sport and movies for entertainment, now there are specialised news (CNN), sport (Eurosport) and movie channels (Sky Movies). Or, whereas people once relied on a national or local newspaper for their information, now there is an abundance of specialised magazines catering for their particular interests. 'Multichannel systems . . . have fragmented the audience into narrow niches based on taste, hobbies, avocations, race and ethnicity.'[52] And this process is likely to continue as individuals become increasingly able to import the information and entertainment that meets their needs as individuals rather than as members of the mass.] Negroponte has even suggested that:

> digital life will include very little real-time broadcast. As broadcast become digital, the bits are not only easily time-shiftable but need not be received in the same order or at the same rate as they will be consumed. . . . On-demand information will dominate digital life. We will ask explicitly and implicitly for what we want, when we want it. This will require a radical rethinking of advertiser-supported programming.[53]

If such a vision of the future proves correct, then this book will appear positively antiquarian. In such a world, there may be very little relevance for the themes discussed here, namely the media's role in the reporting of international affairs and wars and the use of communications in those activities. It will certainly be more difficult to generalise about such matters if, methodologically, we are forced to focus on every point of reception (i.e. every 'wired' individual on the planet) rather than on the point of origin at which such matters emerge (i.e. nation-states, of which there are around 200 today). Fortunately, however, while there are more recognised governments on the planet than at any previous period in history, most of them have yet to embrace the concepts of operating in virtual space, and we remain in a period in which there are still more television sets on the planet than personal computers. That may, of course, change in the life of the next generation (a period which historians use to signify the passage of twenty-five years) and, if it does, it will provide audience researchers with fresh challenges. The growth of the Internet, the proliferation of television channels and increased interactivity are already facts of life in the 1990s, but for the majority of people the digital world is still a little way off.

Even in such a future, however, information will remain a *raw* material; it is what is done with it that converts its mere possession into something else, namely communication (or lack of it). What do we really mean, for example, by the phrase 'information society'? A developed society? When we talk of this being an 'information age', do we mean that there is much more information around than there was in previous periods, or that the only way for societies, and the individuals within them, to develop is to access that information? Then what do they, or can they, do with it? Hence, the frequent assertion that 'information is power' needs to be considered not just in terms of possession but of application. The concept of 'power', itself problematical, need not concern us too much here. Suffice it to say that it is 'widely agreed that power involves the ability to exercise control, to get others to do what they might not do were it not for your presence'.[54] This is not too different from a definition of propaganda I have formulated elsewhere.[55] But propaganda is a particular *type* of power that involves communication and the media rather than economic pressure or the threat of armed force. Having said that, Hans Morgenthau has defined power as 'man's control over the minds and actions of other men', as 'a psychological relation between those who exercise it and those over whom it is exercised'.[56] Of course, not all information is propaganda, not all power is propaganda, and nor is all information power since possession of it operates at a variety of levels, from the trivial to the sophisticated. Knowledgeable game-show contestants, for example, might win prizes for their ability to answer questions, but does that empower them? Sixty per cent of the American workforce might well be involved in the 'info-communications' sector, but this covers a broad church, from word-processing and debt recovery to public relations and advertising. Indeed, this phrase 'info-communications' neatly encapsulates the linkage between the possession and dissemination of information that constitutes the difference between the private and the public spheres. 'The public formed because urban life was sufficiently developed so that strangers were regularly thrown into contact with one another.'[57] Hence, once information begins to be communicated, it becomes a unifying *process*, as common to education and enlightenment as to power and propaganda. But whereas once communications served to turn strangers into friends, or at least acquaintances, now new technology allows strangers to communicate with one another, to gather together in the public sphere, while retaining their privacy and anonymity. In cyberspace, public opinion becomes private opinion, and the concept of the mass – whether it be the public or communications – requires radical rethought.

Because these type of issues will not go away, and indeed will become exacerbated by the march of technology, this book is offered as a series of reflections on aspects of our information age that strike me as important and challenging. Because much writing on the media and communications lacks historical perspective, I have put some of this into the chapters as a foundation for commentaries about new developments. Things are indeed changing and, although we are not seeing an 'end of history', we are undergoing significant transformations that are likely to affect the ways states behave towards one another principally in terms of communications. It is for the reader to decide whether these developments are for good or ill. The history of academic communications research is riddled with a type of pessimism that belies the optimism of the inventors of new communication technologies. Instead I want to establish a framework in which the issues I am dealing with can be looked at realistically and practically.

Edward Said has maintained that 'the first rule for understanding the human condition is that people live in second hand worlds. The quality of their lives is determined by meanings they have received from others.'[58] Anthony Giddens has reinforced this: 'relations with absent others shape our experience'.[59] Let us therefore be under no illusions. This may well be the information age but it is also a media(ted) age and thus an age of propaganda. In fact it has been for some time. This reality is unpalatable to those who cherish liberal notions of a free flow of information as constituting a fundamental human right. But, like free trade, the free flow of information involves competition and the competitiveness of one piece of information over another, and the interpretations surrounding that information involve a struggle for supremacy for hearts and minds that is as much a part of the modern international system as the air that we breathe.

1

INTERNATIONAL
COMMUNICATIONS AND
INTERNATIONAL POLITICS
SINCE 1945

The atomic weapons dropped on Hiroshima and Nagasaki in August 1945 heralded the arrival of a completely new era in international relations in which the framework of political decision-making about issues of war and peace was to be radically different from any period which went before it. Many questions remained about the weapons which had helped to end the Second World War, not least of which was, would they be the cause of World War Three? They undoubtedly communicated a message, the significance of which would become of concern to all human beings. The inevitable proliferation of such destructive technology, especially following the Russian acquisition of the bomb in 1949, meant that in future, wars – at least those between nuclear states – were increasingly unlikely to yield 'winners' and 'losers' in the sense that victory or defeat had been traditionally understood. But out of this realisation there gradually emerged some hope that surely no side would initiate a nuclear strike if, in so doing, it invited its own destruction.

This question hung over the post-war period for almost fifty years. During that time it lay at the heart of thinking about security, defence and diplomatic affairs, and it permeated every aspect of political and social life. But it did serve to concentrate the collective mind, so in that sense it created a systemic bi-polar framework, an order of sorts, around which international events could be not only conducted but also viewed by those observing them. The problem was that this was a framework built on fear. No one who was sentient during this period was untouched by this fear of 'the bomb'. It was not an irrational fear; quite the reverse in fact. But the rationalisation of the knowledge of what such weapons could actually do in light of the fact that they could not be un-invented led to the simultaneous formation of structures for their non-proliferation as well as for justifying their continued possession by nuclear powers. Such justification was essential because, in any nuclear conflagration, for all the later talk about battlefield nuclear weapons, it would be the general public who would constitute the 'front line'. And if the Second World War had been a 'Total War', in which the domestic and military theatres had become substantially

27

intertwined, such interdependence would be nothing compared to what global thermonuclear confrontation would bring. In other words, regardless of what had been said about it in the past, one message of Hiroshima and Nagasaki was that henceforth public opinion really would matter. How, therefore, events were reported and perceived became a critical consideration for politicians, diplomats and soldiers as they went about their business under increasing public scrutiny.

This was essentially the psychological background of what came to be known as the Cold War. Looking back, it is hard to appreciate that this forty-year-long war, this 'balance of terror', was something more than merely the twentieth century's equivalent of a 'Great Game' between the superpowers. But the existence of nuclear weapons, combined with their possession by ideologically antithetical regimes, prompted new rules for international relations in which the control, manipulation and dissemination of information about the other side constituted a permanent and highly bureaucratised 'fourth dimension'. Too readily dismissed as 'propaganda' by scholars, this dimension was not only important in and of itself, it informed the entire environment in which politics, economics, diplomacy and warfare were conducted between 1949 and 1989.

DRAWING THE BATTLE-LINES OF IDEOLOGICAL WAR

It was a dimension in which both psychology and the language of discourse counted for a great deal. During the 1930s, the policies of the Western powers had lacked an appreciation or an understanding of psychology, especially in their dealings with Hitler and Stalin, which frequently put them at a disadvantage and enabled them to be wrong-footed on numerous occasions. These lessons had been learned by the late 1940s when it was realised that dealing with Stalin required not only a psychological understanding of the man but also a strategy for influencing the other side psychologically. Within this context, language assumed an active and highly potent role in defining such concepts as 'peace', 'disarmament', 'deterrence', even of 'independence' and 'liberation'. For the West, a central point which impacted on all other elements of international affairs was their entire concept of 'freedom'. The Atlantic Charter of 1942 had outlined the fundamental principles for why the Anglo-American wartime partnership was fighting: freedom of movement, freedom of thought, freedom of religion and freedom to vote. These were the Four Freedoms. The problem was that they were then fighting in partnership with a Soviet Union whose notion of freedom was determined more by the concept of collective responsibility to the achievement of a Marxist–Leninist state than by an emphasis on individuality. Once the common enemy had been defeated, therefore, such fundamental differences resurfaced, especially in the end-of-the-war conferences at Yalta and Potsdam. Then, as relations between the former wartime allies

28

deteriorated into Cold War over the question of freedom for the peoples of Eastern Europe, the issue of freedom of thought became a burning issue, and extended into significant international documents relating to freedom of information.

Indeed, the fundamental reason why this became such a significant issue in the second half of the twentieth century is inextricably connected to the triumph of democracy over totalitarianism, chiefly at two points: first in 1945 with the defeat of Germany and Japan, and then in 1989 with the collapse of Communist control over Eastern Europe, to be followed two years later by the disintegration of the Soviet Union itself. One difference, of course, was that most people read about the former in the newspapers a day or two later. The latter was seen live on television around the world. This reveals the extent to which the media in a period of fifty years have transformed themselves from being observers of international events to actual participants in them. The speed at which world events came to be reported compressed the time and increased the pressure in which decision-making had to take place during this period. Moreover, the speed at which the international flow of information contributed towards the way these monumental events were being perceived by world public opinion became a much more significant consideration in the decision-making process than in any period before it.

In 1945, the defeat of Nazism and Japanese imperialism was accompanied by the victory of largely Anglo-American democratic ideology over Stalinism in the form of the creation of the United Nations. Regardless of American aspirations, the very idea of such an organisation could never have emerged from the Soviet Union, except perhaps as a front for activities designed to achieve goals other than those for which the UN was designed. This might seem an ungenerous comment but, thanks to revelations which have emerged since the opening of the archives in Moscow, it is not without foundation. The Soviets admittedly had good reasons to mistrust the UN. The creation of an international forum in which the international community could resolve disputes by negotiation rather than force had been tried before in the form of the League of Nations, from which the Soviet Union had been deliberately excluded (until 1934) and to which its principal exponent, the USA, had refused to adhere. But the Second World War would see the formation of a renewed effort with the five leading members of the victorious coalition (USA, USSR, Britain, France and China) holding the five permanent seats of the Security Council, each with a power to veto. It was here that the principal diplomatic squabbles of the Cold War would take place.

The Charter of the United Nations was significant in that it was taken as axiomatic that communications were inextricably connected with the Four Freedoms. And because the Cold War framework is frequently missing from scholarly works dealing with the post-war debate over international communications – just as the communications dimension is usually absent from the

history of the Cold War – it is worth reconsidering the relevant documenta-
tion. The context needs to be understood in terms of two emerging
superpowers with different views about how to achieve post-war concepts of
universalism and collective security in world affairs as a means of assuring
their own national security. In the United States there was a strong drive
towards achieving universal cooperation, which was an extension of
domestic philosophies. The Americans had in a sense been forced into the
Second World War because they had abrogated their international responsibilities during the inter-war years through a policy of isolationism. Given
that that had not worked, there emerged a widespread recognition that the
United States should get itself involved in world affairs so that no one could
launch a sneak attack on them, Pearl Harbor-style, again. This idealism was
soon dashed, as it was realised that the Soviet former wartime ally had
different ideas about how to achieve its own future national security and
avoid a Barbarossa-style attack, in the form of the Red Army staying put on
the German front line and ensuring that its lines of communication
throughout Eastern Europe were also secure. In Washington, this looked
more like self-serving expansion rather than national or collective security.
In Moscow, American aid in west European and Japanese reconstruction
through the Marshall Plan looked like encirclement. Besides, in the
mounting anti-Communist climate of post-war America that culminated
with the McCarthyite witch-hunts of the early 1950s, it didn't take long for
its enemies to point out that the Soviet concept of a universal peace was a
Marxist–Leninist one which took the concepts of struggle and conflict
against capitalism as axiomatic.

The preamble to the UN Charter reaffirmed 'faith in fundamental human
rights, in the dignity and worth of the human person, in the equal rights of
men and women and of nations large and small', while its very first article
stated that the UN's purposes were to include the development of:

> friendly relations among nations based on respect for the principle of
> equal rights and self-determination of peoples, and to take other
> appropriate measures to strengthen universal peace; to achieve interna-
> tional co-operation in solving international problems of an economic,
> social, cultural, or humanitarian character, and in promoting and
> encouraging respect for human rights and for fundamental freedoms
> for all without distinction as to race, sex, language, or religion.[1]

Its principal arm for achieving these goals was to be UNESCO, founded in
1946. The preamble to UNESCO's constitution stated that its signatories,

> believing in full and equal opportunities for education for all, in the
> unrestricted pursuit of objective truth, and in the free exchange of
> ideas and knowledge, are agreed and determined to develop and to
> increase the means of communication between their peoples and to

employ these means for the purpose of mutual understanding and a truer and more perfect knowledge of each other's lives.

Later that year, the General Assembly of the UN adopted Resolution 59 (I) which declared that 'Freedom of information is a fundamental human right and *is the touchstone* of all freedoms to which the United Nations is consecrated; Freedom of information requires as an indispensable element the willingness and capacity to employ its privileges without abuse. It requires as a basic discipline *the moral obligation to seek the facts without prejudice and to spread knowledge without malicious intent*' (emphasis added). To drive this point home, Resolution 110 (II) adopted in 1947 condemned 'all forms of propaganda which are designed or likely to provoke or encourage any threat to the peace, breach of the peace, or act of aggression' while Resolution 127 (II) of the same year called on members 'to combat the diffusion of false or distorted reports which are likely to injure friendly relations between states'. Further resolutions identified the role of the mass media in contributing to the strengthening of trust and friendly relations amongst states.

On 10 December 1948, the General Assembly of the United Nations adopted and proclaimed the Universal Declaration of Human Rights 'as a common standard of achievement for all peoples and all nations'. Designed overall to guarantee freedom, equality and human dignity, the declaration's nineteenth article stated in addition that 'everyone has the right to freedom of opinion and expression; this right includes freedom to hold opinions without interference and to seek, receive and impart information and ideas through any media and regardless of frontiers'. More honoured in the breach, especially in such places as Eastern Europe, the Soviet Union, the People's Republic of China, the southern states of America and (until 1994) South Africa, this document nonetheless provided the ideological framework by which the global community set its aspirations concerning the free flow of information. It also provided the yardstick by which heroes and villains could be defined in the climate of the Cold War.

But it did something else as well. By carving in stone the principle of universal freedom of information, ideas and speech, it highlighted the gap between theory and practice when advanced (First World) societies interacted with Communist (Second World) societies and with those of less developed countries (Third World or LDCs). History appeared to be on the side of the First World in providing not just the confidence to permit democratic processes to operate but also in the means (i.e. the media) by which they could operate. The simple fact of the matter was that more advanced countries had more advanced media systems through which the declaration of human rights could be applied. Moreover, this was very much a public stance. As the battle lines of the Cold War were being drawn in 1947–8, the USA, Britain and the USSR were all re-galvanising their wartime propaganda apparatus to serve post-war ends, including the creation of 'black' or covert organisations whose activities could only be said to have violated these high-minded objectives if it had been known at the time what they were up to.

This is not the place to rehearse the causes and course of the Cold War. It is, however, relevant to identify the degree to which the East–West confrontation was becoming a struggle for allegiances, not just in the developed world but globally. It was a battle fought out on a variety of fronts and, in so far as the media and communications were concerned, on a cultural as well as on a political level. Throughout the entire period, the struggle was portrayed as a genuine contest between different ways of life, between good and evil, and, as with all struggles, presentation to secure and maintain public support was critical, all the more so in a long 'war'.

The Truman Doctrine of March 1947 identified the struggle as one between two seemingly incompatible approaches:

> One way of life is based upon the will of the majority, and is distinguished by free institutions, representative government, free elections, guarantees of personal liberty, freedom of speech and religion and freedom from political repression. The second way of life is based upon the will of a minority imposed upon the majority. It relies upon terror and repression, a controlled press and radio, fixed elections, and the suppression of personal freedom.[2]

Walter Lippmann was especially alarmed at this; it appeared to him to be a rallying cry for trouble. He wrote: 'a vague global policy, which sounds like the tocsin of an ideological crusade, has no limits. It cannot be controlled. Its effects cannot be predicted. Everyone, everywhere will read into it his own fears and hopes, and it could readily act as incitement and inducement to civil strife in countries where the national co-operation is delicate and precarious.'[3] Lippmann found himself opposed by George Kennan who, under the pseudonym 'X', published an influential article in *Foreign Affairs* of July 1947 in which he argued that Soviet motives were fuelled by paranoia and messianic ideology. As has been pointed out, in the United States this debate 'neatly reflected the clashing impulses in the country between divisive fears and conciliatory hopes'.[4]

Certainly the Soviet Union appeared to enjoy a considerable advantage in so far as competing ideologies were concerned, quite simply because, within its own borders at least, it allowed no competition. The Stalinist state was as ruthless in its suppression of opposition as it was rigorous in its control over the media, and thereby the people. Every journalist had to be a Party member and the operation of journalism, from the training of personnel to the granting of licences, was organised by the state. This tended to produce a loyal cadre who could be relied on when it came to the selection – and omission – of news. But if this self-censorship broke down, the Central Committee of the Politburo, the ruling body of the State, could exercise direct control through its censorship agency GLAVIT. The Politburo also appointed the head of the state-owned news agency, TASS, and of the national radio network, GOSTELRADIO, as well as the editors of the state-run newspapers *Pravda* and *Izvestia*. In other words, the Soviet government and the Soviet media spoke with one voice. They did not fight shy of the word propaganda and, even as late as 1988, the editor-in-chief of *Pravda* stated unashamedly: 'our aim is propaganda, the propaganda of the Party and the state. We do not hide this.'

Nor did they hide the fact that propaganda abroad was a principal component of their foreign policy. The defunct Comintern was revived in 1947 as Cominform, to organise a world-wide onslaught orchestrated by the Administration of Agitation and Propaganda of the Communist Party Central Committee (AGITPROP). Language and semantics were pivotal in order to secure 'Marxist–Leninist historical imperatives'. Words thus became weapons in their ideological arsenal to capture the moral high ground over such issues as 'freedom' and 'independence', and thereby set the perceptual framework about 'the West' both at home and abroad, and especially in the 'Third World'. For the Soviets, the struggle was between Communism and anti-Communism; hence the Cold War was started because 'American imperialism sought to nullify the victory of the forces of progress in the Second World War and to impose its diktat on mankind'.[5] For this reason propaganda was seen as 'one of the most important means of the class struggle' in which radio was 'the most effective peacetime weapon of psychological warfare'.[6] Hence, for Moscow, the Cold War 'seriously impedes, if not completely rules out, the flow of truthful information about socialism and breeds negative stereotypes of the Soviet Union'.[7] The objective was quite simply to control the terms of the debates in international affairs and to set the agenda of international discourse as a counter to the West-inspired declarations and organisations set up after 1945. For this the Soviets needed organisations of their own, and numerous 'Front' associations were established, perhaps the most famous of which was the World Peace Council, founded in 1949, which supported the North Korean invasion of South Korea in June 1950 and which was responsible for disseminating fabricated charges of US germ warfare during that conflict. 'Agents of influence', such as sympathetic journalists, academics and even intelligence officers operating in the West, were also cultivated by Moscow in an attempt to get Western opinion-formers to speak on their behalf and in their defence. The KGB conducted widespread *dezinformatsia* (disinformation) through what it later termed 'active measures' in an attempt to discredit Western governments and alienate popular support for their policies *vis-à-vis* the Soviet Union, for example through supporting Western anti-nuclear peace movements.[8] Overt and covert, the Soviets integrated active measures into their foreign policy at all levels. 'As is the case with military, economic and diplomatic instruments, the Kremlin designs and employs these measures to support Soviet strategic objectives and operations.'[9]

33

For the Americans, however, 'covert actions' were seen as related to, but clearly separate from, the conduct of foreign policy. To this extent, the fourth dimension was much more closely integrated into the conduct of Soviet diplomatic, economic and military affairs than it ever was in Washington. While the CIA was charged with the business of combating the KGB on both intelligence and propaganda levels, the State Department in Washington felt that it needed separate machinery to combat Soviet propaganda specifically within the fourth dimension. Hence the creation of the American Cold War propaganda machinery appeared to be a new and somewhat reactive or even defensive measure designed to combat like with like, when in fact the approaches of each side were completely different. The Western concept of peace was an absence of war, whereas the Marxist–Leninist tradition saw war as a continuation of politics by other means. The result of this was to see international affairs in terms of conflict, struggle and competition against any adversaries who did not share the same historical destiny. To this end, the media, together with all instruments of communications and the messages they carried, were identified as part of the same strategy, not separate from it, and thus were much more closely integrated in the Soviet machinery of state than they ever were in the West.

Of course, the totalitarian nature of the Soviet system greatly facilitated this central coordination and integration. In pluralistic Western democracies, where the emphasis was on the separation of powers, when it came to establishing a state machinery for the conduct of international communications the same philosophy was applied. Hence bodies established to conduct external communications were barred from directing their messages at domestic audiences. This was an integral part of the 1948 Smith–Mundt Act, which converted the wartime Voice of America (founded 1942) into the established radio arm of the State Department's international information programme that was designed 'to promote a better understanding of the United States in other countries, and to increase mutual understanding between the people of the United States and the people of other countries'. While professing to adhere to BBC-type principles of broadcasting only news and 'truthful' information, the VOA however suffered a lack of credibility due to the fact that it was clearly the official voice of the American government, that it was state-funded and that ultimately it was directly answerable to the State Department and the President. As such, it was clearly identified with the policies of any given administration, which in turn undermined its stance as being dedicated to the pursuit of any 'truth' that transcended either party political or even US national interests. Hence, Soviet writers could claim that US 'propaganda exposed itself to the world public as both a perpetrator of lies and slander and an organiser of overt subversion'.[10]

As the Cold War unfolded, US President Truman launched his 'Campaign for Truth' in 1950, following the outbreak of the Korean War.

With $121 million dollars appropriated by Congress, the campaign was to be based upon the assumptions laid down in the notorious National Security Council (NSC) document 68 in which Soviet intentions were identified uncompromisingly as leading to world domination. It ran in part:

> The Kremlin is inescapably militant. It is inescapably militant because it possesses and is possessed by a world-wide revolutionary movement, because it is the inheritor of Russian imperialism, and because it is a totalitarian dictatorship. . . . It is quite clear from Soviet theory and practice that the Kremlin seeks to bring the free world under its domination by the methods of the Cold War.[11]

Based on this assumption, the Campaign for Truth would attempt to generate world-wide confidence in American leadership of the free world, counter misrepresentations and misconceptions about US intentions, reassure the international community of American aspirations for peace, while displaying its determination to remain prepared for war and to undermine confidence in Communist regimes. The remarkable extent of this activity was revealed when Winston Churchill returned to power in Britain in 1951 following a suggestion that Western propaganda to the Soviet Union should be stepped up. Truman pointed out in his reply that the US was already conducting the 'equivalent to or exceeded the output of' its domestic broadcasting networks.[12]

The battle-lines were thus drawn. In 1951 Truman created a Psychological Strategy Board to advise the NSC, and in 1953 a personal advisor on what was now being termed 'psychological warfare' was working at the White House for Truman's successor, Dwight D. Eisenhower. In that year also, American information activities were separated from the State Department and the United States Information Agency was formed, directly answerable to the President. The 'Campaign of Truth' became the 'Crusade for Freedom', spearheaded by the newly created, European-based radio stations, Radio Free Europe (RFE) and Radio Liberation (later Liberty, RL), the latter of which was established specifically for Russian audiences. The VOA was charged with the task of multiplying and intensifying 'psychological deterrents to communist aggression'. Reflecting the influence of NSC 68, the VOA's objectives included rolling back Soviet influence by all means, but especially propaganda, short of war.[13] As Eisenhower declared:

> We are now waging a cold war. The cold war must have some objective, otherwise it would be senseless. It is conducted in the belief that if there is no war, if two systems of government are allowed to live side by side, that ours, because of its greater appeal to men everywhere, to mankind, in the long run will win out. That it will defeat dictatorial government because of its greater appeal to the human soul, the human heart, the human mind.[14]

From the standpoint of the 1990s, these seem prophetic words, but they had considerable contemporary resonance, especially following the death of Stalin in 1953 and his successor's call within a few years for 'peaceful coexistence'. At the Twentieth Party Congress in February 1956, Nikita Khrushchev confirmed a drift towards greater flexibility and détente, including the allowance of 'varying roads to socialism', namely a loosening of Moscow's previous iron grip on its Eastern European satellites and a rapprochement with Tito's Yugoslavia.

Although the discrediting of Stalin, of which these policies were a part, was initially supposed to be a secret policy, news of the changes quickly spread. In Poland and Hungary, the opportunity of creating 'socialism with a human face' led to calls for reform. Although the protests in Poland were suppressed by domestic troops, in Hungary a full-scale uprising was exacerbated by international broadcasting from the outside. RFE in particular was felt to have 'aroused an expectation of support' amongst Hungarians at a time when Western assistance was even more unlikely due to the Suez Crisis.[15] Although RFE, backed secretly by the CIA, had the largest audience, the BBC enjoyed a reputation for credibility, especially amongst the better educated and more influential sectors of Hungarian society. Sir Hugh Greene, former head of the Political Warfare Executive's German propaganda service during the Second World War and later Director General of the BBC, felt that 'a dictatorship cannot ignore public opinion entirely and thus by a very gradual process our *propaganda* may affect Soviet policy'[16] (emphasis added). The recognition by international broadcasting professionals that they were in the business of propaganda, though rarely admitted in public, was based on the principle of a former BBC Director General, John Reith, who suggested that 'news is the shocktroops of propaganda'.[17] Or, as a VOA official put it:

> You are not going to kid anybody on the other side of the Iron Curtain or anywhere when you have an official broadcast or a broadcast with a political objective that you are there simply by accident – you will be considered and identified at all times as a propaganda station and I don't necessarily think that that necessarily has a pejorative taste to it. . . . I don't want people looking down the necks of the broadcasters saying ' . . . are you indulging in propaganda?' because the answer should be, without any hesitation, 'Yes, we are, and we hope we are doing it successfully'.[18]

Certainly great care had to be taken by the BBC not to broadcast anything which might be construed as promising Western intervention to assist the Hungarians, not least because its long-term credibility had to be preserved for what everybody knew would be a long war of East–West ideological attrition. When Soviet troops moved in to suppress the uprising, a delicate balance had to be struck between expressing sympathy, horror and indignation on the one hand and avoiding any 'incitement to extremism' on the other.

Whether or not this balance was achieved, by the BBC and VOA if not RFE, this did not prevent *The Times* from accusing their broadcasts of sowing in Hungarian minds 'the seeds of the present struggle' and thus declaring that Hungarians would be justified in feeling 'utterly and completely' betrayed by the West.[19] Hugh Greene, while admitting that 'it was certainly part of our aim to keep alive their links with the west and the belief that somehow, someday . . . things might get better and Russian rule might be shaken off', nonetheless felt that:

> Khrushchev has shaken faith in Stalin much more effectively than we ever could – and perhaps in doing so has helped to show our audience in Russia that we had been telling the truth about Stalin for many years.[20]

The US Senate's Jackson Committee, which had established USIA in 1953, had also recognised the tightrope act that needed to be walked between actions and words in foreign (information) policy. The former would always speak louder, but the latter must not be allowed to fuel expectations of action that was unlikely to be forthcoming due to foreign policy objectives:

> The United States will be judged not only by the things it is able to do, but also by the gap between these and its announced policies. A clear distinction must be made between policies and aspirations. Objectives with respect to which the United States commits itself to act must be clearly identified as distinct from those ends to which we, as a nation, aspire but regarding which the government is not committed to take action.[21]

Thomas Soronson has observed that, 'had that distinction been clearer three years later, the United States might have avoided acute embarrassment at the time of the Hungarian revolt'.[22] It might equally be added that such a rule is still valid. However, as we shall see in subsequent chapters, political administrations can still get into trouble over this, not necessarily any longer because of their official propaganda machineries but because of their nervous relationship with commercial news organisations, and particularly television images.

EXTENDING THE CONFLICT TO THE THIRD WORLD

The 1956 Hungarian crisis, from an international relations point of view, was a relatively minor affair. Although international broadcasting might appear to have threatened to make it otherwise, the crisis was contained and was resolved without any spillage beyond the 'internal affairs' of the Soviet bloc. Khrushchev continued to pursue his policy of 'peaceful coexistence' which, following the Communist takeover of China in 1949, caused a deep resentment in Peking that finally resulted in a Sino-Soviet split in 1960. This was to last until the Gorbachev era in the late 1980s. But the policy of 'peaceful coexistence' was another example of the use of words as weapons, since it was really about peaceful *competition*, especially on the ideological level, and nowhere was this more apparent than in the Third World. In Egypt, for example, the Soviets began to promote their influence in 1955 and supported General Nasser's decision to seize the Suez Canal in the following year. When the British and French colluded with the Israelis to attack Egypt so that they had a pretext to invade in order to protect the Canal, it seemed that Soviet arguments about imperialist aggression carried some weight. However, US disapproval caused Britain to suspend the operation, seriously damaging its position – and its self-confidence – in the Middle East while simultaneously underlining America's leadership of the Western alliance. France, for its part, turned more and more away from Empire to concentrate on Europe. Third-World governments saw the extent to which strong nationalism, in this case Arab nationalism, could defeat former imperialist overlords and watched with interest Nasser's employment of radio in the form of the Voice of the Arabs to achieve these aims. For their part, the British feared the destabilising potential of radio in the 'wrong' hands, and it was noted that with every broadcast which 'boomed forth from the Voice of the Arabs transmitter the British government desperately tried to tighten its grip upon those countries where its writ still ran'.[23]

As the old European empires withdrew from their imperial possessions, sometimes painfully like the British in Malaya, Kenya and especially at Suez in 1956, or the French in Algeria or in Vietnam after Dien Bien Phu in 1954, power vacuums were created which the two extra-European superpowers tried to fill in various ways. The United States, which had always professed itself to be historically anti-imperialist, found that its free-market capitalist politico-economic system enabled the Soviets to portray them as imperialists under an economic disguise. Decolonised and newly independent nations therefore had a choice – which was admittedly something they had not enjoyed before. They obviously would find it difficult to survive independently in an increasingly interdependent world economy delineated by the Bretton Woods system, unless that is they became part of that system. This, the Soviets argued, would merely perpetuate their dependence upon the Western capitalist powers rather than encourage their independence from them. They would thus still be prone to exploitation. Moscow therefore offered help in the form of economic subsidies, advisers and arms supplies to aid their quest for 'independence' and with guidance on how to achieve political and social stability in the transformation from colonial dependency to a Marxist–Leninist version of independence that would dismantle the differences between the fortunate rich and the less fortunate, exploited poor.

The United States saw this as 'psychological warfare' and stepped up its efforts to counter it. This type of activity is described elsewhere in this book but, here, suffice it to say that the danger in the East–West confrontation was that propaganda at times replaced diplomacy as the principal instrument of international communication between the superpowers. Moreover, during the Suez crisis, Radio Moscow had even transmitted personal messages from the Soviet leadership to the British, French and Israeli leaders *before* they had reached their intended recipients by conventional diplomatic channels'.[24] As one scholar has noted:

> Thus 5 November 1956 marks a significant stage in the development of international radio broadcasting as a tool of diplomacy; broadcasting what previously would have been considered private diplomatic communications now became a regular method of conducting Soviet foreign policy.[25]

The humiliation of the British and French over Suez, together with the rift it caused within the NATO alliance, and the emergence world-wide of nationalist movements with Communist inclinations, therefore encouraged the Soviets to step up their propaganda offensive, especially now that order had been restored within the Eastern bloc.

In 1957 the Communist Party of the Soviet Union (CPSU) reorganised its ideological warfare machinery.[26] The Foreign Affairs Department in Moscow was divided into three separate and independent bodies directly responsible to the Central Committee. The Department for Relations with Communist and Workers Parties of Socialist Countries controlled the Soviet satellites in the Eastern European bloc. The Department for Cadres Abroad coordinated all foreign cells in collaboration with the KGB. The International Department dealt with countries in which Communist parties had yet to secure power. According to some sources, including Soviet defectors, the International Department became more important than the Soviet Ministry of Foreign Affairs: it was 'the element in the Soviet decision-making process which gathers information on foreign policy, briefs the Politburo, and thereby exercises, subject to the Politburo, decisive influence on Soviet foreign policy'.[27] It was this body which was responsible for administering, funding and coordinating the front organisations, including the World Peace Council and the International Organisation of Journalists, founded in 1952, whose function was to support Soviet peace campaigns, human rights campaigns and other such causes. In 1957 another front organisation was founded, the Afro-Asian People's Solidarity Organisation, which was to be a channel for Soviet influence in the Third World.

Fearing they would be drawn further into this ideological battlefield, twenty-nine leaders from newly independent 'developing' countries of Africa and Asia decided to form the Non-Aligned Movement (NAM) at the Bandung (Indonesia) conference in 1955. Later joined by Latin American countries, the NAM was to emerge 'as a powerful mouthpiece for developing countries both within the United Nations and in its own fora'.[28] Having said that, as we shall see, it also became a target for the differing standpoints of the Soviet Union and the United States in a debate that was subsequently to dominate debates about international communications, namely the issue of a New World Information and Communications Order.

For Washington and Moscow, 'non-alignment' made as much sense as Swiss neutrality: fine in theory but wholly inappropriate to a nuclear world. Two developments in particular hardened these attitudes. The first was the launching of Sputnik in 1957, which extended the arms race into outer space. Following the successful Soviet launch of the first multi-stage Inter-Continental Ballistic Missile in August 1957, Sputnik I became the first ever space satellite; while Laika the dog was sent into space on Sputnik II. When the American attempt to launch a satellite in December of the same year ended in failure, Washington panicked into believing that Moscow had stolen the march on them, technologically and militarily, and that a 'missile gap' had opened up. While it eventually transpired that there was no such gap, or rather that if anything the Americans remained well ahead of the Soviets in both quantity and quality of nuclear weaponry, especially following the successful launch of Explorer in February 1958, this perception dominated East–West relations between 1957 and 1961. Nothing illustrates more clearly the degree to which international relations were being increasingly conducted through the paranoid spectacles of the Cold War, spectacles which housed mirrors rather than clear lenses. Although the worst excesses of the McCarthy era were over by the late 1950s, and while Khrushchev was attempting to pursue détente, especially following the Soviet leader's visit to the United States in 1959, international communication was being characterised more by misperception than clarity, an indication of the degree to which propaganda had superseded many aspects of foreign policy. This was the background to the two crisis which were to see the Cold War intensify again, namely the Berlin crisis and the erection of the Berlin Wall in 1961, and the Cuban missile crisis of 1962.

The transformation of Cuba from an American dependency to a Soviet satellite following Fidel Castro's takeover in 1959 was bound to fuel tension, especially following the humiliating failure of the CIA-backed Bay of Pigs invasion of April 1961. While the USA's U-2 planes where confirming the non-existence of a missile gap with the Soviet Union, ironically they identified the presence of Soviet missiles on an island just eighty miles from the American coast, with more on the way. This gravest of Cold War crises saw US President Kennedy quarantine Cuba in an attempt to prevent further shipments of Soviet missiles from arriving as the world waited for World War Three. The crisis was eventually resolved at the brink when Khrushchev promised to withdraw his ships and missiles in return for American assurances that they would not attempt to overthrow Castro – at least not by force. Instead, the Americans resorted to 'persuasion', first with the establishment of the 'black', CIA-run Radio Swan, and later, in 1983, with the 'white' station Radio Marti.

The Cuban missile crisis was important because it was probably the last time that a President of the United States 'repeatedly benefited from a cocoon of time and privacy afforded by the absence of intensive television scrutiny'.[29] For example, in this age before commercial satellites, it was possible to keep from the public the news that Soviet missiles were actually already on Cuba, thus avoiding hysteria. Now that the television networks have access to commercial satellites, it is likely that they would have discovered this at about the same time as the government. This would undoubtedly have put extra pressures on the decision-making process in Washington. Moreover, it was taking about eight hours to send messages from Moscow to Washington through the normal diplomatic channels, and to speed things up Khrushchev resorted again to using Radio Moscow. But how different the crisis might have been if Kennedy felt under additional pressure from his own domestic news organisations to 'do something', one can of course only speculate. But we also know that he was prepared to violate FCC regulations when it was decided to get commercial radio stations to carry messages that could be picked up in Cuba itself because the VOA was being jammed. The stations lost valuable advertising expenditure, but their owners 'settled for a White House luncheon with Kennedy' as payment when the crisis was all over.[30] This can be seen either as another example of the degree to which the media were prepared to cooperate with government when necessary in the national interest, or as another illustration of the military–industrial complex at work. As with most things, it depends which side you are on.

Having gone to the brink, the American and Soviet leadership took a good hard look at the other side. The problem was that they were now peering at each other over the Berlin Wall, erected in 1961. Some mutual recognition that their propaganda spectacles were in danger of obscuring their diplomatic vision resulted in the establishment after the Cuban missile crisis of a direct 'hot-line' between Washington and Moscow. But by then, both sides had developed extensive machinery for external radio broadcasting and 'public diplomacy' as they jostled for psychological supremacy from one crisis to another. Before long, with the launching of a series of satellites in the space race of the 1960s, the machinery would also be in place to extend this competition into television, especially following the launch in 1962 of Telstar, the first communications satellite, and of Syncom III which carried live coverage of the Tokyo Olympics in 1964.

As television established itself as a domestic medium in the developed world during the 1950s and 1960s, the principal medium of international communications nonetheless remained the radio. The Soviet Union had always recognised the power of radio in alliance with its world-wide revolutionary zeal to 'spread the word' to the 'workers of the world', but such recognition conversely meant that they feared its power in the hands of others. As a result, Moscow expended considerable efforts in jamming Western broadcasts. In 1945, the Soviet Union had over 1,000 stations devoted purely to broadcasting a wall of noise on the same frequencies as Russian-language programmes emanating from the West. By 1962, the number had reached 2–3,000, and it was estimated by some sources that the Soviets spent more money on jamming than the Americans did on broadcasting.[31] The extent to which jamming was undertaken reflected the ebbs and flows of Cold War tension from Moscow's perspective and provided a good indication of the Kremlin's nervousness at different times. The English-language services to Russia were rarely jammed, so that the Soviet elite in the Russian government (who were amongst the few who could speak English) could stay in touch with what Western governments were saying, if not thinking. The VOA, the BBC World Service and the German Deutsche Welle were collectively nicknamed 'The Voices', and it was a testament to their credibility that the Kremlin should both rely on them and fear them at the same time. At no time did the Western governments emulate the practice of jamming Soviet broadcasts to the West, which not only tells us that they were a useful source of intelligence for Western governments which spent considerable amounts monitoring them but also reinforced the Western Cold War perspective that a free flow of information would ultimately serve Western interests more effectively.

This was precisely what was feared by the growing number of nations in the developing world. The problem was that, as new nations, they needed new communications systems of their own and, to acquire the necessary technology, they needed not only to import the equipment but also to train the personnel. In some countries, such as Libya, the demand for radio and television systems stemmed from spillage of signals designed for foreign military personnel (in this case American) stationed there. But from a governmental point of view, there was the additional incentive that communications were being linked to development and modernity. As Daniel Lerner put it in 1958, 'no modern society functions efficiently without a developed system of mass media. Our historical forays indicate that the conditions which define modernity form an interlocking "system"'.[32] Another pioneer of academic communications studies, Wilbur Schramm, reinforced this, stating that 'without adequate and effective communication, economic and social development will inevitably be retarded, and may be counter-productive. With adequate and effective communication, the pathways to change can be made easier and shorter.'[33] These are a far cry from the more recent ideas about the media creating chaos, but they were widely accepted at the time, especially in new nations either searching for ways to catch up with the developed world or by political leaders in some of those nations who saw an opportunity for sustaining their often tenuous post-independence political positions.

The problem was, however, that once a radio network had been established it became vulnerable to outside influences chiefly in two ways. First, on the overt political level, it became a target in the ideological struggle of the Cold War. In Africa, for example, the initial broadcasting services were short-wave systems (i.e. capable of covering larger distances at the same power as the more expensive medium-wave systems) inherited from colonial administrations. The pattern of external penetration can clearly be seen following the BBC's decision to begin broadcasting to Africa in native languages in 1957, to be followed by Radio Moscow in 1958, the VOA and Radio Peking in 1959, and Deutsche Welle in 1962. In Asia, the battle-lines had been established somewhat earlier, prompted by the Communist victory over the nationalists in China in 1949. In 1951, Radio Peking was broadcasting in thirteen Asian languages, with Taiwan its main target. The VOA and BBC had been broadcasting to the area since the Second World War, but 1951 also saw the CIA establish Radio Free Asia, based in Manila, which was replaced by the Radio of Free Asia which continued until 1966. Japan reintroduced external broadcasting in 1952. Deutsche Welle began its Asian broadcasting service in 1953.

The second level of penetration was less obvious but, if anything, was to cause even greater concern. After all, governments could readily dismiss external broadcasts as 'propaganda' by other governments and therefore alert their peoples to treat it as such. Linking the World Service of the BBC with Her Majesty's Government was common practice – and partly justified, since it was financed by the Foreign Office, although this has never really shaken the Service's reputation world-wide as the most reliable source of international news. However, reliance by newly established broadcasting systems on foreign programme content led to accusations that developing nations were still heavily dependent on the Western powers, rather than independent from them. For example, news-gathering was a highly expensive business. Stations – and even newspapers – could ill afford to deploy foreign correspondents in all the countries of the world. Instead, they would therefore have to rely upon the international news agencies. And the leading agencies were Western: Reuters (British), Associated Press (US), United Press International (US) and Agence France Presse (France). TASS provided a Communist alternative. All this would not matter to those advocates of free-flowing information, but for many developing countries the problem was the image which that information was creating of the 'Third World'.

From the standpoint of London, Washington and Paris, it was hard to see their point. There, the flow of information was seen like the flow of trade; it would flow freely if there was a market for it. On the receiving end, however, it was noticed that the news agencies only seemed to report 'bad news' about events in Less Developed Countries (LDCs). This also applied, of course, to the developed world, but for the newly independent nations desperate for foreign investment the proclivity of the news agencies to report mainly on disasters – 'coups and earthquakes', as one agency employee put it[34] – was hardly conducive to inspiring foreign confidence. By concentrating on famines and floods, it was argued, an imbalanced and detrimental view of what life was really like in such countries was being projected in the West, and this was all the more serious in that the very same view was being imported back into those societies because of their dependence on the international news agencies, damaging self-esteem and national confidence in the process. With such news and perceptions came a disinclination on the part of foreign investors to aid the process of modernity, and there began to emerge calls for a change in such patterns. However, calling for 'developmental news' in which the positive was accentuated was not only against the trend of the events-based type of news reporting that was establishing itself in the television systems of the West, it also looked suspiciously like the Soviet-type model of news, in which the 'good news' – the grain harvest, the production output of factories in the latest Five Year Plan, and such like – was given greater emphasis than news about crime or other ills of society. And this merely rankled with the Western powers waging the Cold War on behalf of their cherished 'freedoms'.

One solution would be for developing nations to establish news agencies of their own, but this was expensive and was really only viable by forming alliances. In the 1960s, therefore, Latin American journalists developed the Inter Press Service to provide a more balanced view of events in that region, which eventually broadened to cover other LDCs. According to one analyst, the IPS was 'the first and only independent and professional news agency which provides on a daily basis information with an LDC focus and point of view. The agency has promoted a new conceptual approach to what is news – stressing the context rather than the event or isolated action . . . on processes rather than on "spot" news as the basis of its news operations.'[35] Later, in 1975, the Non-Aligned News Agency Pool (NANAP) was founded to coordinate the efforts of more than a hundred news services in the Non-Aligned Movement. Other regional arrangements have followed since, with for example the Caribbean News Agency beginning in 1976 and the Pan African News Agency being created in 1979 by the Organisation of African Union. Yet despite the emergence since the 1960s of more than a hundred news agencies, the dominance of the 'Big Four' was never really threatened, while the flow of information between North and South still tends to remain unbalanced in both quantitative and qualitative terms.

Nor was the debate confined to news. Even entertainment programmes, movies at first and television programmes later, appeared to be everywhere – and usually they came from a place called Hollywood. European countries had been concerned about this trend since the 1920s and had attempted to restrict imports by introducing quota systems. But, like the American news agencies following their breakaway in the early 1930s from the major cartel agreements by which the major news agencies divided the world into separate spheres of influence, the American motion picture industry had became a global industry in the space of a generation. It did of course benefit enormously from the devastation wreaked on the European film industries, first during the First World War and then between 1939 and 1945. But clearly there was also something universal about the appeal of American movies. Developing nations also found it difficult to compete with the sheer industrial production-line output of Hollywood films, made to formula in what has been termed the 'classic Hollywood style'. Places like the Soviet Union simply banned their import, but the LDCs found that if they tried to do something similar, it merely incurred the wrath of the State Department and might thus jeopardise American, and thereby Western, aid. Of course, the State Department had long recognised the significance of a phrase popular since the 1920s, namely that 'trade follows the film'. And even though it was not always happy at the image of America which, say, gangster films depicted, the benefits seemed to outweigh the costs, which was why American consuls stationed abroad were required to send reports at least once a year on the motion picture situation.[36] Indeed, by the early 1950s some people were arguing that Hollywood products constituted a Marshall Plan of Ideas which made Walter Wagner's claim of 'Donald Duck as World Diplomat!'[37] seem slightly less ridiculous than it was.

Such arguments began to attract considerable controversy from the 1960s onwards. With American leadership of the Western alliance now firmly established and, at least until the Vietnam debacle, its power untarnished, America in one sense was bound to attract the kind of resentment that had surfaced when Rome had displaced Greece as the then-known world's leading power. But on this occasion, the existence of another superpower in the form of the USSR appeared to provide a check on that power – and it certainly provided an alternative view of the world for those equivalents of the ancient Greeks. But while the United States washed its dirty linen in the full public glare of the media – the Kennedy assassination, the civil rights turmoil, Vietnam and, ultimately, the Watergate scandal – its opponents (both at home and abroad) pointed to its 'cultural imperialism', especially as colour television displaced the black-and-white format as well as the movies as its leading mass medium. In 1962 'the 53 million [television] sets owned outside the United States for the first time surpassed the American total of 50 million'.[38] Indeed, as LDCs continued to attempt to play catch-up in media terms, they found an ideal opportunity to introduce television services of their own as the developed nations switched to colour systems and thus looked for markets to dump their now redundant monochrome transmitters. But again, despite the relatively low costs of introducing modernity in this way, the LDCs found that the price for this was a continuing dependence on

Western programming from back catalogues because importing programmes was infinitely cheaper than producing their own. And if the idea of Donald Duck as diplomat seems fanciful, it would be equally perverse to suggest that watching old editions of *I Love Lucy* was converting millions of Africans to think American. Yet this was in essence what the cultural imperialism debate was about, right up to *Dallas* and *Dynasty* in the late 1970s and early 1980s, and while we should not dismiss outright the arguments that cultural products such as movies and television programmes carry ideologically encoded messages that attack indigenous cultures and create aspirations to emulate the life-styles projected therein, we must equally recognise that exposure to such products can often produce resentment and rejection on the part of audiences. People in foreign countries may have been watching more and more American TV programmes, but the phrase 'Yankee Go Home' was still daubed on the walls of US military bases around the world.

At least we can begin to see why people were now thinking about what Marshall McLuhan in 1960 dubbed 'the global village', even though it was far from a harmonious place. The formation in 1964, following an American initiative, of INTELSAT to provide its initial 19 members with telephone, television, radio, facsimile and data services via satellite earth stations was an indication that Washington was determined that the common language in the village should be English with an American accent. The Soviet Union responded by forming Intersputnik in 1968 to serve the socialist countries, including Cuba, via its Molniya satellites. Like much communications history, technology which was developed as an offshoot of military research (like radio with its initial ship-to-shore applications) was gradually extending into the commercial and private sectors. But, with satellite technology, it seemed that once again the LDCs would be left behind, even though they were now beginning to outnumber the developing countries while their much larger populations fell victim not only to information inequality but also to what was dubbed 'Coca-colonialism'.

By the 1970s and early 1980s, this struggle between the 'core' and the 'periphery' came to a head in the United Nations and UNESCO. No longer happy with client status, LDCs began to assert their independence in media and communications terms, by establishing national and regional news agencies and by asserting their cultural distinctions. Helped, for example, by the wealth created by oil, the Arab League created Arabsat which eventually launched its first satellite in 1985. Indonesia began its satellite service in 1976, launching its first Palapa satellite in 1984. Inmarsat (the international marine satellite organisation) was founded in 1976 to aid global sea navigation. To some extent helped by East–West détente in the period from 1971 to 1979, LDCs were also finding that, once in place, the costs of using such services were dropping radically. For example, in 1964 the cost of a satellite voice channel was £25,000; by 1985 it had fallen to £3,000. INTELSAT

46

broke free from its Cold War shackles, expanded its membership to more than 130 countries, and provided services to around 170 nations by 1988. As costs fell, satellite dishes got smaller, but the gap between the North and South, the core and periphery, still seemed to many to be threatening to open up into a chasm. Hence, old ways of thinking clashed with the new possibilities being provided by communication technologies, particularly in the calls for a New World Information and Communications Order.

THE REAL NEW WORLD INFORMATION ORDER

So much has already been written about the debate over this that it is only necessary here to outline its main issues. UNESCO experts had first identified the phenomenon of 'cultural neo-colonialism' in 1972,[39] and the following year, at the Fourth Conference of Heads of State of the Non-Aligned Countries held in Algiers, there was a call to reorganise the international communications system in such a way as to make it more accessible to all nations and not just to the rich few. Despite achieving political independence, LDCs did not feel that they had secured a position of equality in the international system. A Non-Aligned Symposium in Tunis in 1976 reported that 'since information in the world shows disequilibrium favouring some and ignoring others, it is the duty of the non-aligned countries and other developing countries to change this situation and obtain the decolonisation of information and initiate a new international order in information'.[40] And despite investment in media and communications over the past decade, it had not contributed in any marked way to their economic development, as once promised. Of course it was beginning to in absolute terms, but not relatively. Indeed, here was the rub. Established Second Wave countries were quite simply richer and, to redress the balance of wealth, a 'new world economic order' was required, a call that was endorsed by the UN General Assembly in 1974.

This was perhaps asking for trouble. The facts were plain enough. In 1970, there were 32 newspapers and 9 TV sets per 1,000 people in the Third World, whereas in the First the figures were 314 newspapers and 237 TV sets per 1,000: a disparity of 1:10 for newspapers and 1:25 for TV sets. By the late 1970s, the North American continent accounted for 45 per cent of the world's annual postal traffic and, when Europe and the Soviet Union were included, the figure rose to more than 82 per cent. Eighty per cent of the world's telephones were concentrated in ten North American and European countries.[41] The MacBride Commission, which investigated these inequal-·ities for UNESCO, concluded in 1980 that

The fact that the poorer countries can invest less than the richer countries and that their populations are growing at a much faster rate goes to explain why the gap between the two groups continues to widen. It will be narrowed only by a mighty co-operative effort far in excess of anything being attempted at present.[42]

Other studies reinforced this message, pointing out that 'Tokyo has more telephones than the whole of the African continent',[43] while even by the late 1980s massive discrepancies existed between the proportions of people from different parts of the world owning television sets, never mind such newer technologies as video cassette recorders.[44] The four major news agencies were then estimated to be carrying about 80 per cent of the world's international news every day, with AP serving the media of 115 nations and Reuters of 158.[45]

The restoration of the application of the human rights issue as an international moral barometer, most notably after the Helsinki accords of 1975, certainly became a pivotal issue in the final fifteen years of the Cold War. Yet, although the accords represented the high point of East–West détente in the 1970s, the Soviet Union demonstrated how seriously they took them with the suppression of the Charter 77 human rights group in Czechoslovakia. Having said that, their provisions to improve East–West cooperation in terms of cultural and technological exchanges, as well as improved trade, were designed to aid a freer exchange of ideas and people across Europe while avoiding non-interference in the internal affairs of other states, and as such can be seen as unlocking the door to improved free-flow of information between the two sides of the Iron Curtain. As for the Third World, the NWICO resolution was adopted at the Nineteenth General Conference of UNESCO in Nairobi in 1976, followed by acceptance in the UN General Assembly some weeks later. Rather oddly, it was only then that the detailed research substantiating the resolution was undertaken, chiefly through the MacBride commission, the report of which was published under the title *Many Voices, One World* in 1980. Perhaps under the Presidency of Jimmy Carter (1976–80), the Americans would have remained sympathetic to the promotion of the freedom of information as a fundamental human right. But while the Iranian seizure of American hostages in 1979 might have suggested that a new enemy was afoot, the Soviet invasion of Afghanistan a few months later revealed that the Russian bear was still prepared to show its teeth. The election of Ronald Reagan and his irritability with what he termed the 'Evil Empire' was thus to sound the death-knell for any debates which had Soviet backing.

Under American leadership, then, the Western powers clung to their notions about the free-flow of information and how, eventually, development of communications systems would empower and enrich the LDCs. It seemed to them that the arguments for an NWICO were ideologically motivated, and that this was beyond the pale given the denial of basic freedoms which occurred in many socialist countries and other autocratic or despotic LDCs. Back came the charge, as the Finnish President put it 1973, that:

48

the traditional Western concept of freedom, which states that the state's only obligation is to guarantee laissez-faire, has meant that society has allowed freedom of speech to be realised with the means at the disposal of each individual. In this way freedom of speech has in practice become the freedom of the well-to-do.[46]

Because the increasing number of UNESCO resolutions calling for an NWICO also laid emphasis on the ability of LDCs to help themselves, many chose to go down the route of restricting or taxing heavily imported communications hardware and software. Such attempts to control the impact of alien communications technologies may also have been indicative of the fear of the power of information to undermine the power of the governments imposing the controls. What were they afraid of? Cultural imperialism and continued economic dependency, came the reply. But the free-flow of information would empower individual citizens to make up their own minds and make their own decisions, and allow them to become richer as a result. Not if the international flow of information was imbalanced and biased in the first place, came the reply. Significantly, rarely did international radio broadcasting come into this debate, since many developing countries realised that their case would be undermined if the extent to which they were broadcasting propaganda into neighbouring states became a central issue. Nor was it in the interests of the superpowers to see the debate focus on this aspect, especially following the creation in 1973 of the American Board of International Broadcasting to finance RFE/RL from Congressional funding instead of being under CIA auspices (VOA remained under USIA). An impasse over the NWICO was inevitable, especially when, following the election of Ronald Reagan and Margaret Thatcher to leading positions in the Western alliance at the turn of the decade, the New Cold War displaced the détente of the 1970s.

It has been implied that the NWICO debate was essentially about power, economic as well as political. Information as an empowering commodity was as much recognised by those who possessed and profited from it as it was by those who felt they were denied its possession, and thus exploited by it. Historically, we are used to thinking that the poor revolt against the rich in such conditions. It would be too easy to see the NWICO debate in such terms, but it would certainly be valid to see the Anglo-American withdrawal from UNESCO over this issue as a 'revolt of the rich' in line with arguments put forward elsewhere by Alvin Toffler.[47] The Reagan administration, backed by the media, had become intolerant of UN institutions operating on American soil, especially since they were fuelled heavily by American financial contributions but were now packed with Third World countries consistently passing resolutions in violation of US interests (especially with regard to Israel). The NWICO debate was the principal casualty of this intolerance. The US withdrew from UNESCO in 1985, to be followed by Britain the following year.

This effectively killed off the debate for a decade, but newer technologies were arriving which also began to impact upon international politics. When the Ayatollah Khomeini overthrew the Shah of Iran in 1979, he was greatly aided in his Paris-based campaign by the use of audio-cassettes containing his speeches which could be easily smuggled into Iran and widely distributed throughout the country. No amount of Iranian state censorship and repression seemed able to prevent his voice being heard everywhere, thanks to this imaginative new form of by-passing the traditional media. Elsewhere, new communications technologies were providing clear internationalist opportunities to serve Western interests, as was recognised by Henry Kissinger as early as 1985, when he stated: 'where the control of information is considered the key to political power, cassettes, video machines and computers become threats, not technological opportunities'.[48] Ronald Reagan, nicknamed the 'Great Communicator', was convinced that communications effectively deployed could reinvigorate US policy objectives, especially abroad, that had seemed to suffer a loss of confidence since the humiliating military withdrawal from Southeast Asia in 1973, the fall of Saigon in 1975 and the Iranian hostage crisis. The USIA therefore found itself with renewed backing from a President dedicated to see it 'revitalised' as a front-line weapon, and it was felt that:

> public diplomacy is part of a worldwide transformation in the conduct of international affairs. Traditional secret government-to-government communications have become less important as world leaders compete directly for the support of citizens in other countries. . . . Put simply, instant global communications are breaking down rigidities and isolation, and public opinion is increasingly influential in shaping foreign policy.[49]

There was also the important trend in Western countries during the 1980s towards deregulation in the info-communications sectors, while privatisation of public sector utilities was also gaining ground. Part of this was indeed technologically driven, but the ideological impetus was evident when, in 1984, the United States put pressure on INTELSAT to allow competition in the field of international satellite communication in order to drive down its costs. Ted Turner saw the future with the establishment of Cable News Network (CNN) in 1978, initially lampooned by its rivals as 'Chicken Noodle News'. In Britain, Rupert Murdoch's News Corporation established the SKY satellite television services, and throughout Europe cable and satellite channels exploded. Other technologies, such as the video recorder, the fax machine and the personal computer, were proving all-pervasive, wherever there was the money to buy them, and the transfer of data across borders proliferated on an unprecedented scale as the world economy globalised.

These events were viewed with mounting alarm in Moscow. For forty years, the Soviet authorities had tried to seal off their people from the outside world – by restricting travel overseas and even internally, by arresting dissidents, by bureaucratising the media to serve the interests of the state, by jamming, even by restricting the use of photocopiers. By 1985, 97 per cent of the Soviet population 'enjoyed' access to the system of wired radio sets, on which only state-approved broadcasts could be heard.[50] Imported movies and television programmes, at least from the West, were rare, while domestic news of the West concentrated on all that was bad – which merely whetted the appetite for alternatives. A black market quickly developed in the new technologies, with smuggled tapes and with engineers having a busy time re-tuning radios and TVs so that they were capable of picking up the growing number of satellite services. In Poland, the scene of much domestic dissatisfaction with Soviet rule especially following the agitation of the Solidarity Movement in the early 1980s, a CNN executive described how, as early as 1981, following the initial military crack-down on both domestic and international media, 'we found out that it was possible to pick up an off-the-air signal right on the outskirts of the border'. He continued:

> We took that signal from a little set with rabbit ears and we landlined it to Copenhagen. We had to re-route it then to Rome, Rome satellite to London, London satellite to Maine, Maine downlink landline through Washington, where I happened to be the bureau chief, and I had a Polish translator sit in there on set, landline to Atlanta, at Atlanta the signal would go back out to our subscribers around the world.[51]

Small wonder that, by 1987, it was felt in Poland that 'computers, video and satellite television are attacking the collective unconscious', and it was feared that 'satellite television will demolish the existing structure of information and communications, to the greatest advantage of the greatest industrial and most highly technological powers'.[52]

With the writing on the technological wall, a new style of Soviet leader in the form of Michael Gorbachev bowed to the inevitable once he emerged as General Secretary in 1985. He recognised that wide-scale reconstruction of the Soviet economy was necessary – perestroika – but in order to promote debate about how this should be done, he also introduced the concept of glasnost, or openness. We can now see that this opened the floodgates to greater freedom of opinion within the USSR, which led five years later to the collapse of Communist rule and the disintegration of the Soviet empire. That had never been Gorbachev's intention, despite the 'Gorbymania' of the West which saw it that way at the time. Indeed, regardless of all his early rhetoric about glasnost, when the Chernobyl nuclear accident occurred in 1986 the Soviet media system behaved in its traditional way and it was only when news of it filtered into the Soviet Union from Western sources several days later that the disaster was covered in the domestic media. Nor is it widely appreciated that Gorbachev's Kremlin actually stepped up its propaganda campaigns against the West, with a series of active measures ranging from charges that the AIDS disease was an offshoot of American biological warfare experiments to accusations that rich Americans were plundering the Third World for babies and even spare part surgery.[53]

THE NEW WORLD (DIS)ORDER

Having said that, some important changes were taking place. The Soviet media system began to shift gradually to event-based, Western-style reporting, and the phenomenon of 'investigative journalism' arrived. Live 'space bridge' chat shows between audiences in the US and USSR were permitted and the previously iron grip on information flow within the Eastern Bloc was relaxed. A new independent news agency, Interfax, was formed by journalists, while in 1987/8 all jamming of the BBC, VOA, RFE and RL was halted – the first time since 1945 that all four services could be heard throughout the Soviet system. At the 1988 Gorbachev–Reagan summit in Moscow, Radio Moscow was noted as being less ideologically motivated than before, although it remained critical on points of disagreement.[54] Fax and electronic mail services were opened up with the West, and indeed all forms of two-way communication found it easier to operate.[55] CNN was allowed to distribute its news programmes through GOSTEL-RADIO, and could be seen in hotels from Poland to Hungary. In the former, there were 18,000 satellite dishes and 1.1 million VCRs serving 10 million households with television by 1990, while in the latter there were 15,000 satellite dishes and 0.86 million VCRs for 2.6 million households. In the Soviet Union itself, there were 15,000 satellite dishes and 2.2 million VCRs for 86 million households.[56] These figures might seem small when compared to the levels of penetration that were occurring in the West, but they were sufficiently large to break the hermetically sealed information environment of the previous decades. East Germany had long been able to view West German television, and no amount of propaganda on the part of the authorities about the decadent West could dispel the impressions about affluence on the other side of the Wall before it was finally torn down in November 1989. Within weeks in Rumania, where there were fewer than a hundred satellite dishes in 1990, it only took one person who had seen the Berlin Wall being pulled down to the chant of 'We Are the People' to begin the boos which were then followed by the same chant that precipitated Ceaucescu's downfall.[57] Anyone who witnessed live on television Ceaucescu's bewilderment at what was happening as he tried to address the crowds in Bucharest before they rioted will recall the power which such images conveyed as the third wave clashed with the second.

As events between 1989 and 1991 moved so rapidly, then, Direct

Broadcasting by Satellite (DBS) enabled the peoples of Eastern Europe for the first time to watch, live on television, the dramatic events happening elsewhere in the Eastern bloc as they unfolded – the fall of the Berlin Wall, the advent of democracy in Rumania, Hungary, Poland and Czechoslovakia, the Soviet withdrawal from Afghanistan and the internal collapse of the Soviet Union itself. The key word here is 'live', because live images could not be controlled in the same way as edited productions. In states which controlled their media rigidly, it was always possible to predetermine the events which appeared on television screens in a manner decreed necessary by the state. But in the late 1980s, visitors to Eastern European capitals could notice how those city skylines were being transformed by the arrival of small white satellite dishes. Barely a decade earlier, the USSR had been alarmed at President Reagan's Strategic Defense Initiative (SDI or 'Star Wars'). Little was it appreciated that the real threat was not from SDI but from DBS. Indeed, during the abortive coup in Moscow in August 1991, Gorbachev was able to follow events from his house arrest in the Crimea by listening to the BBC World Service which he had ceased jamming just four years earlier. Meanwhile, the rest of the world was watching his eventual successor, Boris Yeltsin, climb aboard a tank in Moscow to lead the forces of resistance against the plotters – live on CNN.[58] As one official admitted, 'diplomatic communications just can't keep up with CNN'.[59] Or, as a *Washington Post* writer noted, this was 'a genuinely new world order in which the boundaries between cultures have been lowered if not indeed obliterated by television'.[60] If that appears exaggerated, it was none other than George F. Kennan who found it difficult 'to find any other turning point in history that is so significant as this one . . . to the modern communications revolution'.[61]

It is impossible to attribute the changes of the period 1989–91 purely to live satellite television or to increased international communications. But it is equally difficult to see how such changes could have taken place without them. Barry Elliott, former head of BBC Central European Services, claimed in 1992:

> In terms of keeping hope alive and spreading democratic ideas, of really putting it to the people that there were alternatives, yes, I think we did have a role. We were not propounding a change of regime – that wasn't part of our job – but we were stimulating the democratic process, and providing a whole range of views; by reporting strikes and demonstrations that people would not have heard about from their own media we encouraged them to come out and demonstrate.[62]

It was really only in the mid-to-late 1980s, with the arrival of satellite television broadcasting, that forty years of attempting to seal off the peoples of Eastern Europe from alternative images of the West was no longer possible, and so, when the Information Age finally arrived behind the Iron Curtain,

Moscow found that its role was to tear the curtain of authoritarianism asunder. As Edward Shevardnadze stated passionately: 'Praised be information technology, praised be CNN.'[63]

This is not to suggest that the Propaganda Age was finished. In 1989, *Pravda* warned that 'it would be naïve to think that with our restructuring and new thinking, the tasks of certain foreign "voices" have changed. . . . All these methods from the "psychological warfare" arsenal do not, of course, promote trust between countries.'[64] Indeed, in 1987 during the American bombing of Libya, the Voice of America was almost certainly in violation of international laws designed to prevent outside interference in the internal affairs of a state when it broadcast appeals to Libyans to overthrow Colonel Ghadaffi. To 'inform' the anti-Soviet forces in Afghanistan, the Americans established Radio Free Kabul and Radio Free Afghanistan. Moreover, the USIA was extending its brief to international television with the establishment of WORLDNET in 1978. A year later, it was serving eighty-one cable systems in thirteen European countries with daily news and analysis programmes, as well as C-Span (the US government domestic channel) and CNN. The broadcasting service to Cuba was extended to television with the creation of TV Marti in 1990, which the Non-Aligned Movement condemned as 'an aggression and an inadmissible precedent which constitutes intervention in the internal affairs of a state'.[65]

Boris Yeltsin was certainly aware of the need to ride the wave rather than be overwhelmed by it. Shortly after replacing Gorbachev, he even invited Radio Liberty to open up a bureau in Moscow,[66] while the BBC World Service agreed to collaborate with Radio Russia in the making of Russian-language current affairs programmes. All jamming stations were dismantled, with *Pravda* claiming that 'the majority of radio listeners are capable of deciding for themselves what is true and what is a lie, what is information and what is the cunning manipulation of "facts".'[67] The number of telephone circuits to the Soviet Union was also increased to meet demand, and even as internal economic chaos seemed to be the primary target of Western media attention, increased cooperation between the US and Russia was evident throughout the communications sector. The beginnings of an infrastructure plugging the former Second World into the wired circuits of the First was part of the re-establishment of the stability, the order, that helps the day-to-day business of politics, economics and foreign affairs. This is hardly the kind of copy, however, which attracts much media attention.

In January 1992, a joint Russian–US venture, Radio Maximum, was begun in Moscow, to be followed the next month by a Ukrainian–US radio station in Kiev. GOSTELRADIO was replaced by a new company, Ostankino Teleradio, and, to help reconstruction, Warner Brothers donated various films (such as *Superman*) and television series (such as *Murphy Brown* and Bugs Bunny cartoons), while AT&T contracted with a number of the new republics of the Commonwealth of Independent States to install new telephone lines and modernise their telephone systems. When there was talk of shutting down the public diplomacy channels such as RFE and RL, Gorbachev said publicly that he thought this would be 'an appallingly bad idea', while Vaclav Havel of the Czech Republic even wrote to Congress appealing for their continuation.[68] But by then, of course, the major shift was not so much away from what could now be described as the traditional media of press, radio and television but towards personal media – the fax machine, portable audio and videocassettes, laptop computers and Internet access.

As such technology proliferated, the world continued to come to terms with life after the Soviet Union. Russia found itself having to cope with Western media coverage of its war in Chechenya but, to some extent, exploited Western nervousness about a Communist backlash or a return to the bad old days in order to resist Western pressure to do something about stopping the fighting. Influence replaced control as the guiding feature of the Soviet leader's relationship with the domestic media, and it was noted how pro-Yeltsin the Russian media was in his re-election campaign in 1996. To this extent the limits of media coverage remain subordinated to realpolitik. We must therefore be wary of claiming too much for the triumph of the post-1945 concept of freedom of information.

Moreover, even within Western countries, the cultural dimension continues to cause tensions, as was evidenced during the GATT negotiations when the French government took a stance against unrestricted imported American movies and television programmes. But, in the 1990s, McDonald's has opened a store in Moscow and EuroDisney has built a theme park outside Paris, while American media and cultural products continue their global march. 'How can Europe resist?' asked one analyst. 'Chances are it won't. Cultural imperialism or not, millions of Europeans will soon be careering down Big Thunder Mountain, celebrating the Old World's coming of age.'[69] Never mind the fact that millions of Europeans had been visiting Disney World in Florida for at least ten years, or the fact that EuroDisney had a struggle to establish itself, or even that Sharon Stone and Sylvester Stallone have been awarded the highest French cultural awards for their contributions to the cinema, the proponents of cultural imperialism will no doubt continue to behave like the ancient Greeks in criticising barbaric Rome so long as the United States remains the world's sole superpower.

In Tehran, all this makes America 'the Great Satan', while Iran has displaced the Soviet Union as the principal perceived enemy of the United States. But the Americans are not without rivals in either economic or cultural spheres – as Japanese attempts to buy into the American media sector, not to mention the world-wide success of their automobile industry, demonstrate. And the extent to which the Americans are still prepared to go in defence of their interests was apparent during the Persian Gulf War of 1991. That, however, was done under UN auspices in defence of UN resolutions, and this, together with other multilateral efforts, reflects a recognition that the United States can no longer 'go it alone' in quite the same way as it might have been possible to do so in the past.

There remain serious threats to the American ideal of universalism, especially by nationalistic movements jostling for power in countries that have suffered political breakdowns, such as Yugoslavia and the Soviet Union. But democratic forms of government are in the ascendancy throughout the world, and great store is placed on the historical fact that democracies tend not to go to war against other democracies – or at least they haven't so far. This is the real New World Order, a democratic free-market capitalist order in which information has become the lifeblood of the system. Competition and capitalism have always created inequalities, not communications *per se*. And when they operate within a democratic context, the appearance of various competing interests – from political parties to marketing products – provides the impression of wider choice and thus the need for increased decision-making capabilities on the part of individuals – which party to vote for, which soap powder to buy – which in itself generates confusion rather than clarity. That, quite simply, is the price of democracy. The alternative, to which many older people in Russia apparently would like to return, is for the state to make those decisions for them, to guarantee their jobs, living accommodation and pensions. Such human reactions to an apparently confusing world in which more options are available – whether it be, for example, a romantic notion of returning to a 'simpler life' in an English rural idyll – can equally be applied to popular perceptions everywhere about international affairs. Moreover, with the discernible recent shift towards greater concern with global issues such as ecological and environmental factors – as was evident at the Rio summit in 1993 – and international terrorism as issues of universal concern, the simpler life seems further away than ever before as communications increase the connections to those complex issues rather than allow individuals to escape from them. As one writer has put it:

> The nervous system has begun to replace the muscular system in high politics. World politics consists of a great variety of interactions in which actors communicate with the intention to influence other actors. The effectiveness of this interaction depends largely on the quality, credibility and efficiency of the transborder movement of information.[70]

Late twentieth-century enlightened global citizens are against pollution and terrorism, against violations of human rights, against repression and inhumanity, against pollution, against nuclear proliferation. These are now the yardsticks by which heroes and villains are designated. To this list can be added the 'information haves', as long as there are so many 'have-nots'. Herbert Schiller, that renowned defender of the latter, writing of the 'shocking phenomenon' that '20% of the world's population consumes 80% of its wealth and is responsible for 75% of its pollution', stated:

> The main miscreant in this deepening global crisis is a model of acquisitive behavior and consumerist attitude, by the powerful and deadly combination of the media, technology and the market. . . . Images and messages today are the outputs of creative talents, using the most advanced information technologies in their production and distribution, for marketing goals.[71]

Perhaps so. Undoubtedly the looming issues of the post-Cold War Information Age are related to issues of commercialism and competition in the info-communications sectors, not least because of the role they are perceived to have played in the triumph of free-market-enterprise liberal democracy. But whether the messages that are being carried are forces for good or ill, the need for governments to retain an interest in these sectors will ensure the continuation of state propaganda (in its value-neutral sense) as a way of ensuring that ordered presentation of official interests is represented alongside the apparently disordered reporting of them. And, for the moment, that is still most effectively conducted through the agencies of public communications including the media, although a democratic media fails to see itself in such terms. Yet that is why academics like Noam Chomsky and others talk of 'manufacturing consent', of the media as instruments of dominant ideologies, as purveyors of political agendas, while the media seem only too happy to feed off the latest snappy soundbites provided for them by the increasing numbers of spin-doctors employed for precisely these purposes. In short, the media need politics and politicians just as much as the politicians need the media. As for foreign affairs, however, neither side is quite so sure.

2

BRUSHFIRES AND FIREFIGHTERS
International affairs and the news media

Just as the mass media became integral to the everyday domestic workings of the modern state during the course of this century, so also have they come to play an ever-increasing role in the external relations between states. Much has already been written by historians about that increasing role, from the Anglo-German press 'wars' in the build-up to the First World War to the role of newspapers, the cinema and radio in the programme of 'moral rearmament' prior to the Second World War.[1] A growing amount of literature also now exists about how the media came to be deployed as a psychological weapon, at home and abroad, first between 1939 and 1945 and then subsequently during the Cold War. Today, however, if a statesman wants to make a public statement or send a message across the world, he has the option of doing so on CNN rather than through traditional diplomatic channels. As a result, the burning issues of the day appear to be reported 'as they happen', while international affairs are conducted in the full glare of global publicity for a world-wide audience. Such conditions are conducive to improvisation, inconsistencies and U-turns. But, to paraphrase Raymond Chandler, when you make a U-turn, you also make a lot of enemas.

Shortly before he left office in 1977, the year before CNN was founded, US Secretary of State Henry Kissinger suggested that 'the days when statesmen and journalists coexisted in an atmosphere of trust and shared confidences have given way to a state of almost perpetual inquest which, at worst, can degenerate into a relationship of hunter and hunted, deceiver and dupe'.[2] More recently still, during the 1990s, those traditionally responsible for conducting inter-state dialogue can be heard frequently complaining that:

> the new phenomenon of global instantaneous news reporting, particularly by television, has distorted the foreign policies of the western countries in the aftermath of the Cold War by forcing military intervention in such areas as former Yugoslavia, Somalia or Cambodia, while at the same time preventing that intervention from becoming

effective by imposing arbitrary constraints on the level of force used, and on the willingness to risk taking casualties and inflicting them.[3]

Whether the media are really this significant is in fact questionable, but the very existence of such complaints is not just a recognition that an important player has indeed arrived in the international arena but also reflects the feeling that something about his behaviour on the playing-fields of foreign policy has changed matters for the worse.

FOREIGN POLICY IN THE MASS MEDIA AGE

It is frequently said that, prior to the advent of the mass media, diplomacy was the sport of kings and, as such, it had little or nothing to do with public opinion. In 1866, when *The Times* lauded the achievements of those responsible for laying the first trans-Atlantic cable under the banner 'Shrinking World', it identified three principal likely beneficiaries: governments, mercantile interests and newspapers.[4] In other words, public opinion as a concept on a mass scale barely came into its consideration. Hence, in Britain, while democratisation and public accountability advanced only very slowly in the late nineteenth century, 'the foreign secretary and his officials prided themselves on their detachment from the changing moods of public opinion',[5] while such was the special position of foreign affairs within political life that even the House of Commons 'seldom or never presumed to press for an answer when the Foreign Secretary put a finger to his lips'.[6] The First World War changed all that. The diminishing gap between political and public life necessitated by the exigencies of 'total war', combined with the discrediting of 'secret diplomacy' as a cause not only of the war but of some of its more intractable problems afterwards,[7] meant that foreign affairs could no longer be conducted in quite the same sort of seclusion.

Moreover, the modern media had proved to be considerable allies in selling the war and sustaining public support for it.[8] As newspaper baron Lord Northcliffe put it: 'God made people read so that I could fill their brains with facts, facts, facts – and later tell them whom to love, whom to hate, and what to think.'[9] He was to demonstrate what he meant by this especially when he was placed in charge of the government's department for enemy propaganda in 1918. At that stage, the government was forced to draft in newspapermen like Northcliffe and Beaverbrook to conduct their wartime 'public information' activities (just as they had done with literary figures like John Buchan before them[10]) because it had yet to build up a store of professional experience and expertise in the realm of publicity to draw on from its own resources. There had simply been felt to be no need for it before 1914.[11] That was also to change very quickly. The establishment of the League of Nations in 1919, with its dedication to 'open covenants, openly arrived at', combined with extensions to franchise which made it near-universal, and the growing competition which newspapers were subjected to as principal sources of news, first from radio and then from cinema newsreels and later television, all contributed to the advent of a new, more public, era for the foreign-policy-making process. Whereas in Paris in 1919, cinematographic film cameras were denied access to the Hall of Mirrors in order to film the signing of the Versailles Treaty, within six years the Locarno Treaties were signed amidst a blaze of publicity (including silent newsreel cameras), and, by the time of the 1930 London Naval Treaty, such access was becoming the norm. Subsequently, with the advent of sound film, politicians and statesmen could be seen and heard speaking directly to cinema audiences around the world. Radio penetrated the very walls of people's homes. Once-distant places and peoples became more familiar, as news appeared from anywhere and everywhere by a variety of new means in ways that one could only marvel at.

One of the striking characteristics of the relationship between those responsible for conducting policy, at home and abroad, and those reporting on it, was that it tended in these early days more towards cooperation than conflict. There were, of course, occasional clashes, but it would for instance be hard to imagine journalists today emulating the example of their predecessors in cooperating with US President Franklin D. Roosevelt and his staff to conspire (and the word is used advisedly) in disguising the fact that he suffered from polio. As a result, barely a few seconds of film survives showing the man who was President of the United States for twelve years at the height of the cinema newsreel age walking on crutches. Similarly, in Britain, it would be hard to envisage today the kind of press relations which the government enjoyed at the time of Edward VIII's relationship with Mrs Simpson prior to the abdication crisis, with certain newspapers not covering the story because their 'discretion was not in question'.[12] No, the problem for Westminster and Whitehall in 1936 was that the American newspapers were revelling in the affair, news of which, it was realised, would in this ever-shrinking world cross the Atlantic in but a matter of time. One might have thought that, fifty years later, when Margaret Thatcher's government attempted to prevent the publication of Peter Wright's *Spycatcher* in Britain, it would have been realised that copies of the book bought at New York airports would be winging their way to the UK the same day. What destiny lies in wake for future efforts to control the flow of digital data transmission?

Even before the advent, then, of such media-sensitive politicians as Roosevelt in America, Stanley Baldwin and later Winston Churchill in Britain, and of course Adolf Hitler in Germany, international affairs had entered the mass media age.[13] Or was it the other way round? As one Foreign Office official pointed out in 1925:

> The era when it was possible either to lead opinion in foreign politics
> by mere authority or tradition, or to ignore it from Olympian heights,

has long since vanished, and once modern contact, however vulgar, has been established, it is not possible to confine it to an intermittent dispensation of tit-bits of news at the will of one or two minor officials or as a subsidiary function of an unspecialised department. It has become, and must be, practically a never-ceasing intercourse with the publicity world.[14]

Here indeed was a clear early recognition that a new wave was approaching, but there remained a feeling within foreign policy-making elites that diplomacy was too serious a business to be left at the mercy of institutions that pandered to commercial rather than national interests (i.e. newspapers). Walter Lippmann's seminal 1922 study, *Public Opinion*,[15] reinforced this assumption, not least because it argued that the press was doing such a poor job in preparing the public sufficiently for them to share in informed policy-making. Part of the reason for this, again recognised surprisingly early in 1918 by the MP Arthur Ponsonby, was what would later be described as the firefighting tendency of the media (or 'parachute journalism'):

What happened in the press? We see a series of events reported with great fullness; we begin to read of them. The next day the story continues, and we read it with interest; but the day after that some domestic concern crops up . . . And the foreign news is withdrawn, the story stops, and the country is under the impression that that particular issue is over. It may not be at all.[16]

Yet, as high politics, at least in democracies, was forced to become more accountable to the forces of public opinion in whose name it increasingly had to operate, and indeed began to provide it with the legitimisation required for decisions about war and peace, the mass media could not simply be dismissed as erratic – even if they often treated foreign policy issues erratically. Besides, to have ignored them would have meant being left behind in a world that was developing new applications of the power of publicity and advertising thanks to advancements in the discipline of psychology, and therefore new opportunities to use the media for political and diplomatic purposes. Instead, therefore, of being reactive, there was a growing recognition for the need on the part of government for proactivity, which gave rise to ever-increasing state-sponsored media activity – press relations, information departments and the like – in an attempt to ensure that official versions of events prevailed over possible privatised media speculation. This resulted in the practice by government of, if not shaping the media's agenda, then influencing it, rather than allowing the reverse to happen. And, if anything, diplomats were among the first to become aware of this – which is why, for example, in Britain the Foreign Office News Department pre-dates the Press Office at 10 Downing Street by more than a decade.[17]

Of course the press had always been used to greater or lesser degrees by those in authority, most notably by Bismarck and Cavour.[18] Nor was the press automatically uncooperative or hostile, particularly the party political press. In 1893 there was a good example in Britain of the supposed contrast between the journalist, 'whose mere thought was publicity, and the diplomat, who thought always of the effect of publicity upon policy'. Donald Mackenzie Wallace, head of the foreign service at *The Times*, admitted to a journalist colleague:

> I may tell you *between ourselves* that we had a leader written on the decision twenty-four hours before your telegram arrived, but we considered it more 'correct' (in the diplomatic sense) to await the official announcement. For reasons which I need not explain to so experienced a journalist, a considerable portion of our most precious wares are never put into the shop window at all.[19]

This self-perception by journalists as being an integral part of the Establishment, as 'the fourth estate', survived even the Northcliffe 'revolution' of the mass circulation press, although it is all-too-often forgotten by those outside the lobby system or by those without privileged access to inside information. But there is still a loyal cadre of such journalists, whether they see themselves as keepers of the government's conscience, devil's advocates to political policies, custodians of the public's right to know or defenders of some moral high ground. For example, the American press corps, for all its First Amendment rights, knew of the 1961 Bay of Pigs episode in advance but adhered to a White House request not to publish anything about it until after it had happened.[20] Having said that, during the American operation in Haiti in 1993, they proved less compliant, as hundreds of Western journalists defied UN sanctions and a White House demand for a voluntary embargo on live coverage, set up their satellite dishes at Port-au-Prince hotels and, complete with live-link cameras equipped with night scopes, waited to capture the invasion in real time. Something has indeed changed.

The two key elements in this transformation are trust and technology. We are of course talking about a very heterogeneous profession, more so than ever before. Journalism has always been a pretty hierarchical business but, with the changing managerial and occupational practices caused by post-modernisation, the distinctions between 'staffers' and short-term-contract employees such as stringers have become accentuated. With short-term staff, it has become difficult to build up a system of mutual trust, because officials can never be certain that journalists they confide in might have different criteria once their employment contract runs out. On the other hand, staff journalists with whom a relationship of trust can be built over a period of time can usually be relied upon to avoid or delay running with a story if they can be convinced not so much that it is against the 'national interest' but that their own long-term career interests might suffer. And, over time, since cooperation leads to trust, cooperation offers the possibility of future confidences, perhaps leaks, and maybe even scoops. The converse, however, also works: betrayal of trust can lead the well of information to run dry. Officials involved in the great international issues of the day are obviously primary sources of information for journalists trying to do their job; anything spokesmen say, on or off the record, can lead to a story. Indeed, the very phrase 'off the record' displays the degree to which a level of mutual understanding between the professions has built up over the years to ensure that what the official says will not be attributed personally in that story, and those that adhere to it can expect to be spoken to again. But as the nature of work practices change from long-term careers to short-term contractual jobs, it is more likely that everything will be kept *on* the record.

There is something to be said for this, because it begs the question of how objective news reports emanating from official sources actually are. It has been suggested that when such 'in the know' journalists take refuge in the concept of objectivity,[21] this is really 'a defensive measure, an attempt to secure by quasi scientific means a method for reordering the world, independent of the political and social forces that were shaping it'.[22] Consequently, the argument runs, the role of the press has become 'increasingly antipopulist and antipublic':

In a world ruled by interests and regulated by science, the public faded into a spectator. Journalism was diminished along with the public. In theory, at least, news was progressively separated from the truth. News was a blip on the social radar, an early-warning system that something was happening. The truth however became the exclusive domain of science. It was no longer a product of the conversation or debate of the public, or of investigations by journalists. Journalists merely translated the arcane language of experts – scientists in their labs, bureaucrats in their offices – into a publicly accessible language for the masses. By transmitting the judgements of experts, they ratified decisions made by that class – not those made by the public or public representatives.[23]

This is what lay behind the self-styled outsider I. F. Stone's comment about such journalists that 'they know a lot of things that I don't know, but a lot of what they know isn't true'.[24] But such journalists suited the Establishment well, as conduits for its anything but objective agendas. The shift from cooperation to antagonism thus might be said to have benefited purist democratic philosophies more than the cosiness of the media sleeping in the same bed as government officials. Such a stance welcomes the distance created by the disestablishmentarianism of the commercial media, although it remains uneasy at the consequent predisposition to see established institutions become the object of constant media scrutiny and attack. What is felt to have changed the old level of mutual cooperation and trust more than

63

any other event, at least in America, was the Watergate scandal of the mid-1970s, coming as it did at the end of the Vietnam war. In Britain, it was probably Suez in 1956. But the degree to which the corporate nature of the media has prevailed since then, with its increasingly heavy dependence upon advertisers and its drive for profits, has most likely been just as significant, as everyone in the public eye becomes fair game for a media industry driven by criteria quite different from the need to collaborate with its one-time principal sources of news. Because, in other words, there are now so many beds to sleep in, the opportunities for adultery seem infinitely more attractive than the constraints of fidelity.

Certainly, official sources have never been beyond misleading journalists but, once that game is discovered, the cost to the source is likely to be infinitely more prejudicial in the long term. After Watergate, it was not just Richard Nixon who paid the price but the very office of the President of the United States. Anthony Eden suffered likewise in Britain. Thereafter, Prime Ministers were treated with less respect by the media, with first names or nicknames ('Supermac', 'the Skull', Harold, Ted, Jim, Maggie) replacing the appellation of 'Mr'. The loss of credibility by any source in an information age where numerous outlets compete for this very quality is rarely worth taking the risk for. This was in fact quickly discovered much earlier by officials working in the mushrooming number of government press departments in the 1920s, once 'concern with the news media became part of the *routine* of framing foreign policy and conducting diplomacy'.[25] But credibility does not necessarily equate with truth. As one of the first heads of the British Foreign Office News Department informed the press after the First World War: 'You think we lie to you. But we don't lie, really we don't. However, when you discover that, you make an even greater error. You think we tell you the truth.'[26]

This is the tightrope which any journalist has to walk. Through training and experience in the 'school of hard knocks' he or she develops a sense of intuition (a 'nose') for what can be done with any piece of information. However, while the law imposes certain constraints on what can be said, and how, the proximity to the dealings of the 'great and the good', almost by a process of osmosis, leads to a sense of what should be said, and why. If that very contact inevitably pollutes their judgement, when everything in their professional ethos pushes them towards an attempt to be objective, then the moral for the great and the good is that contact is infinitely preferable to avoidance. But with contact comes risk. The risk that what is said may be misconstrued, misunderstood or misrepresented requires, therefore, a degree of professionalism on the part of official spokesmen which makes their job as mediators of official information to the media every bit as difficult as that of the journalists as mediators of that information to the public. As Marlin Fitzwater, the White House spokesman under the Reagan and Bush administrations, warned: 'Reporters are always reporters. Only secondarily are they your friends. . . . Treat them like friends and they will betray you every time.'[27] Moreover, officials need to appreciate that, once in possession of the information, the journalist is rarely the sole owner of it. He has acquired not just a public commodity but also a corporate commodity. Before it ever leaves the news organisation, it is put through a number of selection processes by sub-editors, editors and copy editors which can modify the original meaning or emphasis. As such, whereas the two professions therefore rely on each other, the process of relaying information down the line, so to speak, is fraught with potential problems as the information travels through a series of different human filters.

With the arrival of radio, which allowed for direct government-to-people communication, the number of such filters was potentially reduced. It appeared that the notion of the media as *mediator* might have to be revised, especially now that politicians could speak directly to their constituencies. This perhaps gave radio a higher credibility factor in the minds of the public, as was famously illustrated by Orson Welles's broadcast of H. G. Wells's 'War of the Worlds' in 1938. It was also more accessible to the illiterate and less well educated. Indeed, fear of its power over such people initially prompted the formation of national monopolies or direct state control over broadcasting just about everywhere except North America, where commercialism reigned supreme as an outlet of its free-market enterprise system. By 1938, of the thirty European national broadcasting systems in existence, thirteen were state-owned and operated, nine were government monopolies operated by autonomous public bodies or partially government-controlled corporations, four were actually operated by government – but only three were privately owned or run.[28] Under such circumstances, it was inevitable that international radio broadcasting should become part of the ideological antagonism in the build-up to the Second World War. Equally, as the profession of the radio journalist developed, the capacity to frame radio news in a manner not dissimilar to print was regained once the emphasis shifted from live to recorded programming, first on gramophone and later on tape. Enter once again the editors, the sub-editors and the programme editors. This put on hold the kind of debates we are currently witnessing over the perils of 'real-time' broadcasting.

Radio's unique qualities as an internationalist medium were also recognised from the outset, as encapsulated in the BBC's motto that 'Nation Shall Speak Peace Unto Nation'. Lenin, Hitler and Stalin of course had other ideas,[29] prompting even democracies like the USA – eventually, during the Second World War – to regard external radio broadcasting as a state responsibility, as an instrument of 'public diplomacy' or, as others see it, of 'international propaganda'.[30] Television, on the other hand, as we shall see, was initially viewed in much more parochial terms; even during the first half of the Cold War, its role still seemed confined to domestic consensus-building (which some might see as 'national propaganda')[31] and therefore not really an issue in international affairs until the satellite age.

65

So, by the 1930s, the mass media had already emerged as the interface between the once-secret world of diplomacy and the publicity conscious public sphere. They provided invaluable information for government and people alike, with the foreign department of *The Times*, for example, often being regarded by foreign affairs specialists in the first half of this century as a more valuable source of intelligence than the Foreign Office itself. The emergence in the 1930s of the specialised foreign correspondent meant that men such as Edward R. Murrow and William Shirer became household names in America. Correspondents could go where diplomats dare not, and news from China in the 1930s, for example, kept that country high on the American public agenda.[32] The capacity of the media for 'map-making', as Lippmann called it, often resulted not just from media interest in a given area of the world but because they had been alerted to that area by diplomatic press officers. On their return, most correspondents would not think twice about debriefing State Departments or Foreign Offices about their visits and interviews with foreign officials and heads of state, as the archives only too frequently reveal. This was why, on the outbreak of the Second World War, journalists such as Sir Frederick Whyte, founder and editor of *The New Europe*, and broadcasters such as Vernon Bartlett and Stephen King-Hall, were recruited into the official propaganda machinery.[33] Hence the time-honoured suspicion of the journalist as spy. The level of mutual cooperation, as we shall see in the next chapter, would bear considerable fruit during the Second World War. Indeed, if anything, the period up to 1945 can be regarded as something of a 'golden age' of foreign news reporting. Countries such as Manchuria, Ethiopia and Albania received the kind of extensive media coverage in Europe that would bemuse modern readers, who are but barely informed about the more recent crises in Ossetia, Tajikistan or Georgian Abkhazia. With so much more information about world events now available, how can this be the case?

After the Second World War, with the disappearance of so many metropolitan daily newspapers,[34] even those that did survive started to cut back radically on the number of foreign bureaux they maintained. In 1945, for example, American newspapers employed around 2,500 reporters on overseas assignments, whereas by the mid-1970s this was down to below 500. The *New York Times* had over sixty foreign correspondents in the 1950s but only thirty-four in 1978, while in London *The Times* reduced the number of its overseas correspondents from twenty-six to eighteen between 1965 and 1976.[35] This was partly a reflection of the increasing shift by the public away from the press to television as their principal source of news and information, but what it has meant for the press has been an increasing reliance on the international news agencies as the most regular suppliers of routine foreign news.

And on governments. The Cold War made Moscow and Washington the centres of international news and, in 1979, 182 journalists from forty-six countries were stationed in the former while, in 1983, 480 foreign correspondents from sixty-one countries were stationed in the American capital. This compared with 103 correspondents from twenty-five countries stationed in New Delhi.[36] It has been estimated that almost three-quarters of front-page stories in the *Washington Post* and the *New York Times* were derived from official sources.[37]

Having said that, at the G7 summit in Tokyo in July 1993, an astonishing 11,000 journalists covered the event, reflecting the massive recent proliferation world-wide of media stringers and local freelancers, the so-called 'media circus'. But the number of foreign correspondents on the permanent staff of any given news organisation, people who could justifiably be deemed as foreign policy specialists, has declined, even though there are more such organisations than ever before. A freelance journalist may specialise in one area, but if that area is foreign affairs they are unlikely to get much work. Moreover, if the area of that expertise is, say, Japan, it does not automatically follow that they will be able to report authoritatively on events in South Africa, even though that is where the story might be. Moreover, it is infinitely easier to manipulate non-specialists. Yet in a sense, regardless of the ebbs and flows of organisational change within the news media, none of this really matters, because of television.

If television images are captured on just one camera, they can be used by all the television stations around the world that choose to show them. As one senior diplomat suggested in 1993:

> Media coverage of stories like Somalia and Bosnia has created public issues that probably would not have existed in any significant way 50 years ago. Before World War I, it wouldn't have occurred to anyone that events around Sarajevo or in the horn of Africa could have any remote relevance to America. You might get an inch or two in some of the more cosmopolitan newspapers, but that would be it.[38]

The US-centrism of the American media remains a concern to this day. However, as the American entry into the First World War two and a half years after the assassination in Sarajevo which sparked off that conflict was to demonstrate, seemingly irrelevant events in distant places could have serious and unforeseen consequences for nations. Indeed, nothing could more adequately illustrate the importance of informed foreign news coverage in as much detail as possible. Nor could anything more adequately illustrate the dangers of the post-1945 decline of the specialised foreign correspondent.

The problem is that foreign news gathering is an extremely expensive business, involving the deployment of personnel and equipment for undetermined periods of time in costly foreign hotels and with large expense accounts. Decisions have to be made by news organisations as to whether the stories are important enough – and sufficiently relevant – to command public interest at home. How can they know, especially as foreign policy *issues*, the stuff of diplomacy, sometimes never flare up in the form of *events*, the real stuff of journalism? Besides, sending journalists to one spot means not sending them to others. More usually, it is cheaper to rely on the news agencies with their permanent bureaux stationed overseas. Yet anyone who has seen these wire service bulletins knows that they are the most basic reports of information, usually quite short, and containing only the bare details. Once issued, it is left to the journalists who receive them to 'spice them up' according to their house style. In other words, different customers in the media receive the same information and repackage it in such a way that it becomes barely recognisable from the original bulletin. The appearance of heterogeneous coverage thus masks the actual homogeneity of much foreign news gathering. The four major suppliers – Associated Press, United Press International, Reuters and Agence France Presse – owed a good deal of their continuing prominence to historical longevity, and a little of it – at least in the case of Reuters and Havas, the precursor of AFP – to government subsidies. As international news gathering developed into a valuable commodity, governments and media alike thus became their direct customers, serving the public only indirectly. The agencies may have found that supplying factual information was necessary to keep those direct customers happy, but as suppliers of a raw commodity they were none the less in an enormously powerful position as 'gatekeepers' of international news. Again, credibility was vital to their success, yet how much news they gathered and how much they distributed were quite different.

Gatekeeping is really about filtration and, even in purely quantitative terms, by the time the torrent of news gathered from the available reservoir has been distributed to customers it is, by comparison, a stream. By the time it reaches the public it has become a trickle. Even the major news agencies 'rarely filed reportage with depth comparable to that from a daily's own foreign bureau'.[39] More recently still, international news agencies have been undergoing significant changes. UPI was bought out by a Middle Eastern consortium in the early 1990s, which does not appear to have aided its survival. TASS, the official agency of the former Soviet Union, is essentially finished as a major global player, and certainly discredited as a conveyer of credible information. Only twenty per cent of Reuters' income now comes from news distribution as it shifts to being the major world supplier of global data and economic information.[40] However, despite the existence of nearly a hundred other news agencies world-wide, they show few signs of breaking the global domination of the three remaining principal players, AP, Reuters and AFP. Reuters has acquired VISNEWS, the largest world-wide supplier of video news footage. All that has been said of gatekeeping with regard to printed material applies to TV footage as well. These organisations therefore remain the prisms through which most international news enters the public domain, even today. To borrow I. F. Stone's distinction, although they gather a lot of news, a lot of what they gather never reaches the wider public.

The eventual global television and newspaper audience of these organisations is colossal, well in excess of two billion people, but to illustrate the degree of filtration that goes on we can draw on a study made in the early 1970s. In June and July 1971, all the information sent from AP bureaux in Latin America to AP's headquarters in New York was analysed. It revealed a tendency to mirror customer-led (i.e. media subscribers') demand for events-based news rather than to reflect any sense of the public's need to know about issue-based trends elsewhere in the world. The actual amount of foreign news which was filtered out by AP editors prior to distribution to subscribers in the United States would have terrified Walter Lippmann. Although sporting items were by far the most numerous of stories coming in, with 23.23 per cent of the total items in the categories identified, and foreign relations came second, with 19.19 per cent, by the time AP redistributed the news to its domestic 'A' wire, all sport had been eliminated and foreign affairs had been reduced to 6.25 per cent. Crime stories, 13.81 per cent of incoming material, shot up to 47.66 per cent of its output to domestic customers.[41] Although far from conclusive, and very much coming from an era before CNN, these figures do reveal the degree to which the American news agencies and media map the outside world for the American public and reorder the 'reality' of what goes on there. Crises which may have been festering for some time seem to explode very suddenly on to our public consciousness, with the result that the context, and therefore an informed understanding of the realistic policy options available to the government, is missing.

PUBLIC OPINION AND FOREIGN POLICY

But how intrusive the media actually are at other times is easy to exaggerate. Again, foreign affairs presents special problems, as does the emergence of a modern public opinion in theory as distinct from practice. After all, how many people are really interested in international affairs? One might argue that this is an irrelevant question, for, while it may still be true that media coverage of foreign affairs reflects the relative disinterest or lower priorities of the public as a whole, officials have none the less become more accountable to that public as democratisation has unfolded during the course of the century. More people can vote now than could a hundred years ago, and although there have really been only two general elections in Britain during that period in which foreign affairs featured prominently on election platforms,[42] and remembering that the 1940 American Presidential Election was fought out on an isolationist ticket, developments in international economics, politics and technology, especially during and after the Second World War, conflated or even obliterated once previous distinctions between domestic and overseas policies in whatever dimension they took place. This

increasing interdependence, combined with the increasing interconnectedness of national with international affairs, is what is meant by globalisation
which takes place in every area from political economy to environmental
issues.

By way of illustration, nowhere perhaps was this more evident than in the
area of defence issues. Voting taxpayers contribute to the cost of national
defence, which often involves the deployment of troops and equipment overseas to protect 'national interests'. Increasingly, those troops are being asked
to go overseas to serve the 'international community' on behalf of the
United Nations or other multilateral alliances. Defence policy and foreign
policy thus become closely interconnected with the necessity to command
public support for such deployments. Between the two World Wars, it was
because Britain no longer possessed the military resources required to safe-
guard her world-wide interests when faced with three simultaneous threats –
in Europe from Nazi Germany, in the Mediterranean from Fascist Italy and
in the Far East from imperialist Japan – that the policy of appeasement was
seen by the government as the only viable alternative. Or at least until rearmament was more advanced. The problem was how to convince a
predominantly pacifist public, scarred by the 'war to end all wars' and the
deprivations of the Great Depression, that their taxes needed to be expended
on armaments when the government's policy was one of peace. And this had
to be done without frightening the public too much as to the real vulner-
ability of British interests, exposure of which would merely have alerted her
potential adversaries and brought on that which the government was trying
to avoid. Thus was developed the notion that rearmament was an 'insurance
policy', and that 'Britain Must Be Strong' in order to avoid war.[43]

Again, when that policy failed and the Second World War broke out, the
distinction between defence, foreign policy and public opinion was obliterated in the form of the bomber. Bombers – despite the myth of a 'strategic'
bombing campaign against specific industrial and military targets – involved
civilians in matters of life and death, in questions of war and peace, because
bombers failed to discriminate between the public and other sectors of the
community. Factories, for example, are built in towns and the workers live
nearby. Bombs dropped from a height of 20,000 feet cannot be expected to
avoid causing, in the current military jargon, 'collateral damage'. Such
weapons eradicated the traditional space between domestic and foreign
affairs, and not just in the war of 1939–45 but also in the decades that
followed. As the Cold War heated up, the arrival and proliferation of
nuclear weapons meant that foreign policy decisions about peace and war
had the even greater capability of affecting every citizen, not just in one
country but throughout entire continents. In other words, the maintenance
of large defence budgets required justification to a taxpaying electorate that
constituted the front line in any potential nuclear confrontation. Whereas on
the one hand this required considerable attention to proactive media

strategies on the part of government institutions in order to sustain public and media support for continually high defence expenditure, on the other it required a large degree of secrecy about the whole area of defence. Hence most legislation in free societies involving the curtailment of press and media freedoms stems from defence or security matters. And most early critics of how the American government achieved this balance during the Cold War were able to latch on to the notion of a 'military–industrial complex' that conspired with the media to manipulate the public.[44]

This balancing act was considerably easier in the Soviet bloc, where state-controlled media could be relied upon to voice the desired views of authoritarian regimes. For that reason, the Soviet media became an invaluable source of intelligence for Western analysts, with considerable expenditure being devoted to monitoring them and no attempts to jam their external broadcasts. By contrast, the Soviet regime spent vast amounts of money on attempting to seal off their publics from exposure to Western media, ranging from jamming to bans on the use of photocopiers. Hence the Cold War became as much a struggle to influence the public opinion of the oppositional bloc as it was a great game of defence one-upmanship. And while this might have appeared to have worked in certain towns which declared themselves 'nuclear free zones', the reality of nuclear fallout was always likely – as the Chernobyl accident of 1986 demonstrated – to be somewhat different. But defence issues at least provided the impression of an increased level of public interest in international affairs.

This may seem odd because a recurring, if perhaps regrettable, fact of life is that foreign affairs infrequently commands a high priority for domestic news organisations. Media professionals believe, rightly or wrongly (one suspects the former), that the majority of their customers in the audience are not particularly interested in events foreign. One survey from the early 1960s in the United States put the figure at around 15 per cent of the population constituting a potential 'foreign policy public'.[45] Whether this figure has increased or diminished, especially now the defence issue has a lower priority in the post-Cold War era, is impossible to tell. It is probably about the same, if not slightly high. Hence, specialised diplomatic correspondents are a rare breed, a small band of brothers who tend to feel under-appreciated and over-stretched, while many mass circulation organs simply do not employ them, choosing instead to rely on the wire services. The staple diet of an evening newscast or a morning newspaper still tends to be domestic news, and foreign affairs are all too often covered either in a fire-fighting manner or in a short segment under the category 'The World in Brief'. Tabloid press coverage of foreign affairs on a daily basis is even more sketchy, except when Japanese subways are subjected to gas attack or when a glove belonging to the likes of O. J. Simpson doesn't fit. Foreign affairs are quite simply *foreign* and, with the spectre of nuclear confrontation diminishing with the collapse of the Soviet Union, they are perhaps becoming even more so.

So what is all this talk about globalisation we hear so much about today? The notion of the global village suggests that we know so much more about our neighbours than previous generations, and that this increased knowledge can only generate greater mutual understanding. But is this really the case? Even the broadsheets, which attempt a more extensive daily analysis of foreign affairs for the interested reader, simply don't have the space for really thorough coverage. More specialised journals such as *Foreign Affairs*, or weekly publications such as *Time* and *Newsweek*, do provide more detailed analysis, but, inevitably, the more specialised the publication, the smaller the audience: niche products for niche audiences. In Britain, the most consistent analyst of foreign affairs is probably – and significantly in that its focus is economics – the relatively low-circulation *Financial Times*. And it has to be remembered that those publications which can command global audiences – such as *The Economist* – still tend to be read by a relatively small proportion of national populations as a whole. It is these people who are at the vanguard of globalisation. These are the elites who care about foreign events because they recognise that the flapping of a dictator's arms in one part of the world can possibly influence foreign, economic or military policy elsewhere in the world a month or so later. These are the real citizens of the global village, who watch their neighbours' behaviour because they realise it can affect their own livelihood in some way, and these are the people who rely heavily on the international media, including the news agencies, the wire services and a multiplicity of other specialised sources. Indeed, such groupings are finding that they now have to rely increasingly upon specialised data provision services, quite simply because the kind of information they require does not receive coverage in the mass media. And it is these types of niche publication which tend to be most influential in terms of their impact upon the foreign-policy-making elites. What role for the mass public and the mass media in these circumstances?

Because the majority of people do not normally read more than one newspaper, whereas scholarly researchers and global villagers must, the parameters of the information reaching any individual will be determined by the nature of the newspaper that is read, supplemented perhaps by radio reports heard in the car on the way to work and by evening television news bulletins watched in the home. Since 1963, most surveys indicate that the credibility of television news reporting is higher in the minds of the public than that of newspapers. That at least is the case in advanced Western countries, whereas in the developing world, where perhaps state-controlled media enjoyed less credibility, the BBC World Service still commands huge audiences (around 140 million in the mid-1990s) because of its historical reputation for accuracy. Whether it would continue to be so if it were more widely appreciated that the World Service is funded by the British government through the Foreign Office is another matter. And whereas an audience of 140 million might be a huge audience in some terms, it is still a tiny fraction of the world's population as a whole.

Foreign affairs thus remains a preoccupation of a small but influential group of people struggling to come to terms with what can appear to others to be the chaos of the post-Cold War era. The arrival of the *mass media* 'circus' on the international scene, it is felt, has contributed to that chaos by its erratic, ill-informed and spasmodic coverage. The complaints that one hears from diplomats about the media are in a sense, therefore, a fear of lost control, a yearning for an era when it was possible to conduct foreign affairs in relative isolation from the mass public and in a state of relative coopera-tion with the media establishment. On the other hand, perhaps they exaggerate the degree to which the media have become in their eyes more of a loose cannon than they were in the past. Indeed, one journalist has even accused his fellow reporters of being 'mindless agents of foreign policy':

> They are mainly conduits for a system of institutions, authoritative sources, practices, and ideologies that frame the events. I have concluded that reporters play a relatively small part in the creative process of discovery, analysis, and representation involved in news production and issues well before they, the mythical watchdogs, have a chance to do anything resembling independent analysis or representation.[46]

This has received academic support from Edward Herman, who agrees that the media 'serve mainly as a supportive arm of the state and dominant elites, focusing heavily on themes serviceable to them, and debating and exposing within accepted frames of reference'.[47] Moreover, now that the media estab-lishment is demassifying and commercialising, the ability of professional press officers to manipulate non-specialised freelancers and stringers is likely to increase.

DIPLOMACY AND THE MEDIA

International news reporting has lost many of its past constraints. Certainly, looking back, we can indeed appreciate just how much news during the Cold War was influenced by what have been termed the 'files' and 'boxes' of 'negotiated reality' originating in Moscow and Washington.[48] Robert Cutler, Eisenhower's first national security assistant, put it thus:

> In this world, where freedom as never before struggles rawly for survival . . . [the news media] must make clear how they will contribute to our survival; they must prove to us that the widespread public disclosure of our secret projects will make the free world stronger, and the neutrals better disposed, will rally the subject peoples [of Eastern Europe] and will put the Communist regimes at a disadvantage.[49]

World news was therefore very much a reflection of what Washington and Moscow wanted world news to be. And if the media agenda reflected this Cold War agenda, it was also convenient as well as economical to report the world in simplified terms. As a result, 'that worldview recognised only three or four trouble spots, with much of the rest of the globe missing from the media's collective radar screen, out of sight and largely out of mind'.[50]

Is it any different now? Certainly, neither diplomacy nor the media any longer enjoys the convenience of a Manichean world through which international events, rightly or wrongly, were seen through bifurcated spectacles. The trouble spots of the world are now all the more confusing because they do not seem to be related to superpower rivalry. But this does not automatically mean that they will command media attention. Some will, and for what can appear to be mysterious reasons. Small wonder that in a New World Order in which the need for governmental agenda-setting and for official propaganda through the media might therefore ostensibly appear to have diminished, it can seem that the 'dogs of journalism' have been let loose to savage world events, apparently at random, creating disorder. Hence phrases such as 'New World Disorder', 'the do-something factor' and the 'CNN curve' assume a recurrence when the latest crisis from nowhere suddenly appears on the nightly television news.

The conceptual relationship between the practice of diplomacy and the media production process – despite the relationship between the individuals involved – has rarely been a comfortable one. On the one hand, diplomacy is about negotiation between states in an attempt to resolve their differences, often involving lengthy and tedious consideration of issues that require specialist examination. It is about the routine implementation of foreign policy decisions made by politicians in an attempt to avoid conflict and resolve differences. It involves diplomatic dialogue by professional career diplomats who normally operate quietly, out of the glare of the media and therefore of public attention, and who feel relatively safe in the knowledge that their routine, everyday activities rarely command much public interest or scrutiny. After all, such activity – the writing of diplomatic despatches, the gathering of highly specialised intelligence, round-table negotiations, face-to-face conversations between ambassadors – is hardly the raw material which makes for excitement on the part of the media, let alone the public. This is because, in general, the media thrive on conflict rather than conflict resolution. Diplomacy therefore is not normally high on their agenda.

Of course, the exception to general media indifference is when diplomatic relations threaten to erupt into a crisis. When diplomats receive a phone call from a journalist, it provides a clue that 'trouble' is brewing. This is how many traditional diplomats have regarded the media when their proactive practices have broken down. It is then that they begin to see journalists as intruders, potential mischief-makers who can jeopardise their quiet, methodical ways of working by publicising or exaggerating some disagreement or point of legitimate negotiation. Diplomats know that the media thrives on bad news, and believe that the normally low priority given by the media to matters of foreign policy is hardly conducive to the kind of consistency of contextual understanding which they believe their activities merit. They also appreciate the dangers that can result from sudden media attention when the telephone rings.

While serving as British Foreign Secretary in the late 1980s and early 1990s, Douglas Hurd complained that 'when it comes to distant but important events, even all the Foreign Office cables do not have the same impact as a couple of minutes of news video. Before the days of video cameras people might have heard about atrocities, but accounts were often old and disputed. The cameras are not everywhere. But where the cameras operate, the facts are brutally clear.'[51] Unfortunately, they are not. The kind of foreign policy issues which the media seize upon – wars, crises, famine, disasters and the like – are invariably infinitely more complex than the media can ever possibly convey in the time and space available to them. However, 'once CNN is on the story, the media drumbeat begins, public opinion is engaged, and a diplomat's options recede. So it is important to look at which kinds of messages have been usurped by the media, and which have not, to distinguish between the public message and the private one.'[52]

The public message as conveyed by television is surrounded by phrases such as 'seeing is believing', 'a picture is worth a thousand words', 'the camera never lies' – all of which invest television with qualities for delivering truth and understanding to all who watch it – qualities which, quite simply, it has yet to possess. And while it is undoubtedly true that television audiences have a clearer idea of what foreign lands and statesmen *look* like than the generations prior to the invention of the photographic image (moving or otherwise), there is perhaps another phrase of greater pertinence to TV's role in foreign affairs, namely that 'In the kingdom of the blind, the one-eyed man is King'. It is this very *in*ability of television to provide a full or complete picture of the context and complexities of diplomacy that makes it such an erratic and unpredictable player, a crowd-pleaser which has signed on principally for two reasons: the speed at which it operates, and the drama which this can convey as a method of increasing the size of the audience it can reach.

What has just been said, however, invests television with powers which, as a value-neutral technology, it does not possess. What we are talking about, therefore, is people. The relatively low priority given to foreign affairs by the media professionals on a day-to-day basis is in fact a mixed blessing for the diplomats. On the one hand, it means that they can usually operate without the media in their hair, yet, on the other, they can use the level of media attention as a barometer by which to set their own priorities in a given crisis. Whether either of these aspects is particularly desirable is another matter, but both have become a fact of modern diplomatic life. Given that media coverage of foreign affairs has, at best, been arbitrary and perfunctory, there is hardly any way that diplomats can predict which crisis will receive media attention and which will not. There are various potential ingredients which any diplomat needs to be aware of, but this requires some appreciation of what constitutes 'news' in the minds of professional media organisations and what drives those organisations at any moment in time. Human interest stories have become particularly compelling, more so than in the past.[53] As the military are only too aware, the question of access is also pivotal (more of this in Chapter 3). But in times other than war, if the diplomats do ever find themselves in the front line of media attention, denial of access invariably tends to cause more trouble than it is worth. Any journalist worth his or her salt who is met with a stark 'no comment' will merely dig deeper, because they assume something is being hidden from them, and when that happens they enter the world of diplomacy less as an observer but as a potential catalyst capable of reordering the diplomatic agenda.

This suggests, as has already been explained, that diplomacy needs to be in the business of crisis management and what is now termed 'spin-doctoring'. If we borrow Chaos Theory's most overused cliché, namely that the flapping of a butterfly's wings in China can affect weather patterns in New York, modern diplomacy in the media age can be seen partly as the monitoring of butterflies by observation, consultation and negotiation, to prevent storm clouds from brewing. The media, on the other hand, thrives on hurricanes. While on the constant look-out for human interest stories, in foreign affairs it is not always apparent to the media that there is a story until a storm cloud has already formed: a line of bedraggled refugees, a mass grave, a starving child. The enormous fuss over 'Operation Irma' in 1992 – the saving of a young girl caught up in the war in former Yugoslavia – was nicknamed 'Instant Response to Media Attention' by those who had to implement the rescue. The problem for diplomats is that, once the media become interested, their contribution is inherently inclined more to seeing the storm erupt than to seeing it go away. There is, of course, no hard and fast rule on this; there are plenty of recent examples of stormy crises which have failed to attract mass media attention – Ngorno-Karrabach, the Sudan, the civil war in Afghanistan – not because the media was denied access but because various judgements had been made concerning the costs, safety, or 'infotainment' value of the event. But when the mass media do decide, for whatever reason, that a given crisis is worth covering, its potential to disrupt the routine priorities of diplomacy comes into sharp focus.

This is felt to be especially true of live television. When, for example, in 1993 a US diplomat described the crisis in the Sudan as 'Somalia without CNN',[54] he was pointing to the entrance of this privately owned international news channel into the once-secret world of diplomacy, with its ability, if not to set, then to re-order the agenda of international politics. His message was clear: if TV cameras were present at the scene of a flashpoint, then the international community was more likely to respond than if they were absent. If this is true, then it says a great deal about the sensitivity of modern politicians to a medium which, in so far as diplomatic practitioners are concerned, still tends to be regarded more as a hindrance than a help.

This is because, in free societies, the press on a day-to-day basis cannot be expected to be uncritical of government policies. Foreign observers, including diplomats, scrutinise national media reports for clues concerning the strengths and weaknesses of a government, including the degree to which it enjoys domestic popular support. Most diplomatic practitioners would argue that diplomacy has to take a long-term view and not be hamstrung by the short-termism of political elections. When politicians do decide to adopt a long-term position in the media age, as in the case of the Truman Doctrine when anti-Communism was used to stir up public support for US foreign policy, then there is a danger that the government can lose some of its subsequent flexibility in diplomatic negotiations. On this occasion, because the government was now expected by the domestic American media to be tough on Communism wherever it confronted it, its foreign policy was to some extent pre-determined throughout the 1950s and 1960s. Only the bitter experience of Vietnam allowed Nixon and Kissinger to develop greater flexibility in the era of détente and the 'opening to China'.

Scrutiny of domestic media opinion by foreign analysts makes media criticism all the more irritating to diplomats from the country being scrutinised; it gives away too many 'secrets', and such publicity can also undermine negotiating positions. So while official press departments attempt to influence the way in which domestic and foreign journalists cover a given issue, there is a recognition that the extent to which this can be done to the benefit of the source is limited by the unpredictable and ultimately uncontrollable nature of the free media. For this reason, governments themselves conduct their own direct media activities designed to influence the image of a nation abroad. Over the years, two approaches have been identified as essential: long-term activity in the form of cultural diplomacy, and short-term public diplomacy in the form of external radio, and now television, broadcasting.

CULTURAL AND PUBLIC DIPLOMACY

Today, most governments in advanced countries operate radio and television services of their own. These are the 'external services', the official voices of national policies designed for overseas audiences, now firmly entrenched as a responsibility of the state in the information age. Most enjoy a quasi-autonomous position within the diplomatic establishment. It has even been suggested that the hostility of many diplomats towards their own external broadcasting services is 'because they don't control it. They think it upsets the governments in the countries where they broadcast.'[55] However, because the independent commercial media naturally cannot be relied upon automatically to reflect national, long-term diplomatic interests, governments themselves have decided that they must engage in public international communication on a day-to-day basis. Some even hire media advisers and public relations firms for specific campaigns.[56]

Given the dominance of the Anglo-American media world-wide, the source of so many charges about 'media imperialism', it might seem strange that the British and American governments should bother to involve themselves in such 'public information' activity. After all, if the media are so effective in projecting an Anglo-American (more American, it has to be said) hegemonic view of the world throughout the globe, and that view is felt to benefit those nations' interests to the detriment of others at a political, economic and cultural level, this might even suggest that governmental media operations by those states are unnecessary. However, while it may appear that the involvement of the commercial media in international affairs, especially the advent of global television news services like CNN, might have rendered redundant the overseas information services, or at least rival them, in fact they merely reinforce the need for them.

In most countries, regardless of their political persuasion, there is a sense that the psychological dimension of the way they are perceived by the outside world cannot be left to the media. In authoritarian regimes, there tends to be less concern that the domestic media might create an adverse impression quite simply because the media are already under pretty strict official regulation or control. In such societies, the outside world can scrutinise that domestic media on the reasonably safe assumption that the media is serving as a mouthpiece for the political regime. For example, if one picks up a copy of a newspaper produced in Beijing, Tehran or Pyongyang, it will provide important clues not just about what the Chinese, Iranian or North Korean governments want their citizens to read about but also what they don't want their people to read about and discuss. Hence, the Taiwan–China crisis of 1996 may have received considerable media attention around the world, but not in the People's Republic of China itself. In more open societies, however, governments cannot always be certain about which stories secure media coverage, despite all their efforts to shape the political agenda of their free media. The democratic media may be influenced by political communications but it does not follow that they are forced to become uncritical outlets for political propaganda.

Foreign nations glean a good deal of their information about other societies from their national media. In that respect, the British royal family is not merely the property of the British press but of the global media. Similarly, whereas a Foreign Office in a free society might lament a televised documentary critical of another country, it can do nothing to prevent transmission of the programme unless national security issues are involved. It might make representations to the television company responsible for the programme, warning, for example, that it might offend the ruling family of such and such a kingdom, but it can do little else until the programme has been aired and protests received. To such regimes, it remains extremely difficult, for example, to explain that the BBC is not the British government – or at least that the domestic broadcasting services of the BBC are paid for by the licence payer. The World Service is different. And just as diplomats cannot always rely on free domestic media to reflect positively upon the image of another nation, nor do they have any control over which slices of the domestic media foreign nations seize upon to illustrate what a dreadful (or wonderful) place their country is. It is for this reason that most governments engage in what the Americans term 'public diplomacy' and what is termed elsewhere variously as 'overseas information policy' or 'national self-advertisement'. Hence the British Council, like the BBC World Service, is paid for by taxpayers from the vote of government departments.

Cultural diplomacy, an invention of the French in the late nineteenth century, is a governmental activity which attempts to by-pass commercial media images by appealing directly to the peoples of foreign societies on an ostensibly non-political level. Its principal instruments are language teaching, educational exchanges and other forms of cultural contact – all of which seem pretty innocuous, which is precisely why it is subject to periodic political attacks calling for its reduction or cessation. Why should taxpayers from any given country which engages in it subsidise an activity that does not directly benefit them? Because, comes the reply, it does benefit them in long-term, if somewhat nebulous, ways. If foreigners have direct experience of a nation's culture, through an ability to speak its language, read its literature, scrutinise its cultural forms preferably in their natural surroundings or at least in their own localities, then those foreigners are more likely to understand and appreciate that any media images they are exposed to do not tell the whole story about that nation. Their appreciation may even translate into empathy and friendship, leading to greater mutual understanding. Hence government sponsored or supported organisations such as the British Council, the Alliance Française, the Dante Allighieri Society or the Tokyo Foundation all initiate cultural and educational exchanges, participate in international exhibitions, establish libraries in overseas countries, and sponsor travelling drama, music and lecture tours, all in an attempt to increase a level of international understanding and appreciation that can, it is argued, aid foreign policy in the long term. And because this activity has proved vulnerable to political attack, there is also an economic justification for it. This suggests that if Nation X subsidises a student from Nation Y to study a subject like engineering for three years or more in X, then upon graduation he or she will return to Y in a fast-track career which may see that person ultimately in control of an engineering firm which, when it needs to make a foreign order, will automatically look to Nation X because of the goodwill generated towards it during that person's period of study. Cultural diplomacy is therefore good for business as well as for international cooperation – which is why it now attracts so much corporate sponsorship in societies such as Japan and the United States.

All this might seem naïve were it not for the fact that, over the past hundred years, developed countries in particular (because they can afford it) have come to realise the importance of such activity in their foreign policy objectives. It tends not to be a mass activity; rather, it is directed at the future movers and shakers, the elites, of foreign societies, whether they be the political, military, economic, cultural or diplomatic leaderships of the future. However, French cultural diplomacy did not prevent the Algerian war or the defeat at Dien Bien Phu; nor does the work of the British Council prevent its overseas offices from being the first to be smashed up in any local anti-British demonstration. This indicates that cultural diplomacy is very much an adjunct of conventional diplomacy. If the latter fails, the former suffers; but the former is considered worth trying in an attempt to lubricate the workings of the latter.

To this extent, cultural diplomacy is very much a political activity designed to serve national interests in an ostensibly cultural guise. It is a reflection not only of the broadening popular base of the foreign-policy-making process but also of the increasing role of ideology in international affairs. The British Council, for example, was established in 1934 under the auspices of the Foreign Office as a direct response to the aggressive ideological circumstances of the pre-Second World War period. Its role was defined as follows:

> To make the life and thought of the British peoples more widely known abroad; and to promote a mutual interchange of knowledge and ideas with other peoples. To encourage the study and use of the English language; ... To bring other peoples into closer touch with British ideals and practice in education, industry and government; to make available to them the benefits of current British contributions to the sciences and technology; and to afford them opportunities of appreciating contemporary British work in literature, the fine arts, drama and music.[57]

Its aims remain essentially the same to this day. Anyone who pretends that it is anything other than a different facet of the struggle for hearts and minds fails to recognise the significance of operating at different psychological levels within the fourth dimension.

One interesting aspect of post-war debates about cultural imperialism is that they hardly ever analysed this phenomenon. This is surprising since here there is hard evidence that governments from advanced countries spend their taxpayers' money to promote and disseminate their national cultural products abroad, including to Third World countries, often with very little direct benefit to those taxpayers. Perhaps the problem for the cultural/media imperialism school of thought was twofold. Official cultural diplomacy is generally recognised to be beneficial through its quest to improve international understanding, and this barely squared with the emphasis of their argument that media products undermined indigenous cultures. Second, the thrust of their argument was anti-American and, of all the developed nations' governments who engage in this type of activity, the Americans engage in it only through the United States Information Agency (USIA), originally founded in 1953 to serve Cold War purposes. They have no equivalent of the British Council. Under the 1961 Fulbright–Hayes Act, the aim of the USIA is defined as the spreading of information abroad about the United States, its people, culture, and policies, and conducting of educational and cultural *exchanges* between the United States and other countries. Most Americans are therefore unaware that, in this back-door kind of way, the USIA is operating on American soil. In 1993, twenty-three US government agencies spent at least $1.4 billion on more than a hundred international exchange and training programmes. This tends not to tally with a major feature of the media/cultural imperialism thesis, namely that it is a uni-directional flow from the core to the periphery. Certainly, USIA's programmes include the VOA, now broadcasting world-wide in forty-nine languages, and the WORLDNET television service, but it also embraces the Fulbright scholarship, International Visitor and other educational exchange programmes, the American Speakers Abroad programme, publications translated in more than fifteen languages, the Wireless File, and a network of overseas operations, including libraries and cultural centres. The USIA also encourages private philanthropic organisations such as the Carnegie Foundation to promote educational exchanges.

Of course, powerful, but privately owned, American multi-national corporations have proved enormously successful in exporting goods, such as Coca-Cola or McDonald's hamburgers, and cultural icons such as Madonna or Michael Jackson, throughout the world. And although such activity might benefit the profits of those organisations, this does not mean that the American government is always happy with the image of America contained in, or generated by, media and cultural products raised on its own soil and then exported abroad. After the Second World War, the State Department felt that Hollywood, for example, was misrepresenting America to the world through such pictures as *Tobacco Road, The Lost Weekend* and *The Grapes of Wrath*, which dramatised some of the country's most pressing social ·problems. 'The motion picture industry is potentially the most valuable ally in the conduct of our foreign relations and conversely it is a first-class headache,' wrote US Assistant Secretary of State William Benton in 1946.[58] Because the State Department was especially averse to that much-loved American phenomenon, the cowboy film, it even produced a documentary

81

of its own for Thai audiences depicting how American ranchers worked very much in the same vein as the Siamese sheepherders at whom it was targeted.[59]

Today, more than a hundred nations engage in external broadcasting. But the end of the Cold War, the spread of democracy and more open markets is prompting a re-think. As propaganda services, external broadcasts might appear to have become redundant once the Cold War was 'won'. However, after much debate in the early-to-mid-1990s, there is a recognition of the need to use them for 'consolidation propaganda' purposes. Public and cultural diplomacy will remain in the business of winning the support of foreign peoples to further national political, economic and security interests. But because it is about addressing those peoples and not their governments, new communications technologies like the Internet provide opportunities to reach them directly and individually. There is an increasing shift from radio to television as TV at last becomes the norm in many parts of the world. Radio will undoubtedly remain the principal medium in the least-developed of Third World countries, but for the wired cities, organisations like the Voice of America, the BBC World Service and Deutsche Welle all have sites on the World Wide Web. The US Advisory Committee on Public Diplomacy reported in March 1995 that:

> People all over the world now have more power to shape events and the actions of governments than at any time in history, making public diplomacy as essential to U.S. interests as diplomacy between governments. Governments increasingly understand that publics have great power to influence events and decisions. They realize that communication with foreign publics often has much more impact than the exchange of diplomatic notes.

The report went on to point out that, although public diplomacy has not replaced government-to-government diplomacy, 'traditional diplomacy has been changed decisively by the communications revolution'.

> Today, governments must win the support of people in other countries, as well as leaders, if policies are to succeed. They must cope with constituent pressures at home and with the consequences of public pressures on other governments. They must mobilize coalitions and support for policies in multilateral organizations. Because what they say at home will be instantly reported abroad, policy explanations must be consistent and persuasive to domestic and foreign audiences alike.[60]

This was because, quite simply, 'we live in a world of information abundance, instant communication, and porous borders. The Information Age has replaced the Industrial Age.'

Heads of state increasingly converse by telephone, ambassadors appear more frequently on the national television services in the countries in which they are stationed, and foreign policy is increasingly conducted in the public domain, and in real time, reducing the time previously available for deliberation – all these trends point to the need for an *increased* emphasis on public and cultural diplomacy. More information, of course, does not automatically produce greater understanding. But if the motives, nature, culture, character, traditions and interests of a nation are better understood and appreciated, and if this is achieved by bringing foreigners to that nation to visit, study or simply experience that society and its people, there is a much greater chance that its actions will be better understood. Of course, there is always the chance that this can backfire. Increased contact with one's neighbours in the global village does not necessarily mean that they will get on with one another. Familiarity can breed contempt. But cultural exchanges which take place between better educated sections of communities, who are thus more likely to resolve differences by negotiation rather than force, are less likely to harm diplomacy and indeed may even help it. That is why the American government brings almost half a million foreign students each year to its shores. Another form of cultural imperialism, perhaps? Or is it simply a recognition that direct, personal contact with the world's surviving superpower is infinitely more beneficial than the frequently distorted image of the United States that appears on television screens around the world?

TELEVISION AND DIPLOMACY

Until comparatively recently, the role of television in international affairs appeared to be limited to providing a 'window on the world' for national or local audiences that anyway were assumed to be largely divorced from or disinterested in occurrences in foreign fields, except perhaps during international sporting events or when nations went to war. Television, in other words, was traditionally seen more as a passive observer of foreign affairs – and a somewhat arbitrary one at that – than as an active participant in them. Now, however, there is a growing debate about the role and impact of television on the foreign-policy-making process, especially in light of the Gulf War of 1991 and more recent events in Bosnia and Somalia. Television is beginning to be regarded as potentially a quite significant player in international affairs. How valid is this, and what, if anything, has changed?

There appear to be a few obvious answers to the second question. Since the 1980s, the arrival of new technologies which enabled pictures and data to be transferred around the globe – instantaneously – in a variety of formats, deregulation in domestic communications systems and their greater accessibility to foreign satellite systems and services, the internationalisation of television news and other services targeted at global audiences, and the increased portability and affordability of those services, have all been discernible trends. True, communication technologies have always been characterised by innovation in so far as spatial and temporal compression are concerned, but never quite with the pace and on the scale we are now witnessing, thanks to microchip capacity being doubled roughly every eighteen months. The current buzzwords of 'multimedia' and 'convergence' have become every bit as important to media scholars as 'globalisation' is to the discipline of international relations. However, we need some disciplinary convergence to appreciate that, above all, it was the end of the Cold War which coincided with the arrival of live television broadcasting as a norm, creating a completely new and, by comparison, chaotic international environment for both diplomacy and the media.

Television's first post-1945 decade identified it as an increasingly important phenomenon in the national life of a nation; internationally, few spoke of it in terms other than those related to domestic issues. All that changed in 1957. That year, Khrushchev gave an interview on American network television (CBS's 'Face the Nation') in which he announced his plans for 'peaceful competition', prompting fears that he had scored a new kind of international propaganda coup.[61] At that time no American statesman could retaliate in kind – not just because the Soviet authorities would never have allowed it, or even because of technical limitations, but because television had yet to reach mass penetration in the Soviet Union. Instead, they would have to rely upon external radio broadcasting.[62] It was only with the launch of Sputnik in 1957 and the Space Race which followed that a new era for international broadcasting occurred, with implications far wider than the transmission of the 1964 Tokyo Olympics to a world-wide television audience.[63] For example, television news reports from Southeast Asia gave Vietnam the status of being the first 'living-room war',[64] not just for self-flagellating American audiences but for horrified viewers around the world. The students who chanted 'The Whole World is Watching' at the 1968 Democratic Convention in Chicago reflected the realisation that communication technology was indeed making possible Marshall McLuhan's 'Global Village'.[65] As Henry Kissinger recalled:

> Television was just then coming into its own. The regular evening broadcasts were attracting audiences in the tens of millions, far more people than even the most popular print journalists could hope to reach in a lifetime. And they possessed the advantage of visual images to provide a running editorial commentary. The newscasts reflected a craving for drama and showmanship that, even with the best of intentions, could not always be balanced, if only because it was technically impossible to cover the atrocities the Vietcong were committing in areas under their control. The news anchor turned into a political figure, in the sense that only a president could have reached as many people – and certainly not with such regularity.[66]

In the lifetime of a generation, then, television emerged as a discernible feature in international cultural affairs. But it was also impacting on politics.

We have seen how numerous surveys indicated that most people, wherever they were, now trusted television more than any other medium as their most reliable source of news and information.[67] From 1962, when only 29 per cent of Americans found TV their most credible news source, to 1980, when the figure was 51 per cent (as compared to 22 per cent for newspapers), the rise of the medium as a political player on the domestic scene was as dramatic as the decline in interest by the press in foreign affairs.[68] Henry Kissinger's view was that the 'print media have almost no impact at all. The *Los Angeles Times* could do a great exposé, but it would stir up only a few people. A few big columnists may have influence in Washington, because everybody reads them and they are a common point of reference. But the big power is TV reporting.'[69]

Yet this was still only true for countries with advanced media systems. LDCs were – and many still are – a long way from the kind of mass public access to television which sees over 90 per cent of homes in possession of a TV set. Indeed, the Soviet Union was only beginning to approach this position by the 1970s.[70] Once that occurred, however, the kind of spillage of TV signals across neighbouring borders, between say Canada and the USA, or West and East Germany, began to cause concern on both cultural and political grounds.[71] To exploit such new markets, made increasingly possible by the deregulation that took place in the 1980s, international *commercial* narrowcasting television services emerged such as CNN and, for younger audiences, Music Television (MTV). That these media were indeed American meant that US television programming reigned supreme around the planet, a common point of reference for peoples from Salford to Singapore. In this sense, 'Dallas' and 'Dynasty' constituted an extension of what has been termed a Marshall Plan for Ideas.[72] Or so it can appear at cursory viewing. In fact, while it is true that American-produced television programmes do export successfully to just about every country on earth, this does not mean that they *dominate* the programme output of most national television stations. In comparison to the amount of programmes imported from other countries, US programming certainly is more clearly in evidence than that of any other nation, but any glance at the prime-time daily viewing output of television stations from Albania to Zaire reveals that locally produced programmes still tend to dominate the schedules. If one excludes movies (made originally for cinema and not for television or video) and quiz-shows (admittedly often modelled on US formats), the figures are surprising small and rarely reach above 20 per cent. This is not to suggest that American productions do not feature prominently in day-time or late-night viewing, but rather that at prime-time, when local audiences are at their highest, the tendency is not towards Americanisation or US programme domination, as many writers have suggested.[73]

In 1980, some indication of its capacity for damaging diplomatic relations was seen when the British Independent Television network planned to screen a critical documentary entitled 'Death of a Princess'. Although documentaries tend to command relatively small audiences, the Saudi Arabian government protested and tried to prevent the programme from going on air. Despite British governmental insistence that it had no power to intervene in British television programming policy, tension was exacerbated when Fleet Street attacked the Saudis for trying to do precisely what Whitehall maintained it could not do itself, namely 'muzzle the press'. Consequently, the British ambassador in Riyadh was asked to leave and diplomatic relations were temporarily suspended.[74] Undisclosed diplomatic sources in London feared that the Saudi move was 'not only a protest to Britain, but also a warning to other countries not to show the film and to restrain their media from casting Saudi Arabia in a bad light'.[75]

Even this example now seems archaic. Advanced broadcasting systems which sold their programmes abroad could always be foiled, because cans of film had to be physically carried and hence their import could be banned. Moreover, the variety of television transmission systems in use around the world (PAL, SECAM and NTSC)[76] also remained a useful device for barring access to unwanted foreign television signal spillage. But, again, technological developments in the 1980s rapidly overcame such obstacles and the switch from analogue to digital systems we are now undergoing will obliterate such factors altogether. In the meantime, newer means of disseminating information, such as domestic video recorders and cameras with a cassette barely larger than a cigarette packet, became increasingly harder to detect, as President Marcos of the Philippines discovered in 1986 following his ban on all foreign media. Video cassettes of Japanese and American TV news reports were smuggled in by foreign exiles, thus maintaining 'information access' during the People's Revolution.[77] Yet because such activity still involved people taking physical risks, political leaders began to realise just how fluid the international information environment was becoming thanks to electronic communications. Hence in Panama in 1989 General Noriega found it impossible to prevent the import by fax machines of American newspaper reports. Now, with the even newer technologies of the 1990s provided by computer-mediated communications, whereby pictures can be compressed and digitised for transmission over the Internet, prevention and detection have become a potential nightmare for those wishing to control the flow of international information.

Why bother? Is it because, as that overworked idiom has it, information is power? Power to do what? Certainly, many Eastern European leaders are on record as saying that improved access provided by international communication technology to alternative ways of seeing and perceiving what the West was really like helped to end their oppression.[78] When asked about the influence of RFE in Poland, Lech Walesa's reply was, simply: 'Could there be an earth without a sun?' Communist propagandists now claim that they were always chasing Western tails on this: 'In propaganda, you have to be first to put a spin on a certain event', claimed Alexander Shalnev, US bureau chief of *Izvestia*. 'You guys [at the USIA] were saying the first words on almost every subject. We were always on the defensive. In propaganda, you have to be on the offensive all the time to be successful. We lost it completely.'[79] The Chairman of the Board for International Broadcasting, the parent organisation of RFE/RL, claimed: 'I have talked with Yeltsin, Havel, Walesa, people in the streets who would come up and tell me that they huddled in closets for 40 years to listen to our broadcasts. It helped make possible, I think, what we see today ... the fall of the Berlin Wall, the new and emerging democracies ...'[80]

In Czechoslovakia, East Germany, Hungary, Rumania and elsewhere in Europe, the events of 1989–91 did appear to demonstrate that television and the other new media had become significant as events in one country reached the public of another by a variety of channels, thereby not only by-passing previous national controls but also encouraging the belief that change was possible. During the period between 1974 and 1994, over forty countries adopted some form of democratic government. Balanced against this, however, we do have the example of the Tienanmen Square uprising in 1989 when Chinese officials were seen, live on CNN, pulling the plugs in an attempt not only to re-establish control over their domestic information environment but also to shape the outside world's perception of what was about to happen. The latter failed as spectacularly as the pro-Democracy movement itself. The real power remained with brute force. Tanks, not television, decided the outcome. Indeed, it was Gorbachev's refusal to apply brute force in 1989 and 1991 (contrary to his predecessors in Hungary in 1956 and Czechoslovakia in 1968) which ultimately allowed the monumental changes in Eastern Europe to take place, not the media.

None the less, the fear that an unfettered flow of information from outside sources can serve as a disruptive factor promoting change survives. It was behind Beijing's pressurisation in 1994 of Rupert Murdoch's Star Asia satellite television service to drop BBC News bulletins from its schedules.[81] Because its reach is global, instantaneous and virtually unstoppable (it only takes three satellites in orbit 23,000 miles up to cover the entire planet with satellite footprints),[82] Direct Broadcasting by Satellite is feared far more than radio ever was as an invasive and destabilising factor by regimes of all persuasions – whether manifesting itself in French concerns during the GATT negotiations over unlimited American programme imports or the Iranian government's decision in 1995 to ban the sale and possession of satellite dishes. Britain banned the sale of decoders capable of receiving the kind of hard-core pornography television services supplied to other European subscribers. Many nations are therefore beginning to see the advantages of cabled systems by which satellite signals are received at a central dish 'farm' before re-distribution to customers, thereby making them easier to control than the DBS option. But DBS cannot be un-invented, and because the dishes are getting smaller all the time, certain authoritarian regimes, including China, have placed responsibility for monitoring this development under the auspices of their internal security ministries rather than their telecommunications authorities.

Perhaps the key word in all this is 'fear', rather than 'factor'. 'If knowledge is power then diffusion of knowledge must result in a diffusion of power and the control of this process is, in itself, a form of power.'[83] While it is hardly surprising that those governments which fear the power of the media to shape the perceptions of their domestic populations, to the point that they exercise strict state control over those media, should also fear the power of international communications to undermine that very control, we do need to remind ourselves that the important element here is indeed control, not television. After all, command and control of communications has historically been seen to be as essential to the maintenance of political power as it has to the achievement of military success. The internationalisation and the commercialisation of the media can therefore appear to be the latest threats to the continuation of that control. But this was precisely the ideological motivation behind the Reagan–Thatcher determination to herald a new era of deregulated media and communications. It was also why in the mid-1980s the US and Britain both withdrew from UNESCO, which had been the principal forum for the international community's debates about freedom of the press and the free flow of global information. It seemed to them that a New World Information Order was being called for by states which proved reluctant to practise such concepts within their own societies.[84] Market forces and consumer capitalism would decide the issue, not political regulation.

It is this belief that the media serve as forces for freedom and democracy, a belief consolidated by the role of glasnost in the collapse of the Soviet Union and the ending of the Cold War, which has given satellite television a new status in international affairs, its role being almost that of an instrument of political warfare. But we also need to remember that the medium is *not* the message. The *message* is the message. The medium, in so far as foreign policy is concerned, is deeply flawed.

THE LIMITS OF TELEVISION IN FOREIGN POLICY

Although scholarly attention has only recently begun to appreciate it, television is in fact a highly deceptive medium. We are, of course, talking mainly in this context about news, current affairs and other 'factual' programming; entertainment or fictional programmes, such as movies and soap operas, which command infinitely larger audiences, are not the main object of attention here.

At the most basic of levels, the obvious needs to be reiterated: television cameras can only 'see' what they are pointed at. They provide, at best, mere snapshots of reality and, at worst, illusions of reality.[85] For we are dealing with what is primarily a picture-driven medium that requires certain fundamental preconditions for it to operate effectively and simultaneously. These range from the ability of the camera operator literally to turn on his camera (requiring electrical power) at the right time (requiring judgement, experience, light and luck) to capture the right sort of events (i.e. those which are visually or narratively exciting) from the best possible angle (requiring access, professionalism – and, again, luck). What goes on behind the camera operator's back or when the camera is turned off does not constitute part of the visual record. When the right combination of these exacting circumstances comes together, there is the chance that the pictures *might* form the basis of a story for eventual transmission to a wider public – provided they can be sent home successfully, with the necessary equipment working and the satellite time booked. But the process does not end there. For newsgathering, like diplomacy, is indeed a process requiring a team of professional individuals making judgements about the available pictures prior to them ever being seen by an audience. In the editorial rooms, the pictures sent in from reporters in the field can be synthesised, chopped about and re-ordered with a new commentary. In other words they are editorialised until they are whipped into a comprehensible story. Depending upon the nature of the target audience, that story may be told in differing editorial styles, prompting accusations that, on many commercial, advertising-driven stations, news stories are determined more for their entertainment value than for information purposes ('infotainment').[86] More serious reporters try to combat this by editing their packages in the field – which again is easier to do now, thanks to portable equipment, and which is giving rise to the phenomenon of 'multi-tasking' within the broadcasting industry.

But whether in the field or back at base, according to differing broadcasting traditions, some pictures may still be omitted on grounds of 'taste and decency'. During the Gulf War of 1991, for example, close-up pictures of the horribly burned remains of women and children killed in the bombing of the Al Firdos installation in the Al-Amiriya suburb of Baghdad were omitted ('self-censored')[87] by some Western broadcasters for the same reason that they would not use similar pictures of the victims of a plane crash.[88] Pictures of the aftermath of a mortar attack on a bread queue in Bosnia in 1992 were treated likewise, in a 'sanitisation' process which, according to one analyst, meant that those news reports would 'never have the same impact on the political process'.[89] In other words the shock value of horrific television pictures is reduced by a broadcasting tradition which is keen to avoid offending or upsetting its audience. Hence 'the doings of the world are tamed to meet the needs of a production system in many respects bureaucratically organised'.[90]

Moreover, when all the decisions have been made, often at great speed in order to meet the transmission deadlines of news bulletins, there is the frequently overlooked problem of how individual members of a mass audience perceive the end result. We all too often forget that mass audiences consist of individuals. Hence the pictures may be common to all, but each individual will perceive them differently according to his or her particular background, education, gender, sensibilities, judgement, perceptions and prejudices. Thus, there is a twin process of what psychologists term cognitive dissonance taking place: by the media professionals themselves, and then, subsequently, by the audience. Yet all this only becomes possible if the news organisation has made the expensive decision to send its reporters to the scene in the first place (if it has no correspondent permanently, and again expensively, stationed there), usually with costly equipment and hotel bills needing to be justified in terms of the story's significance and attention-keeping capabilities. This in turn gives rise to the 'firefighting' tendency of the media; capturing the explosion itself live on-camera is rare enough – more usually it is its aftermath – but the causes of the fire, the context, are usually too complex for television to convey adequately. The media, after all, concentrate on *events* and are at their weakest when tackling *issues*. Reporting an event in an ethnic conflict, such as a tribal massacre, does not automatically help to explain the context of that massacre and thus distorts its significance. Equally, when the flames are out and the media have gone, the issues still remain. And erratic coverage is further guaranteed by the recent trend towards making economies. 'In television, the cutbacks are more dramatic. The three main [American] broadcast networks virtually have opted out of regular, noncrisis coverage of international affairs . . . CBS no longer assigns a full-time reporter to the State Department. Overseas, television relies increasingly on free-lance video footage and stringers, some of whose connections are suspect.'[91]

It is often felt that when the broadcast pictures are of dreadful scenes, universally perceived (if that ever happens), they can provoke audience outcries and calls to 'do something' to stop the slaughter taking place before their eyes. However, this also invests television with a power that it may not inherently possess. Before the plugs were pulled, television images of the student demonstrations in Tienanmen Square tended, in the words of one US official, to demand of the world community 'a solution we couldn't provide. We were powerless to make it stop.'[92] This strikes at the very heart of the problem, one which continues into the 1990s. As one scholar has written, 'the projection of images of deprivation and suffering onto television screens creates a clamour for action which can not be satisfied without exertions or risks that go well beyond those justified by any sense of national interest or even reasonable humanitarian concern.'[93] This was why, despite months of shocking pictures from Rwanda, beginning in April and May 1994, including footage of scores of bodies floating down rivers and the hacking to death of a woman, for twelve weeks of 'terrifying tribal genocide the Clinton administration and other western governments . . . actively resisted the flow of horrific pictures that documented the mass slaughter'.[94]

The crisis in Zaire in late 1996 was a perfect illustration of how the phenomenon now works. The sight of people on the move in their tens of thousands attracts the concern of the NGOs and other aid agencies, which issue press releases, thus attracting the interest of the media with the prospect of a human tragedy of enormous proportions (this after two years of relative media disinterest in Rwanda). Suddenly, Zaire starts to feature nightly on the television news bulletins and the pictures of lines of innocent women and children start to harrow, especially when border clashes caused by the huge movement of people threaten to engulf them in war. Concerned politicians, on this occasion from Canada, offer to lead a humanitarian force while the UN bungles through its cumbersome bureaucratic procedures. Just as it makes a decision to intervene, pictures emerge of people returning home as the crisis on the ground alleviates. Local politicians say there is no longer any need for military intervention, the journalists go home and the crisis evaporates from the media's – and therefore from the international political – agenda. Until the next time, that is.

When television does manage to cover a story that is unpalatable to those in authority – such as the Al-Amiriya bombing in February 1991 – there is a disingenuous tendency to shoot the messenger.[95] I say disingenuous because blaming the medium for the message it carries not only deflects attention away from the story itself, it disguises fears about the impact which the message *may have* on the general public. In the Gulf War, for example, the fear was that by showing pictures (even sanitised ones) of what modern weapons can do to real people, audiences might be sufficiently shocked into doing something to stop the war.[96] This is a remarkable, and deeply flawed, testimony to the continuing influence of the 'Vietnam Syndrome', namely the belief that the US military could have won the war in Southeast Asia had in not been 'stabbed in the back' by hostile media back home.[97] As we shall see in the next chapter, there simply is no evidence to support the assumption that critical television coverage can change public opinion *en masse* from a pro-war to an anti-war stance, during the Vietnam war or any other war. But the belief that it can has given rise to the enormous efforts now being expended by military establishments on 'Public Affairs' or 'Public Information' activity to shape, via the media, the outside public perception of what they do in times of war and crisis.[98]

When individual members of the audience do decide to do something in response to television pictures – whether it be sending food parcels to the hungry, organising pop concerts to raise money for famine relief, or protesting to their elected representatives or in the streets – it invariably depends more on the motivations of those individuals as individuals rather than on the pictures themselves. But even when one man watches a news report of a famine in Ethiopia and is sufficiently disturbed by it to organise a pop concert attended by 100,000 people, which in turn is watched live on television by tens of millions of people around the world, the power of the medium cannot simply be dismissed. Just because we do not yet know precisely how to measure media effects does not mean that those effects do not exist.

This becomes even more complex if one considers the view of Benjamin Netanyahu who, while deputy foreign minister of Israel, invoked the Heisenberg Principle 'whereby if you observe a phenomenon, you actually change it':

> Television is no longer a spectator.... We now have the Heisenberg physics of politics. As you observe a phenomenon with television, instantly you modify it somewhat. And I think [therefore] that what we have to make sure of is that the truth is not modified, and that it is constantly fed to the leaders and the publics in democratic countries.[99]

This may well be so, but it is also a justification for official 'information management'. Because the assertion behind it is difficult to prove at an empirical level, even with public opinion-polling, attention has consequently been forced to focus on television's role not as a catalyst but as a participant. Douglas Hurd, while British Foreign Secretary, even suggested that 'the public debate is no longer run by events, but by the coverage of events'.[100] Similarly, Marlin Fitzwater, US President Bush's press spokesman, claimed that in international crises 'we virtually cut out the State Department and the desk officers.... Their reports are still important, but they don't get here in time for the basic decisions to be made.... The normal information flow into the Oval Office was vastly altered by live video images.'[101] If this is so, especially given the flawed nature of the medium, then small wonder that there is growing concern.

Hurd went on to admit that 'working with the media has added a steadily growing extra dimension to the business of government, and in particular to the business of diplomacy'.[102] But we have to ask whether this is because officials recognise that the media really have become participants or because they fear that they might become so. Moreover, does this fear say more about them than it does about television? Some months earlier, Hurd had said that, 'like it or not, television images are what forces foreign policy makers to give one of the current 25 crises in the world greater priority'.[103] This was dubbed 'Hurd's Law' by one critic, who felt that because 'there were no TV cameras in southern Iraq during the [Shia] uprising [in the aftermath of the Gulf War, there was] therefore no serious pressure on western governments to intervene'.[104] The uprising to the north, by way of contrast, was different, because John Major saw the plight of the Kurds on TV news reports, prompting him to suggest Operation Provide Comfort to the Americans.[105] In October 1993, when pictures taken on a portable hi-8 video camera – not, significantly, by a professional journalist[106] – of a dead US serviceman being dragged through the streets of Mogadishu, 'switchboards to the White House [were] jammed with callers, most favouring tougher restrictions on the media and calling for an immediate US withdrawal from Somalia'.[107] President Clinton duly obliged. Operation Restore Hope, which had been launched amidst a media blitz on the Somalian sea-shore, collapsed on the sword of unpalatable media images from a back street in a place few of those callers to the White House had heard of before.

So television can serve as an occasional catalyst in foreign policy – but only when politicians allow it to do so. Restore Hope failed essentially because American forces on a humanitarian mission turned it into a man-hunt for General Aideed. That policy decision, combined with the proliferation of methods for collecting images about its consequences, was the source of the failure, not television. Nonetheless, Boutros Boutros-Ghali's view is that: 'Today, the media do not simply report the news. Television has become a part of the event it covers. It has changed the way the world reacts to crises.'[108] If it really is being allowed to set agendas for diplomatic initiatives,[109] again given its limitations, this is a recipe for disaster. 'We are under no pressure to do something about crises that are not on TV', one British official has admitted.[110] Yet if it is difficult enough for psychologists to establish a direct causal link between television and human behaviour generally, how can we talk with certainty of a 'do something factor'? One might only conclude that television's 'power' to set the agenda is determined more by those taking notice of it – or who are afraid of it – or who are willing to grant access to it – than it is by any inherent qualities which it may possess as an instrument of mass communication and persuasion.[111] There is more evidence that such people are more likely to be the politicians and the officials in the audience than members of the general public at large. And despite the argument that decision-makers simply do not have the time to watch television, and are therefore not influenced by it,[112] – and how many busy diplomats and politicians have the time to sit and watch the evening news? – no matter how hard they try television does intrude into their daily routines. If wives, sons or daughters don't tell them over the dinner table about the shocking pictures they have witnessed in that night's news programmes, their press officers almost certainly will the next morning. It doesn't matter whether the reports were accurate, balanced, contextualised or even significant – which they might not be – only that they have been transmitted and that they might have provoked a reaction. George Stephanopoulis gave the game away when he admitted that: 'in the White House . . . We have 24 hour news cycles . . . CNN assures you that you are forced to react at any time, and that's going to happen throughout the time of the Clinton presidency.'[113]

The journalist Nik Gowing has written that 'officials confirm that information often comes to them first from television or text news services well before official diplomatic and military communications channels can provide data, precision, clarification and context'.[114] US President Bush even went so far as to say: 'I learn more from CNN than I do from the

CIA',[115] while his press secretary claimed that 'in most of these kind of international crises now, we virtually cut out the State Department and the desk officers. . . . Their reports are still important, but they don't get here in time for the basic decisions to be made.'[116] Here, then, is the real source of the change. The speed at which modern news-gathering can – though not always does – occur places increased pressure on the decision-making process, which in turn complains that it cannot cope sensibly with the kind of knee-jerk solutions demanded by the pictures.

AGENDA-SETTING IN REAL TIME

If, in the traditional world of diplomacy, television is still regarded as a nuisance, real-time coverage adds a further threat: it means that the public is often made aware of an event at the same time as the politicians, who are accordingly forced to respond in a manner which runs counter to the diplomatic traditions of working methodically, systematically and slowly. According to Lee Hamilton, 'television also encourages policy-makers to react quickly, perhaps too quickly, to a crisis. . . . Television, critics say, leads not to sound foreign policy but sound bytes masquerading as policy.'[117] Hamilton was Chairman of the US House of Representatives' Foreign Affairs Committee when it examined this issue in 1994. His view was that 'there can be little doubt that television has had an impact, perhaps a profound impact on the conduct of US foreign policy'. He continued:

> Spurred by technological advances ranging from satellites to cellular phones, vivid images of conflict and deprivation are sent instantly to American homes from the world's trouble spots, whether in Haiti or Somalia or Bosnia or the Persian Gulf. These televised images quickly become a central part of the foreign policy debate. They affect which crises we decide to pay attention to and which we ignore. They affect how we think about those crises, and I have little doubt these televised pictures ultimately affect what we do about these problems.[118]

Once again, therefore, we appear to confront a contradiction. There is more information available today than ever before, more effective ways of gathering and distributing that information and, thanks to portable communications technology such as the satellite phone, camcorder and laptop computer, greater opportunities for non-professionals to make an input to the traditional flow of communications. Yet there are several indications that people cannot handle this information overload. Instead, people make choices about which pieces to absorb – through their choice of a newspaper or selection of a newscast. Very few people watch CNN continuously; people want access to news twenty-four hours a day, but they do not want to watch it for twenty-four hours at a time. And what they do watch, thanks to another piece of portable technology, the channel-hopping zapper, has to interest or concern them or else they tune out, or rather they tune in to a 200-channel universe of choice. Foreign policy remains the interest of relatively small numbers of people; it always has, despite talk of global villages and information superhighways. But live coverage of foreign policy issues makes it more exciting for more people, which merely makes it all the more likely that control over those issues will be diffused to an audience beyond the traditional elites.

It is often assumed that the public is prone to responding emotionally to dramatic events by clamouring for something simply and quickly to be done – to stop the horror before its eyes – while the politicians in the audience have to weigh up the options in a more considered way. However, politicians who believe in the power of television are increasing in number, and they, too, are members of the audience. Of the massive amount of live information now available, one senior White House adviser has noted that 'there's really no time to digest this information, so the reaction tends to be from the gut, just like the reaction of the man on the street'.[119]

The arrival of Electronic News Gathering (ENG) since the 1980s, of *instantaneous* news reports and live coverage from once remote places, does therefore appear to have transformed diplomatic practice. This is still most acutely felt in the United States where CNN has emerged as the most dynamic development of the American media scene prior to the arrival of information superhighways. Once lampooned as 'Chicken Noodle News' – reflecting the audacity of the experiment barely two decades ago – CNN has defined itself as the 'town crier in the global village'.[120] Its external arm, CNN International, had a revenue in 1994 of $100 million, as compared to $13.6 million at the time of the Gulf War,[121] and has made it an unavoidable player in international affairs.

CNN executive Tom Johnson maintains that 'our goal at CNN is neither to assist nor inhibit the diplomats of any country as they seek a solution for this or any crisis. It is our goal to provide fair and balanced reporting of all news and all views that are relevant to the events of the day. . . . Diplomats aside, all of us can only benefit from this open access to information.' Not everyone agrees. Real-time reporting exacerbates all those inherent weaknesses of television as a medium for conveying complexity. One need only recall CNN journalists, donning their gas masks in Jerusalem as they reported live on a chemical attack during the Gulf War, to see the problem. As Edward Bickham, a former special advisor to the British Foreign Office, has pointed out:

> The power of television in foreign policy is a mixed blessing. As a medium it plays too much to the heart, and too little to the head. It presents powerful, emotive images which conjure strong reactions. . . . Anecdotes about individual suffering make compelling television, but they rarely form a good basis to make policy. . . . Foreign policy should be made by democratic governments,

accountable to Parliament, not in reaction to which trouble spots the news gathering organisations can afford to cover from time to time. . . . Reactions to the priorities of the news room are unlikely to yield a coherent or sustainable foreign policy.[122]

Yet a senior US presidential advisor has admitted that this is precisely what can happen in the White House. 'High-level people are being forced essentially to act or to formulate responses to policy decisions on the basis of information that is of very uncertain reliability.'[123] Are they, however, being forced, or are they merely allowing this to happen? Either way, this can't be right. We are being presented with a scenario of Washington's agenda being determined by Atlanta, rather than vice versa, which – if correct – will in turn be determined more by CNN's ability to break stories first with pictures rather than by any sober calculation of US national interests. This scenario also fails to take into account the recent attention which governments like the US Government are giving to 'spin-doctoring', and the media agenda-setting on the part of American politicians whose growing skill at this was all too evident during the Gulf War.[124] One State Department official even admitted that the Clinton administration's strategy before 1995 was 'to keep Bosnia out of the headlines. Every day it's not in the news is another day of success',[125] even though it took two mortar attacks on Sarajevo's marketplace and the lines of fleeing refugees from Srebrenica – all in full glorious technicolor – to expose the strategy as a failure. At least on this occasion.

Traditionally, public diplomacy was paid for by governments to ensure that their views were projected to the wider world as a corrective to any media misrepresentation, and in the past five years both Britain and the US have extended this into television (BBC World Service Television and WORLDNET). Public diplomacy therefore has, if anything, become an even more essential function of governments to provide calm as a corrective to the chaos frequently caused by real-time, fire-fighting reporting 'as it happens' on the part of commercial news organisations. The precondition of this, however, is a coherent foreign *policy*. 'If an administration has thought its foreign policy through and is prepared and able to argue the merits and defend the consequences of that policy, television and all its new technologies can be dealt with.'[126]

CNN has been described as 'a common frame of reference for the world's power elite . . . A kind of world-wide party line, allowing leaders to conduct a sort of conference call heard not only by the principals but also by their constituents across the planet.'[127] The televised interviews between Presidents Bush and Saddam Hussein during the build-up to the Gulf War would certainly appear to confirm the validity of this. However, it has been pointed out that 'when politicians wish to mediate they use diplomatic channels, secure and private; when they wish to confront they use open forms of mass communication'.[128] But the clearest indication of the dangers of them relying

96

on live television for their information came on 15 February 1991, when news networks around the world rushed to break the story of Saddam's offer to withdraw from Kuwait before his speech had even finished, let alone considered, prompting premature celebrations of war's end before the full details of the Iraqi president's offer (including the withdrawal of Israel from the Golan Heights) become known.[129] Therefore, it is hard not to agree that 'instant access from the battlefield to the conference table and back again has enormous political implications, both good and bad'.[130]

It is for this reason that many analysts are beginning to call upon the media to reconsider their role within a global real-time society, one which is not a slave to commercialism or technological wizardry:

> The news media's greatest challenge is to explicate a concept of globalism and global news coverage with dedication to the idea that all parts of the world should be represented, lest we lose the chance to be fully informed. It is no longer satisfactory in a global society to attend only a few countries at a time. The educated and informed person who is conversant in the global society must know not only what is happening in all parts of the globe, but also across thematic topics such as global economics, environment, technology and ideology.[131]

Idealistic words, perhaps, and desirable ones certainly, but it is doubtful how realistic this is. Besides, is it not simply a call for propaganda on behalf of globalisation? Certainly, as the drift from print to television continues, it might appear that a medium inherently incapable of conveying complexity is being asked to do the impossible – unless, that is, drastic restructuring of news and current affairs takes it away from the trends of commercialisation and back to a public service ethos. For, as it has been pointed out:

> This is a good place to debunk the much repeated idea that television is a medium best suited to transmitting emotions, and that it either 'cannot' or is not 'good' at transmitting ideas. . . . The answer to why we see what we see on television lies in a combination of how audiences have come to conceive of the medium, what audiences want to watch (or have grown accustomed to watching), and what the people who control and sponsor television believe needs to be created and broadcast in order to maximise profit.[132]

Restructuring the way foreign news is reported, however, may simply produce a mass turn-off or switch-over because, as a former publisher of the *New York Times* put it, 'the fountain serves no purpose if the horse refuses to drink'.[133]

Broadcasters remain convinced that they understand their audience best, and thus are best placed to cater for their needs. As Ed Turner of CNN has argued, 'we continue to collect evidence that television news does have an impact on the conduct of foreign policy, but no one knows how much'.[134]

And because CNN is an all-news channel, he defends it as giving fuller coverage than that which the entertainment networks are able to provide:

> If we were to take a strong story-line, compress it into a formal documentary, pre-empt the news hours, and run it for say two hours on any night, chances are quite high that very few people would watch. That is the way of the world, rightly or wrongly. But if you take the same information, the news and opinion and build it around a live-from-the-scene reporter or anchor, and inject proper live shots from other aspects of the story, I believe you can not only attract a sizeable audience but also perform some important and effective services for the viewers.[135]

So, on the one hand we have CNN as a force for increasing popular interest in foreign affairs by making it exciting, while on the other there is the argument that this is merely placing undue pressure on politicians into making over-rapid decisions. To this charge, Ed Turner's argument is simple: 'if no comment is proper for our satellite signal, then an intelligent policy-maker will tell us "no comment". If this limited stress is unacceptable, then perhaps we need some new leaders.'[136]

As has been suggested, the 'no comment' approach is that which is most likely to arouse journalistic suspicion that something is being hidden. It also leads to massive speculation on what *might* be going on by the endless parade of 'talking-heads' that CNN and stations like it use to fill their air-time with. Such speculation can often do more harm than good, especially if foreign leaders are watching it and misread the signals of so-called informed 'experts'. It is simply not an option, therefore, for diplomats or politicians any more. Yet at least Turner conceded that journalists, too, face a major challenge in the age of real-time television, namely that of 'will we be smart enough to use the technology wisely? Will we be astute and honest as programmers and as editors of this journalism? It will be expensive and it will be difficult, but given the track record of the free world's journalist, I believe the answer is yes. We are cranky and we are impertinent and not infrequently wrong in this elusive search for truth. But taken as a whole, the answer is yes.'[137] An analysis of the track record of the free world's journalist at war, especially during the Gulf War of 1991, does, however, suggest a different answer.

3

ILLUSIONS OF REALITY
The media and the reporting of warfare

'There are times', the BBC correspondent and self-confessed 'war zone thug' Martin Bell has written, 'when journalism seems almost privileged, like having a front seat at the making of history'.[1] The corollary to this, of course, is that there are also times when journalism takes a back seat or even fails to enter the auditorium at all. And, if we take the point a little further, events which go unreported are thus in danger of becoming the hidden history of our mass-media century.

Wars, one might think, would not normally fall into this category. This is because, even by their simplest definition in international law as armed conflicts between two or more states or factions, they appear to be precisely the type of event upon which the media thrive. After all, wars involve the deployment of troops and weapons in a manner which makes for exciting copy and pictures (the more high-tech the better); they produce a stream of human interest stories of tragedy and heroism; they provoke heightened emotions such as patriotism, fear, anger and euphoria; and they involve winners and losers. When a nation is at war, newspaper sales increase, television and radio news programme ratings go up, while extremes of popular and media support or opposition reach new heights of intensity and polarisation.

Thanks to the media, each new generation of news consumers remembers 'its war', big or small, right or wrong, wherever it is fought, as its own. Would this be true for generations prior to this mass-media age? Perhaps, but only for those most directly involved: the soldiers themselves, their families and friends. Yet how much has actually changed? Certainly, thanks to Martin Bell and his colleagues, the media do appear to enable us to take a front seat at the making of history on the shirt-tails of journalism. However, from the music hall jingoism of the Boer War era to the television coverage of Bosnia in the 1990s, wars fought somewhere else really only become 'our wars' because the media creates what is in fact an illusion of participation in them. In other words, with the (even then only partial) exception of the 'Total Wars' of 1914–18 and 1939–45, most people's experience of warfare during this century is also to a large extent indirect, as witnesses to history via the media rather than as actual participants in it.

THE FIRST FLAWED ROUGH DRAFTS OF HISTORY

Just how central the media are as observers of the world around us can be seen in the popular iconography of twentieth-century warfare. Tanks rolling across trenches in France, the bombed-out ruins of Guernica, Spitfires in dogfights above Southeastern England, the mushroom cloud above Hiroshima, helicopter gunships over the Vietnamese jungle, the last moments of the *Belgrano*, cruise missiles travelling down a Baghdad street as if following an A–Z map of the city – all have been burned into the public consciousness by media images, and they remain enduring symbols of 'our wars'. But, for the troops in the field, the pilots in the air and the sailors at sea, the experience was altogether quite different.[2] Indeed, although experience and observation are not the same thing, the media, especially the audio-visual media of cinema and television, are capable of conflating them into one. In this media age, then, we need to remember that some soldiers fight wars and some civilians get caught up in them. The rest of us merely observe – but only whenever there are journalists present. When they are absent, for those not directly involved, wars – usually other people's wars – become 'forgotten wars'.

What makes the media focus on some wars and not others will be examined a little later. First, we need to appreciate some fundamental aspects of war reporting and the image of warfare that is relayed to the public by the media. At the forefront of our minds should be the point that, although the media do provide most of us with our 'first draft of history', it is, at best, very much a *rough* draft.

Naturally, we need to distinguish between the copy of reporters in the field and that of the analysts and columnists back home who produce the op-ed pieces about them. The former are at the battlefront, experiencing all the operational dangers and restraints of working, *inter alia*, with armed forces, while the latter are able to take a broader, more distant, view, especially since they have access to the political establishment and the public climate back home which helps them to provide a slightly wider context. But time, that friend of the historian, is the enemy of the journalist. With any journalistic piece, no matter how accurate or insightful it may be, there will almost always be a need for considerable subsequent re-writing of the story by historians before its wider historical significance can be fully understood or appreciated.

This should again alert us to the limits of journalism as an observer of events. The imperatives of speed to meet deadlines against competitors, problems of access to all the events as they happen, and a broader recognition of the causes and course of the events being covered, often prove to impose impossible demands on journalists in their role of mediating information to the public about matters of historical significance. And just as the fact that an event attracts media attention at any given time does not necessarily mean that it will retain its significance in the annals of history, the converse is equally true. Even those wars which do attract media attention can be seen subsequently in a very different light from that which was presented by the media at the time. Obviously, more information comes out about the event after it is over, which re-defines the way we look at the past and often prompts heart-felt re-evaluation of the way we saw the event at the time. This is because, quite simply, it does takes *time* to understand the wider context – and time, to the journalist, is a precious commodity that is measured more in deadlines numbered in hours – and today even seconds – than the relative luxury of the months or years required for historical research and personal reflection.

In a commercial business, news is a highly perishable commodity. But to sustain that business, credibility is essential. This places enormous pressure on the journalist to get the story right, regardless of the deadlines. In a war, this can prove almost impossible because of the sheer number of forces at work deliberately attempting, whether by commission or omission, to influence the way in which that story is being perceived by the outside world. A further problem for historians who come to it later therefore is not just that the first journalistic rough draft rarely tells the whole story and is infused with these various influences, but that once it has entered the public sphere via the media it also becomes extremely difficult to modify or revise it. Contemporary historians, especially of the revisionist tendency, are only too familiar with the problems associated with this, especially with the retort: 'it wasn't like that; I was there!' As we know, memory can play extraordinary tricks. But the real point is that relatively few people are physically present at historical events; the majority rely heavily upon the media for information about them. And too rarely is it appreciated that media reports have been subjected to so many forces competing in the attempt to shape their nature that their value as 'eyewitness' news is ultimately quite limited.

Again, we are in danger of homogenising a very diverse profession. A reporter from a twenty-four-hour news radio station, or one from, say, *Soldier of Fortune* magazine, will be looking for information of a different order to that sought by someone from BBC Television News or CNN, who, in turn, will have a different (perhaps a political) angle than someone from, say, the *Sun* or the *New York Times*. Likewise, local newspapers will be looking for local angles. Television needs pictures. We have seen that, because foreign reporting is an expensive business, many organisations prefer to rely on the wire services from Reuters or the Associated Press, or some might use stringers who are on the spot. In this age of global television news services, many national stations will simply run CNN's coverage, and pay for its use – infinitely cheaper than establishing their own separate foreign-news-gathering operations. But there are two implications of this that came to the fore during the Gulf War of 1991. The first is that the world television audience, so obviously a culturally, politically and economically diverse body, became increasingly dependant for its principal news coverage about the war on the homogeneous and ubiquitous CNN. The second implication stems from CNN's emphasis on live coverage, especially of official press conferences. When political leaders and military officials can speak directly to a world audience via live television, why bother with the rest of the vast media corps? Indeed, live TV by-passes that press corps and undermines its traditional role as mediators of information from news source to point of reception. Reporting an event 'as it happens' under the banner 'Breaking News Story' often requires reporters to talk without thinking or to speculate on causes and consequences that might not yet be fully understood. In other words, live television coverage threatens the traditional role of the pluralistic media as considered mediators of news to the public via various means and in various styles. Further, it may replace their mediation with a single, almost monolithic, instantaneous, yet endlessly recyclable (and possibly inappropriate) version of events. People may continue to rely on multiple news sources – the morning paper, the car radio, the evening television news. But if all these outlets in turn are relying on the same source, whether it be Reuters or CNN, monopoly masquerades as plurality. And if the driving imperative is speed of reporting rather than context, then snapshots masquerade as panoramas.

But however the news is gathered and packaged, warfare presents the journalist with very special problems. For example, most combat veterans testify to the veracity of two major features of war: long periods of boredom, punctuated by unimaginable brutality. Neither of these characteristics is particularly conducive to the business of journalism. The result is that the *reality* of war invariably is largely absent from the media record. Journalism thus, in this somewhat paradoxical sense, perpetuates hidden history even about the wars it does decide to cover. This in turn raises interesting questions about the image of war which remains, not least because that image is so enduring and at the same time the source of so much controversy.

FRAMING THE MILITARY–MEDIA DYNAMIC

War, then, appears on the surface to be good for the media business, and especially for television. But whether the media help the business of waging wars (let alone the writing of their history) is quite another matter. Most military personnel would certainly share this scepticism. Soldiers tend to regard the media as a troublesome nuisance hindering the serious business of waging war, and it is no coincidence that the arrival of the war correspondent as a profession – William Howard Russell of *The Times* during the Crimean War – prompted the introduction of modern military censorship.[3] Prior to that, reports from battlefields tended to be written by field officers for publication some time after the event, with the result that they were very

102

much an official 'record' designed more for posterity and propaganda than for informing the public – which was thereby divorced from the conduct of war, both spatially and temporally. It is noticeable that the iconography of warfare prior to the twentieth century was predominantly romantic or heroic – Goya's paintings, and the work of some other artists and the new breed of photographers notwithstanding – and depicted an activity that was 'natural' and 'glorious'. Battlefields, after all, were still at that time places where individuals and states earned their place in history. The arrival on those battlefields of civilian journalists like Russell, with their ability to communicate to the public *their* vision, a civilian vision, of what was 'actually happening' with unprecedented speed, posed a serious challenge to that prevailing, almost regimental, iconography. Even so, it is worth noting in passing that the popular image of the 'Glorious 600' members of the Light Brigade charging to their deaths in the Crimea remains more enduring in heroic terms than the horrified reports about conditions in the British army which were sent home by Russell – a point which should serve as our first corrective concerning the alleged long-term adverse impact of the media on the image of war. In other words, despite the horror, the iconography of glory remains.

None the less, it would be fair to suggest that, thanks to advent of the war correspondent, warfare in the eyes of the public would never be quite the same again. The military, who knew and feared this, especially if increased scrutiny resulted in an increase of popular anti-war sentiment, thus embarked upon the long road of censorship or, as they now prefer to call it, 'security review'. Their time-honoured justification for this is made in terms of preventing valuable information from falling into enemy hands, but the fact remains that they were also motivated essentially by the wish for a large degree of damage limitation – not merely on the battlefield itself but amongst the watching civilians far beyond it.

Throughout the centuries, soldiers who have experienced the realities of battle have feared that non-combatants would – not unreasonably – fail to understand their killing business. With the advent of the mass media this fear increased, not least because journalists theoretically possessed the capacity to demythologise the cult of war and all its distancing imagery. But, as we shall see, they need not have worried. It was not just that slaughter needed to be rationalised;[4] journalists quickly discovered that it also had to be rationed. The reality of war was so stark, the boredom so numbing and the killing so brutal, that reporters found they had to negotiate between conflicting pressures: the public's increasing desire to know on the one hand, and the need to present a tolerable and 'acceptable' face of warfare that would preserve both public support – and continued media consumption – on the other.

Since 1914, governments of all persuasions have attempted to resolve the problem of sustaining popular support by establishing institutions to manipulate information reaching the public, via the media, from war zones.[5] During the First World War, a 'Total War' in which the gap between the domestic and fighting fronts was narrowed substantially, the press corps was carefully husbanded in what became the first modern paradigm for the military–media relationship. Journalists were largely confined in lavish castles away from the fighting ('chateaux warriors'), while the new moving film cameras were denied access to areas in which the death and destruction were taking place. Elaborate official propaganda machines worked hard to sustain public support over four long years by trying to regain the traditional distance between the fighting and civilian fronts which communications and the media now threatened to compress. The war correspondents who occupied the ever-shrinking space in between were thus seen as potential enemies within the military gates rather than as allies in the service of democratic freedoms – itself a relatively novel concept at the time of the First World War. But, again, if the idea was to project an image of war quite different from its brutal realities, this once again failed in the long run, since the Great War holds a unique – and perhaps undeserved – place in the twentieth-century psyche as one of futility and unnecessary sacrifice.[6] That war, perhaps more than any other, is said to have marked an 'end of innocence' about the real nature of war, a 'rite of passage' to a more realistic public perception of what modern weaponry can really do to real people. However, such an impression could *not* have been gleaned *at the time* from the media whose record of patriotic jingoism and the demonisation of adversaries through atrocity stories was unparalleled up to that point.[7] If there was a new realisation, it came subsequently as an *ex post facto* rationalisation of the enormous sacrifice and loss that had taken place and which touched almost everybody.

However, from this anachronism, a myth was born, namely the assumption that a sanitised version of war via the media helps to sustain public support for it. Moreover, can we place any credence on the converse assumption, now so prevalent among critics of the media, that if only the 'reality' of war could be shown, public support would be undermined? Those with a fondness for counterfactual history often suggest that if television cameras had been present on the Western Front, that brutal conflict would not have lasted as long as it did. Yet this misses two fundamental points. In the first place, the military authorities would never have let such cameras anywhere near the fighting. And second, it assumes that 'the camera never lies'. But there is also a third and much more significant issue. Despite the growth of pacifism towards the end of the First World War and the post-war traumatic horror of the war's losses and consequences, the public and the media in the victorious countries for the most part continued to support the war. The Allies did not experience the internal collapse of Austria–Hungary, or the revolutionary uprisings in Germany and Russia, which contributed so much to the defeat of those nations. The degree to which media support and public support are connected will be tackled at the end of this chapter. Here, the point is that in the national wars of the twentieth century, the media tend to be every bit as patriotic as the public they are serving. They are not uncritical in this support, but when 'our boys' are fighting, the instinctive reaction of press and public alike is to support them. To make certain of this, by the end of the First World War the press barons Beaverbrook and Northcliffe were even placed in charge of the official British propaganda machine. They were so appointed by the Prime Minister, David Lloyd George, who was the first British politician of the twentieth century to believe in the power of the press to shape events. For him, this belief was instinctive, intuitive, rather than based on scientific audience research – such a factor was still a long way off. In other words it was an assumption, based on his own experience, that the press could make or break politicians. His successors likewise have come to believe that the media can win or lose wars.

The actual record of media coverage of military involvement is, however, quite different from the myth. It is in fact more one of cooperation than conflict. This has been largely forgotten – due mainly to the American experience of the Vietnam war, to which we shall return shortly. But it is an undisputed historical fact that the media have helped the prosecution of national wars during this century far more than they have ever hindered them. And the reasons for this lie not just in the development of ever-more-sophisticated methods for controlling and manipulating the media. Whereas in authoritarian regimes the state-controlled media are straightforward mouthpieces of government policy that could therefore be expected automatically to support a war effort, in free societies even during wartime such control has its constitutional or legal limits. This makes the record of democratic media support for national wars this century all the more remarkable, and begs further examination.

Much has already been written about the processes by which first the press and then the mass media came to constitute a 'fourth estate' in the body politic of democratic nations. At the micro level, however, there are still remarkably few academic studies of reporters in the field. Fortunately, there are numerous memoirs by journalists describing conditions in the field, especially during times of war. Military memoirs reinforce the impression that the military–media dynamic has always been characterised by tension. However, in the opinion of General Alexander, who took command of British North African forces in 1942:

> The press correspondent is just as good a fellow as any military officer or man who knows a great many secrets, and he will never let you down – not on purpose – but he may let you down if he is not in the picture, merely because his duty to his paper forces him to write something, and that something may be most dangerous. Therefore he must be kept in the picture.[8]

Indeed, the record of most war correspondents in the Second World War is one of wholehearted support for the war effort – whatever side they were on. In Britain, for example, despite strict censorship procedures, the number of occasions on which the media clashed with the government in six years of 'Total War' was remarkably few.[9] And when American correspondents after Pearl Harbor encountered bad news, they often failed to report it, 'not because disclosure might help the enemy in playing to Allied weakness, but simply because it reflected negatively on the Allied performance'.[10] Hence General Eisenhower could refer to the 500-strong press corps attached to his command as 'almost without exception . . . my friends'.[11] This is where patriotism and propaganda coincide, and in wartime the record of the journalist's profession as patriots and propagandists is every bit as noteworthy in democracies as it is in authoritarian regimes. The difference is that in one the media volunteer to serve this role and in the other they are compelled to do so. The system of voluntary censorship adopted in Britain and the United States in the Second World War did not, however, extend to combat zones, where field censorship of what modern war does to real people was particularly tight.[12] The military might argue openly that this was essential to prevent relatives and friends being offending by the sight in the media of their loved ones in anguish, but the legacy of historical iconography – the element of public morale – also survives in this process. Hence only enemy dead were shown in cinema newsreels, and even then in not too much detail. This means therefore that the degree to which the media's showing of the realities of war while it was happening could adversely affect morale and promote anti-war sentiment remains largely to be seen. It has, quite simply, never happened.

This is not to deny that the media have proved quite successful in conveying a *sense* of the fighting. But just as the military fear what would happen to public morale if the 'whole truth' were known, so also do the media fear the risks of alienating their customers if the 'whole truth' were told. It is here that the interests of the war correspondent and the soldier in the field coincide, although it is rarely acknowledged as such – perhaps because the military mind rarely grasps this and because the media dare not acknowledge it. But the Korean War (1950–53) provides a revealing example of how problems can emerge from this core issue. Because of their largely cooperative track record in the Second World War, there was no initial American censorship imposed on reporters in Korea. However, when journalists in the field found that the guidelines they had imposed upon themselves failed to discourage critical copy back home on the part of their colleagues who wrote op-ed pieces in the relative comfort of their own offices, which in turn began to incur popular disquiet about the unpatriotic media coverage, it was they who approached the Department of Defense for clarification, not the other way round. The resultant censorship system in the field proved similar to that of the Second World War, with military censors on the spot reviewing every word and image prior to release for publication. Once this system began to operate, the military's predisposition towards secrecy over publicity resurfaced. This was despite the fact that it was still taking several hours at best, and several days at worst, to get copy out of the theatre of war and back to base. However, the military approach was not confined to censoring reports of troop movements or other operational details for fear of aiding the enemy; it quickly extended to issues of morale, not just in theatre but back at home as well. General MacArthur, for example, refused to allow any media criticism on topics raging from troop behaviour to UN decisions.[13] After all, the guiding principle established by the democracies fighting in the Second World War was that news rather than views could be censored, which allowed for a degree of media debate and criticism that would foster the illusion that no censorship was taking place. This in turn was excellent propaganda for the moral stance of a democracy at war. But in Korea this was undermined, reflecting in the process a growing awareness by the military that they had become a part of society, not separate from it, and had thus become more accountable to society. It does, of course, need to be borne in mind that the America engaging in the 'police action' of Korea was undergoing the sordid era of the McCarthy witch hunts at home, in which dissenting voices were reduced to whispers or even silence out of fear. Nonetheless, it is ironic that the introduction of censorship, and the establishment of the Press Advisory Division of the Public Information Section of the UN Command, actually reduced military–media tension, not increased it.[14] Having said that, this failed to prevent the war from becoming increasingly unpopular.

This was due in no small part to the fact that media attention on what troops do in modern battles was becoming partially responsible for the growing public accountability of armies. During wars fought with conscripted troops, this was perhaps to be expected, but in wars fought by core professional units, it continues to cause some resentment, especially as the troops are deployed largely as a result of political decisions. For Britain, as was suggested in the previous chapter, the watershed came during the 1956 Suez Crisis[15] and for America it was the Vietnam War. The democratic media on both occasions proved more critical than supportive of national policy than they had ever been before, with the result that the media bore the brunt of the blame for failure by those framing and implementing the policy, rather than the policy itself.

How fair was this? Certainly, after Britain abandoned National Service in 1962 and the Americans abandoned the draft in 1973, the military found that, when it went to war, journalists with no previous military experience were turning up with little idea of the realities of fighting a war and making unrealistic demands that could not be accommodated, which in turn merely caused media criticism that was resented by the military. This increasing lack of mutual understanding has been the source of ongoing tension which, when combined with the US experience of Vietnam, has poisoned military–media relations for the past twenty years and which is only now beginning to see some signs of improvement.

Some rare members of the military have placed the blame for this upon themselves: 'through fear of reinforcing the basic antimilitarism of the American people we tended to . . . downplay battlefield realities. . . . We had concealed from the American people the true nature of war at precisely the time that television brought its realities into their living rooms in living color.'[16] In the United States, Vietnam thus stands pivotal in this debate, the first 'television war' in which the modern public could observe modern warfare in all its lack of glory. Television stands accused of having stripped away the delusions of the past about the nature of real war, bringing to Americans the 'end of innocence', and, as a result, has completely changed the operational considerations of military commanders when they come to deploy their troops in battle. There is only one problem with all this. It is mainly nonsense.

THE MYTH OF THE VIETNAM SYNDROME

Vietnam has been labelled the 'Uncensored War'[17] because, unlike other twentieth-century wars, relatively few restrictions were placed upon the media's ability to report what was going on throughout the entire conflict. This is not to imply that the US government did not engage in 'news management', and indeed it proved quite effective in promoting media support for the war in the early stages of significant US troop deployment between 1963 and 1965. This was despite the fact that, during this period, 'US information policy was still in a process of evolution' and was operating on such primitive directives as that which decreed that reporters 'should not be transported on military activities of the type that are likely to result in undesirable stories'.[18] Thanks to the advent of television, this 'first television war' did appear to have an audio-visual immediacy and, it is thereby assumed, a potential impact on domestic support for the war. The problem was that, in the long term, the impact was felt to have been negative. James Reston of the *New York Times* wrote: 'Maybe the historians will agree that the reporters and the cameras were decisive in the end. They brought the war to the people . . . and forced the withdrawal of American power from Vietnam.'[19] Then again, maybe not.

The Vietnam conflict crept on to American television screens only gradually, almost serendipitously, reflecting the extent of the US military build-up there. In 1963 there were 16,000 American troops in Vietnam and about twenty American foreign correspondents to cover their contribution. By 1968, these figures had risen to half a million men and 637 journalists. The presence of the latter, legend has it, had adverse consequences for the performance of the former. From 1965 onwards, following CBS's Morley Safer's report showing US Marines burning peasant huts with Zippo lighters, images of burning monks, napalmed children, deadly helicopter gunships and executed Vietcong appeared nightly in the living-rooms of civilian homes far removed from the fighting, making Vietnam the most visible war yet seen in history. On the surface, it looks like a recipe for disaster, and indeed, for many, it was. But it is also the stuff from which myths emerge. And, indeed, many did.

The most deeply rooted myth, which has become almost impossible to budge in military thinking, is the widely-held belief that the media in general and television in particular helped America to lose the war in Vietnam. Even twenty years or more later, in 1995, one American survey found that 'although . . . that opinion is no longer held by top civilian and military leaders of the nation's defense establishment, it is still widespread amongst military officers', with 64 per cent believing that 'the news media coverage of events in Vietnam harmed the war effort'.[20] This line of thinking runs as follows: how could Superpower America suffer the first and only military defeat in its history to a Third World enemy that was inferior in just about every way, from military equipment to moral justification? The answer surely could not lie in the inadequacies of the US military or the policy it was forced to implement; it must lie elsewhere. The military must have been forced to withdraw due to a collapse of public support at home, a collapse fuelled by hostile coverage by the media, and particularly by television. This is, in fact, an argument not dissimilar to that deployed by military professionals in the defeated Germany of the 1920s, including an ex-corporal who exploited the 'stab-in-the-back' thesis on that occasion by generating a Jewish–Bolshevik conspiracy fuelled by enemy propaganda. Defeated nations always search for rationalisations for their failure – for the Vietnam 'Syndrome', as it has become known, is indeed a rationalisation, as distinct from an explanation, of the failure of American forces to secure a military victory in Southeast Asia.[21]

The actual reasons for that defeat are beyond the scope of this study. However, evidence to support the 'demythologisation' of media culpability needs to be provided. In general terms it needs to be remembered that, for the Americans, the Vietnam war essentially lasted ten years, from 1963 to 1973. For the first five years, the media is generally held to have been supportive. One recent judgement has it as follows:

> because Project Beef-Up [i.e. escalation of US involvement] directly and openly violated an international treaty, Washington unrealistically wanted to fight on the sly. And it wanted the reporters to go along with the fiction, to play the ostrich. The emperor was naked, but it would become unpatriotic to say he was wearing no clothes. When the policy didn't work, American officials clammed up, covered up, and lied – not only to the public and the press but eventually to themselves.[22]

The so-called turning point at which media support is felt to have been lost was the 1968 Tet Offensive. Thereafter, relentlessly hostile media coverage is said to have forced the inglorious withdrawal of 1973. But it is important to note that this was *five years* after Tet, a period as long as American involvement before then – and longer than US involvement in World War Two. If five years of media support was followed by five years of media opposition, then Washington can only be said to have been uncharacteristically resilient when faced with such hostile media criticism. There is indeed sufficient evidence to suggest that questioning media coverage of the Tet Offensive – in fact a military victory for the Americans but said to have been projected as a defeat by the media – prompted US President Johnson not to stand for re-election in 1968.[23] But the victor in that election, Richard Nixon, who was committed to ending the war and who demonstrated what he meant by this by extending it into Laos and Cambodia, was *re-elected* in 1973. Again, if the media was so hostile, it was clearly having little impact on public opinion. Indeed, it is also largely forgotten that a 1967 Harris poll for *Newsweek* found that 64 per cent claimed television coverage had made them more *supportive* of the war, while only 26 per cent said it intensified their opposition, and there was even an upsurge of support in the polls after Tet.[24]

Seemingly trivial examples can often reveal wider truths. In the ten-year period of the war, only one Hollywood film studio was prepared to tackle American involvement in Vietnam head-on. This in itself undoubtedly reveals that the war was indeed controversial; imagine 1941–45 with a similar Hollywood track record! However, that film, *The Green Berets* starring all-American hero and conservative icon John Wayne, was not simply an overtly propagandistic justification for American military involvement, it was also a box-office success, grossing $8 million domestically.[25] Given that it was released in 1968, at the supposed height of popular/media opposition to the war, something isn't quite right here. Let us therefore turn to the specific details.

In the early stages of the US military build-up, the Joint United States Public Affairs Office (JUSPAO) was established to meet the needs of newsmen, who, it needs to be reiterated, largely supported the war. Hordes of inexperienced journalists attempting to make a reputation for themselves proved to be easily 'managed' by JUSPAO, which exploited their dependence on news from the fighting fronts in the north. Military censorship was not much in evidence in what was certainly the least censored major war of the twentieth century – the exception to the rules on war reporting which had been the norm since the Crimean conflict. One significant consequence of this abnormality was the gradual opening up of a credibility gap as a few journalists started to check the 'facts' issued by official American sources in Saigon. They found an increasingly wide discrepancy between JUSPAO's official battle accounts and casualty figures and their own observations in the field. It was at this point, conventional wisdom has it, that people began to realise that the Pentagon was lying and that journalists were telling the truth – which perhaps helps to explain why only four journalists ever had their accreditation withdrawn by the South Vietnamese government throughout the entire war! The official early evening briefings – timed to facilitate reporting by domestic TV news bulletins – earned the nickname 'Five o'clock Follies', as the credibility gap widened from around 1965 onwards. This in turn was exploited by Hanoi, where journalists were permitted to see only what the authorities wanted them to see. The North Vietnamese began to realise that, despite inferior military equipment and technology, the propaganda tradition of Communist warfare could exploit democracy's cherished freedoms and its new love affair with television. If Hanoi could win over the journalists and other high-profile visitors, or at least make them sceptical about America's ability to win, then the war could be won in New York, Chicago, Los Angeles, San Francisco and, above all, Washington.

Then came Tet, 1968. The media coverage during and after that offensive supposedly reflected the mounting hostility of American newsmen towards United States involvement. General Westmoreland, the American commander, was to state in 1979:

> The American media had misled the American people about the Tet offensive and when they realised that they had misjudged the situation – that in fact it was an American victory – they didn't have the courage or integrity to admit it.[26]

Television pictures at the time of Tet certainly did portray a view different from that being conveyed by the political and military authorities in Washington and Saigon. Walter Cronkite, the distinguished and respected anchorman of CBS News, watched with disbelief as the Vietcong stormed the American embassy in Saigon, exclaiming: 'What the hell is going on? I thought we were winning the war.'[27] The credibility gap had now reached America itself. Cronkite's real point was that 'to say that we are mired in stalemate seems the only realistic, yet unsatisfactory, conclusion'.[28] President Johnson's response was that, with the loss of faith by people of Cronkite's standing and influence, he would not stand for the 1968 Presidential election. True, polls indicated that he was losing more and more of middle America's support, while young America took to the streets in protest. Anti-war propaganda by a growing vocal minority now jostled with the patriotism of the majority, while the media attempted to steer a middle course in the tradition of objective reporting. Nonetheless, as Professor Daniel Hallin, the leading scholar of this subject, has pointed out:

> Before Tet, editorial comments by television journalists ran nearly four to one in favour of administration policy; after Tet, two to one against. Before Tet, of the battles journalists ventured to describe as victories

111

or defeats, 62% were described as victories for the United States, 28% as defeats, 2% as inconclusive or as stalemates. After Tet, the figures were 44% victories, 32% defeats, and 24% inconclusive.[29]

So a change had taken place and it is a change which, on the surface, can be seen not so much as a transformation of loyalty but a diminution of it. But even these figures still show majority support in the war reports, as distinct from the editorial pieces. In other words, the American media did not necessarily become anti-war after 1968; US-based journalists merely became less willing to accept uncritically the official version emanating from Washington and Saigon. And while it is true that 'journalists became more inclined to report information critical of official policy . . . there were certain basic elements of the structure and ideology of American journalism which persisted more or less unchallenged through the Vietnam period, and make it very hard to sustain the thesis of an actively oppositional news media'.[30] The evidence suggests that journalists continued to be reliant upon official sources of information, despite the opening up of a credibility gap, and the only real change was that more and more attention was being given to the vocal – and visible – minority which was opposing the war. And whereas the media might be accused, therefore, of magnifying the significance of that minority, the evidence suggests that, although the media 'did give increasing coverage to the opposition as the war went on . . . this coverage was not particularly favourable. . . . Whatever tendency there may have been for journalists to become more sceptical of administration policy, *it does not seem to have been translated into sympathetic coverage of the opposition.*'[31] The simple fact of the matter, therefore, is that the media have since shouldered a large proportion of the blame for actually doing their job more efficiently than they had been before 1968, when they had been uncritically supportive.

President Nixon's 'Vietnamisation' of the war involved a reduction in the number of American forces as a concession to public opposition, while bombing offered the hope of victory through air power – as it had done in 1940 and 1943. Yet, as the Second World War had shown, bombing, even on the scale the Americans were prepared to adopt in 1969–73, does not destroy the morale of the enemy; in fact quite the reverse. It is rather an attempt to demonstrate to domestic opinion that the military is capable of hitting the enemy – a propaganda of the deed – at a time when it is losing the propaganda battle and the conventional military struggle.[32] The continuing return in body-bags of young American conscripts belied the official pronouncements that the war, against a fanatical but inferior enemy, was being won. Repeated media coverage of such homecomings fuelled the anti-war movement while alienating public confidence in central government's ability to tell the truth – a process which received further confirmation during the Watergate scandal. Yet none of this should be taken to mean that the public had lost its faith in the institution of government.

112

William Small, Director of CBS News in Washington, felt:

When television covered its 'first war' in Vietnam, it showed a terrible truth of war in a manner new to a mass audience. A case can be made, and certainly should be examined, that this was cardinal to the disillusionment of Americans with this war, the cynicism of many young people towards America, and the destruction of Lyndon Johnson's tenure of office.[33]

On the last point, there can be little doubt. The 1960s saw democratically elected politicians becoming increasingly sensitive to what they saw as the power of television to sway public opinion. Whether television in fact possesses such power has preoccupied academic researchers ever since. But the point is that many politicians, much more so than in Lloyd George's time, *believe* that the media is invested with such qualities and, although that belief may say more about them than it does about, say, television's actual impact upon society, it does mean that politicians rather than the media have largely shaped the agenda for debating the subject. And so a real war, uncensored, enacted every day for ten years in full colour on a hundred million TV sets throughout America, might indeed appear to be a recipe for disaster in terms of domestic public opinion. Before 1968, surveys reveal that a majority of those viewers were encouraged to support the efforts of their boys 'over there' by the coverage. Thereafter, however, following prolonged exposure to the horrors, did such coverage undermine popular support? Some research indicates that prolonged exposure to media violence leads to the anaesthetisation of people's sensitivities, turning off their minds rather than the TV sets.[34] The pictures may have been horrific, but were they having an impact? The students may have chanted 'the whole world is watching' in their anti-war demonstrations, but was television capable of converting the desensitised, the indifferent or the patriotic into like-minded souls? Undoubtedly, the collapse of *political* consensus over the Vietnam War resulted in growing opposition within the United States itself, but whether television caused that collapse is doubtful. However, once it had collapsed, and opposition reached the Senate and the Presidential elections, the media was bound to pick it up. Hence,

the case of Vietnam suggests that whether the media tend to be supporting or critical of government policies depends on the degree of consensus those policies enjoy, particularly within the political establishment. . . . News content may not mirror the facts, but the media, as institutions, do reflect the prevailing pattern of political debate: when consensus is strong, they tend to stay within the limits of the political discussion it defines; when it begins to break down, coverage becomes increasingly critical and diverse in the viewpoints it represents, and increasingly difficult for officials to control.[35]

In short, we have a classic case of shooting the messenger for the message being carried. Because political opposition to the war increased, perhaps as a response to mounting public opposition, the media merely reflected that – for which they, not the politicians, have been blamed. But then it is not in the interests of military men to blame politicians, at least not in public. The media are a much easier target. Yet as the politicians abandoned the policy that had placed the military in Southeast Asia, 'remaining behind in South Vietnam to retrieve whatever national face they could, those of their members most emotionally tied to the failed policy fixed their anger upon the news media, the most visible exponent of the society that appeared to have rejected them.'[36] But because, thanks to Watergate when the power of the media was at the forefront of the 1970s mind, politicians have come to fear the media as well, this has served to unite politicians and soldiers in the belief that television can have a tremendous impact on their activities, that in fact it forced the American withdrawal from Vietnam, whereas it is their activities in the first place which attract the media's attention. In other words, if any one group can be blamed for losing the war, it was the politicians, not the military or the media – and certainly not the media in the field.

None the less, in Vietnam, some of the dangers of war-reporting in the television age did emerge. Reporters and cameramen were unable to present a 'true' image of the war by virtue of the circumstances in which they operated. The 'limitless medium' does in fact suffer from several significant limitations. Whisked in and out of combat zones by any helicopter on which they could hitch a ride, reporters in Vietnam were looking for the kind of exciting footage demanded by their editors without searching the proper context in which the action needed to be seen. Interestingly, *Time* magazine launched an attack on the Saigon press corps for covering 'a complex situation from one angle, as if their conclusions offered all necessary illumination' as early as 1963.[37] After then, television coverage became even more prominent. Visual excitement on the small screen does not automatically make for adequate or contextualised reporting, especially with television companies back home competing for ratings in short, sharp newscasts. Bias, naturally enough, affects the entire reporting process – from the direction in which the camera was pointed in the first instance to how the film was subsequently edited and packaged, and even to how the images and messages were received by individual members of the public. Although there were comparatively few censorship restrictions on what newsmen could cover in Vietnam, they often acted as their own censors by not including material that might offend the senses of taste and decency amongst their audiences. But as Peter Braestrup has pointed out, 'television people have been saying for years that they brought the truth home, the horror of the war. But the fact is that from August 1, 1965, to August 1970, only about 3 percent of television network news stories showed heavy combat with dead or wounded shown on the screen. Most of it was aftermath coverage.'[38] If

114

the horrific images emanating from Vietnam had any impact at all, it was likely that it was their *cumulative* impact which served to shape popular perceptions about the war over a period of time, rather than any specific military 'turning point' coverage. None the less, scenes of a little naked girl screaming in pain from napalm burns, or of the execution of a Vietcong suspect by a Saigon Police Chief, are the very stuff of which atrocity propaganda is made. The problem in Vietnam was that such atrocities were being committed by 'our side' rather than by the enemy. 'It was this horror, not the reporting that so influenced the American people.'[39] The My Lai massacre may not have been filmed, but the very fact that it happened reinforced the overwhelming visual 'evidence' that the war was about something more than the authorities pretended. The comparative shortage of equivalent material from the enemy side – the difference between rigid media control and unfettered media access – meant that Americans began to fight amongst themselves about the respective merits of the war, and many could only draw one conclusion. In short, television helped to simplify a complicated war. Because it has been developed along patterns of behaviour by largely commercial considerations, television relies upon sensational coverage, generalisation and selection. But to extrapolate from this that the war was lost on television, or, further still, that television makes it nearly impossible for democratic states to conduct war successfully,[40] was to prove patent nonsense. Yet this is exactly what happened. 'Despite its manifest irrationality, the power and pervasiveness of this belief have made it a significant factor in modern military–media relations.'[41] So has the belief that 'the camera never lies'.[42]

ANTIDOTES TO THE VIETNAM SYNDROME

It isn't only the camera. And yet, if truth – as is frequently asserted – is the first casualty of war, one question we need to ask is: who else is lying? It may be a truism, but quite simply, if the journalist is absent from an event there is no story, which means he has to rely on third-party sources for his information. But when he turns up for the show, he can still be spoon-fed with the version of the story desired by his source. Better to go into the field to see for himself. That is how journalists die. War zones are extremely dangerous places, all the more so for the inexperienced who don't know the difference between incoming and outgoing artillery fire. Soldiers are at least trained for this, whereas very few news organisations prepare their personnel for the realities they will face. Moreover, every year since 1945, there have been somewhere between twenty and thirty-five wars taking place around the world at any given time. These have been small wars, low intensity conflicts and civil wars – most of which fail to command media interest in the rest of the world. Two or three might invite the interest of Western news organisations; most will be more likely to appear under the caption 'the world in brief'. This is hardly the kind of background information required for a journalist who is suddenly despatched to a combat zone because something has happened to bring it further up the agenda of the news organisation concerned – a massacre, a breakthrough, hostages or whatever.

Once any given conflict is deemed 'newsworthy', however, journalists flock to the war zone like sharks to an injured fish. There is then a kind of feeding frenzy where the intense competitiveness of the media business becomes the driving force behind the coverage. As one old foreign correspondent once remarked: 'Whenever you find hundreds of thousands of sane people trying to get out of a place and a little bunch of madmen struggling to get in, you know the latter are newspapermen.'[43] Today, we would add to the latter radio and television correspondents. During Operation Desert Storm in 1991, an astonishing 1,500 journalists swarmed to Saudi Arabia – more than the troop contributions of most coalition members and three times the number of reporters present on D-Day in 1944 – with another 1,500 waiting for accreditation by the time the war ended. Why was this, especially when there was a crisis going on at the same time which would have far more significant consequences for the course of the twentieth century, namely the crisis in the Baltic which precipitated the break-up of the old Soviet Empire? Indeed, the American networks were winding down their Eastern European bureaux when Saddam Hussein invaded Kuwait in August 1990. It was becoming an expensive business for, in their terms, very low returns. And what are those terms? One of the answers to this question we have already identified: pictures. War and military build-ups present great photo-opportunities: troop movements, high tech equipment and possibly even the chance of some action shots – the fast-moving, picture-based material on which television thrives.

As General Dugan, the head of air operations in Desert Storm, put it: 'Now, 1,500 is not an unmanageable number, but it is a number that cries out for management.'[44] The sheer size of the press corps in Saudi Arabia reflected the massive proliferation of media outlets since the Vietnam era much more than it did the likely long-term historical significance of the Gulf War. Not all of these people could be allowed to accompany the troops, in the same way that there is only a limited number of places in the public gallery of a courtroom. And after their experience in Vietnam, the military would have preferred to have kept the press away altogether. Accordingly, General Winant Sidle, who had previously served as chief military spokesman at JUSPAO in 1967–9, was asked to investigate how in future conflicts involving American troops the press corps could be 'accommodated'. In 1982, the British had appeared to offer some solutions.

During the Falklands War, only twenty-nine journalists and crew were permitted to accompany the Task Force – all of them British. The foreign media were to be served by the Reuters representative. Even that small number was only agreed reluctantly by the Royal Navy. The British armed forces seemed to have inherited all the preconceptions and misconceptions about the media from the American experience in Southeast Asia. Their price for conceding a media presence was that the journalists would be totally dependent upon the Navy in two vital aspects: travelling to and from the war zone, and communicating their copy from the Task Force back to London. Invariably, military communications took priority, with the result that delays were inevitable. 'Hot news', the lifeblood of modern journalism, became 'cold news' or no news at all. Indeed, it took longer for one report to reach home than a despatch had taken to reach London from the Crimea, 130 years earlier.

After the war, the House of Commons Defence Committee which investigated its media coverage conceded that there had been more to the censorship than mere 'operational security', namely the 'furtherance of the war effort through public relations'.[45] During the war itself, the philosophy underlining this appeared to take the form that late news is no news for the media, which in turn is good news for the military. With some film reports taking three weeks to reach London, the BBC for example was forced to use pictures from other sources. When Argentinean footage was used to fill the vacuum created by British censorship, the BBC was accused of disseminating enemy propaganda. When footage from British journalists did finally arrive, it had been sanitised by the censors shadowing the journalists with the Task Force. Phrases such as 'horribly burned' were cut out, news of setbacks such as the loss of HMS *Sheffield* were delayed, even the substitution of the word 'cleared' for 'censored' were all part of an attempt to present a particularly one-sided, and highly favourable, view of a war with little bloodshed. As one public relations officer told an ITN correspondent with the Task Force: 'You must have been told you couldn't report bad news before you left. You knew when you came you were expected to do a 1940 propaganda job.'[46]

This type of comment reveals the eternal tension between the military and the media in wartime: secrecy versus publicity. The Ministry of Defence spokesman during the Falklands War, Ian McDonald, epitomised the traditional military preference for secrecy. His policy was never to lie deliberately but never to endanger the safety of the troops by disclosing information which might prove to be of the slightest use to the enemy. He also knew that, thanks to the increasing internationalisation of the media, the Argentineans would be watching. If a denial served to deceive the enemy, then well and good. But tension with the media increased when the military deliberately used them as instruments for deception. On this issue, the Chief of the Defence Staff, Sir Terence Lewin, stated:

I do not see it as deceiving the press or the public; I see it as deceiving the enemy. What I am trying to do is to win. Anything I can do to help

117

me win is fair as far as I'm concerned, and I would have thought that that was what the Government and the public and the media would want, too, provided the outcome was the one we were all after.[47]

The British experience in the Falklands and the American mythology about Vietnam came together during the US Invasion of Grenada in 1983. Regardless of the Reagan administration's insistence that the rapidity of events prevented any time for accommodating the media, the resultant media blackout only served to strain US military–media relations still further. An unusual degree of military control of the invasion was provided by Washington which, a decade after Vietnam, not only guaranteed exclusion of the press corps but also created the resultant speculation and confusion that filled the vacuum. Mounting protest eventually resulted in a few journalists being flown in after the invasion was all over and well away from any military action. These few were supposed to share ('pool') their reports with the hundreds of others of their frustrated fraternity, which they did not always do. The end result was a vicious fight within the press corps itself. When the event was all over, they switched from fighting amongst themselves to attacking the military. It was a disastrous low point in twentieth-century US military–media relations. The irony was that public support for the invasion was high. Clearly, the legacy of the Vietnam myth of media culpability had entered mainstream American opinion, which, polls revealed, now trusted the military more than the media.[48] Clearly, the general public also believed that the military could win wars whereas the media could lose them.

Grenada demonstrated that the question of access was the critical issue in the military–media dynamic. In the past, access had been agreed, albeit reluctantly in some cases, because the needs of the military to retain popular support for their actions was accepted as a consequence of modernisation and democratisation. But with access came some concessions, namely a degree of field censorship. Vietnam is supposed to have broken this rule and in the process poisoned military–media relations. But as Grenada demonstrated, it had not necessarily soured the relationship between the military and the public. The military might have taken some comfort in this had its institutional memory understood the relationship between the stark realities of war and the public image of it as projected by an historically cooperative media. Rather, with Vietnam very much in its mind, it looked to ways of controlling the media rather than cooperating with them. This defensive knee-jerk reaction to what was in fact a myth merely served to create in Grenada the very situation that was felt to have existed in Vietnam. It was therefore almost a self-fulfilling prophecy that military–media relations after 1973 would be adversarial, that the military would be reactive rather than proactive. And this was happening at a time when radical technological developments were indeed providing opportunities for undermining the very controls which the military now sought to put in place, but which could only be done under conditions that were bound to generate friction with an adversarial media not only capable of by-passing them but almost determined to do so. Preparing for the next war by looking to the lessons of the last one may be a time-honoured form of military planning, but developments, especially in portable satellite communications, during the 1980s provided unprecedented possibilities for war reporting that, in the light of Desert Storm, really do make the Falklands and Grenada conflicts look even more like nineteenth-century wars than they did at the time. War was about to become 'live'. But did this mean it was about to become 'real'?

REAL WAR AND MEDIA WAR

Before examining this most significant of recent developments, we need to return to some further conceptual aspects of the military–media dynamic that inherently create problems for analysing the media image of warfare. Methodologically, they are as important for the historian embracing this brave new world of 'evidence' as they are for even the most casual media observers of war. For once a war breaks out, it is not always immediately apparent that in fact two wars start to take place: the 'real war', in which real people die, and what might be termed the 'media war', in which the realities of war, such as death and destruction, are both distant and distanced from a non-participating mass audience by the very nature of the media as mediator. Real war is about the sound, sight, smell, touch and taste of the nasty, brutal business of people killing people. Media war is literally a mediated event which draws on that reality but which, in and of itself, is confined merely to a third-party or an audio-visual – and thus a desensitising – representation of it. Some theoreticians have labelled this phenomenon of war a 'pseudo-event',[49] that is, an illusion of war's real-ities, disseminated, even manufactured, by the media for the edification, almost in a gruesome way the entertainment (the 'infotainment'), of a mass audience which can never experience its horrors at first-hand but which participates in war as a distant spectacle. This is the stuff upon which French intellectuals like Jean Baudrillard and Paul Virilio thrive.[50] Suffice it to say here that, undoubtedly, any media image of war is very much a flawed window on to the battlefield. What is perhaps surprising is that anyone should see it as otherwise.

In wartime, the media in fact serve a variety of roles at a variety of levels. With information, they can convey a *sense* of the fighting to a public divorced from its actual horrors; with entertainment, they can provide a degree of relief or escape to a public more directly involved, such as, for example, in a blockade or a bombing campaign. Even television news bulletins try to end on a slightly upbeat note ('And, finally . . . ') to avoid depressing an audience too much and to be followed (to take an extreme example) by *Sgt Bilko*. Here we are mostly concerned with the points at which war and the media interact directly in the form of war reports. And because they mediate information about the progress of a war to the public, the media can serve not just as providers of 'straight' news and information but also as agents of propaganda and disinformation. This is because the very processes by which war reports are gathered, packaged and disseminated are subject to a wide spectrum of influences ranging from the physical location of journalists in the battle area to standards of taste and decency in the editorial offices far beyond it. In between they are subjected to such influences as censorship and self-censorship, the means by which information is communicated from the war zone to the outside world, deception campaigns, official information policy and propaganda. These are indeed the pollutants which constitute that overworked idiom, 'the fog of war'. These are also the reasons why historians need to re-write those first rough drafts.

In short, whatever impression we gain of a given conflict via the media is not necessarily an accurate representation of what is actually happening. The gap between war's image and war's reality remains extremely wide. This is perhaps best illustrated when the experience of the soldier collides with the perception of the civilian population in whose name he is fighting. In the near-contemporaneous novels concerning the First World War, ranging, for example, from *All Quiet on the Western Front* to *Goodbye to All That*, each contains some reference to that collision. The soldier on leave finds himself uncomfortable amidst a civilian population which is infinitely more bellicose than himself because it has been subjected to media images of a conflict that he can barely recognise from his own direct experience. Soldiers returning from a tour of duty in Vietnam were disoriented when the cheering crowds who had seen them off a year earlier now ignored or jeered at them. The process by which this image–reality gap is created needs to be understood, therefore, from the starting point at which the information is gathered right the way through to its final point of reception by an audience.

Without getting into post-modernistic theories about the relationship of 'truth' to 'reality', we need to appreciate that no one journalist can report the whole truth, just as no single news story can cover the whole picture. Each constitutes one piece in a mosaic. A journalist can only report what can be seen, or is allowed to be seen. *Newsday* reporter Susan Sachs said of her experience in the Gulf War of 1991 that she could 'only get an ant's view of the war. And we're all under the naive impression that by piecing together the pool reports and briefings, we can present a real picture of the war. Yet, all the parts do not make up a whole.'[51] This phenomenon has been neatly labelled by another journalist 'tactical myopia'.[52]

Equally, if two or more journalists are present at the same event, they will not necessarily report it in precisely the same way. The emphasis, manner, tone and insight each journalist brings to bear on a given story very much depends upon the personality, experience, education and location of that journalist. For example, a film camera can only 'see' what it is pointed at; whatever is going on beyond the angle of vision does not constitute part of the image. The decision to point the camera at x and not y is a human decision based upon judgement derived from professional training and experience. Even the decision about when to start the camera rolling is a judgement call. Moreover, two cameras standing side-by-side, regardless of whether they are rolling at the same time or not, will produce a variation. The operator will also be working for, or on behalf of, a news organisation which has particular institutional interests and emphases which may affect the angle adopted for the story. And if bullets or bombs are being fired at the camera operator, the human temptation to take cover is invariably greater than the journalistic imperative of keeping the camera rolling. There does exist footage by cameramen who didn't take cover, some of whom were killed in the process. The resultant images are dramatic precisely because they are the exception to the norm. Robert Capa, the famous war photographer, was fond of saying that 'if your picture isn't any good, you're not standing close enough'.[53] For most journalists, however, being read is better than being dead – and it is worth noting that perhaps Capa's most famous photograph in *Life* magazine, that of a Spanish Civil War soldier 'the instant he is dropped by a bullet through the head in front of Cordoba' (so ran the caption) was in fact of a soldier stumbling in training![54] That small detail aside, the essential point is that news stories, as distinct from graphic images whether faked, lucky or otherwise, have a lifespan considerably shorter than that of human beings.

A news report, then, is by definition merely a slice of the action. The BBC's John Simpson has put it thus: 'It is rather like an account of a football match written from a seat near one of the goals. Whenever the play was down at my end I had a superb view of it. But when it moved to the far end of the pitch I only knew what was happening when I heard the crowd roar.'[55] One might retort that the journalist could always jump on to the pitch to follow the play, but on a battlefield that is a very dangerous business. Bullets and bombs do not discriminate between military personnel and journalists. Hence those journalists who are prepared to trade protection for unfettered freedom to roam the battlefield don uniforms and accompany the troops as accredited reporters. Once in uniform, however, in the eyes of the enemy the journalist has clearly aligned himself with the soldiers whose uniform he shares. He thus becomes a spy. But the whole business is a series of compromises by both sides. The military provides limited access, 'security review' and protection, while in the same process the media concede their unfettered freedom of movement and copy in return for relative safety. They accompany the troops, sharing a good deal of their risks in order to get the best possible slice of the action they can.

121

There are a number of other important operational factors which can affect the nature of war reports. First is the often overlooked fact that most modern battles are fought at night. There is indeed footage of the battle of El Alamein, for example, but when one looks at it one sees merely a black screen punctuated by flashes of stroboscopic artillery fire with momentary glimpses of the guns' silhouettes. One sees nothing else of the battle itself. Indeed, for the 'documentary' film of the battle, *Desert Victory* (1943), combat sequences had to be re-enacted for the cameras by troops far from the battlefield – in daylight.[56] Another famous piece of battle footage, the going-over-the-top sequence of British troops leaving a trench with one soldier falling back apparently killed in the 1916 film, *The Battle of the Somme*, was in fact faked by the cameraman, Geoffrey Mallins.[57] These examples from two World Wars are, of course, from the age before hand-held television cameras equipped with night vision lenses. Today, such technology makes news-gathering of actual battles technically more possible, but only under certain conditions. For example, camera crews accompanying troops into battle still risk life and limb, but they can hardly ask an army to stop moving while they can set up their equipment to get the right kind of picture angles. Moving ahead of the troops to anticipate their movement within their desired angle of vision is obviously out of the question with the enemy around, never mind moving into the line of fire of the very troops they are accompanying! Having said all that, modern cameras equipped with night lenses are capable of taking dramatic battle footage, as anyone who saw the combat images – taken by official combat camera operators, not journalists – shown in the BBC TV series on the Gulf War that was broadcast in 1996. But that was five years after the event. At the time, the military only released images of a clinical, clean, sanitised war. The needs of the present outweighed the accuracy of the historical record until long after the event was over.

In the process of news reporting, a third type of conflict also breaks out at the interface between real war and media war. This is the conflict of interests between, on the one hand, the military whose job it is to fight the war and, on the other, the media whose job it is to report on it. The one invariably disagrees with the other on how this is best achieved. As Martin Bell has put it, 'our instinct is to publish and be damned, their's is to censor and be safe'.[58] The priorities of those responsible for fighting war and those responsible for reporting it are obviously quite different, epitomised by the difference between the equipment they carry. New technology may have replaced the sword and the pen with rocket launchers and portable camcorders, but soldiers are still trained to kill while reporters have progressively appeared to make that task much harder by virtue of the publicity they afford to an activity which no longer seems as 'glorious' or as 'natural' as it had once been. Because the media are felt to be largely responsible for exposing the brutalities of conflict to a population that once seemed happier to regard wars in heroic terms, they have been invested with a critical capacity which fosters anti-war sentiment. If this is true – and as we have seen there is much to question in it – then the camcorder has indeed proved mightier than the cruise missile. Yet if this is more assumption than fact, there is a need to understand the fundamental dichotomy between real and media war in order to ascertain the source of such myths and to identify why and who the investors in such assumptions are.

Real wars are multi-faceted, complicated and brutal events in which the participants themselves rarely have the full picture of what is going on while it is actually happening. An individual soldier, for example, might know what is happening in his segment of the battle area, but he is at a loss when it comes to events perhaps even only a few hundred yards away. Not even the commanders have every piece of information at their fingertips, although the struggle to maximise that situation is at the heart of modern strategic planning in 'command and control' warfare. We cannot therefore reasonably expect the media to do something which the generals can not. What function, then, can the media serve? If we employ the analogy of war as a mosaic or jigsaw puzzle, for genuine understanding of the complete picture not only do we need to know how many pieces there are but also how they fit together. For the public, that is the role of the journalist at war while it is taking place; afterwards it becomes the task of the historian. The problem in any given ongoing real war is not only that one individual cannot know what all the pieces are, they cannot even know how many of them there are until it is all over – and often not even then. Similarly with ongoing media war, we can never have all the pieces. Nor can the military, and indeed in situations like the conflict in Bosnia information gathered by journalists can be extremely useful intelligence for the armed forces. As Martin Bell has written:

> We know things they need to know, both for informed decision-making and for their own safety. Others may see this differently, but for me it is not unprofessional behaviour or a breach of whatever codes are supposed to govern us, to pass information to them. I have always wished to be declared redundant as a war correspondent and become a peace correspondent instead.[59]

This is yet another example of the extent to which key journalists are still more inclined towards cooperation than competition. And, as Colonel Bob Stewart recognised, 'the media in Bosnia sometimes served the useful purpose of being present to record agreements – there were sometimes no other records. Being held accountable in the forum of world opinion can occasionally be a powerful means of persuasion and agreements made on camera are more difficult to break.'[60] It depends, of course. Saddam Hussein has never felt bound by the televised pictures of the 'cessation of hostilities' agreement signed in the desert at Safwan at the end of the Gulf

War. But the point remains that journalists, like the military, normally have to work with an incomplete picture and with an unknown number of pieces. It is not, therefore, so much a question of journalists lying; it is inherent in the process of war-reporting that they simply cannot tell the whole truth.

REAL-TIME WARS: DESERT STORM

Today, because it is technically possible to transmit information instantaneously from a battlefield using portable communications equipment, it might appear that there is a greater opportunity to overcome this. But, once again, that equipment still needs to be set up, the satellite air-time booked, and all the equipment needs to be working – hardly ideal circumstances in which to capture live images of war. For this reason, journalists invariably recognise that their reports will not be in real time, at least not from scenes of actual fighting, but will rather be recorded packages of the best available pictures combined with voice-over report, usually edited on the spot once the movement of battle has slowed down or stopped. Modern-day videotape and portable editing suites allow for this. But how those packages then reach editorial headquarters for consideration varies considerably. Again, theoretically, a print journalist can call his head office on a satellite phone and dictate his copy verbally. Better still, he can now type his copy on a portable laptop computer connected to a modem and, with a few keystrokes, a 2,000-word despatch can be uploaded to a news office in seconds, whereas, just a decade earlier, it would have taken an hour's dictation on whatever public pay phone was nearest to the action. Audio-video material can likewise be transmitted digitally. This is all a far cry from the days when a newsreel cameraman, having set up his heavy equipment and filmed his raw footage, would have to beg or bribe someone else leaving the war zone by the fastest land, sea or air route available to deliver his cans of highly flammable nitrate film to his headquarters, whereupon it would be cut, edited and a commentary – written by someone else – added. Or is it?

During the Gulf War of 1991, 'the first *live* television war', a selected band of journalists was granted permission to accompany the coalition forces in the field to cover Operation Desert Storm. (The Iraqis refused any equivalent access for their 'Mother of All Battles', although they did, uniquely, permit journalists from coalition countries to remain behind in Baghdad once hostilities broke out.) As a result of General Sidle's deliberations in 1984, the 'news pool' system had been devised whereby a limited number of self-selected correspondents would accompany the troops into the field in Military Reporting Teams (MRTs). In Saudi Arabia, the American, British and French forces – but only those out of the thirty contributing nations – allowed access to these pools provided they

124

consisted of around fifty reporters and crews, who would then compile their reports for use by the rest of the world's media corps. Although the number eventually rose to about 200 pool reporters, this was but a fraction of the 1,500 or so journalists who flocked to the region to cover the war but who were forced instead to stay behind in hotels in Riyadh and Dharhan (the 'hotel warriors'[61]). The journalists didn't like this arrangement because it ran contrary to all their traditional professional competitiveness to get a scoop over their rivals, but most went along with it because limited and shared access was better than no access at all. 'We were pack journalism forced into a girdle. When it came undone, so did we.'[62] This was because the pool journalists found that, despite all their modern communications equipment, there were still considerable technical problems in reporting the war. Mischievously, the military minders, the American Public Affairs Officers and the British Public Information Officers, told the journalists not to use their mobile phones because they would 'radiate signals to the Iraqis',[63] thereby giving their positions away and thus making them all vulnerable as targets. When, during moments of calm, journalists in those pools which permitted satellite transmission tried to set up their equipment to send out edited packages, they were told to do so well away from the encampments, for the same reason. Although no sensible journalist in a such a position would want to take risks for fear of losing his own life, let alone the lives of the very troops who were protecting him, another game was afoot, namely the legacy of the Vietnam Syndrome. Most journalists were unaware of the technical possibilities of their high-tech equipment, especially its interface with military communications systems. Even if the Iraqis had been able to monitor such transmissions, the point was that the military were suspicious of journalists in their midst and wanted to influence the way in which the war was being reported in their favour. When, for example, a British television crew tried to escape their minders and transmit copy back to London unsupervised, their transmission was intercepted by an airborne AWACS electronic warfare plane, and they were promptly arrested.[64] The American army simply refused to permit satellite equipment in their pools, prompting one reporter to claim that 'each pool member is an unpaid employee of the Department of Defense, on whose behalf he or she prepares the news of the war for the outer world'.[65] The US Marines, with their more open and accessible approach, received much more favourable coverage than the US Army deployments, which had the experience of Vietnam still ringing in their ears – a lesson which has not been lost since. As one Marine in Desert Storm put it, the news media were accepted as an 'environmental feature of the battlefield, kind of like rain. If it rains, you operate wet.'[66]

Some journalists, the self-styled 'unilaterals', did decide to break away from this system and did manage to get stories which ran at odds to the official line – about coalition troops not being equipped with adequate maps and so on. Some Iraqi troops even surrendered to the *Independent*'s Richard Dowden, *Life* magazine's Tony O'Brien and photographer Isabel Barnes.[67] But how far such freelance activity contributed to a wider understanding of the war must remain open to doubt, since unilateralist copy often seemed out of synch with the overwhelming unanimity of the official line, creating confusion rather than the clarity they intended. Moreover, the unilaterals were a small minority. Most journalists in the region were only too mindful of the experience of a CBS crew which went missing across the Kuwaiti–Saudi border days after the war began and spent the next forty days in an Iraqi prison cell. Only a year earlier, the Iraqis had executed a journalist – Farzad Bazoft of the *Observer* – who had gone investigating inside Iraq for himself.

The system for getting copy back from the pools for shared use in Riyadh was also fraught with delays – and indeed this proved to be the main source of friction in a war which was in fact characterised more by military–media cooperation than by conflict. If only the journalists had read a little more about the history of their profession. A World War Two veteran correspondent had warned as far back as 1950: 'The war correspondent, no matter whether he works for the press or for broadcasting, is dependent above all on his communications; he must keep in touch with his cablehead or his wireless transmitter or else he cannot do his job. This obviously limits his movements. If he chooses to go "swanning" with the forward troops his chances of getting his story off are much reduced.'[68] Most of the literature on the media war in the Gulf has concentrated on clashes stemming from this fundamental point. Having said that, the actual record of military–media cooperation during Desert Storm was more in the tradition of the Second World War than of Grenada. But because of the technologically determined expectations of this being a live war, disappointment was inevitable. Once journalists in the pools had filed their reports in the field, their copy was then supposed to be taken to Forward Transmission Units, in fact located to the rear – often well to the rear – of the MRTs. These FTUs had direct satellite links with newsrooms around the world. But once allied ground forces, after weeks of preparatory air strikes, moved against the occupying Iraqi forces in Kuwait, their advance was so rapid 'that the system of getting our copy back to the transmission unit's satellite phones 50 kilometres back broke down completely. It was days before London got the first battle reports from the [British] 7th Armoured [Division] and by then the war was virtually over and we had to hurriedly compose retrospectives'.[69] Accordingly, the Reuters correspondent, Paul Majendie, who was attached to the American 1st Armored Division, felt his assignment had been a 'total disaster' from a journalistic point of view because 'the problem was the totally inadequate method of getting the stories back'.[70] Likewise, Edward Cody of the *Washington Post* complained that 'you turn over control of your copy to them [the military despatch riders] and they don't

126

care whether it gets there [i.e. to the FTUs] or not. It's not part of their culture.'[71] At another level, Colin Wills of the *Mirror* found that the minders of his pool with the British 7th Armoured Brigade, unlike those of the 4th Armoured Brigade who were willing themselves to drive back to the FTUs and hand in the copy personally, proved unwilling to cooperate, and instead he was forced to rely on 'pressing bits of paper into soldiers' hands and hoping they would get there'.[72]

There was another source of friction which came to cause some resentment, particularly after the war was over when the extent to which the media had been used in deception became apparent. During the war itself, the media was used in the campaign to deceive Saddam Hussein into thinking that the coalition was preparing to liberate Kuwait from the waters of the Persian Gulf by a sea-borne assault by the marines. Hence, prior to the ground war, greater freedom to report naval preparations was extended to journalists while greater secrecy was simultaneously imposed in the desert, from which the coalition was in fact planning its main assault. Just as the British had equipped Singapore defences to point out to sea, only to see the colony fall from a land assault in 1942, so also did Saddam's forces gear their heaviest defences on the Kuwaiti coastline only to see coalition forces swing round by land behind them in an enveloping movement. This was General Schwartzkopf's celebrated 'Hail Mary Play'. The difference between this time and 1942, however, was that in 1991 Saddam could theoretically glean intelligence from his enemies' relatively open sources of public information, including global television coverage of daily briefings by coalition spokesmen. And in those briefings, every clue was given that the assault would take place from the sea rather than by land. If he had bothered to read *Newsweek* a week or so before the actual ground war began, he could have seen the entire battle plan for himself.[73]

Herein lies one of the great contradictions of war in the information age. It can hardly be denied that the Gulf War saw more information given to more media outlets than ever before. Perhaps uniquely, it was possible to glean what was actually going on from scouring the sheer multiplicity of media sources at the time. But there was so much of it, accurate or speculative, that it was virtually impossible for most people to read the clues. Certainly, the Iraqi intelligence services must have been hopelessly confused, although there is some evidence that they were able to launch their first counter-attack at the end of January 1991 against the coastal town of Ras Al-Khafji because they had seen footage of the town empty on CNN.[74] But clearly they did not see the 'Hail Mary Play' coming.

Deception has formed part of warfare since the Trojan Horse, but the *active* incorporation of the media into such exercises is a relatively recent development and, it has to be said, a dangerous one at that. If the free media, even the patriotic media, discover that they are being used for such purposes, they are likely to distance themselves from the exercise, even from the illusion that they are still operating relatively freely from military restrictions which they are willing to comply with on grounds of safety and operational security. The media may not expect to be told the whole truth during wartime, but they do expect to be told as much of the truth as can be told without jeopardising military operations and the lives of troops. Interestingly and paradoxically, in the Gulf War, some British pool journalists were in fact told of the entire battle plan for the ground war several days before it occurred:

> We knew of the entire battle plan a week before the land war started. On a professional level, needless to say, it was very frustrating. To be in the know and not be able to file a word was like being the secret of alchemy and at that same instant being struck dumb.[75]

The BBC's Kate Adie has confirmed this,[76] adding that:

> On some occasions we held back footage because part of an operation might not have been completed, and transmission could endanger lives; on some, we held footage because the involvement of specific forces would have betrayed the position or thrust of an action. For instance, British artillery alone fired Type 110 guns on the first day of the major ground bombardment. We held the footage 24 hours, until US 110s had fired, so as not to give away the precise location of the British guns, which was central to the deception tactic in the invasion of Kuwait.[77]

The time-honoured use of the media in deception has been to tell them *nothing* of what was actually happening in any military campaign until after it was all over, so as to prevent the enemy finding out. Traditionally, censorship has rested on the military assumption that the media could not be trusted with such information and, for the most part, the media have got used to being told less than the whole truth. Yet the significant departure from this practice in the Gulf War, which would none the less alarm many military officers around the world, indicates a growing sophistication on the part of some senior military personnel at the military–media interface. Nor, as we have seen from the pre-Vietnam era, is this realisation a particularly recent phenomenon.

In other words, on the battlefield soldier and civilian journalist are mutually dependent. The aims of the respective professions may be fundamentally different, encapsulated by the saying that 'when the military make a mistake, people die, but when the media make a mistake, they run a correction', but they are not mutually incompatible. For the people on the ground, cooperation is infinitely preferable to conflict. Whether this can be justified back home remains, and is likely to remain, the source of considerable debate. In particular, the use of the media in deception campaigns in the Falklands and the Gulf, the active use that is, can only be done with extreme caution and in such a manner that the media are unaware of it, or delude themselves into thinking that they are still observers of war rather than participants within it. And, as the Gulf War demonstrated, just because journalists have the equipment to transmit live reports from the front, it does not automatically follow that they are able to do so. Even when they are, there are still problems with the slice of 'reality' their cameras depict.

Take the example of the Scud–Patriot duels in the Gulf War. During the first stage of the conflict, the air war, nothing much was happening in the media pools in the desert, and so the hotel warriors in Dharhan were forced to accept the repetitive pool reports about troop preparations and morale, etc. Despite the briefings held for them about the air attacks, the vast majority of journalists quickly realised that they were completely dependent upon military statements for news about the progress of the war. The message was simple: this many sorties flown today, that many bombs dropped; 'we are winning, and we will go on winning'. To reinforce this, the military began releasing video footage taken from cameras mounted on planes and laser-guided bombs which demonstrated the unprecedented accuracy of modern air war. But it was the military who had taken these pictures, not the media. The only corrective available was from those Western journalists allowed to remain in Baghdad, and their reports seemed to confirm that allied bombing was indeed only targeting military installations and that 'collateral damage' was minimal.[78]

But that was Baghdad. To the journalists in Riyadh, it was clear that so many sorties and so many bombs must be taking place elsewhere, and little information was forthcoming about these from the briefings. After the cheering prompted by the gift of military video releases, frustration began to set in. This was clearly the military's war, and the military's version was the only one to be permitted. Then, on the first Saturday of the war, in the early hours of the morning local time, the Iraqis launched their first Scud attacks against Israel and Saudi Arabia. Apart from the fact that this demonstrated that the war would not be quite as one-sided as was being projected, and the Iraqis were capable of hitting back, it also allowed the journalists to report on the war for themselves. Now it was their war, and there followed a media 'Scudfest' in which reporters were seen bravely staying at their posts as incoming Scuds exploded against the night sky, while their anchors back home pleaded with them to take cover in the air-raid shelters. In Jerusalem, reporters donned gas masks while they continued to transmit live from the war zone. The journalist as hero prompted public admiration in the United States for Arthur Kent, for example, who was dubbed 'the Scud Stud' and the 'Satellite Dish'. Even when Patriot missiles were quickly despatched to intercept the Scuds, the reporters stayed at their posts to film the duels, as spectacular 'fireworks displays' of exploding munitions enabled the journalists at last to report the war for themselves.

The problem, once again, was that this was all largely irrelevant to the 'real war', and much of it again was nonsense. Jerusalem, as any self-respecting Middle East correspondent should have known, would never have been an Iraqi target – and nor was it. The Scud attacks were largely a military side-show, although it has to be said that the prominence given to them by the media forced the military to re-deploy valuable resources to hunt their launchers down. It even emerged after the war that the Patriots did not actually hit their targets but exploded close to them, forcing down debris which often caused more damage than the warheads might have done. Live war in the Gulf may have been exciting stuff for the media and public alike, but the real war was being fought somewhere else – and that war we did not see. Nor, when the ground war began, did we see the decisive final phase until after it was all over.

OUR WARS AND OTHER PEOPLE'S WARS

There is a need now to pause here in order to distinguish between what might be termed 'our wars' and 'other people's wars'. 'Our wars' are those which involve 'our troops' possibly fighting alongside 'our allies' against a clearly identified enemy and 'their allies'. 'Other people's wars' are different, in that outside media coverage of them differs fundamentally in character. This is not to suggest that the media are above taking sides in other people's wars (who could doubt that the majority of Western reporting during the wars of Yugoslavian succession were anti-Serb?) but rather that there is a greater level of disengagement about the issues involved even though they may invoke a similar emotional response to the human suffering. All wars are nasty, brutal affairs, but other people's wars are about other people's business which may have little or nothing to do with 'us'.

'Our wars' are wars of the greatest emotional engagement with the combatants – both military and civilian – involved. There is of course a further distinction between conventional warfare, in which civilian participation is limited to observation of the conflict via the media, and 'Total War', which involves actual participation. The 'Total Wars' of 1939–45 and, to a lesser extent, 1914–18, in which the entire resources of the nation had to be mobilised for survival, let alone victory, were different in that the traditional distance between soldier and civilian was narrowed almost to the point of extinction. If global thermo-nuclear war had erupted during the Cold War era, it would have been likewise. 'Total War' involves the entire population, whether in the form of mass male conscription into the armed forces or of a civilian population mobilised to contribute to the war effort, for example by replacing the lost male workforce with female workers in war industries and by evacuating children from potential targets of bombing. As such, the sense of mutual identification between military and civilian combatant is intensified, as distinct from other types of war in which professional armies consisting of volunteers are watched most intently by their civilian relatives and friends.

For such people, media coverage of limited wars can be intrusive, which is why there are guidelines in reporting pictures of the dead and injured casualties of war. Opponents of war who criticise the media for 'sanitising' such images miss this critical point. A rule of thumb in the two World Wars was only to show pictures of enemy dead; that way, relatives could not discover the loss of their loved ones from the media, although they could see that the war was inflicting casualties on the other side. People understand that, in war, people die. Whether they want to see it on their television screens is quite another matter.

Equally, in 'our wars', the journalist walks a very thin tightrope attached to two cliff edges labelled 'objectivity' and 'patriotism'. His journalistic responsibility to stand back from a story and analyse it objectively can prove incompatible with his audience's subjective desire to see everyone support the national war effort. Bad news about the progress of 'our side' invariably prompts calls to shoot the messenger. But democracies have evolved during the course of this century which cherish notions of freedom of speech and opinions. In wartime, most people accept the need for some restrictions upon those democratic 'rights', but the issue remains just how far should they go. Should they suppress all bad news in the name of patriotism, even though this often occurs in the name of operational security? Examples of this occurring in the past are numerous. Casualty figures have often been minimised, and defeats simply omitted from the public record. Following the retreat from Mons in 1914, the British War Office withdrew the permits of film camera crews, while in 1940, while still First Lord of the Admiralty, Winston Churchill, refused to release news that HMS *Nelson* and HMS *Barham* had sustained serious damage.[79] Such instances of suppression are only possible when the military are in complete control of information reaching the public domain from the war zone. Modern communications technology has weakened that control, whereas modern political imperatives have increased the likelihood of access being granted to journalists.

Access is, indeed, the key to all this. In Vietnam, the media were granted virtually unlimited access to go wherever they wanted to go, at their own risk. Tragically, as a result of war reports that were perceived as being more and more critical, various and ever-more-controversial ways of influencing the outside perception of a crisis in a manner beneficial to its military–political conduct have evolved since the 1970s: to exclude the media altogether, as in Grenada; to delay their arrival, as in Panama; to make them totally dependent upon the military for their safety, transport and communications, as in the Falklands; or a combination of all these, as in Desert Shield/Desert Storm.

In other people's wars the role of the media, if anything, is to make such conflicts more our own than would otherwise have been the case. In the Spanish Civil War (1936–39), for example, British Movietone's newsreel coverage of the bombing of Guernica showed pictures of the devastated city

131

under a commentary which ended: 'This was a war, and these were homes – like yours'.[80] The message was that the aerial bombing of cities – then a new and terrifying weapon – was of concern to all citizens of all countries. Despite international efforts at non-intervention in Spain for fear of the conflict spreading, it was clear that Fascist Italy, Nazi Germany and Soviet Russia were all contributing to the civil war. The newsreel coverage brought this home to cinema audiences in neutral Britain and France, and prompted some members of those audiences to volunteer for the International Brigades. This was their way of 'doing something', but most viewers just watched with horror as a European civil war foreshadowed things to come in the Second World War – during which Franco's Spain was, ironically, to remain neutral.

Media coverage of other people's wars is characteristically less susceptible to censorship by militarily non-participating governments. It is, however, still subject to manipulation by the warring parties. More recently, in another European civil war zone, the wars of the Yugoslavian succession, attempts to manipulate journalists were endemic in an effort by the warring factions to secure the moral high ground for their cause. Hence, in Bosnia-Herzegovina, the Bosnian Serbs attempted to portray themselves as the victims, rather than the aggressors – as victims variously of German, Albanian, 'Islamic fundamentalist' but, above all, Croatian and Bosnian 'fascist' conspiracies. One might have thought that, in a global information environment, it would be much easier than before to verify or discredit such stories, but when international journalists wanted to check for themselves on one alleged atrocity involving necklaces made from the fingers of Serbian babies, they were quite simply refused access to the alleged scene. The famous ITN footage of emaciated Moslem prisoners of war, which caused an international outrage in 1992, was banned on Serbian TV. Similarly, the Croatians and Bosnian factions were likewise keen to steer the media coverage in their favour, not just within areas under their control but on the international arena as well. The Bosnian Moslems, for example, provided increased foreign journalistic access to their civilians on the march from the fallen 'safe havens' of Srebrenica and Jeppa in the summer of 1995 to demonstrate that they, indeed, were the victims in this conflict, while Serb protests that they were merely retaliating to (off-camera) Bosnian army attacks were drowned beneath the sea of devastating footage of Bosnian civilian suffering.

Regardless of whose war it is, therefore, the question of journalistic access remains critical. If a journalist is not present at an alleged defeat or massacre, it can only be reported second-hand, which minimises the impact of the story. The absence of pictures minimises it still further. The converse is equally true. Modern communications technology facilitates increased access to scenes of horror and destruction that would have been inconceivable a century earlier. The ability of the media increasingly to bring home such scenes has widened the arena of warfare beyond those directly involved in or directly affected by the fighting. The media turn all wars that they can get access to into a matter of wider public concern. This, in turn, makes it all the more essential for the warring parties to control that access because their battlefront is no longer confined to the battlefield itself.

In other people's wars, journalists from countries not directly involved are the target of concerted attempts to manipulate world opinion in favour of one side at the expense of the other. But is this really any different from what goes on in our own wars? The most effective way of controlling the media is simply to deny them access. But the advent of the war correspondent as a specialised profession has made this increasingly difficult to justify, especially as such reporters seemed to be catering for a demand amongst a public whose support for any war effort could only be sustained by satisfying the hunger for information. The watershed of the Crimean War was significant in that the public could no longer accept uncritically the official pronouncements of the military spokesmen. An increasingly literate, educated and enfranchised public demanded third-party mediation and the press filled this requirement as a watch-dog. This is not without its irony. During the Gulf War of 1991, surveys in the United States indicated that the public was more prepared to accept the announcements of military spokesmen than the versions provided by the press. Because the 1991 audience could see those spokesmen live on television in the comfort of their living rooms thousands of miles from the scene of fighting, the military were actually bypassing the media's traditional role as intermediary between soldier and civilian, established since the Crimea. The media did not help themselves by being seen to ask stupid questions live in press conferences. Indeed, live television made such conferences public conferences, rather than press conferences, with the role of the correspondents reduced to that of questioner. Nor is this decline of public trust in the media's capability to report on wars 'in the public interest' confined to the United States. During the Falklands War, the excesses of the tabloid press, especially those of the *Sun* with such headlines as 'GOTCHA' and 'UP YOURS, GALTIERI', resulted in a fall in circulation.

The Gulf War surveys revealed another significant trend, namely that the public was prepared to tolerate military censorship of war reports, at least until after the war was over, if that would reduce the risk of casualties. Casualties of war fall into two categories for the media: military and civilian. Military casualties are to be expected, but if they are 'our' casualties, then the military feel, first, that there should be as few of them as possible and, then, that the media should not give undue attention to them. During the Gulf War, a news embargo was imposed upon the media coverage at the naval base in Virginia where body-bags arrived home. This again is very much a legacy of Vietnam. The point here is that there has been a growing recent trend that wars can only be fought with a minimum of military casualties, for fear of undermining popular support. The public, it is frequently assumed, cannot stomach huge casualty figures, especially if

133

the dead and wounded are given prominent media attention. Although one suspects that the validity of this assumption varies from country to country, in accordance with their military experience and history, it remains at the root of military assumptions about the role of the media in wartime, namely that they are more of a threat than an aid to combat.

How valid this is depends very much on the degree to which the public bases its support for involvement in a war upon 'just' reasons. If the war is felt to be 'just', then casualties are regrettable but 'justified'. This applies even to civilian casualties, although the extent of military nervousness concerning non-combatant casualties, especially 'innocent women and children', is even more marked now than ever before, especially if cameras can get to the scene. During the Second World War, for example, the Strategic Bombing Offensive against Germany was deliberately couched in terms very different from the reality. It was a *strategic* air campaign, directed at *military* and *industrial* targets, rather than at *civilian* areas. The head of Bomber Command, Arthur Harris, wanted in 1943 to make a stark public admission that 'the aim is the destruction of German cities, the killing of German workers and the disruption of civilised community life throughout Germany'.[81] He was unsuccessful. The illusion had to be maintained that the Royal Air Force was an instrument of precision bombing capable of hitting precisely what it was aiming at, resulting 'in a more or less constant concealment of the aims and implications of the campaign which was being waged'.[82] Accordingly, news reports, photographs and films were poured out to illustrate 'successful missions' against factories and other military/industrial targets, rather than hits on the residential areas in which those targets were invariably located. This not only served as a justification for the huge numbers of bomber crews which failed to return home but also provided a moral counterpoint to the British experience in the Blitz. Given that the British public had clearly been targeted indiscriminately by German bombers then, they might have suspected that the RAF's line about the discriminating nature of allied bombing was as patently untrue as we know it to have been. But in the absence of pictures from the scenes of destruction, the illusion could be sustained.

During the Gulf War, great emphasis was again placed upon the ability of high-tech coalition bombing to hit its targets accurately. Thanks to advances in military technology, it is certainly true that cruise missiles and laser guided bombs could hit their intended targets with an accuracy unprecedented in military history. Moreover, thanks to new communications technology, those weapons could be equipped with video-cameras. For the first time, audiences could see for themselves how 'smart' weapons homed in on military targets with uncanny accuracy prior to the screen going blank. Such footage not only gave the impression that the coalition could hit precisely what it was aiming at, but it could thereby discriminate between military and civilian targets. This fitted well with the line pursued by coalition leaders that this was a war fought not against the Iraqi people but against the regime of Saddam Hussein and those forces which supported him. The problem was that, of all the bombs deployed during the Gulf War, the 'smart' ones formed only about 8 per cent of the total. The remainder, old-fashioned 'dumb' weapons of indiscriminate destruction, were not seen on television screens. No journalist was permitted to accompany a bombing mission during Desert Storm, while the Iraqis refused journalistic access to those areas subjected to mass bombing.

Air power is a notoriously difficult phenomenon for the media. On the one hand, it contains the raw material of spectacular reportage, from the air aces of the First World War to the helicopter gunships of Vietnam and the Gulf. Cameras mounted on board aircraft can produce the kind of exciting footage matched by no other war technology, as anyone who has seen William Wyler's 1943 colour documentary film of a bombing raid over Germany, *Memphis Belle*, will appreciate. On the other hand, by its very nature, most coverage has to consist of interviews with pilots and crews before and after missions, aircraft taking off and landing and, if camera crews are permitted, bombs being released. The Gulf War saw cameras mounted on the bombs themselves. But none of this allows for images of the impact of the bombs once they have exploded; when the bomb hits its target, either from a distance of 30,000 feet, or after homing in through cross hairs, the screen goes blank. Thereafter, there is little indication of the sheer destructive power of high explosive until after the smoke has cleared. The time between the moment of impact and the scrutiny of bomb damage can never be captured on film, and it is in that space, after all, where people die. That reality of war evades media war.

The Iraqis did try something unprecedented in the history of war when, following the outbreak of the air-war phase of Desert Storm, they allowed journalists from belligerent countries to remain behind in Baghdad. Saddam Hussein also believed in the Vietnam Syndrome. He believed that, once the bombing began, it would result in massive devastation to civilian areas which, if filmed, could cause a public outcry in the very countries responsible for the bombing and lead to the cessation of the war. Captured pilots were accordingly paraded on Iraqi television declaring their disapproval of the war, and the broadcasts were duly retransmitted around the world by CNN. Iraq's solitary baby-milk manufacturing plant was destroyed by coalition bombing, putting paid to the myth that the coalition was not fighting the people of Iraq, and images of the bombed-out installation, too, were duly retransmitted by CNN. The war would thus be won in the hearts and minds of world public opinion rather than on the killing fields of Kuwait. But Saddam miscalculated. The coalition decided not to carpet bomb the Iraqi capital but only to use precision weapons – and these invariably hit their targets. The captured pilots ploy enraged public opinion, while the baby-milk plant, the coalition claimed, was a chemical warfare factory.

CNN was accused of spreading Iraqi propaganda rather than of reporting the war. But doubts remained. The coalition was only targeting military installations but the Iraqis refused to accompany Western crews to such sites. Why suddenly change that tactic now with the 'baby-milk plant' if it really was a chemical weapons facility?

One new element of camera-mounted bombs combined with TV crews inside enemy territory was bomb damage evaluation. As one pilot stated:

> It certainly was interesting for us to come back and land and watch the [TV] replays of what it's looking like from another perspective. Knowing where some of the broadcasts were coming from, and seeing the skyline . . . we could actually pick out who some of the bombs belonged to. . . . There was some good in having good old Peter Arnett on the ground.[83]

Arnett, veteran war reporter from the Vietnam era now working for CNN, was only too conscious of the Iraqi attempts to manipulate him. But, like the other Western journalists in Baghdad, he was put to his greatest test on 13 February 1991 when two laser guided bombs crashed through an installation in the Al-Amiriya suburb of Baghdad, killing around 400 people. All Iraqi censorship restrictions were lifted that day and the journalists were told that they could say, hear and film anything they wanted to. Because the badly burned bodies being brought out of the charred building were clearly civilians – 'innocent women and children' – here was the crucial test of whether the coalition's line about minimising 'collateral damage' to the Iraqi people could be sustained.

In the space between the reality of war and the media image of war, this was the defining moment. For the first time, the Iraqis had the kind of images which fuelled their belief in the Vietnam Syndrome – all the more effective for them being taken by Western, rather than Iraqi, television crews. Because those crews arrived within hours of the explosion, there were no clumsy efforts at blatant propaganda, as with the freshly painted 'baby-milk plant' signs written in English three weeks earlier. And all existing censorship restrictions were lifted that day. The problem was that the images were so graphic that Western broadcasting standards of taste and decency militated against their full use. As the pictures were beamed around the world by satellite, most editorial rooms bred on a Western tradition realised that they would have to take out the graphic close-up images of horribly burned children prior to transmission. They would not show comparable images of a motorway crash or an air disaster, so why should war be any different? Despite such self-censorship, however, the shock of what was shown still created an outcry, with the *Daily Mail* the next morning accusing the BBC of being the 'Baghdad Broadcasting Corporation'. As coalition spokesmen attempted to control the spin – they had hit what they were aiming at; it was a military bunker, not a civilian shelter; they did not know why civilians were inside – the press attacked the messenger. Television was the enemy, just as it had been in Vietnam. However, even the sanitised pictures from the Amiriya bombing failed to shake popular conviction that the war against Saddam was indeed just and that, although regrettable, civilian deaths were inevitable.

Research conducted by the Institute of Communications Studies at the University of Leeds into the public reaction to the Amiriya bombing suggests that we should regard the media less as a window and more of a mirror. This research took several stages. First, a series of groups composed of people drawn from all socio-economic backgrounds was shown the ITN and BBC news reports that were transmitted on the evening of 13 February 1991 concerning the bombing. Incidentally, both the BBC and ITN received more complaints about their coverage that night than at any other moment in the war. All our groups remembered the coverage vividly, and had distinct reservations about the wisdom of it being shown. They were then shown the unedited footage that was available to the broadcasters from the satellite feeds out of Baghdad – footage that was considerably more graphic in terms of its close-ups of the badly burned victims than that which was actually transmitted but which had been 'self-censored' by the broadcasters on the grounds of 'taste and decency'. Having seen what was actually available to the broadcasters, all our groups changed their minds, feeling now that the broadcasters had behaved more responsibly than they had hitherto assumed. None of the groups wanted to see such unedited material on their television screens, although some members did argue for showing it late at night. All were concerned to protect children from such scenes, and a few were even angry at the Leeds researchers for showing it to them. No one changed their minds about the rights and wrongs of the war.[84] The overall response can be summarised thus: we know that people die in war, but we don't want to see it in full glorious Technicolor on our television screens in the same way that we wouldn't want to see close-ups of the victims of a motorway or plane crash.

The second phase was to push this a little further, especially in the light of arguments forwarded by some critics of the Gulf War as a 'sanitised war'. Their argument was that, if the realities of war were shown on television screens, as they were supposedly shown in Vietnam, then the public would see the horrors for itself and be so offended that public opinion would militate for its cessation. The assumption was remarkably similar to that of the Vietnam-inspired American military with its belief in the power of television to change public opinion – and therefore its rationale for keeping such horrors off the screen. Accordingly, ten groups of subjects were assembled and given crash courses in video-editing. With a technical assistant, the groups were then provided with the Amiriya bulletins from British, French, German and American newscasts and asked to assemble the story for themselves. The groups were also given the raw satellite feed footage. *None* of them chose to use the graphic footage of the charred bodies in their final product. All found it too horrific, and the similarity of judgement between audience and professional broadcasters concerning this decision was remarkable.

Given that public support for the war held steady at around 80 per cent, it was felt that we had highly representative groups. However, to test our findings still further, an anti-war group was assembled and asked to undertake the same exercise. This was the only group which seriously considered using the raw satellite material – but equally it was the only group which failed to complete its assignment.

What does all this tell us about the relationship between war and the media? In the first instance, it suggests that, in Britain at least, the public receives the media coverage it wants. It might only have realised this once it had been exposed to the complete picture – which in itself suggests that the media have some educating of their own to do about how they operate in such circumstances. During the Gulf War, many news bulletins were prefaced with the remarks that 'this report contains some scenes which you might find disturbing', but perhaps they need to state more explicitly that 'this is nothing compared to what we could have shown you'. The dilemma arises about how to demonstrate that fact on air. This could be done late at night in current affairs and news analysis programmes, but domestic video recorders and bedroom television sets make it unlikely that all children will remain guarded from such scenes. Moreover, most people would not be thankful even for that type of coverage, given the number of complaints which the broadcasters received about the pictures they did show. Finally, the reaction of the anti-war group would suggest that dissent and war opposition are infinitely more complex reactions than support. But the response of that group does indicate an equal belief to the military in the potential power of the medium to act as a tool for propaganda.

The question, therefore, is whether war correspondents serve as war propagandists, either wittingly or unwittingly. Propaganda implies a subjective viewpoint, whereas correspondents plead commitment to objectivity. But how can they be objective when their main or sole provider of information is a warring faction which releases its information to serve specific aims? The answer is to release only beneficial 'facts' and to censor those 'facts' which might jeopardise operational security. During the course of this century, there has been a growing recognition of the need to release 'facts' under the guise of the 'public's right to know'; that is the whole point of democratic accountability. Yet, as we have seen, this is problematical. If the public chooses not to exercise its right and instead subordinates its desire to see victory rather than the truth, in whose name are the media operating? If they work with the military to provide only that information which the military wants to see released, they are, by definition, working as propagandists on behalf of the military. Moreover, if that information coincides with what the public wants to hear, they are providing propaganda to a public which wants that propaganda. How different from a propaganda state is this?

CONCLUSIONS

The Leeds Gulf War research allowed scholars to test for the first time some of the fundamental problems that have hounded the military–media–public-opinion matrix throughout the wars of the twentieth century. Its findings suggest that television audiences have a high degree of sophistication in their appreciation of the horror of war, but that television, at least while a war is being waged, is not an appropriate medium for conveying that horror. Audiences watched the news for 'facts' about the progress of the war and not for the fact that people were dying in the most horrible ways. They knew, understood and regretted this, but the knowledge was abstract, almost philosophical, rather than specific in terms of the information and images they had received. It was not so much a matter of turning off but of turning away from this reality. Death was inevitable, regrettable but necessary. They didn't need their favourite source of domestic entertainment to make that uncomfortable blend of emotions – and knowledge – more unpalatable than it was.

So, based upon the Vietnam-inspired belief that TV images of death and destruction could adversely affect public support, were the coalition and the Iraqis right to forbid cameras from being anywhere near the real killing fields of the war, where the real death and destruction was taking place in southern Iraq and occupied Kuwait? From an audience point of view, the answer is probably yes, but not for the reasons that made this happen. The real war was kept off television screens because that is what the military wanted, which happens to have been what the people supporting them wanted as well, whereas the media war projected an image of a high-tech, clinically accurate 'video-game' war in which the screens went blank once the laser-guided bombs had passed down a ventilator shaft. This fitted well with the long-standing accepted iconography of warfare as an heroic exercise, especially if the war was felt to be 'just', and the media played well their part in this tradition. On the two occasions when there were indications that this was a war which was killing civilians – the baby-milk plant and Amiriya – there were no dead at the former site (bombed at nighttime, so no workers present) while the dead at the latter (also bombed at night, but for some still-unknown reason sheltering civilians) were only shown covered by blankets. It was the moment which the Iraqis had been waiting for to expose as false US President Bush's repeated assertions that this was not a war against the Iraqi people, while it was the moment most feared by the Americans with their Vietnam-inspired preconceptions about the impact of real war on television. For that reason alone, it would be reasonable to suggest that the Americans would not have targeted the Amiriya installation had they known so many civilians were inside, because they did know that the Iraqis would

139

escort the Western journalists to such a site. What, indeed, is remarkable is that there were so few such occasions. The decision to target Baghdad only with precision weapons was made with television images in mind as much as the decision to carpet bomb the Iraqi troops in the field was made because television cameras were absent. When the ground war finally came, President Bush was to call a halt after 100 hours because he feared the impact of television images of the 'slaughter' on the 'Highway of Death' out of Kuwait City. Yet again, this is a striking example of the fear which politicians possess about television's ability adversely to influence a public opinion which, one suspects, would have preferred to see the war fought to a more decisive or 'satisfactory' conclusion, namely the removal of Saddam Hussein. Of course, such an option would have been infinitely more complex than perhaps television would have been able to convey, but the record of the coalition's media managers during the war suggests that it might have been possible with a cheerleading media – and a cheerleading public.

The Gulf War was in many ways fought to exorcise the demons of Vietnam. Despite the tension between the US Army and the US media in Desert Storm, no post-operational analysis could deny that, overall, the media had done a good job from the military's point of view. This was partly due to skilled media management, but it was mainly because, unlike in Vietnam, the public supported the administration's reasons for prosecuting the war, while the administration, in turn, had allowed the military to conduct the war their way. This was not total, as the decision to end the war when it did demonstrated. It was, moreover, a short war with remarkably few coalition casualties. For those who worry about what would have happened if it had gone on longer with higher casualties, one can only point them to the experience of Vietnam for at least the three years between 1963 and 1966, and, in many respects, to the period thereafter once it has been demythologised. The record of the democratic media in 'our wars' of the twentieth century suggests that a supportive media can be expected, especially if they have clear guidelines and access to plenty of information.

The media and war have become inseparable; they have a symbiotic relationship. The old view that the media were harmful to the prosecution of war is not only invalid but irrelevant. The media are not only here to stay but are acquiring new technologies which will enable them to gather and disseminate more information than ever before. The US Army Field Manual recognises that 'dramatic visual presentations can rapidly influence public – and therefore political – opinion so that the political underpinnings of war and operations other than war [OOTW] may suddenly change with no prior indication to the commander in the field'.[85] The lessons of Grenada reveal that if they are denied access, the military equivalent of 'no comment', the media will redouble their efforts to gain it, causing more trouble for the military than they might have done if they had been taken along in the first place. Indeed, the post-Desert-Storm inclination of the US military to be more proactive in media terms appeared to bear fruit in the Haiti operation of 1994. Then, media representatives were assigned to military units spearheading the planned invasion to 'Restore Democracy'. Once the invasion was called off, and because the media had defied the White House appeal for a news embargo, the Joint Task Force leadership aboard the USS *Mount Whitney* was able to watch CNN in order to ascertain what was happening on the island. As the Field Manual states, 'The importance of understanding the immediacy of the impact of raw television coverage is not so commanders can control it, but so that they can anticipate adjustments to their operations and plans.'[86] There is at last a recognition that 'the media can be trusted if the military's explanation of events is valid and makes sense. The proof? From all the reporters briefed on the operational plan prior to the start of Uphold Democracy, there were no leaks. None. Reporters understood the ground rules and knew that a story released ahead of time could endanger US forces.'[87] It was those who were not 'in the know' who presented the gravest cause for concern, but they didn't really matter anyway. Just like the unilaterals in the Gulf War, if the media agenda can be set and shaped in an overpowering and attractive manner, deviants will be, well, deviants.

In 1964 one writer noted how political leaders in Southeast Asia regarded the press as 'an element of psychological warfare and therefore [one which] must be rigidly controlled. Adverse reporting about a regime tends to give aid and comfort to the enemy and must therefore be eliminated.'[88] At that time no one would have claimed that this was appropriate for democratic societies, although many may have harboured private desires that this could be done. Today, there is a growing realisation that the only way forward is through cooperation. The military is catching up with the world which diplomacy feels it has lost. There is now a recognition that the democratic media will not simply stay away from our war zones, and that if they are kept away this will merely raise their suspicions either that there is something to hide or that they are not being told the whole story, which in turn will only make journalists more determined to get there anyway. The phrase 'no comment' merely stimulates the journalist to go searching for a story which might not exist in the first place. The military has therefore come to realise that providing access to the media has become an essential part of warfare in the information age. Getting journalists to understand what happens in battles, even to the point of deciphering the military jargon used there, remains a serious problem, especially in those military establishments which have abandoned conscription but, as the Gulf War demonstrated, they have also become easier to manipulate. The military might well argue that that is a problem for the journalistic profession, and is not their responsibility. However, as the media generally become less and less interested in military affairs, and the number of specialised defence correspondents who understand them more remains a relatively small elite, the number of inexperienced journalists who are likely to turn up when the armed forces are next called into action is going to be very much a military problem. As one American journalist has warned:

> You can just about bet on it that as our military gets smaller and smaller, so it gets involved in smaller conflicts. In the meantime, the breadth of media who want to go to that conflict gets larger. We've become a society of voyeurs. Everybody wants to see it; not too many people want to understand it.[89]

It is therefore in the interests of the military to find ways of accommodating the media in the next war, not least because in the post-Cold War world it has become imperative to explain and justify the presence of military forces in any given theatre in all its complexities, and it is incumbent on them to do this either directly through the medium of television or indirectly through the media corps.

In 1995, a series of proposals emanated from the Freedom Forum First Amendment Centre in the United States which provides a clue as to how matters may proceed. This independent think tank brought together an experienced journalist and an experienced soldier to consider the issues in light of the lessons of the Gulf War and conflict situations since. Their report, with the remarkable title 'America's Team: the Odd Couple',[90] proposed that in future there should be no field censorship; its existence merely caused friction and, given modern technology, it was likely to prove impossible in practice anyway. This would, of course, require a level of trust on the part of the military and a level of understanding as to operational restraints on the part of the media. Some might feel that this is asking a lot of journalists, but one only needs to bear in mind the level of military–media cooperation in the past conduct of 'our wars' to be reassured that it is more likely to happen than not. One also needs to exorcise the myth of the Vietnam Syndrome. None the less, because both military and media personnel change their jobs after a given 'tour of duty', the lack of institutional memory on both sides needs to be addressed so that the wheel is not constantly being reinvented, and the same old misunderstandings resurface to cause friction. Hence an office devoted purely to this issue was established in Washington DC to act as a 'facilitator' for mutual misunderstandings and misconceptions. It was also proposed that increased contact between the two sides was essential – for example Officer Training Corps on university campuses should liaise more closely with journalism students. Similarly, the status of the Public Affairs Officer should be upgraded within the military hierarchy, so that it would become a job soldiers wanted to do rather than feeling they had been side-lined into a career dead end. Conversely, it was suggested that journalists attend the National War College and other military educational establishments.

All this was designed to improve the sense of mutual military–media understanding. To control the numbers of journalists likely to want to go to war, a modified pool system was proposed in the form of an 'Independent Coverage Tier System'. Each tier would consist of fifty journalists, with 'news organisations reaching the largest number of people . . . [having] priority'. This may be controversial because, in the media, quality of reporting and quantity of audience do not always go hand-in-hand. For example, would a reporter from a relatively low-circulation, quality (and therefore influential) national daily newspaper be denied access to the tier because someone from a mass audience populist cable TV station has already secured the slot? Having said that, the proposals would create multiple tiers – an 'A Team', a 'B Team' and so on – which could be mobilised depending on the size of the operation involved, and determined by the military commander's ability to transport and protect a given number of tiers. This number might only be one, and therefore the 'A Team' would consist of representatives from the leading wire services, television and radio networks, magazines and national newspapers. Ten per cent of places (i.e. five slots) would be reserved for independent freelancers and a further 10 per cent for foreign journalists from countries also involved in any joint operation.

It is certainly an imaginative proposal, but whether, as the report states, the result would be 'more accurate and better-quality coverage of military operations, with the American people as the ultimate beneficiaries'[91] very much remains to be seen. After all, in the Second World War the Wehrmacht was prepared to accommodate teams of cameramen and journalists to get the best available front-line coverage. Then, they were called Propaganda Kompanie (PK) Units and they undoubtedly produced some of the best war footage ever taken. But whether the German people were ultimately best served by that coverage was quite another matter. More recently, a senior American officer has suggested that:

> Soldiers are trained to deal with the bestiality of battle; the American people are not. Soldiers, in fact, fight and die on the battlefields of the world to keep that kind of horror off the playing fields of America – not so some can work on ratings and Pulitzers by beaming it into our living rooms. We do not degrade the dignity of our worst criminals by showing their execution on television; why are our soldiers given less consideration?[92]

Although the actual historical record belies this, the fear survives because of live television. Yet, as the Gulf War demonstrated, live television may create some special circumstances but it does not automatically follow that death and destruction will appear 'in our living rooms' or that popular support for the war will alter as a result.

Moreover, if the Odd Couple start working together to set in stone a system which has anyway worked out pretty favourably for the coverage of national wars fought by democracies in the past, our wars – whether they be real wars or media wars – are in danger of becoming one and the same thing. If that happens, however, it is likely that the resultant imagery will sit more happily alongside the traditional historical iconography of glory rather than the literal reality of guts. Other people's wars, or at least the two or three that news organisations decide to cover at any given time, are much more likely to become the brutal, nasty, televised affairs so feared by the Vietnam Syndrome generation: Bosnia, Rwanda, Chechenya. Even then, thanks to questions of taste and decency, it is unlikely that the full horror – the reality – can be shown. No matter how much existing standards deteriorate – or 'adapt to the needs of a changing audience' – in the quest for ratings, it is unlikely that decent people will accept the real reality. Moreover, thanks to media prioritisation, the majority of wars going on in the world at any given time will simply fail to command public attention. It is only when the boys from our village go to war, whether it is ours or someone else's, that the locals begin to think global.

4

MIND GAMES

Information warfare and psychological operations

We have seen in the previous chapters how the media have emerged as participants in events, largely at what might be regarded a strategic level – in other words as willing communicators of information and images from scenes of war and peace to a wider civilian populace which constitutes 'the audience' *beyond* those zones. In this way, to borrow an analogy from T. E. Lawrence, information flows as 'circle beyond circle',[1] or perhaps we should say wave upon wave. We now turn to the role of communications *within* crisis situations and combat theatres at what might be seen as the tactical or operational level, namely within the very first circle itself. As such, this involves the communication of information by military organisations to support their objectives on the ground in ways quite different from the kind of media management arrangements made by government press departments and their Public Affairs, or Public Information, Officers out in the field.

We have also seen how the culture of the soldier and that of the journalist are quite different, some might even say antithetical. To the military, the media are too often seen as outsiders looking in. Thus the impressions gained, or given, about what is going on within the first circle are important to the media, purely for outside purposes in the circles beyond. This is essentially why soldiers, trained to fight, tend to regard media relations as a distraction from the real business for which they are paid. This is particularly the case in societies which have abandoned conscription, which merely exacerbates the insider–outsider divide. For example, in recent years media interest in the military at times other than war has been episodic, and when it has occurred it has revolved around such issues as homosexuals in the armed forces, the role of women, and criminal acts by soldiers against the civilian populace (as in Cyprus, Japan or Northern Ireland) or even against new recruits (Canada). Such high-profile media attention is hardly felt to be conducive to a balanced public debate about the *real* issues affecting the armed forces in the 1990s, namely what role there is for them in the post-Cold War world. Moreover, the adverse publicity which such incidents have attracted can be seen as a failure in military public relations on the one hand while providing clear evidence of the need to improve such activity on the other. In other words, if the military have become more adept at PR during times of war, at other times their expertise in this area leaves a lot to be desired. This merely demonstrates that the impressions gained about the first circle in the circles beyond it have become more important to the military for *inside* purposes.

THIRD-WAVE WARFARE

However, as insiders involved in military operations, the military also have to consider the state of mind of people caught up in their fighting business, whether they be the troops on their own side (requiring attention ranging from armed forces radio for morale purposes to command and control capabilities for conveying orders around the combat theatre) or that of their direct opponents (requiring, *inter alia*, deception, intelligence and psychological warfare operations). However, like media management, the information age has also made this an area fraught with problems. Again, the fluidity of modern information inevitably means that, when discussing communications within the first circle, we cannot but avoid returning to strategic questions and indeed to the media. The dividing line between Public Information activities at the wider level and Military Psychological Operations on the ground is, in other words, no longer as clear as it has been in the past.

This is because, in much contemporary strategic thinking, the very notion of conflict is undergoing such significant transformations that even the concept of the traditional 'battlefield' is changing. Although battlefields can still be places in which people are directly involved in combat, whether they be soldiers or civilians (or both), and, as such, communicating with them remains an important element of determining what happens there, the military no longer enjoys a monopoly in terms of communications technology within them. And we are not just talking about journalists. Amateur radio operators (hams), for example, can tune in to military frequencies or indeed to like-minded souls within the combat area and report what they hear to the outside world, while all sorts of other information spillages (for example, by amateur camcorder footage or from mobile phones) mean that communications within a combat zone now assume not just a tactical but a strategic significance as well. Information flowing around a battlefield for tactical or operational purposes by the military thus seeps out by a variety of sources to a wider strategic civilian audience beyond it, whose reactions to that information can in turn directly impact on the course of events back at the scene of conflict. In 'the next war', it is not inconceivable that a news organisation could mount a camera on a pilotless aerial drone and send it to film scenes of battle, which could be broadcast live to a global audience – who might include enemy commanders who could adjust their battlefield deployments accordingly. This hypothetical situation would demand that the drone be shot down by the military, thereby risking the hostility of a 'free press' who would undoubtedly scream loudly about violations of their First Amendment rights or some other freedom, but the damage might already have been done on the battlefield itself, never mind beyond it.

In short, battlefields, even of the traditional variety, have become extremely porous places. This is especially true given the sheer variety of modern operations involving military forces, for example in humanitarian exercises where civilians from non-governmental organisations (NGOs) like the International Red Cross are also at 'the front line'. It might therefore be more appropriate to start thinking now in terms of 'battle spaces' in which instantaneous communication technologies are not only obliterating previous distinctions between tactical and strategic information, and between military and civilian perceptions of what is happening there, but also between the 'battle front' and the 'home front'. Besides, the latter, thanks to communication technology, has now become a 'global front' with a real-time audience.

This is a huge issue and, to understand it, it might help if we start in the combat theatre itself. Here, in the first circle, military planners talk of Command and Control Warfare or C^2W. Essentially this is about the effective integration, organisation and deployment of resources 'to deny information to the enemy, influence, degrade or destroy adversary C2 capabilities while protecting C2 capabilities against such actions'.[2] In the Third Wave, we must now add to this Communications, or C^3W, plus Intelligence, C^3IW, and finally Computers, C^4IW. Indeed there is a school of thought which has it that 'neither mass nor mobility' may any longer determine the outcome of battles and wars; 'instead, the side that knows more, that can disperse the fog of war yet enshroud an adversary in it, will enjoy decisive advantages'.[3] Of course, in purely military terms, the most effective form of C^4IW is physically to destroy the enemy, which can be achieved by disrupting the enemy's C^4IW capabilities, thereby removing his ability to fight. However, because many analysts believe that military affairs are undergoing a significant revolution thanks to the new technologies, this is no straightforward affair, not least because 'the enemy' may no longer be readily identifiable. Where, for example, is the front line in a terrorist campaign? How, and indeed where, should one engage the perpetrators of the Lockerbie tragedy? Is a computer hacker who inserts a virus into a military computer system a soldier or a terrorist? Conflict, like information, is creeping from one circle to the others beyond it – many of which are no longer confined to what have been in the past regarded as traditional military activities.

These realisations and possibilities are driving much military thinking in the 1990s, particularly in the United States, about concepts of Information Warfare or 'infowar'. One analyst at the American National Defense University has argued that we should now start thinking about seven different but interconnected forms of warfare, all of which fall under the umbrella of information warfare: command and control warfare, intelligence based warfare, electronic warfare, psychological warfare, hacker warfare, economic information warfare and cyberwarfare.[4] Within these categories, notions of conflict cross a spectrum of relationships ranging from cooperation to competition, conflict, and war.[5] Even in a state of cooperation, as in a coalition, for example, two parties may wish to protect ancillary information from disclosure to the other. Also, infowar theory incorporates the possibilities of 'corporate wars' fought between competing trans-national corporations, although here we shall be dealing largely with military applications, not least because it is the American Department of Defense (DoD) which at the moment is proving to be the main engine for driving the thinking about this. And while it is true that the tendency in US military planning since 1945 has been to theorise in terms of spectrums of conflict (graduated nuclear escalation) that do not always apply in practice (hence the mess of Vietnam), it may be that this conceptual device is perhaps too rigid for concepts of infowar. This is because the majority of conflicts in the 1990s are, in fact, intra-state struggles, in which ethnic, nationalistic and tribal forces compete for power – often with a brutality the visibility of which is made all the more shocking courtesy of global television news services. And because of the television cameras, what we used to call civil wars are fought in battle spaces that become a matter of global concern, prompting the international community to 'do something' to stop the horror before their eyes, especially when they embrace 'innocent civilians'.

The post-Cold War era is seeing a variety of these 'conflicts other than war', ranging from humanitarian operations in Somalia and Northern Iraq to the peace-enforcement operations in Bosnia, and even democracy-enforcement in Haiti. One striking characteristic of American armed forces' involvement in such operations has been the increasingly central role being given to Psychological Operations, or PSYOPS. The renewed emphasis on this use of targeted information to assist military operations has already made it a significant, if barely noticed, informational player in today's turbulent international environment. And if it is only military analysts who have taken note of the renewed emphasis on this activity within the first circle, it is only a matter of time before others beyond are affected by the inevitable seepages.

Indeed, in the waging and winning not just of wars but also of what are termed 'military operations other than war' (MOOTWs), many analysts believe that in our post-industrial, third-wave information age 'information warfare will dominate twenty first century conflict . . . Achieving information dominance over an adversary will [even] decide conflicts long before resort to more violent forms of warfare is necessary.'[6] Nor is this mere science fiction. On 1 October 1995, the US Air Force created the first Information Warfare Squadron, the 609th, at Shaw Air Force Base in South Carolina.

SOME DEFINITIONS AND OPERATIONAL PRINCIPLES

In a manner evocative of the unfolding of nuclear strategy after the end of the Second World War, much of the thinking about infowar is still evolving and it will undoubtedly take time for the doctrine to be worked out fully. But it is already clear that certain assumptions form the basis for what is emerging. In the battlefield deployment of what have been termed 'word weapons', 'paper bullets' and 'munitions of the mind', the emphasis has historically been placed on the communication of information – and thereby ideas – in association with the exercise of violence. The former is certainly more economically viable than the latter; paper is undeniably cheaper than the uranium tips of modern artillery shells and bullets. So are computers. This, therefore, makes the software of information an attractive proposition in an era of defence expenditure reductions and changing strategies. Equally, there is a moral case to be made that persuading people *not* to fight is infinitely preferable to killing them, and we now hear more and more of 'non-lethal weapons' in an attempt to reduce casualties – on both sides – and thus minimise gory images which might upset or alienate the audiences within the circles beyond who have no stomach for the realities of war. Despite the issues outlined in the previous chapter, because some of those realities are now more likely to be witnessed than at any time in the past – due to the increasing commercialisation and competitiveness of media in possession of high-tech communications equipment – the waging of infowar assumes strategic proportions. Indeed, this combination of economic, moral and technological determinism is driving much of the contemporary thinking which places greater emphasis on communication(s) as an instrument for 'attacking the intellectual battlespace' in new concepts of 'war' such as 'hyperwar', 'netwar', 'cyberwar', 'virtual war' – and 'infowar'. While it may seem strange that highly dubious assumptions – about the inability of the public to sustain casualties, for example, and the impact of violent images on popular support for war – are at the root of all this, stranger still are some of the implications that are emerging from the new thinking. In particular, PSYOPS assumes a new significance, not just at a tactical level but also as a strategic tool. For, while it is still at the moment mainly deployed as an ancillary to military operations, some thinkers are looking to a time when persuasion might even replace violence. The basis for this assertion already exists in the current official definitions.

During the Second World War, it was recognised that 'psychological warfare is not a magic substitute for battle, but an auxiliary to it'.[7] Military historians would be the first to argue that words alone cannot win wars but, by attacking the fighting morale of an enemy force, proponents of PSYOPS aim both to reduce 'the cost of the physical battle' and to render 'the enemy easier to handle after surrender'.[8] When the targeted audience is an opposing military force, this is termed Tactical PSYOPS support in the battlefield area, although that audience also embraces 'observers and key communicators in the target area'. This can of course include journalists as well as military communications personnel. The aim is to support 'immediate and short-term objectives in direct support of tactical commanders'.[9] All well and good; this is tried and tested. The problem for PSYOPS is that it anticipates operating at three other levels, three further circles, and it is at those levels that potential problems emerge. As operational support, the objectives of PSYOPS are mid-term: the 'target audience is regional. In support of theater operations units assume responsibility for strategic PSYOP in the region.'[10] Consolidation PSYOPS is designed to assist 'in the reorientation and education of occupied areas'.[11] In other words, the target audience is the civilian population who are subjected to re-education and rehabilitation along lines designed by the victors. Finally, at the strategic level, PSYOPS is designed to promote long-term objectives: 'target audience is normally global in nature'.[12]

What does that mean? The current official American definition of PSYOPS runs as follows:

> Planned operations to convey selected information and indicators to foreign audiences to influence their emotions, motives, objective reasoning, and ultimately the behaviour of foreign governments, organisations, groups and individuals. The purpose of psychological operations is to induce or reinforce foreign attitudes and behavior favourable to the originator's objectives.[13]

Here, the use of the word 'foreign' fails to delineate between enemy and friendly, while the definition also avoids separation between soldiers and civilians, or between tactical and strategic activity. It might also be noted that US institutions are expressly forbidden to conduct PSYOPS on US soil.

The present NATO definition is noticeably and, due perhaps to the plurality of intra-alliance views on the subject, even markedly broader: 'planned psychological activities *in peace* and war directed at enemy, *friendly and neutral* audiences in order to influence attitudes and behavior affecting the achievement of *political* and military objectives'.[14]

Many people would label this as propaganda, and indeed that is what it is. Philosophical objections to the use of the word 'propaganda', based either on its historical abuse or on a conceptual misunderstanding of its real nature, should consult the introductory chapter to this book. But even the relationship between propaganda – traditionally regarded as having been directed at civilians – and psychological operations – traditionally seen as directed at soldiers – appears to be changing. In 1950, one US Army training circular maintained that strategic propaganda 'is the long-range "artillery" of psychological warfare'.[15] During the Cold War, most Western countries regarded propaganda as a 'fourth arm' of *defence*, and placed it alongside military, naval and air power. Psychological warfare, on the other hand, was a 'fifth arm' of *attack*, which sees economic power added to the list.[16] It is worth noting in passing that the Soviet Union made no such distinctions.

By using words such as 'warfare' involving 'defence' and 'attack', however, we remain vulnerable to limiting our understanding of today's PSYOPS to predominantly wartime circumstances. Psywar certainly remains part of the PSYOPS concept. However, if communications is the fifth dimension in inter-state *conflict*, it remains the fourth dimension of inter-state *relations*. Propaganda at a strategic level is merely the process of targeted persuasion within that fourth dimension, in *peace* as well as in war, and in all the contingencies in between. Hence strategic propaganda could just as necessarily be directed at friendly and neutral states as at readily identifiable enemy states. Psychological warfare, on the other hand, has traditionally been thought of as being targeted at hostile, or potentially hostile, nations merely in times of crisis or war. As such it tends to be seen as a sub-branch of strategic propaganda, rather than the other way around as suggested by the 1950 training circular mentioned in the previous paragraph. During the Cold War, the military argued that all propaganda had to be subordinated to psychological warfare, rather than *vice versa*. And if now, with the end of the Cold War and the redesignation of former nuclear enemies, one might have thought that psywar could once again be relegated to being the tactical branch of strategic propaganda directed specifically against an enemy in a combat situation, one needs to think again.

Because current military practitioners of PSYOPS define their activity broadly as the planned and targeted use of information to influence human attitudes and behaviour, they have come to believe that traditional battle-fields no longer provide the only environments in which PSYOPS can be employed and indeed can – and must – form part of these other types of operations involving military forces. Nor, equally, are enemy soldiers the only target groups for their attention; in infowar theory, 'nobody is a soldier and everybody is a combatant'.[17] A sceptic might say therefore that everyone can be shot, but there is a recognition in Western military thought that such action could no longer command public support for very long, especially if television cameras were present. The corollary, therefore, is that everyone must be persuaded not to fight, so that there will be no need to shoot them. This makes infowar and PSYOPS an essential ingredient of pre- and post-war phases, as a part of diplomacy. To counter any alarm which this may provoke, many American officials argue that contemporary PSYOPS is now so different from its World War and Cold War antecedents that the shib-boleths of the past must be discarded, and anyone who doubts this need only look at the children's colouring books and bumper stickers produced to promote awareness of mines by IFOR in Bosnia.[18]

This is a startling assertion. But is it only held in the rarefied atmosphere of Defense Colleges on the North American continent? NATO, which is after all a military alliance of sixteen democratic nations, also makes in its definitions the distinction between 'strategic' activities – designed to support the achievement of national, or multinational, objectives, i.e. propaganda directed at a wide audience in support of policy – and 'operational' or 'tactical' activities, i.e. those designed to support operations in the theatre of military operations. Psychological Consolidation Activities (PCA) are defined as 'planned psychological activities in peace and war directed at the civilian population located in areas under friendly control in order to achieve a desired behaviour which supports the military objectives and the operational freedom of the supported commanders'. Battlefield Psychological Activities (BPA) are defined as 'planned psychological activities conducted as an integral part of combat operations and designed to bring psychological pressure to bear on enemy forces and civilians under enemy control in the battle area, to assist the achievement of tactical objectives'. Finally, Strategic Psychological Activities (SPA) are defined by NATO as 'planned psychological activities in peace and war which normally pursue objectives to gain the support and co-operation of friendly and neutral countries and *to reduce the will and the capacity of hostile or potentially hostile countries to wage war*' (my emphasis).

To understand this in its proper perspective, we do indeed need to see PSYOPS today in terms of the employment of communications technology designed to aid various types of military and other operations rather than identifying it purely with the combat propaganda or psywar of the past. For this reason, current American thinking sees PSYOPS as a tool which can

> significantly enhance our ability to maintain peace, expand dialogue and understanding, encourage the process of democratisation, lessen tensions, inhibit proliferation, contain conflict, end it as rapidly as possible and with the minimum loss of life, and accelerate the re-establishment of stability and peace.[19]

Terminology is certainly a problem here. While PSYOPS or PSYOP remain terms preferred by the US military (the two acronyms are used interchangeably), other NATO members still tend to fight shy of the label due to its historical associations, typically resulting in the creation of a host of euphemistic acronyms ranging from 'Operational Information' (OPINFO) to 'Civil–Military Affairs' (CMA). The US military establishment, however, feels that if it merely created a euphemism of its own, and someone discovered that what was being done was really PSYOPS, then this would merely undermine its credibility – and credibility is vital to the successful application of PSYOPS.

In a global environment fraught with danger, then, the informational dimension has thus become every bit as significant as the traditional military, economic and diplomatic aspects which influence international relations. Indeed, it is this fourth dimension which constitutes the 'intellectual battlespace' of the New World Order's struggle for hearts and minds. Yet, while PSYOPS forms one part of the spectrum of persuasive techniques intended to promote national interests, ranging from propaganda to public information, international information and public diplomacy, in practice it remains a term still used mainly by the military. Non-military organisations continue to fight shy of the label, even though the distinctions are often clearer in theory than in practice. While there is also a tendency in all this to regard PSYOPS as a new wonder weapon which can do just about anything, the American experience in 1991 during Operation Desert Storm, termed the 'first information war',[20] did serve to convince many senior military planners that PSYOPS should be a major part of the shape of things to come. Strategic applications of PSYOPS are inevitably going to remain a highly controversial area. On the other hand, they need not necessarily be so, but only if one appreciates fully the operational principles which have evolved from democratic historical experience during the course of this century.

FROM PSYWAR TO PSYOPS

The psychological dimension to aggressive human conflict has always been an important feature on the battlefields of history.[21] Information and messages generated by sounds, symbols, gestures – even, in more superstitious times, religious relics and omens – have a long tradition of military deployment in calculated attempts to affect the progress and outcome of battles in a way that is favourable to one side at the expense of another. Of course, rational theorists have also understood the significance of such techniques in pre-empting the need to resort to war. After all, it was Sun Tzu who wrote in the fourth century BC that 'to subdue the enemy without fighting is the acme of skill'.[22]

Once war breaks out, however, psychological weapons are deployed in an attempt to influence the use of other types of munitions. Yet, because their deployment embraces issues of morale (civilian as well as military, friendly as well as enemy) as a factor in determining victory or defeat, there have always been ethical concerns as to how this is achieved – by fair means or foul – as well as doctrinal issues about when to use it, and at what level. Most standard histories of warfare still tend to overlook the relevance of this activity,[23] both on the battlefield and beyond, despite the fact that the combined military application of communications and psychology can be identified as far back as biblical times. But although the psychological arsenal available to military commanders has obviously expanded with the twentieth-century explosion in communication technologies, many of the techniques employed none the less remain time-honoured. Indeed, Joshua's use of trumpets outside the walls of Jericho had its modern parallel when, during the 1989 US operation in Panama, recorded rock music was played through loudspeakers at high volume outside General Noriega's compound (including the song by Martha Reeves and the Vandellas, *Nowhere to Run, Nowhere to Hide*). And, just as the British consul in Bern spent a good deal of his time between 1914 and 1918 placing leaflets in bottles to float down the Rhine, PSYOPS officers did likewise in the waters of the Persian Gulf in 1991.

These examples might not appear to be the stuff by which spectacular military victories are achieved but communications have come a long way since this type of activity was first conducted on a scientific and systematic basis during the First World War. Then, psywar was essentially a matter of printed material. Radio was added to the armoury in the Second World War, and in the decades that followed, satellite television, computers and other forms of high-tech communications were enlisted into psywar's ranks as warfare extended into the electro-magnetic spectrum. Psychological warfare techniques have been a feature of the small wars of the Cold War era, especially in Korea and Vietnam, and in the counter-insurgency conflicts in Kenya, Malaya and elsewhere.[24] In such contests, psywar could be regarded essentially as combat propaganda. However, the very bi-polar and global nature of international competition during the Cold War, an ideological contest in which public opinion at large was pivotal and mass communications outlets were widely available, new and broader concepts of psywar were felt to be required.

The story throughout is one of a constant struggle for acceptance as a legitimate weapon of war, never mind peace. In September 1914, following German airborne leaflet dropping raids over Nancy and Paris, newspaper baron Lord Northcliffe suggested that the British should retaliate in kind, only to be rebuffed by General Wilson who said that this was 'a minor matter – the thing was to kill Germans'.[25] Soldiers were in the killing business, not in the emerging discipline of psychology. After four years of war, however, when all other methods of breaking the deadlock had been tried and failed, the First World War essentially became a question of 'which people will lose heart first?'[26] When in 1918 Northcliffe was placed in charge of the newly created British enemy propaganda department based at Crewe House, he was determined that the answer would be 'the soldiers and peoples of the Central Powers'. Leaflets in their millions began to be dropped daily over enemy lines, while other techniques such as loudspeaker teams were also being deployed in an effort to speed up an end to the bloodshed.[27] This worked particularly effectively on the Italian Front, targeted by Crewe House as being more likely to yield immediate results in light of indications that the Austro-Hungarian Empire was on the verge of internal disintegration. Armed with promises of self-determination for the subject nationalities inspired by US President Wilson's Fourteen Points, Crewe House coordinated a massive leaflet campaign designed to foster further unrest amongst the Austro-Hungarian forces. Mass desertions followed, prompting the Austro-Hungarians to order machine-gun sections to stem the tide of their own defectors. By August, almost a million leaflets a day were being dropped over Austrian lines and they contributed significantly to the collapse of the regime in the following month.[28]

Crewe House next turned its attention to Germany, receiving a little assistance from the Americans who likewise joined in, establishing the Psychologic Sub-Section of G-2 in the War Department, with a Propaganda Section within the Military Intelligence Branch at GHQ in the field.[29] It was here that they began developing rudimentary techniques for evaluating the impact of their leaflet and loudspeaker output in the form of prisoner-of-war interrogations: 'of the thousands of prisoners who passed through the examining cage of a single American corps during the first fortnight of the Meuse–Argonne campaign [1918], it was found, upon examination, that one out of every three had our propaganda in his pocket'.[30] Messages varied from the futility of continuing the struggle and the inevitability of defeat to promises that the German people would be treated fairly provided they discarded their rulers. Thus began the technique of trying to separate the enemy population from their governing regime, which in turn provided the German leadership, present and future, with rationalisations for the defeat which came in November 1918. General Ludendorff claimed that 'we were hypnotised by the enemy propaganda as a rabbit is by a snake', while General Hindenburg wrote that 'besides bombs which kill the body, his [i.e. the enemy's] airmen throw down leaflets which are intended to kill the soul. . . . Unsuspectingly many thousands consume the poison.'[31] While such statements, together with the paeans of praise heaped upon the British propaganda effort by Adolph Hitler in *Mein Kampf*, must be treated with a degree of scepticism, the idea took root that 'good propaganda probably saved a year of war, and this meant the saving of thousands of millions of money and probably at least a million lives'.[32]

In light of this experiment, some military writers as early as 1920 were predicting that, in future, physical combat would be 'replaced by a purely psychological warfare, wherein weapons are not used or battlefields sought'.[33] None the less, within ten years a popular backlash against all forms of activity associated with war had taken root within democracies. Propaganda was no exception, as reflected in Lord Ponsonby's rather bizarre statement that 'the injection of the poison of hatred into men's minds by means of a falsehood is a greater evil in wartime than the actual loss of life. The defilement of the human soul is worse than the destruction of the human body.'[34] Any propaganda operations, including psychological warfare, had to be conducted under another label, or in far away places: for example, unrest in Western Samoa at the turn of the 1920s prompted the Royal New Zealand Air Force to drop several thousand pamphlets 'by hand, in rolled bundles of fifty to a hundred, and at a height just above the coconut trees'.[35] The new Soviet regime in Russia, however, while it remained dedicated to fostering world revolution until

Stalin displaced Trotsky at the end of the 1920s and introduced the idea of 'socialism in one country', had no such qualms. The Soviets having identified the British empire as one of their primary targets for propaganda, targeting 'oppressed working class people', Whitehall needed to do more than merely rely, as hitherto, on strong governance in those areas shaded red on the world map.

This was a new form of warfare, a 'political warfare' which became a function of the secret intelligence services during the inter-war years. To the British, political warfare meant 'that aspect of intelligence in which information is used aggressively to manipulate opinion or to create special conditions by purely intellectual means'.[36] It was clear that this was a way of the future, in peace as in war. By the outbreak of the Second World War in 1939, therefore, plans were already under way to establish an enemy propaganda department and, indeed, on the opening night of the war, the first mission by the RAF was an air raid over Germany – to drop leaflets, not bombs. Campbell Stuart, a stalwart of Crewe House, was brought back initially to head the unit known as Department EH (Electra House) – the codename reflecting the secretive aura which now surrounded such activity. When Winston Churchill became the UK's Prime Minister in 1940 at the height of Nazi military success in Western Europe, he believed that unconventional warfare could do what the other armed forces could no longer do pending an invasion, 'set Europe ablaze'. This required the establishment of a Special Operations Executive, divided into two branches: SO1, which dealt with propaganda, and SO2, which dealt with espionage and subversion. After considerable political infighting, SO1 became the Political Warfare Executive (PWE), a civilian agency which, under its cover name of the Political Intelligence Department (PID) of the Foreign Office, conducted all British propaganda directed at enemy and enemy-occupied countries from 1941 onwards. The Ministry of Information, which had been established in 1939, continued to conduct home and allied propaganda. Thus organisational separation between propaganda – home and foreign – and psychological warfare – between foreign enemy and foreign friendly audiences – was achieved. Whether or not this was desirable is another matter.

So much has already been written about propaganda in the Second World War – the greatest propaganda war in history – that there is merely a need here to draw out the characteristics which affected its subsequent use.[37] By far the most important element in British wartime psychological warfare was the BBC. In 1943, an internal BBC document discussing the European service maintained that 'we can carry out intellectual liberation without waiting for its physical counterpart'.[38] The Germans preferred the term *geistige Kriegführung*, intellectual warfare, even though their approach to propaganda was based on the premise that it needed to be addressed to the lowest common denominator and that intellectuals would not be a worthy target because of their ability to identify propaganda when they were confronted with it. Indeed, the very discursive nature of democratic society led to the inclination to base propaganda upon reason rather than emotion, upon 'truth' rather than falsehood, and upon persuasion rather than coercion.

The British continued to use the term 'political warfare' centred around the PWE until the Americans joined the war after 1941, when the word 'psychological' gradually replaced it as Psychological Warfare Branches (PWBs) were established in the various theatres as military agencies. A few months before Pearl Harbor, Washington had established the Office of the Co-ordinator of Information (COI), which began broadcasting to enemy and enemy-occupied countries before the United States entered the war. After Pearl Harbor, the COI was divided into two branches: the Office of War Information (OWI) dealing with 'white' or overt propaganda and psychological warfare, and the Office of Strategic Services (OSS) for 'black' or covert activity, special operations and intelligence. Liaison between the OWI and the PWE was established early on, issuing joint psychological warfare directives from the autumn of 1942 onwards. The largest PWB was set up in North Africa in November 1942 on the direct order of General Eisenhower. This was a joint Anglo-American, combined military–civilian, unit. As part of the preparations for the invasion of Europe, a Psychological Warfare Division was established at the Supreme Headquarters of the Allied Expeditionary Force (PWD/SHAEF), the forerunner of SHAPE.[39] This implied greater inter-allied cooperation than was in fact the case, but, where the British and Americans were at least agreed in their overall approach to psychological warfare, or at least that disseminated by overt methods in which the source was clearly acknowledged, was that leaflets or broadcasts should be based as much on the truth as possible. Both nations recognised that falsehoods or false promises have a tendency to backfire. Hugh Greene, who was involved in this activity from 1940 on into the Cold War era before becoming Director General of the BBC in 1960, put it thus: 'tell the truth within the limits of the information at our disposal and to tell it consistently and frankly. . . . It is a strategic weapon and must not deviate from the truth for tactical reasons.'[40]

BLACK PROPAGANDA VERSUS WHITE

Many practitioners from the 1939–45 era and beyond are on record as insisting on the axiomatic nature of truth in democratic propaganda. We must be neither naïve nor precious about this, not least because few practitioners point to the parallel conduct of black campaigns. 'As near as possible the whole truth' may have been the rule in the OWI and MoI, but this principle fails to embrace the complementary work of the black propaganda organisations. For example, Britain's Political Warfare Executive, and especially Sefton Delmer's unit, ran a series of black radio stations (called

Research Units) which gave the impression of conversations between underground cells of disaffected soldiers inside occupied Europe. They were in fact broadcast from British soil. Also, allied agents would risk life and limb transmitting rumours ('sibs')[41] designed to sow seeds of doubt in the minds of eavesdroppers. The latitude given to such propagandists not only in their choice of language but in their actual content was considerable; they did not need to worry quite so much about lies, for example, because their material was not obviously coming from allied sources. Rather, the main criterion was *credibility*, and if that involved graphic language and gossip by seemingly ordinary people expressing their private reservations about their rulers, then so much the better from the point of view of authenticity. Moreover, because the broadcasts seemed to be coming from inside Germany or German-occupied territory, it was also possible to express views that ran counter to the official line. For example, following the Casablanca Conference of 1943, allied policy was one which would require 'Unconditional Surrender', which implied that no amount of negotiation would be possible for Germany to end the war, not even if the German people rose up against their Nazi rulers.[42] Black propagandists, on the other hand, could suggest that 'we' get rid of 'Hitler's gang' and 'our' situation might then well improve.[43] This was highly secretive work – by necessity – and tended towards the realm of the secret intelligence services. White propagandists worried that the credibility of their work might be undermined by the discovery of this 'black game'. The organisational separation of black and white activity has remained ever since.

Because it is normally apparent who the source is, white activity needs to be based upon credible truths. This does not mean that it is based on the whole truth. The selective deployment of truth as a weapon was learned during the course of the First World War but found its apogee in the Second World War with the allied 'Strategy of Truth'. As Daniel Lerner has pointed out:

> A strategy of truth ... is not synonymous with honesty. Conversely, there is no known national propaganda apparatus which operates according to a strategy of dishonesty. The word to be emphasised, in the first instance, is not 'truth' but 'strategy', for truth in propaganda is a function of effectiveness. The basis of operations described by the phrase is expediency, even if its rationalisation to the public is usually made in terms of morality. Propagandists do not decide to tell the truth because they personally are honest, any more than they decide to tell lies because they are dishonest. Given a particular audience to be reached with a particular policy, the basis for decision is an estimate of what will work.[44]

This hits the nail right on the head. Successive generations of psywarriors have learned that, to be effective, **PSYOPS** needs to be credible and rooted in a reality that approximates to the 'truth'. Eighteen months before the end of the Second World War, an internal BBC directive put it thus:

> Certainly we have refrained from falsifying good news to make it appear less good or bad news to make it seem worse in an exaggerated quest for so-called objectivity. . . . And yet, although we have constantly sought to be honest and balanced we have (inevitably perhaps) in all but the actual fighting news tended to approach each topic and item from the point of view of 'does this help or hinder our cause?' 'Is this good propaganda?' . . . The test must be . . . 'is this important?', 'is this something which a citizen with a right to full information and to form his own judgements ought to know about?' It is both our duty and in our interests to give our listeners full information now that there is no danger of the full unvarnished truth setting the weak-nerved and unstable in a panic and thus imperilling our chances of survival (as was once the case).[45]

Although white propaganda, whether by leaflets or radio, serves as the official voice of the sender, and is therefore clearly identifiable as 'propaganda' in the eyes of its target, experience has repeatedly reinforced the significance of making the output predominantly information-based. It may take some time for the reliability of the source to be built up, which invariably means being able to deliver only what is promised. This might make white activity more cautious than black, and it is certainly essential for white propaganda to stick more closely to official policy. Moreover, white propaganda struggles to compete with the targeted authorities' propaganda resources. Hence, radio signals can be jammed and laws passed forbidding people to pick up leaflets. Because it clearly originates from the enemy, resistance to its messages is automatically higher. White propaganda, therefore, is always forced to compete on its opponent's terms. If that opponent is an authoritarian regime with a state controlled media, in peace as well as in war (since democracies also must impose degrees of state control over the media in wartime), then the provision of alternative and credible news has a greater chance of receptivity. Hence the BBC managed to build up a considerable audience for its German Service in Nazi Germany during the Second World War, which was to serve it well during the Cold War.

Between 1939 and 1945, when the external broadcasting services were finding their feet and learning the operational principles of white radio propaganda, they employed journalists whose inclination was towards publicity rather than secrecy. Their principle, derived from the Western journalistic tradition, was to tell 'the truth, nothing but the truth and, as near as possible, the whole truth'. One American employed by the OWI put the dilemma as follows:

159

Our real difficulties came over a choice between giving the news and withholding it, between the practices of journalism and the dictates of war, between the urge to inform and the passion to save lives, between common honesty and plain humanity.[46]

So, by inclination and experience, white propaganda conducted by democratic regimes evolved less around the principle of truth and more around credibility. 'On any long-term basis, credibility is a condition of persuasiveness and credence is associated with a reputation for truthfulness. Democracy, by its nature, is a long-run operation, and its distinctive function as government by consent must be affiliated with a strategy of truth.'[47]

All sides in warfare posture as truth-tellers. In Marxist thinking, for example, it was claimed that propaganda had to be truthful because its main task was 'the enlightenment of the selected audiences, especially by rational methods for influencing their consciousness'.[48] Nor is white propaganda always above deception. A calculation has to be made as to whether white propaganda can be used in the service of a tactical deception without damaging the strategic credibility of subsequent output. We shall see how this occurred in the Gulf War when leaflets and broadcasts from overt coalition sources deliberately deceived the Iraqi forces into believing that the frontal assault against them would come from the sea rather than by land. The media was used likewise. In the Second World War, similar techniques were used within the overall deception plan accompanying Operation Overlord. The Germans had to be convinced that the invasion would take place at a location elsewhere than the Normandy beaches, and the deception plan (Operation Fortitude) did this spectacularly.

By 1944, then, psychological warfare was also being conducted to supplement military operations, both from outside and in the field. Five Mobile Radio Broadcasting companies were set up to accompany the troops invading Europe, field newspapers such as *Nachrichten für die Truppen* were being distributed, leaflets containing safe conduct passes (*passierscheinen*) were dropped by plane, leaflet bomb and balloon and, following the capture of Radio Luxembourg in the autumn of 1944, the black radio operations by 'Soldatensender Calais' were supplemented by Luxembourg's powerful 150 kilowatt transmitter.

A further indication of the significance of credibility over truth can be found in an example of a psywar leaflet distributed by combat propaganda units with the Fifth Army in Italy. The leaflet showed photographs of German prisoners playing billiards in comparatively luxurious surroundings in a prisoner of war camp. 'Although it was true that prisoners in American P/W camps received eggs for breakfast, further testing showed us that this notion was so preposterous to the Germans on the other side of the firing line that they simply laughed at the idea.'[49] 'Instead of picturing captivity in the U.S. as the outrageous idyll which it really was', the emphasis was subsequently shifted to the slogan: 'It's no fun being a prisoner-of-war!'; and then to: 'Better Free than a Prisoner of War, Better a Prisoner of War than Dead'.[50] From such exercises, methods for evaluating effectiveness began to emerge. Within all the debate about the effect of communications upon audiences that has been raging for over fifty years, too often is it forgotten that psychological warriors were amongst the first to develop a systematic procedure for measuring the impact of communications on their target audience. This basically involves six criteria. These are:

- the number of leaflets in the possession of captured prisoners-of-war;
- their ability to recall and comment on messages contained in leaflet and radio messages;
- favourable comment, especially in discussions behind the lines prior to surrender;
- detailed description of why the soldiers decided to desert or be taken prisoner;
- the degree to which the enemy was preoccupied with counter-propaganda, including plagiarism of psywar themes employed;
- comments by enemy commanders from captured documents.

Despite the flaws in such methods – captured prisoners, for example, would frequently say what they thought their interrogators wanted to hear – one analysis could conclude from such criteria that 'Allied strategic propaganda contributed greatly toward driving Italy out of the war'.[51]

Similar assessments could not, however, be made for Germany or Japan. Target audiences in both those countries were both military and civilian. For the latter, a major theme of propaganda towards the end of the war was the futility of resistance. One American leaflet dropped by the millions over Japan ran as follows:

These leaflets are being dropped to notify you that your city has been listed for destruction by our powerful air force. The bombing will begin in 72 hours. The advance notice will give your military authorities ample time to take defensive measures to protect you from our inevitable attack. Watch and see how powerless they are to protect you. There is nothing they can do to stop our overwhelming power and iron determination. We want you to see how powerless the military is to protect you.[52]

Despite such appeals, and perhaps because 'Unconditional Surrender' inhibited anything more sophisticated, Japanese morale failed to crack. It took two atomic bombs to force surrender. Likewise, the Germans fought to the bitter end. In the overall balance, psychological warriors defended their work by arguing that they had been useful, 'in co-operation with the major arms, in bringing about the surrender in battle of 4,900,000 well-trained and well-indoctrinated German soldiers'.[53] Of those interrogated, 54.5 per cent admitted that they had read allied leaflets, had listened to allied broadcasts or had heard allied front-line loudspeakers. But there were no mass uprisings amongst the German or Japanese people. If strategic bombing could not succeed, we should hardly be surprised that strategic propaganda failed to break enemy morale. Quite simply, the policy of Unconditional Surrender denied the psywarriors their most obvious message, namely that there was a way out for ordinary Germans or Japanese who wanted to come over to the allied side. The policy denied the kind of propaganda message which had already proved to be the most successful: surrender or die. German troops considering surrender could only hesitate if they believed that they would be treated in much the same way as the Nazi leadership, namely as war criminals. In turn, this gave some credence to the Nazi propaganda line that German soldiers did not desert but were only captured, and that the morale of the armed forces held steady. Regardless of its tactical successes here and there, Unconditional Surrender was the greatest single obstacle for psywar, and demonstrated that most fundamental of axioms: propaganda and policy must be conducted in harmony; the one formulated without due consideration for the other is a recipe for failure.

Like other persuasive techniques, PSYOPS can essentially take three forms: black, white and grey. Black propaganda must not be confused with deception, although it often is.[54] Black activity is that which emanates from a source whose real origin is disguised; it claims to originate from a source different from the true one. Born of a lie, black PSYOPS can, and frequently does, lie – and it is this very specific covert branch of propaganda which has tarnished the image of other forms of official persuasion in the public mind. Because its source is secret, black activity has greater leeway in terms of policy and content. Because it purports to originate from somewhere else, it can say things that might not otherwise be approved of by the originating government. Rumours, scandal, gossip, even pornography, have all come within its historical remit. Great efforts, therefore, have to be expended on concealing its origins; hence this type of activity tends to be conducted by the secret intelligence services, while information regarding its practice remains extremely difficult to come by.

Covert propaganda is a dangerous business. A black operation must remain covert if it is to remain effective – which is why its targets must necessarily expend so much energy on exposing the genuine source, to expose black as white. The problem is that, in so doing, they run the risk of publicising the original black propaganda still further. This is also dangerous for the source because, if it is so exposed, not only is its credibility undermined, thereby jeopardising future operations, but the motives of the administrating political authority are also brought into question. Hence governments publicly distance themselves from their black propaganda organisations in a conspiracy of silence, which in turn allows those organisations greater freedom to go about their business increasingly divorced from policy, public accountability and, some might say, from reality. The secret is to remain secret, not to get caught out. Its objective is to penetrate the communications systems of the enemy and inject any information – true or false – which might disrupt the enemy's performance – politically, militarily, economically or psychologically. Provided the source is kept secret, the recipient interprets the information – which can range from a joke spread by secret agents to slogans daubed on walls – as an indicator of internal discontent or criticism rather than as a propaganda effort by an outsider. Propaganda originating from a distance, as with literature or radio and television, must appear, therefore, to originate from within rather than without. An effective method during the Second World War was to produce black material which would then be torn up by agents and scattered, which resulted in much wider dissemination of the content than might otherwise have been the case.[55] Covert distribution, therefore, is as vital as covert attribution. Moreover, to retain credibility, it must be based on an element of the truth, or at least the lies should be interspersed with credible truths. Although democratic regimes remain justifiably nervous about such activity – the dangers of being found out infinitely outweigh the advantages that might result, which is why in the United States today covert operations can only be sanctioned by Presidential approval – in wartime black propaganda has been justified as a necessary weapon to ensure victory.

During the Cold War, for example, it was part of the great struggle between the CIA and the KGB. As we now know from defectors, black Soviet PSYOPS – which the Russians termed 'active measures' (*aktivnyye meropriyatiya*) to cover its real nature – were designed to discredit their opponents and involved the planting of stories in the world's media such as the allegation that the AIDS virus had been produced as an offshoot of American experiments in biological warfare. Another story, which was still cropping up in the mid-1990s, that children in Third-World countries were being murdered in order to supply transplant organs for rich Americans, was also a KGB active measure from the final stages of the Cold War era.[56]

White PSYOPS, with which we are mainly dealing here, largely out of necessity due to the clandestine and therefore inherently secret nature of its black counterpart, is that which is disseminated openly by clearly identifiable sources. It therefore acts as the official voice of the sender, which is why it is essential for policy and propaganda to work hand-in-hand. The example of the Fourteen Points in the First World War also acts as a reminder of two further factors: the need for inter-allied coordination of both policy and propaganda; and the need to consider long-term, as well as short-term, implications. In his war memoirs, General Ludendorff noted that 'Good propaganda must keep well ahead of actual political events. It must act as pacemaker to policy and mould public opinion without appearing to do so.'[57] When the United States entered the war in 1917 as an associated power to the Allies, and President Wilson announced his Fourteen Points, his was the first real declaration of war aims designed to explain to American and wider opinion why America was fighting. The partners in the Anglo-French alliance were not wholly in agreement with all the points (the British government, for example, disliked the clause relating to freedom of the seas), but their propagandists had at last been provided with a policy statement around which they could develop their propaganda messages. Accordingly, the Points were widely exploited in propaganda directed against the enemy, particularly in the campaign targeting the subject nationalities of the Austro-Hungarian Empire. The promise of national self-determination proved greatly appealing and contributed significantly to the collapse of Germany's ally to the south.[58] Short-term propaganda, however, was to produce long-term policy implications when, at the 1919 Paris Peace Conference after the war, representatives of the Czechs, Yugoslavs, Poles, Romanians and other 'oppressed nationalities' all turned up demanding that allied wartime propaganda promises be converted into peacetime political realities. The resultant formation of the newly independent states of Central and Eastern Europe along ethnographic, rather than sound strategic, borders was to create long-term consequences that were not even resolved by the Second World War.

Grey activity fails to identify any source specifically. It specialises in not telling the 'whole truth'. Because it is anonymous, paradoxically it lacks the credibility of both white and black – it could be from anywhere, so what credence can it have? At least with white activity, the source is identifiable, even if it is official propaganda. Hence democratic governments, which purport to be based on consensus rather than coercion, are more inclined philosophically to tell the truth rather than to lie. Moreover, such governments prefer to conduct white activity through services which are quasi-independent from government. The British conduct some of their white activity through the BBC, for example, while the Americans use the Voice of America. These organisations frequently contain material which is critical of their governments, which merely enhances their credibility as reliable sources of information.

PSYWAR IN THE COLD WAR ERA

Black propaganda continued into the Cold War era. 'There is nothing remarkable in this sequence. The cold war is merely a synonym for intelligence operations. Military means are used only occasionally, and then at the periphery of the conflict. In a large measure, diplomats and propagandists are used to wage its hottest battles.'[59] Indeed, most of the post 1945 studies of psychological warfare took it for granted that it was both a necessary and a legitimate response to the growing political, military and ideological threat posed by international Communism.[60] Having wound down the overt psywar machinery against Nazi Germany, it was but a matter of time before covert psychological operations found a place in the CIA following its creation in 1947.[61]

In 1950, following the North Korean invasion of South Korea, US President Truman established the Psychological Strategy Board in the White House to coordinate the wider effort, both overt and covert.[62] This was a rare recognition that information warfare must be coordinated at highest levels of government and decision-making. In the five years since 1945, most of the psywar personnel involved in the Second World War had returned to civilian life, while in the US military this type of work had returned to obscurity. As a result, rapid improvisations had to be made once the Korean War broke out, although in the end the dropping in tactical theatres of such publications as 'Parachute News', combined with strategic radio broadcasts from transmitters based in Japan under the umbrella label of 'The Voice of the United Nations', meant that quite an extensive campaign had been conducted.[63] Experiments were also made with loudspeaker planes – C-47s which would attempt to bellow out messages to enemy troops above the roar of the plane's engines. By 1951, a much more effective organisation was established, reflecting the growing commitment to psywar in the field. Operation 'Moolah' was felt to be particularly successful; $50,000 and political asylum was offered to any North Korean pilot who would fly a Soviet-built jet to UN-controlled territory, with a further $50,000 dollars for the first one to do this. In September 1953, Lieutenant No Kon-sok, braving UN anti-aircraft fire, flew his MIG-15 into Kimpo airfield. He refused the cash.[64] The problems for US psywar in Korea were that great emphasis was placed on surrender in a war which made surrender particularly difficult, that quality was sacrificed to quantity, and that a 'side-show mentality' meant that psywar was not taken seriously enough by the higher level of commanders in the field.

At the strategic level for the Cold War, there followed a bolstering of the white machinery, first in the US State Department where an International Information Administration was established, and then, in 1953, with President Eisenhower's decision to establish the autonomous United States Information Agency (USIA) with the Voice of America as its white broadcasting arm. Radio Free Europe and Radio Liberty were established as grey organs,[65] although the former also contained a clandestine 'Desk X' headed by Ladislas Farago to combat Communism behind the Iron Curtain, using black techniques.[66] Military PSYOPS was also to gain a boost with the establishment in 1952 of a Psychological Warfare Centre based at Fort Bragg.[67] The degree to which these various activities were coordinated remains open to considerable doubt, with each branch going their separate ways until the Bay of Pigs disaster exposed the myth of a coordinated psychological effort.[68]

A decade after the end of the Korean War, the Americans started once again to become embroiled in Southeast Asia. In the Vietnam war, PSYOPS

– as psywar had now become officially known – none the less assumed its traditional forms: leaflets, radio and loudspeaker broadcasts. The very first Air Commando combat loss, in February 1962, was a C-47 on a leaflet-dropping mission. More efficient methods for airborne loudspeaker broadcasts were developed so that 'programs broadcast from 3,000 feet high are clearly audible from the ground. Broadcasts are often pleas to the guerrillas in the jungle to surrender. It is an eerie thing to hear a C-47 droning high overhead, from which a monstrous celestial voice is enjoining the sinners to repent'.[69] However, the PSYOPS effort was only really stepped up in 1965 when it was decided that it would be coordinated centrally by the Joint United States Public Affairs Office (JUSPAO) in Saigon, which also handled relations with the media. Whereas JUSPAO was to get into a terrible muddle with media relations, at least the PSYOPS effort enjoyed the advantage of being at the right hand of the policy-makers in the field itself, and of having the support of the military commander, General Westmoreland.[70]

In 1966, the 5th Air Commando Squadron was formed to deal purely with psywar against a Vietnamese enemy whose own techniques in areas of counterinsurgency warfare were considered to be superior. 'Effectiveness can be judged by the fact that the VC [Viet Cong] shot at the psywar aircraft more than at any other, except those of Ranch Hand [the defoliant aircraft]. They also banged pots and pans together in hamlet streets to drown out the speakers, and cut off the hands of the villagers caught reading leaflets.'[71] The *Chieu Hoi* (Open Arms) amnesty campaign was deemed a success in terms of the numbers of Viet Cong soldiers who, using safe passes, defected to the South Vietnamese government.[72] In 1964 and 1965, Chinese and Vietnamese recruits flew on PSYOPS missions during 'Project Duck Hook, inserting and resupplying almost two dozen teams of agents behind enemy lines'.[73] One technique employed in this operation was to parachute blocks of ice containing animal blood into the jungle, whereupon they would melt and be discovered by forces of the North Vietnamese Army who would accordingly redeploy ground forces to find the non-existent downed pilots. This more accurately falls into the realm of deception operations, although innovative if somewhat bizarre PSYOPS techniques such as the dropping of ping-pong balls and bars of soap with messages implanted into them were tried. The general scepticism about risking the lives of aircrew on such missions remained, however, even after the launching of 'Project Combat Spear' and the use of PSYOPS in the highly secret MACV-SOG operation (Military Assistance Command, Vietnam – Studies and Observation Group) in 1967.[74] Aircrews also dropped thousands of small transistor radios, pre-tuned to the 50,000 watt station based at Pleiku, while the policy of Vietnamisation after 1968 also saw television sets deployed for the first time in public places, showing popular Hollywood entertainment films.[75]

In the war 'for the hearts and minds' of the Vietnamese people, US

PSYOPS was a combined civil–military effort, as it had been in the Second World War, which was an important recognition of the need to target not just troops. Despite the view of one JUSPAO chief in 1968 that 'it must be recognised that propaganda and psychological warfare are the primary weapons system of the era and that the function of military operations is, in essence, limited to supporting them',[76] PSYOPS was still seen as a support weapon for the military effort, not *vice versa*. This was perhaps a mistake, because the war proved militarily unwinnable. On the other hand, it was unlikely that psychological operations alone could have succeeded because, despite support for it at the highest levels, US policy over Vietnam was itself vague and confused. Moreover, as JUSPAO recognised: 'The North Vietnamese soldier in South Vietnam presents a particularly difficult target. . . . He has a relatively high state of indoctrination, reinforced by a range of psychological controls . . . the product of a closed, totalitarian society'.[77] For this reason, PSYOPS against the North Vietnamese Army was felt to have been largely unsuccessful, although the campaign against the Viet Cong saw more results – in all about 200,000 defectors between 1963 and 1974. Of these, 79 per cent claimed to have understood and believed some or all of American leaflets, and 87 per cent said they understood and believed the loudspeaker messages.

None the less, PSYOPS in Vietnam, like any other military activity associated with that war, was undervalued as a result of American defeat. In the words of one document, 'the end of the United States' involvement in the Vietnam War marked the beginning of a decade-long period of decline and atrophy of military psychological operations'.[78] On a strategic level, however, their use in the Cold War became if anything more important, although the 1970s saw the Soviets seize the initiative in this area. Indeed, the very theory of conventional deterrence itself can be seen as a classic PSYOPS exercise. From the Western perspective, it rested on credibility: of capability, intentions and readiness. To deter a Soviet attack, Moscow had to be sent the message that not only did the United States possess the capability of retaliating, but that it intended to do so if attacked, and that it was militarily and psychologically ready to do it. The nature of this message changed with changing circumstances – for example, in debates over first-strike capability and over massive retaliation versus graduated deterrence, but the essence of the message remained the same: that launching an attack on the West would result in consequences too great for it to be worthwhile. The Soviets countered with attempts to demonstrate US aggressiveness and scored a spectacular coup with branding the neutron bomb as a 'capitalist weapon', effectively preventing US President Carter from deploying enhanced radiation weapons in Europe. During the following decade, when efforts were made to employ Reagan's Strategic Defense Initiative to aid deterrence, it was said that 'the fact that the derogatory term "Star Wars" has been publicly attached to the SDI program has aided the Soviets considerably in their propaganda campaigns against it'.[79] One suspects, however, that 'Star Wars' did more for the American strategic propaganda effort against the Soviet leadership than perhaps anything else.

The year 1980 saw a dramatic change. With the Soviets becoming increasingly embroiled in their own version of Vietnam in Afghanistan, US President Ronald Reagan's determination to support non-Communist regimes around the world as part of his new Cold War against the 'evil empire' of the Soviet Union heralded the revival of PSYOPS. Perhaps not surprisingly for a man who had been weaned on the mass medium of the cinema, in 1981 'the Great Communicator' announced his national security strategy as being comprised of diplomatic, economic, military *and* informational components. Reagan made communications a top priority. In so far as PSYOPS was concerned, it needed considerable attention.

When US forces invaded Grenada in October 1993 in Operation Urgent Fury, PSYOPS was initially improvised, but once fighting got underway, loudspeaker teams from Fort Bragg attached to the 82nd Airborne Division worked hard to minimise civilian casualties by informing the island's populace of the 'benevolent' intentions of the 'liberating' forces. Because Grenada's only radio station was destroyed early in the operation, PSYOPS teams had to do this with outdated and cumbersome radio equipment, while leaflets mainly consisted of the time-honoured surrender pass and, for the first time since the Second World War, counterfeit enemy currency was reproduced to attract attention to other PSYOPS messages. The currency in question was that of Cuba, not Grenada, reflecting US concerns that it was the alien 'construction workers' who were more likely to prove troublesome than the indigenous islanders, who were the target of calming and reassuring PSYOPS when the fighting was over ('consolidation' PSYOPS). Having said all this, PSYOPS in the Grenada invasion was characterised more by improvisation than advanced planning, and its lowered post-Vietnam status was such that it was grouped together with Civil Affairs and Public Relations activities.

In early 1984 President Reagan ordered the US Department of Defense to rebuild its military PSYOPS capabilities, which resulted in the DoD PSYOPS Master Plan, approved by Secretary of State Casper Weinberger in 1985. It was this document which extended the brief of PSYOPS beyond merely war situations to embrace peacetime and crisis situations, in other words contingencies short of war. For the first time in two decades, a small PSYOPS directorate was established in the office of the Secretary of Defense, while military PSYOPS became a responsibility of Special Operations Forces rather than of Military Intelligence. In El Salvador, for example, after an initial reluctance to employ PSYOPS, a C-5 PSYOPS Directorate was established within the El Salvador Armed Forces (ESAF) in 1983 with the help of American advisors from Fort Bragg. By January 1985 it was conducting a nation-wide multimedia campaign, designed to increase civilian support for the government forces while undermining the credibility and effectiveness of the rebel guerrilla forces of the Faribundo Marti Front for National Liberation (FMLN). Increased numbers of FMLN defectors followed, and the campaign was stepped up when the ESAF established Radio Cuscatlan by mid-1986 to counter Radio Venceramos, the FMLN station, which, until then, had had the radio propaganda airwaves pretty much to itself. Nonetheless, PSYOPS was awaiting a discernible success for it to be fully recognised by policy-makers at all levels. In 1989, it found one in Panama.

For the first time since Vietnam, PSYOPS planning was integrated into the overall operational planning process from an early stage, and at the highest of levels. As a result, a PSYOPS Task Force was created and a twenty-man team was in place on the ground when the invasion took place. It was only too apparent that it would be needed if clarity of US intentions was to prevail not only in battle but also over the propaganda disseminated by General Noriega's regime. For example, the Panamanian government-controlled newspaper *Critica* contained such anti-American stories as one about African bees, angered by blatant US disregard for Panamanian sovereignty, attacking US troops, many of whom had been deployed solely because they carried the AIDS virus.[80] Because of the large numbers of American citizens in Panama, PSYOPS had also to embrace civilian as well as military personnel, and so the seizing and reactivation of Panama's TV-2 station by US Special Forces was critical. Before that was achieved, prepackaged broadcasts were transmitted into the area by flying television stations aboard converted C-130 aircraft called Volant Solos, operated by the 193rd Special Operations Group of the Pennsylvanian National Guard. It transpired that most Panamanians watched CNN for their news and information, and so this type of targeted military information was essential given that the media was being carefully husbanded under the new Pentagon Pool System – which effectively meant CNN and its colleagues were being kept well and truly away from the fighting. But this was a foretaste of problems to come. Meanwhile, three days after the invasion, the full PSYOPS Task Force arrived and loudspeaker teams accompanied all ground forces, stressing the legitimacy of US actions, countering rumours and anti-American propaganda, and maintaining that the US had no quarrel with the people of Panama but only with the corrupt Noriega regime and its paramilitary forces. A 10 kilowatt radio station, 1760, was established to spread these themes, although, because many Panamanian commanders had actually been trained by the Americans, PSYOPS teams discovered the value of telephoning known adversaries personally to persuade them to surrender, which became known as the 'Ma Bell' technique. In fact, 'cease hostilities' was a preferred message to 'surrender or die', while money-for-arms incentives were the subject of leaflet, poster and broadcast campaigns. Indeed, particular attention was paid to local cultural sensitivities, especially in the

PSYOPS-produced news-sheet *Perspectivas*, although the outside world saw only barbaric cultural imperialism when US forces played loud rock music into the compound where the opera-loving Noriega took his last stand before capture. Once that had been achieved, PSYOPS became an integral part of Operation Promote Liberty, designed to promote the fledgling democracy established in Panama.[81] Having imposed this by force, persuasion took over.

PSYOPS REBORN: DESERT STORM

The Gulf War of 1991 proved to be the major watershed in the revival of PSYOPS. Planning began almost as soon as the invasion of Kuwait had taken place in August 1990. The PSYOPS plan in theatre was code-named BURNING HAWK, and, after considerable bureaucratic wrangling, it was finally approved a month before the outbreak of the war, with the intention of creating 'a synergy of information and military action to amplify the effectiveness of coalition units, while degrading that of Iraqi forces'.[82] In terms of cost-effectiveness, almost $16 million was spent to help the capture of 87,000 Iraqi soldiers and to persuade another 160,000 to desert. In other words, for a mere 0.03 per cent of the $60 billion cost of the war to the coalition, 44 per cent of the Iraqi army was persuaded to discontinue fighting.[83] 'Among the final results . . . was the institutionalisation of a methodological process for planning and implementing PSYOPS.'[84]

On 20 December 1990 General Schwarzkopf warned that PSYOPS was 'going to be absolutely a critical, *critical* part of any campaign that we must get involved in'.[85] There were to be three phases. The first was to project US resolve, consolidate support, dissuade Iraqi regional support and promote inter-coalition solidarity. Phase two would reinforce coalition defensive efforts and persuade Iraq troops to stop fighting. The third phase was to support offensive operations and promote local, regional and international understanding and support. Included in the first two phases was the production of a videotape, 'Nations of the World Take a Stand', which was distributed in four languages throughout the Middle East and Southwest Asia under the auspices of the USIA. Two hundred copies of this were even disseminated in Baghdad.[86] This was strategic PSYOPS – and it was an operation in which it was explicitly stated that the liberation of Kuwait would be effected' by the US Marines from the sea. But the main effort was at the operational level. After several weeks of war in January and early February 1991, the coalition began to step up its carpet bombing of enemy troop positions in Kuwait and southern Iraq as part of its preparations to 'soften up' the opposition before the actual ground war began. This was the war that was kept hidden from the media – by both the Iraqis and the coalition. None the less, Iraqi conscripts were considered to be a prime target for an additional supporting psychological campaign which might just save their lives – and, of course, thereby reduce American casualties. The need essentially was to convince them of how they were being used as cannon-fodder by Saddam Hussein, to demonstrate that further fighting was futile, and to show them how to surrender safely. As the post-war interim report on the conduct of the war to Congress indicated: 'the PSYOP effort was focused on breaking the Iraqi will to resist, and on increasing the fears of the Iraqi soldiers, while pointing out that the Coalition was opposed not to the Iraqi people, but only to Iraq's national policy'.[87]

In the Gulf War, it was the Americans who were best equipped to conduct this work on behalf of the coalition. It was only as recently as March 1990 that the American Department of Defense had updated its 1985 Psychological Operations Master Plan, and the detailed revisions to the 1987 field manual in light of the Panamanian experience were still under way. The DoD Master Plan indicates how much emphasis successive Republican administrations had placed upon revitalising psychological operations as a 'military force multiplier' during the final stages of the Cold War. Each of the military Services developed its own doctrine for conducting psychological operations (and these doctrines remain secret), but all were influenced by NATO's Joint PSYOPS doctrine (which has been published). By the time Iraq invaded Kuwait, therefore, the United States was unique amongst coalition countries in having both the philosophy and the resources to employ these 'munitions of the mind'. The 8th Psychological Operations Task Force began to prepare itself from September 1990 and eventually embraced more that 650 personnel, including sixty-six PSYOPS loudspeaker teams (mainly from the 9th PSYOPS Battalion, whose motto is 'Win the Mind – Win the Day') who provided tactical support for every ground unit throughout the land war at the end of February 1991.[88]

On 21 January, the *Daily Telegraph* reported that, according to the CIA and other agencies conducting psychological warfare operations against the Iraqis, morale among the Iraqi troops could be a deciding factor in the length of the anticipated ground war. US Senator Sam Nunn, chairman of the Senate's Armed Services Committee, was quoted as saying: 'I certainly think it's possible there could be a psychological breakdown there and if that happens, it could go very rapidly'. Apparently President Bush had issued three secret directives between August and December outlining the PSYOPS campaign incorporating increasingly organised Kuwaiti resistance groups inside the occupied country with a combined use of strategic 'black' (possibly CIA) and operational/tactical 'white' (Central Command) radio stations and leaflet propaganda.[89] As part of the preparations for this, thousands of transistor radios, along with audio tapes (and even video tapes), had been smuggled into Kuwait and Southern Iraq via Jordan with the help of nomads so that the enemy could listen to coalition broadcasts.[90]

There were to be three principal methods of dissemination: radio, leaflets and loudspeakers. The 8th Psychological Operations Task Force was located at CENTCOM in Riyadh, while the Psychological Dissemination Battalion, the 6th and 9th Tactical PSYOPS Battalions, and loudspeaker teams from the 18th, 19th, 244th and 362nd Reserve Tactical PSYOPS companies, were stationed near Dharhan's King Fahd International Airport. There, they had at their disposal C-130 aircraft for disseminating leaflets as well as two EC-130 Volant Solo aircraft.[91]

On the strategic level, one of the coalition's problems was that the government of Bahrain refused to allow American broadcasts in Arabic from the Voice of America's medium-wave transmitter in that country. Short-wave transmissions in Arabic, with their far greater range, were doubled to about fifteen hours a day when the war began, but receivers were too expensive and too few and far between in Iraq. If the coalition wished to address the medium-wave receivers possessed by the majority of Iraqi civilians, they would need access to the Bahrain transmitter. The obstacle was that the Bahrain government believed the Voice of America's Arabic service was too *friendly* to Saddam, with its information minister revealing to Bruce Gelb, United States Information Agency director (in charge of VOA), on 28 January that he was unwilling 'to take the risk of allowing others to talk on your behalf in a language you cannot monitor or understand'.[92] This was felt to be a reference to Middle Eastern journalists working for the VOA whose loyalties were considered dubious and whose credibility was suspect. It was therefore left to the BBC's World Service, broadcasting in Arabic from its medium-wave transmitter on the island of Cyprus, to bear the brunt of the coalition's 'white', or overt and information-based, broadcasts. 'Black' propaganda broadcasts, on the other hand, which gave the appearance of coming from somewhere else, appeared to be emanating from disaffected groups inside Iraq and Kuwait when in fact they were coming from transmitters within areas controlled by the coalition.

Black psychological warfare radio stations, presumably transmitting from somewhere in Saudi Arabia, such as the allegedly CIA-run Voice of Free Iraq and various Kurdish and possibly even Iranian stations, called upon the Kurdish and Shi'a Iraqis to rise up against the 'Saddam Hussein gang'.[93] Coalition black propaganda cleverly blamed Saddam for bringing the forces of the 'Great Satan' into the area, and insisted he must be punished for this.[94] The official coalition line was that this was a war to liberate Kuwait and not to overthrow Saddam Hussein. Allied leaders stated repeatedly that the coalition was not fighting the Iraqi people, which meant that, officially at least, the coalition would not be able to utilise demonisation propaganda against the enemy population as a whole. Instead, the coalition chose to separate out the Ba'athist Party and its 'storm-troopers', the Republican Guard. These were ones who were holding the Iraqi people back from peace and prosperity. And these were the ones who must be overthrown – not by the coalition, but by the Iraqi people themselves.

The Voice of Free Iraq (*Sawt Al-Iraq Al-Hurr*) started broadcasting from a clandestine location on 1 January, although test transmissions had been picked up by the BBC Monitoring Service at Caversham since 21 December 1990. Claiming that its facilities had been donated by the Syrians, Egyptians, Saudis and other members of the Gulf Cooperation Council, the station was unashamedly anti-Saddam. From 26 January, the station identified itself as the 'Radio of the Iraqi Republic *from Baghdad*, the Voice of Free Iraq', the first part of this identification being identical to that of the official Iraqi national radio service.[95] Yet it remained unclear as to who precisely was running this operation.[96] On 30 January, it broadcast the following statement:

> After all this destruction you are seeing around you, Iraqi brother, you must be wondering: what did we gain, what did we reap in the Saddam Hussein era? . . . And was it good for Iraq? Who is going to rebuild Iraq which was rich with its resources and great with its wealth, after all this destruction you are seeing around you. . . . As soon as he finishes a war, he takes us into another war, and as soon as he finishes with a problem, he creates another problem for our country, and as soon as he finishes a massacre, he initiates another massacre.[97]

The message was clear: the Iraqi people should rise up against Saddam Hussein so that the country could return to the peace-loving community of nations.

Nor was such an appeal confined to the civilian population. On 31 January the Voice of Free Iraq broadcast an appeal by the 'National Committee for the Salvation of Iraq' to the troops in the field:

> Our heroic army! Oh sons of our brave armed forces! The tyrant has issued the order for the destruction of Iraq and its brave army, and has escalated his threats. By bragging about his missile capability, air defences and aircraft, our army has now become exposed not just in Kuwait but also in Iraq, and is being subjected to air bombardment which, God forbid, may lead to a great catastrophe liable to blow away Iraq, its people and army. . . . Onwards to revolution, Oh fearless soldiers, and on to rebellion, Oh heroic officers. Aim your rifles at the tyrant's heart and at the heads of his filthy myrmidons. Hasten to the salvation of Iraq.[98]

On other occasions, opposition groups (fictional?) transmitted messages in tones similar to those heard on Iranian broadcasts made by Sh'ite clerics in support of fundamentalist viewpoints. A spokesman for the 'Islamic Call Party', for example, maintained:

> It has transpired that, behind this aggression, America is aiming at destroying Iraq for the benefit of Israel. If the declared objective of America is the liberation of Kuwait, then why all this destruction of

173

Iraq we are witnessing? Is this meant for Israeli security through the breaking of the Iraqi military machine? We say to the Iraqi people that American law does not permit the planning for the assassination of a foreign head of state, but this law permits the destruction of a people and removing of a country like Iraq from the political map. This would seem strange to wise minds.[99]

The PSYOPS radio network organised by the 4th Psychological Operations Group (Airborne) – 4POG(A) – revolved around the clandestine Voice of the Gulf (*Sawt Al-Khalij*), which began transmissions in late November 1990 on both medium wave and FM, occupying some of same frequencies as those used formerly by Kuwaiti radio (now the Iraqis' Mother of All Battles station).[100] Purporting to be a purely Arab station, broadcasts from two transmitters in Saudi Arabia, at Abu Ali and Qaysumah, were supplemented by the Volant Solo aircraft protected by AWACs and fighter escorts for eighteen hours a day, and for forty days of the war. This was military-to-military communication, often intruding into the frequencies used by Iraqi units – although this is frequently denied, especially when civil wavelengths are involved. 'The emphasis here was to attract an enemy audience through the accuracy of the program's news items concerning the Gulf conflict.'[101] Interspersed with readings from the Koran and patriotic music were direct appeals to the troops to surrender, such as the following:

> Why don't you save your life and that of your colleagues by coming to the Kingdom of Saudi Arabia, as the war is going to finish soon and then you will be able to return to your homeland and your family? And when you come, dear Iraqi soldier, it will be at the invitation of the command of the joint forces and operations theatre. You will be a guest of this command . . . while enjoying the usual Arab generosity, security, safety and medical care.[102]

This was all a fairly one-way process at the time war started. Following the invasion of Kuwait, the Iraqis had set up various strategic (and therefore short-wave) stations, such as the Voice of the Peninsula and the Arabian Gulf (first heard 29 August 1990), the Voice of the Egypt of Arabism (first heard 11 August) and the Voice of Arab Awakening (first heard 13 October), to address the Arab-speaking world, including members of the coalition military. Holy Mecca Radio, a black Iraqi station targeted at Arab anti-Saudi listeners, was not heard after 18 January, the transmitter presumably having been knocked out by allied air strikes. The Iraqi Voice of Peace station (first heard 11 September) which directed its energies at English-speaking coalition military personnel and whose broadcaster, 'Baghdad Betty', had accused the cartoon character Bart Simpson of sleeping with the wives of American troops prior to the war, was not heard after 20 January – to the lament, no doubt, of many troops.[103] The Mother of All Battles station, which began transmitting in Arabic for domestic Iraqi audiences from 25 January and was joined two days late by the main domestic radio station, The Voice of the Masses would also appear to have been knocked out by 5 February. Because these stations had all used powerful short-wave frequencies, their appeal was clearly to the wider Arab world. It was the Mother of All Battles station, for example, which gave full play to Saddam's pronouncement that every Iraqi, Arab or Moslem who engaged in terrorist activities against coalition interests would be considered a martyr,[104] and which boasted of its triumphs in the holy war against the infidel. The Iraqis even managed to disseminate twelve leaflets of their own, all of which were badly conceived and grammatically incorrect.[105] The degradation of Iraq's capacity to spread propaganda both inside Iraq and beyond by means other than via Western journalists would appear to suggest that the coalition considered this a significant part of their overall bombing campaign. One can only speculate as to the feelings of the planners concerning reporters in Baghdad who were undermining this effort, especially since reports from Iraq provided faces to the enemy people and bombing victims which coalition propagandists would sooner have remained anonymous.

A further problem for the allies was how to supply the Iraqi people with alternative sources of reliable (i.e. coalition) information about what was going on. Accordingly, the Voice of America began transmitting in Arabic on the same frequency as Radio Baghdad, which became harder to pick up as the allies extended their bombing; by mid-February only one transmitter was operational on the short wave, and jamming (about three times more expensive than broadcasting) made this even more difficult to receive.[106]

PSYOPS had also entered the computer age. For the first time, electronic publishing systems were used to create and transmit propaganda material, especially into occupied Kuwait where the Iraqis had failed to detect fax machines being used by the resistance movement. 4POG used its PAT (PSYOP Analyst Terminal), an Intel-chipped PC with image scanner and colour laser printer, to produce leaflets from a single location for any target within the theatre of operations. Whereas in the past, the production of leaflets had taken days, even weeks, now it could be done in hours – a matter of considerable significance in any propaganda campaign where timing is essential to the effectiveness of the message.

The main focus of the coalition's psychological warfare activities was, however, designed to encourage Iraqi troops to defect, desert or surrender. Before the war, 4POG(A) had experimented with leaflets scattered by balloon along the Kuwait–Saudi border.[107] After the war, it also emerged ·that experiments had been made before the deadline of 15 January with 'The Wave', in which leaflets were placed inside 12,000 bottles and dumped into the Persian Gulf by a smuggler from the United Arab Emirates in the hope that they would be washed ashore in Kuwait. But once the war started, most of the leaflets were to be disseminated by aircraft or by leaflet artillery rounds. The M129 leaflet bomb, for example, is capable of delivering between 54,000 and 60,000 packaged leaflets to a target area and can be dropped by F-16 or C-130 aircraft, whereas up to 2,000 leaflets can be packed inside a special 155mm artillery shell. In spite of all the high-tech kit, however, the soldiers who painstakingly have to load the leaflets by hand into their containers await the technological breakthrough which will ease their lot.

The most common form of leaflet was the 'invitation card', illustrated with cartoons and designed 'to play on the feeling of Arab brotherhood that we hope will survive this conflict'.[108] Another highly effective method was to drop leaflets by aircraft prior to a B-52 air strike, announcing precisely when the raid would take place, and then again after the bombing saying 'We kept our promise'. Others depicted Saddam riding a bedraggled barefoot soldier like a horse, or anxious Iraqi parents worrying about the safety of their sons.[109] Yet others carried messages such as: 'Desert Storm is coming to your area. Flee immediately'; 'The 16th Infantry Division will be bombed tomorrow. Leave this location now and save yourselves'; and 'Leave your equipment or defend it and die! The choice is yours!' On the reverse of many leaflets were the following instructions:

CEASE RESISTANCE – BE SAFE

To seek refuge safely, the bearer must strictly adhere to the following procedures:

1 Remove the magazine from your weapon.
2 Sling your weapon over your left shoulder, muzzle down.
3 Have both arms raised above your head.
4 Approach the Multinational Forces' positions slowly, with the lead soldier holding this document above his head.
5 If you do this, you will not die.[110]

Reports suggested that, by the start of February, five million leaflets had been dropped giving details of how to surrender.[111] By the end of the war, a total of something like 29 million leaflets would be dropped over Iraqi lines, an astonishing figure which meant nearly two for every member of the Iraqi population or about 50–60 for every enemy soldier within the theatre of operations.[112]

Only days after war's outbreak, the coalition air forces began to concentrate on pounding the Republican Guard positions in Southern Iraq and Northern Kuwait. It was here that B-52 bombers, some of which would soon be flying from Fairford air base in Britain, concentrated the indiscriminate 'carpet bombing' of the well dug-in, heavily protected and privileged 'elite' units. Similarly, thanks to rapid achievement of air supremacy, allied planes were targeting frontline Iraqi conscripts. Poor weather often hampered the ability of precision-guided munitions and aircraft to hit strategic targets inside Iraq, and so combat missions were frequently diverted to attacking positions inside Kuwait, 'so there was no time, from day one on, that the Iraqi ground forces were not under heavy air attack'.[113] As General Schwarzkopf had insisted: 'I can assure you that when and if we have to fight a ground war, I'm not going to fight his [Saddam's] war. He's going to fight our war.'[114]

PSYOPS was to play an integral part of that bombardment. On 6 February, leaflets were dropped stating 'Flee and Live or Stay and Die'. The next day, a BLU-82 bomb was dropped on the target area. At 15,000 pounds, this weapon (also known as a 'Daisy Cutter' or a 'poor man's nuke') is the size of a Volkswagen Beetle car, and its massive explosion resembles the detonation of an atomic bomb. Subsequently, more intimidation leaflets were dropped, stating: 'You have just experienced the most powerful conventional bomb dropped in the war. It has more explosive power than 20 Scud missiles. You will be bombed again soon. Kuwait will be free from aggression. Flee south and you will be treated fairly. You cannot hide.' Eleven such weapons – 'the mother of all bombs, for the mother of all wars' – were dropped in all.[115] A major success of this characteristic example of psychological warfare operation was the defection of an Iraqi commander and his staff, who raced across the border to surrender before a second 'Daisy Cutter' could be dropped on their position. One of them brought with him the maps of the Iraqi minefields along his section of the Saddam Line – an invaluable intelligence coup that was greatly to help coalition troops once the ground war started.[116]

In the weeks that followed, almost three-quarters of the defectors crossing the Saudi border stated that their decision to give themselves up had been influenced by allied leaflets and broadcasts. Post-testing of prisoners of war found that 98 per cent of the test group had been exposed to allied leaflets, that 80 per cent said they believed the message, and 70 per cent said they were influenced by leaflets to defect or surrender. As for radio,

58 per cent said they had heard the PSYOPS broadcasts (even though radios were banned in Iraqi combat units), 46 per cent said they believed what they heard, and 34 per cent were induced to surrender by them. As for the use of loudspeakers, 34 per cent said they were exposed to them, 18 per cent believed the message and 16 per cent attributed their decision to surrender to them.[117] But the actual bombing itself must have played the major role in their decision; prior to the war, there was nothing like the same number of desertions, even though the PSYOPS campaign had hardly got under way. In all, it was officially estimated that PSYOPS messages 'persuaded approximately 44 per cent of the Iraqi army to desert, more than 17,000 to defect and more than 87,000 to surrender'.[118] Even accounting for exaggeration, these are remarkable figures by any standards.

The absence of any real aerial resistance on the part of the Iraqis none the less still fostered the illusion in some quarters that a ground war might be averted. Although Iraq's nuclear capacity was said to have been destroyed at the outset of the air war, and much of its chemical and biological manufacturing capability undermined, there was still a fear that Iraqi troops in the field possessed chemical weapons. As this anxiety increased, coupled with a growing media impatience about the lack of information coming out of Riyadh and Washington, on Wednesday 23 January General Colin Powell made a timely declaration that coalition strategy was to 'cut off and kill' the Iraqi army. In the most forthcoming briefing of the war up to that point, Powell and US Secretary of Defense Cheney reiterated General Schwarzkopf's point about fighting the war on their own terms, declaring that the aerial bombardment would go on: 'time is on our side', said the Defense Secretary.[119] The major questions, therefore, were 'when?' and 'where?'

As for the latter, it should have come as no surprise – to the Iraqis least of all – that the attack eventually took place where it did. A careful examination of the informed Western media would have provided ample clues. As early as 27 January, for example, the *Independent*'s correspondent Phil Davidson travelled across the 300-mile allied front, and his observations left him in no doubt that 'in the battle to free Kuwait, US armour and infantry will thrust forward across southern Iraq'. While Baghdad may or may not have been reading the *Independent*, a similar strategy had been outlined more than once by military strategists interviewed on CNN, which was certainly avidly watched there. That the location of the attack still came as a surprise, therefore, was a tribute to the overall military deception operation, designed to convince the Iraqis that the liberation of Kuwait would take place from the sea rather than by a land attack swinging west.

As for the question of 'when?', on Sunday 28 January, Dick Cheney elaborated on his position in a televised interview. He said that the United States had 'always assumed' it would need a land war to expel Iraqi troops from Kuwait 'but we don't want to do it any earlier than we have to', by which he meant 'after we've done enormous damage to his ground forces – after they've been significantly weakened'.[120] Apart from the carpet bombing of the Iraqi entrenchments in Kuwait and southern Iraq, this was to be achieved by cutting supply lines and, as the war approached the end of its second week, the coalition turned its attention to attacking bridges and supply columns. On Monday 28 January, allied war planes were reported to have caught an Iraqi military convoy moving across the open desert in Kuwait, destroying twenty-four tanks, armoured personnel carriers and supply vehicles – in fact the largest known single success against Iraqi armour since the start of the war.[121] It was also at about this time that pool reporters noted that something had changed in the field:

> the usually hypersensitive US censors have permitted information to be released about the unpreparedness of sections of the American force, leading to the suspicion that a full scale disinformation may now be under way to try to fool Saddam about the date of any attack.[122]

Perhaps the most controversial aspect of the PSYOPS campaign in Desert Storm was the degree to which its messages encouraged the civilian population in Iraq to rise up in an attempt to overthrow Saddam Hussein. All along, coalition themes had insisted that this was a war against Saddam and not against the Iraqi people. But undoubtedly the impression was given to people in cities like Basra that if there was an uprising to overthrow the Iraqi leadership, the coalition would help. Used for the first time since the First World War, this ploy again produced disastrous consequences. When the Kurds to the north and the Shi'as to the south did revolt, coalition support was not forthcoming (except in the form of humanitarian aid to the Kurds). The sense of justifiable betrayal amongst these peoples, especially when Saddam's forces began ruthlessly to suppress the insurrectionists, was once again a lesson that propaganda must not get out of step with policy. Because US policy had never openly declared that the intention of the war was anything other than 'the liberation of Kuwait', the degree to which US PSYOPS forces on the ground subordinated strategic aims to tactical expedients was the greatest black mark on the overall campaign. It added force to the reservations of many air force officers, who regarded leaflet drops as 'bullshit bombs'.

MILITARY OPERATIONS OTHER THAN WAR IN THE NINETIES

Towards the end of the Gulf War, the Kurdish population staged an unsuccessful revolt against the Iraqi regime and, when the revolt was crushed, they were forced to flee to the mountainous northern sectors of the country close to the border with Turkey. Following widespread media attention to the plight of the Kurdish rebels, on 5 April 1991 President Bush directed that the United States mount a massive humanitarian relief effort which was to later become a multinational effort, Operation Provide Comfort. Black PSYOPS had encouraged the revolt; now white PSYOPS was deployed to persuade Iraqi forces not to interfere with the efforts of the non-governmental organisations conducting humanitarian operations and, later, to do likewise with PKK (the Kurdish workers' party) forces. Pallets of food were air-dropped to the refugees with instructions on how to prepare the ready-to-eat meals, 'a gift from the United States. . . . Remember, in the name of Allah, remain orderly and fair while food is being distributed.'[123] Other leaflets explained how the operation was 'in accordance with UN Resolution 688, and because it is right in the eyes of Allah', and that the operation's soldiers were 'armed for self-protection only. They are not armed for offensive purposes or in support of any armed faction in the region.' In the organisation of the refugees into camps, details were issued about why guns were forbidden, rules were set relating to life and behaviour in the temporary communities, and instructions given about health and sanitary arrangements, about staying off convoy routes and about how to avoid mines. Finally, in the process of returning refugees from Turkey, safe conduct passes were printed which stated:

> Please allow the bearer of this pass safe passage. They have been shel-tering in Turkey, and are returning home with the assistance of international forces. This person is not a collaborator. This person is an innocent civilian caught in circumstances beyond their control.[124]

In all, over five million PSYOPS products were distributed throughout the operation and, in the opinion of John Shalikashvili, Chairman of the Joint Chiefs of Staff, 'much of the success achieved during Operation Provide Comfort can be attributed to the successful integration of psychological operations in support of the overall humanitarian assistance mission'.[125]

The American intervention in Somalia from 9 December 1992 provides another revealing example, both of the value of PSYOPS in support of peacetime humanitarian missions and of the dangers which occur once that support is withdrawn. It also provides, as we have seen, an example of the limitations of PSYOPS when operating alongside unfettered freelance news journalism, which in the end turned out to have a greater ability to influence policy beyond the theatre of operations itself. Somalia also provided numerous bizarre examples of news journalism in the New World Information Disorder. Few people who saw them will forget the television pictures of US Marines coming ashore at Mogadishu beneath the blaze of flashguns and camera lights deployed by representatives of global news organisations waiting for them on the beaches. Certainly few Americans will forget the images of a dead US soldier being dragged through a Somali warlord's camp several months later, images which prompted the withdrawal of US troops. In between, however, a much lower-profile information campaign was conducted in the country by a Joint PSYOPS Task Force consisting of 125 members of the 4th PSYOP Group (Airborne) from Fort Bragg and several of its subordinate battalions.

Fresh from the success of Desert Storm, these US PSYOPS forces were an integral part of the planning for the humanitarian intervention of American forces under the umbrella of the United Nations Task Force (UNITAF) – 'a coalition of the willing', as President Bush termed it, eventually comprising twenty-two nations. The PSYOPS Task Force worked directly for the UNITAF commander, Lieutenant General Robert Johnston, who was 'extremely interested in having PSYOP up front for this operation, because I thought the most useful part of PSYOP would be that it would prevent armed conflict'.[126]

The first PSYOPS soldiers flew from Fort Bragg to Mombassa where they joined the US 15th Marine Expeditionary Unit aboard the USS *Tripoli*. At the outset of the operation, a Marine CH-53 Sea Stallion helicopter dropped 220,000 leaflets explaining that the arriving US forces were part of a UN international humanitarian relief effort, but the extent to which this aided a peaceful landing remains unknown. Because of the complete social and bureaucratic breakdown of Somali society, PSYOPS teams thereafter did find that they were the only means of providing any form of communications between the UN forces, the organisations implementing the humanitarian mission, and the Somali people themselves. Their stated objectives were to reduce the number of casualties, prevent local factional interference with relief operations, assure the local population of impartiality, and stress the desire not to intervene in internal politics and crowd control. Language was a serious problem at first, but a sole Somali-speaking US Navy sailor was found and he was teamed up with a dozen Somali civilian linguists from America to produce the initial output before local inhabitants were recruited into the PSYOPS Product Development Centre.[127] Once this team got going, 7.2 million pictorial-based versions of thirty-four different leaflets were produced and disseminated to twenty-six target areas in ninety missions. Essentially, there were two types of leaflet: the 'handshake leaflet' depicting an American soldier shaking hands with a native Somali; and the 'convoy security leaflet' which stressed that, if necessary, force would be used to protect the convoys. Post-testing of the former demonstrated considerable effectiveness. On the reverse ran the words:

United Nations forces are here to assist in the international relief effort for the Somali people. We are prepared to use force to protect the relief operation and our soldiers. We will not allow interference with food distributions in our activities. We are here to help you.[128]

The first type of message would be dropped a few days prior to the arrival of UNITAF forces in each town, followed by the second type instructing the locals not to block roadways carrying relief convoys. In addition, eight loudspeaker teams travelled the country with tapes pre-recorded by native linguists, supplemented by helicopter-mounted loudspeaker systems. As one observer commented: 'it took enormous effort to enter a foreign country, portray the US military in a positive light, translate the message into the local language, and distribute that message via print, loudspeaker teams and radio broadcasts'.[129] A daily newspaper, *Rajo* (Hope), produced from 20 December 1992 onwards with an average daily circulation of 28,000, was distributed in each humanitarian relief sector. In all, 116 issues were produced, a total of 2.1 million copies distributed to twelve cities and towns. A cartoon in *Rajo* featured a Somali named Celmi (after the Somali-born US sailor) and his 'wise friend', the camel Mandeeq, whose conversations with each other reinforced the UNITAF themes of impartiality and fairness in doing all that could be done to aid the process of resolution between the warring factions. US Ambassador Robert Oakley stated that 'we are using Rajo to get the correct information into the hands of the Somali population and to correct distortions. . . . The faction leaders, I know, read it very, very carefully. Every once in a while, Aideed or Ali Mahdi . . . draws my attention to something that appeared in the newspaper. So they're very, very sensitive to it and they know its power.'[130]

To counter hostile radio propaganda by the warlords – such as accusations that the foreign powers were present to exploit Somali natural resources in a new wave of imperialism – 'Radio Rajo', broadcasting from the US Embassy compound, went on air twice daily from 20 December onwards on AM and medium-wave frequencies to serve as the voice of UNITAF. Short-wave transmissions were added from 6 January 1993. A month later, however, the Italian task force set up Radio Ibis FM in Mogadishu – complete with its logo of a singing banana over a map of Somalia and its theme music from the 'Indiana Jones' films – to cheer up the Italian troops by playing pop and Pavarotti interspersed with health tips and news. Because of Italy's colonial legacy in Somalia, it quickly built up an audience amongst the Somali people; rival warlords even wrote in praise of the station. The American PSYOPS people were annoyed at first, not least because Ibis contrasted with the earnest tone of Rajo with its readings from the Koran, American army communiqués and traditional Somali folk music. One Italian officer was quoted as saying that 'at first the Americans ordered us to switch off Radio Ibis, stating, correctly, that propaganda was within their domain. But we've reached a compromise. Every day they bring a 45-minute cassette with their communiqués and folk songs, and we broadcast it.' And, added the commentator, 'every day, for 45 minutes, the Somali audience plummets – only to rise again as soon as Indiana Jones introduces Pavarotti in concert'.[131] An important lesson was thus learned, namely that, to sustain an audience, PSYOPS must not only be credible but entertaining. Sustaining an audience forms part of what is termed facilitative communications, the maintenance of an audience by messages which are not in themselves designed to generate specific responses but which keep open the very channels of communication for when such messages are required.

PSYOPS support for specific elements of the operation also proved effective. When, in December 1992 and again in March 1993, UNITAF decided to clear the streets of Mogadishu of abandoned and destroyed vehicles to improve road contact with market areas, leaflets, handbills and posters were printed to explain what the engineers were doing and why. A 'pastoral scene' leaflet was used to encourage displaced persons and refugees to return to their homes in support of NGO resettlement programmes and 'to help break the cycle of dependency and to encourage self-sufficiency'.[132] Mine-awareness products, from leaflets to colouring books for children, were also produced with the message: 'report, don't touch'. In the view of Marine Lt. Gen. Robert B. Johnston, the UNITAF commander, 'PSYOP really worked well to convince . . . [Somalis] that we were there with the military capability to take care of the factions, and that we were going to provide support and safety.'[133]

Such official sources inevitably paint a rosy picture. The problems really came when the American mission appeared to move from friendly persuasion to aggressive action, when humanitarian assistance appeared to be transformed into political–military intervention following the disastrous decision to arrest General Aideed, turning the entire operation into a man-hunt. This time it was the policy which dictated the failure of the propaganda. Moreover, when the United Nations Operation in Somalia (UNOSOM II) assumed command from UNITAF on 4 May 1993, it decided to reduce the number of PSYOPS personnel in UNITAF from over a hundred to just five, reflecting UN distrust of PSYOPS.

Likewise, in Rwanda, there was no concerted use of information warfare to influence the situation in a positive manner. Here, the major enemies were clearly starvation and anarchy, but another enemy was Radio Mille Collines, a Hutu-operated radio station which was brutal in its incitement to genocide. The only attempt to counter its broadcasts was made by the French unofficial organisation, *Reporters Sans Frontières*. One can only speculate how many lives might have been saved if the UN had established its own radio station in the area.

It was the view of Lieutenant General Henry Shelton, commander of the Joint Task Force 180 which went into Haiti in 1994, that the integration of PSYOPS early in the overall planning for Operation Uphold Democracy 'was critical to the successful execution of the operation':

Long before any American military forces stepped ashore, PSYOP helped us quickly accomplish our political and military objectives by laying the foundation for transition from forced entry to semi-permissive operations. Without a doubt, PSYOP won the hearts and minds of Haiti's citizens, as well as setting the stage for the peaceful accomplishment of the Joint Task Force's mission. There is no question that PSYOP saved lives, on both sides. . . . It proved to be the unsung, yet vitally important, factor in this operation – a true force multiplier.[134]

The Haitian crisis began nine months after President Jean-Baptiste Aristide's election with two-thirds of the vote in December 1991, when a military coup headed by General Raoul Cedras seized power and forced Aristide into exile. There followed political repression and the execution of Aristide supporters, forcing many of those who had voted for the President to fear for their lives and flee. Many fled by boat in an attempt to reach the United States. Between November 1991 and July 1992, psychological operations officers were despatched to provide information as a calming factor to almost 35,000 Haitian boat people intercepted by the US Coast Guard at migrant camps established at Guantanamo Naval Base in Cuba. Interrogations attempted to ascertain whether they were political or economic refugees; health checks revealed a high number to be HIV positive.

Some pro-Aristide leaflets had been dropped over Haiti in October 1992 but the issue, which was receiving massive media attention in the United States, became embroiled in the Presidential election which saw Bill Clinton replace George Bush in November 1992. Because (then) Governor Clinton had criticised as inhumane President Bush's executive order to repatriate the Haitian boat people, a renewed exodus was expected after the election until the President-elect announced he would continue his predecessor's repatriation policy in January 1993. The following months saw attempts to find a political settlement, UN sanctions against Haiti, PSYOPS plans being drawn up, until finally, in May 1994, General Cedras was installed as provisional president of Haiti.

The psychological preparation of the area began the following month, following a renewed flow of Haitian refugees trying to reach Florida in flotillas of ramshackle boats. On 18 June, A 4POG Military Information Support Team (MIST) was despatched to Washington to coordinate its work with State and Defense Department officials, together with people from the National Security Council and the CIA.

> The goal of the MIST was to create an information environment in support of US objectives to restore democracy to Haiti, to allow President Aristide to present a message of reconciliation to his constituents, and to outline plans for his return to power. This information campaign was of particular importance because of the steady diet of disinformation and misinformation provided by the Haitian military regime to their people.[135]

When, in July, the UN Security Council passed an American-sponsored resolution calling for the formation of a multinational force to use 'all necessary means' to restore Haiti's elected but exiled government under President Jean-Baptiste Aristide, the green light for the PSYOPS campaign was given. Messages developed by the Washington group and coordinated with the Haitian government-in-exile were sent via commercial and secure telephone lines to 4POG teams at Key West and at Roosevelt Roads Naval Air Stations, in Florida and Puerto Rico respectively, where they were digitally converted into audio tapes. These were then passed to the crew of one of two EC-130 Commando Solo (the upgraded Volant Solo) aircraft from the 193rd Special Operations Group, each of which began flying in 12-hour missions over Haitian air space from 15 July onwards, transmitting the radio messages on FM in Creole (the language mainly spoken by the poorer sections of the population) interspersed with popular music, news and panel discussions. The call sign of this service was Radio Democracy. 'The day of return is not far', declared Aristide in his very first transmitted speech. 'Will there be vengeance? Will there be any violence? No.'[136] Because of initial reports that few local people could hear the broadcasts, 10,000 multi-frequency radio sets were air-dropped in Haiti for distribution among the target audience. When Cedras's spokesmen claimed that the broadcasts were having no impact at all but complained of unauthorised flights over Haitian air space, the Americans knew that reception was increasing. The message of the additional Radio AM 940 was that Haitian citizens would no longer be allowed political asylum in the US after 5 July, but offered the hope that democracy would be restored in Haiti. 'Our objective', one anonymous participant stated, 'is to create a credible and entertaining show that broadcasts pro-democracy, pro-Aristide messages and gives the people hope that things are getting better. We are trying to target as many people as possible, the poorest Haitians.'[137] Because the Commando Solos were also equipped to transmit television pictures, TV Democracy subsequently began to broadcast taped audio-visual messages into domestic receivers on the island. Leaflets were dropped in their millions, while, in addition, loudspeaker messages were put out by US Coast Guard ships, stressing the dangers of boat migration in poorly constructed vessels in shark infested waters. At the holding camps at Guantanamo Bay, the MIST produced a Creole-language newspaper, *SA K'PASE*, while Radio Creole transmitted a mixture of news and entertainment on 97.5FM.

All this was to create an 'information environment' to prepare for the invasion by force in September 1994 of American troops to depose Haiti's military regime. It encouraged the Haitian police to disassociate itself from the military coup d'etat. The invasion was averted at the last minute following an agreement worked out with the Cedras regime by a delegation headed by ex-President Jimmy Carter, which permitted the peaceful entry of American troops in Operation Uphold Democracy. Cedras agreed to step down by 15 October, the USS *Harlan County* containing the 'Haiti Assistance Group' was turned back, and the UN mission was aborted.

Instead, US forces entered Haiti peacefully on 19 September, Cedras and his staff left Haiti on 13 October, and Aristide returned to power two days later. PSYOPS personnel claimed a major triumph for the power of persuasion over violence: 'the unprecedented success of the campaign was clearly evident in the warm embrace extended to US forces by the Haitian population, the minimal acts of violent retribution, and the absence of even a single US combat casualty during the introduction of US forces'.[138]

When the mission stopped being an invasion, PSYOPS officers had to change their approach at the eleventh hour. Tactical ground teams under the front name of 'Public Awareness Liaison' (reflecting the continuing nervousness of Washington about the overt deployment of PSYOPS) were sent in by helicopter in advance of the main US forces to ensure that the arrival of the latter was peaceful and that civilian order remained calm. Once the main force had arrived, a Joint Psychological Operations Task Force was established to oversee the handing in of weapons (in exchange for cash) and the minimisation of revenge and retribution while the Haitian police and military 'were reminded of their constitutional duties to serve the people and, for the most part, were persuaded to avoid the unnecessary use of violence. The citizens were also instructed on how to conduct themselves in mass demonstrations in a democracy.'[139] The message was spread throughout the island in 760 ground missions and sixty-seven helicopter missions by loudspeaker teams. Among the themes stressed by this extensive hearts-and-minds mission were: that the American forces were not an invading force but rather a part of a mission 'to ensure that all Haitians may live in a secure and peaceful environment'; exhortations to 'help us to help you'; humanitarian assistance campaigns, such as the 'Adopt a School' and 'Adopt an Orphanage' programmes; and reinforcement of 'the image of US forces as a military which assists rather than oppresses people (a concept not easily embraced by the Haitian masses)'.[140] This was a classical campaign of 're-education' involving the peaceful seizure of Radio and TV Nationale, which was then handed over to the new Haitian government. But because of the lack of sophistication amongst the indigenous population, messages were also disseminated in novel ways such as on soccer balls, t-shirts and badges. In this way was the transition from a largely American operation to a multinational force under the aegis of the UN Mission in Haiti achieved by the spring of 1995.

PSYOPS officials cringed at the suggestion that all this was propaganda, instead 'likening what they do to an "information campaign" or even launching an advertising campaign'.[141] Indeed, it could be argued that the PSYOPS people themselves had been engaging in such a campaign by their unprecedented release of information and material about this operation and their work in general.[142] 'Propaganda is more like putting out false information from an unknown source or a false source', claimed one officer. 'We identify ourselves as "Radio Democracy" and we make it clear it's an

American broadcast.... This is essentially an information campaign.'[143] Another argued that 'there is not really a fine line between truth and propaganda and what we do. We transmit information so that people can make informed decisions'.[144] A PSYOPS commander in Haiti maintained that 'we used them almost like artillery. We peppered the battlefield before we sent in manoeuvre forces. We used them to inform the public of what we were doing ... and ... to prepare the public for actions that were going to happen.'[145]

This is not that far removed from what another writer on propaganda had claimed, half a century earlier:

> The place of artillery preparation for frontal attack by the infantry in trench warfare will in future be taken by revolutionary propaganda, to break down the enemy psychologically before the armies begin to function at all. How to achieve the moral breakdown of the enemy before the war has started – that is the problem that interests me.[146]

For the author of this extract, this was the ultimate object of propaganda. His name was Adolf Hitler. Once again, therefore, we see the necessity for analysing propaganda in neutral terms, as a process of persuasion which can only be judged by reference to the intentions behind the process.

This can perhaps be best illustrated by a review of the wide variety of other PSYOPS missions conducted at the civilian–military interface during the course of 1993. For example, a US PSYOPS team supported the UN and the Cambodian Mine Action Centre by producing 'an extensive variety of mine awareness products such as leaflets, posters, bulletins, banners and cards ... to educate the people about the dangers of unexpended munitions'.[147] Again, in March 1993, when the US Coast Guard towed a refugee ship with over 500 Chinese as part of Operation Provide Refuge to Kwajelein Atoll in the Marshall Islands, PSYOPS personnel were despatched to liaise with the refugees and to produce newsletters and information boards for them.[148] A fifteen-member PSYOPS Task Force was despatched to Bosnia and was responsible for almost a million leaflets dropped on the night before the first American air-drops of relief supplies, explaining that the aid was impartial and humanitarian in nature, together with safety instructions to keep away from the parachuted food pallets until after they had landed. In Ethiopia, a PSYOPS unit produced ordnance awareness and first-aid handbooks for a joint mine clearance operation with the local forces. All this was conducted out of the glare of media attention – until early 1997, that is, when the International Red Cross scored a spectacular publicity coup world-wide by getting Diana, Princess of Wales, to champion the cause of mine awareness in Angola. Meanwhile, the military experts continued their work quietly. In a joint combined medical readiness training exercise in Senegal (MEDFLAG), PSYOPS personnel supplied the American Special Forces teams with 'military information and electronic newsgathering support as well as materials on Senegalese cultural norms' to assist in the 100,000 'informational booklets, posters and pamphlets providing information on personal hygiene, health and sanitation'.[149] PSYOPS MISTs were deployed to Barbados, St Lucia and Grenada to work with local committees in developing drug awareness campaigns; media ranging from bumper stickers to television commercials were used as part of the fight against narco-terrorism. In Bolivia, the Dominican Republic, Guatemala and Jamaica, other MISTs were deployed to work alongside anti-drugs campaigns directed at schoolchildren using colouring books, videos and other media. In Bolivia, they were said to have helped to decrease the number of hectares that were used to cultivate coca. In Belize, cholera prevention materials were supplied. In Venezuela, PSYOPS personnel developed information campaigns supporting 'democratisation, professionalisation of the military, civil–military relations, and counterdrug operations'.[150]

In Bosnia prior to the Dayton Peace Agreement, however, no coordinated psychological operation was conducted to support the humanitarian efforts either by the military, civilian, non-governmental or voluntary organisations. Episodic leaflet drops by US PSYOPS MISTs barely constituted a coordinated effort, and the absence of any activity in this direction provided a useful counterpoint to the critics who worried about 'Big Brother' and 'Uncle Sam' working side-by-side. By not preparing the psychological environment, there was a danger that the entry of peacekeeping forces could have been jeopardised by factions uncertain of the identity or motives of the arriving forces, or by those who had something to lose as a result of the deployment of peacekeeping forces. The ground was thus laid open for hostile propaganda portraying peacekeeping forces as opportunistic aggressors, interfering and patronising colonisers who wish to exploit natural resources.

The summer of 1995, which saw the fall of Srebrenica and the subsequent events which led to the Dayton Peace Agreement, altered the environment in the former Yugoslavia into one of peace enforcement. The decision was finally made to deploy American ground forces to join the Implementation Force (IFOR), and with them went PSYOPS personnel. Radio IFOR (formerly Rock of the Balkans) was established, at first broadcasting prerecorded news and IFOR messages for six hours a day; this time rock music was included in the programming, indicating that the lessons of Somalia had been learned. TV IFOR soon followed, producing news items for transmission and re-transmission on the post-war reconstructed local TV stations. A dual-language newspaper, the *Herald of Peace*, was produced with an initial print run of 5,000 and rapidly reached a circulation of 100,000 within Bosnia. Because the region had been riddled with hate propaganda for three and a half years, information products derived from the Western tradition of Anglo-American fact-based propaganda were not unwelcome, while colouring books for children which incorporated join-the-dots drawings of grenades and land mines attempted to reduce the post-war carnage. Posters, bumper-stickers and even youth magazines (especially the popular *Mirko*) were produced to spread the message of reconciliation and reconstruction. In areas where people were attempting to return home, posters were displayed asking the question 'Feeling harassed?', followed by the message 'Don't let anyone harass you. Contact the IPTF [Implementation Task Force], they can help.' At the time of writing, the PSYOPS effort in Bosnia had received very little media attention, perhaps because it was being conducted under the pseudonym of the IFOR Information Campaign 'as a convenient and generally acceptable euphemism for psyops, thereby negating the concerns in some quarters over the application of psyops in support of IFOR'.[151] What is already clear, however, is that the successful deployment of PSYOPS in Bosnia in support of Operation Joint Endeavour, by the US, the UK, France and Germany, is having considerable influence on emerging doctrine about 'Wider Peacekeeping' and 'Peace Support Operations'.[152]

CONCLUSIONS

Part of the problem with PSYOPS, as with other aspects of military affairs, derives from attempts to work out planning strategies for the New World Order that has yet to settle down to recognisable patterns of behaviour. Everyone is agreed that the informational dimension will play a central role – not just in its own right but also in the way it impacts on other elements of inter-state relations. This makes it difficult to delineate responsibility to a central authority such as a special unit within the United Nations, which is the logical thing to do in planning any targeted information activity since the pitfalls of speaking with many voices make that activity prone to greater confusion rather than clarity. Moreover, a central authority dealing with information to serve national or international objectives in a complicated world suffers from two further disadvantages. First, it would have to deal with the legacy of history and the records of Nazi propaganda ministries and Soviet committees. Second, a separate authority would be unlikely to command the respect of other government departments or NGOs which see themselves as better placed to release information about the specific aspect of international relations for which they have been traditionally responsible. Even in the two World Wars, Britain, the United States and Germany were all unable to resolve this central problem, with the result that 'national' propaganda themes emerged from a variety of sources rather than a single point. Within the informational dimension itself, there are competing forces which maintain that they are better placed to deal with certain types of specialised information. The logic of all this is to ensure greater inter-agency coordination – always easier to achieve in theory than in practice, especially at the civil–military or insider–outsider interface.

Because of their greater historical experience in such activity and perhaps because, as Trotsky put it, war really is the locomotive of history, military thinkers have concentrated their minds more on the role of PSYOPS as, to use the jargon, a 'combat force multiplier'. As one would expect from professional propagandists, they package their activity in undeniably attractive terms. For example, they argue that if, in dangerous circumstances, attempts are made to encourage enemy soldiers to defect, desert or surrender, thereby saving their lives in the process, there is a moral case to be made that this is a more acceptable activity than actually killing them. Or, as one officer has put it: 'Our motto is "electrons instead of bullets" '.[153] This gains even greater moral authority now that PSYOPS is being applied increasingly to embrace civilians caught up in a conflict. For instance, in planning for an NCEO, a 'non-combatant evacuation operation' – i.e. the evacuation of civilians from combat situations to a safe haven – it is claimed that PSYOPS 'can reduce interference by the local populace and military forces . . . explain the purpose of the US/allied action to counter confusion and misinformation, and assist in crowd control'. Further:

> PSYOP themes should emphasise that US actions are in accordance with international law and US/allied forces are in the country only to protect the evacuation of US/allied citizens and not to occupy the host nation or take sides with any faction.[154]

Using PSYOPS for such situations is likely to become even more essential for organisations like the UN, especially as in June 1996 the International Red Cross was predicting that the number of people around the world fleeing crisis situations was like to double to 50 million within ten years.[155]

Certainly, in purely military situations, PSYOPS still essentially embraces targeted military information forming an integrated supporting role in C^2W. More recently, however, the Pentagon's consideration of C^4I planning has started to attract attention. In the press, there are sensational claims: 'Info warriors hope to transform the way soldiers fight. Their goal: to exploit the technological wonders of the late 20th century to launch rapid, stealthy, widespread and devastating attacks on the military and civilian infrastructure of an enemy.'[156] This involves the full range of communications technology, from flying television stations to the injection of computer viruses into enemy screens and hard disks. 'Modern armies are so dependent on information that its possible to blind and deafen them in order to achieve victory without fighting in the conventional sense.'[157]

There are wider implications beyond the sheer technology, and these depend upon one's individual perspective. For example, it is possible to argue that, because PSYOPS supports national objectives, it is being used during the 1990s to support American foreign policy objectives based on the premise of consolidating 'victory' over Communism in a New World Order – although such explicit statements cannot be found in any of the public documents. Instead, they speak of a re-dedication to fostering 'democratic peace and prosperity'. Is this, therefore, a new form of ideological activity designed to influence the competitive global political, economic, military and informational environment in a manner favourable to US national objectives? Other nations are beginning to realise that they avoid entering this dimension at their peril,[158] although they call it something else. For these reasons, PSYOPS is increasingly being seen as an additional, and perhaps even indispensable, informational tool to aid not just the old-fashioned concepts of war-making and peacekeeping but also newer, more proactive policies of peacemaking, peace-building and peace enforcement – all at a strategic level.[159]

For this reason, many believe that the UN should embrace PSYOPS as part of its activities:

> With the introduction of non-lethal weaponry, and an increased reluc-tance on the part of national governments to place their armed forces in harm's way (especially when involved in United Nations opera-tions), psyops has an even more important role to play. This is true in conflict and in the period before conflict begins. The use of psyops in UN peacekeeping as an instrument of UN policy (rather than that of participating countries alone), is overdue. . . . The UN should use psyops as it does diplomacy: as an interlocking tool that, along with other means at its disposal – including force – can be used to limit casualties and assist in achieving aims set by the UN Security Council.[160]

At a tactical or operational level, there are powerful arguments for doing this. The problem, once again, comes at the strategic level.

In the so-called New World Order, the American conduct of PSYOPS is less negative in intention than the psywar of the Cold War and other wartime situations, in that it tends to be more promotional of the values which helped democracy survive those struggles. It was always thus in a sense but, with a clearly identifiable enemy in the form of the old Soviet Union, it had an ideology to shoot down as well as one to sell: a form of negative advertising. While now being more 'pro' than 'anti' since the demise of Communism, the emphasis has also shifted to a global rather than bi-polar environment, in which the threat of global nuclear war may have diminished but which still continues to suffer dangerous regional clashes fuelled by the forces of nationalism, or what might be termed the unfinished business of the old imperialistic orders of the past two centuries. Moreover, while supporting notions of pro-democracy, human rights and peace-building, there none the less also remain several forces which threaten the new emerging order, namely nuclear proliferation, terrorism, drug trafficking and, where the latter two meet, narco-terrorism. With the most advanced info-communications system in the world, the United States is particularly vulnerable to 'info-bombers' who could disrupt the computerised infrastructure of the economy. So psychological operations remains about the business of the targeted use of information to induce results favourable to those undertaking the effort, but the enemies are now identified as transnational threats to a global community rather than ones emanating from a specific regime targeting a specific nation. At the moment, this is used to justify the role of the US acting as a global policeman on behalf of the majority of nations who share similar values of 'freedom', 'free enterprise' and 'human rights'. States which threaten such 'universal' values will accordingly remain the primary targets of US PSYOPS.

From once being an activity which fuelled uncertainty in the minds of the enemy, psychological operations is now more about indicating intentions and generating information about the presence of military forces. Those intentions must remain the object of scrutiny. As for the propaganda itself, one is ultimately left with a choice. Is it better to persuade people to do something, to kill them, or to allow them to kill themselves by doing nothing? And, in so far as infowar is concerned, is the command, control and manipulation of information preferable to more lethal means of resolving disputes? The feeling that they are underpins the renewed emphasis on both activities. These are the difficult choices being arrived at in a complex and confusing world, a response to the changing nature of disputes since the end of the Cold War and the political dilemmas they create. However, many of their new applications are still being worked out. As one official warned in 1994:

> There is currently no common understanding of what psychological operations are and what they are not. It appears that we do not clearly understand the difference between the conduct of military PSYOP as a unique operation and other activities that have a PSYOP effect whether intended or not. As things now stand, almost anything can be called a psychological operation.[161]

After all, 'PSYOP is communication and therefore covers the entire field of human action'.[162] Perhaps a new phrase is need to mark a cleaner break with the past and with its past associations. Psychological Activities (PSYACS or PSYACTS) perhaps. Or, 'we might consider the term persuasive communications to mean the same thing as psychological operations'.[163] However, one authority has pointed out that 'our documents are replete with implications that DoD PSYOPS plays a far greater role in "strategic" PSYOP than it actually does or will in the near future'.[164] Emerging infowar theory threatens this. If we are to see wider applications at a strategic level, the involvement of the media is inevitable, and they might not like it unless the traditions of the strategy of truth are preserved. Indeed, one of the features absent from public pronouncements about C^4I, one suspects, is that what is really meant is C^5I: command, control, communications, computers, intelligence – and CNN!

CONCLUSION
Back to the future

This book has not been kind to the media or to journalists, either those in the past because they worked too closely with diplomats and soldiers or those of more recent times because they help to perpetuate the appearance of chaos and, in fact contribute to it, rather than provide explanations for the turbulence which has always affected international affairs. New communication technologies, as we have seen, provide genuine opportunities in our changing international environment for individuals to by-pass the traditional media. Yet certain fundamental questions remain:

> Will the time come when men, irrespective of their physical dispersion over the earth, can actually hear, seé, smell and touch the achievements of the human mind and the beauties of nature around the globe without having to leave their own local habitats? In such a world, what place will there be for such concepts as political *isolationism*, national *self-sufficiency*, and competitive *militarism*? Or will the devotees of these vestiges of a bygone age, fortified by the awe-inspiring products of science and invention that they so tragically misuse, destroy the fabric of civilisation ere the dream is realised? The race would seem to be between destructive nationalism on the one side and constructive internationalism on the other.[1]

Those words, remarkably, were written over fifty years ago. It is a race which is still on. It is also one in which the use and abuse of communications will undoubtedly continue to feature prominently.

But an additional question we need to add to this list is 'what role will the media play in this race?' I am not alone in thinking that, 'given the realities of globalism, the media have a special challenge to make international news and global interrelationships not just palatable but compelling enough to draw the kind of keen reader and viewer interest they warrant'.[2] The writer Michael Crichton, on the other hand, thinks this might even be irrelevant as he regards the media as a dinosaur whose extinction is imminent thanks to the arrival of the new digital technologies that allow people to by-pass their traditional sources of information about the world around them and go directly to the source itself. He argues:

> The media are an industry, and their product is information. And along with many other American industries, the American media produce a product of very poor quality. Its information is not reliable, it has too much chrome and glitz, its doors rattle, it breaks down almost immediately, and it's sold without warranty. It's flashy but it's basically junk. So people have begun to stop buying it.[3]

Certainly, polls indicate that the public is now more prepared to trust the sources of information than the messengers who carry it, that Desert Storm's soldier-spokesmen were trusted more than the reporters who reported on what they were saying. Or perhaps it would be fairer to say that twice as many Americans said that 'military censorship is more important than the media's ability to report important news'.[4] Yet, despite the decline of public confidence in media institutions, millions of people still buy newspapers and they still watch television. Like junk food, there remains a mass market for it. But equally, the rapid rise of on-line information services and Internet service providers in the past five years indicates that there is also a growing market for alternatives. So while the media attacks the Internet for being the domain of paedophiles and terrorists, they may well find that, within the life of the next generation, they could be displaced by it. Certainly, even though most major media organisations now have home pages on the World Wide Web, they have been slow to realise the ramifications of this discernible world-wide shift away from mediated to personal, interactive, computer-mediated communication. In the United States, and increasingly elsewhere, this has not been so for the military or diplomatic establishments.

It has been suggested that 'modern man feels helpless, and justifies this feeling by looking at the frightening world around him. Like a hypochondriac, he uses the undeniable threat of real danger to rationalize an even greater anxiety than a balanced view might warrant.'[5] I would suggest that the media are largely responsible for this, for, although the world is a much safer place than it was before, when tens of thousands of nuclear warheads were pointed at the great cities of the world, people are still either indifferent to or afraid of the chaos that they perceive around them. Fear – of crime, of flying, of war – is disproportionate to the realities. Whether manifesting itself in a 'fortress America' mentality, a British fear of the European Community or an EC fear of 'mad cow disease' from Britain, complicated issues are communicated to the public as if they were simple events, with very little media responsibility for those issues once they are no longer deemed 'newsworthy'. In this way the media set the popular agenda not so much in terms of telling the public what to think but in prioritising what they should think about.

International affairs in an increasingly interdependent globalised world have become important because events in one part of the world now impact more on people elsewhere, but still the media affords them comparatively little attention, except at times of crisis and war. Could we realistically expect any better from the media? Given the general level of popular disinterest in foreign affairs, the answer is probably 'no'. After all, why should the media suddenly start devoting more column inches and longer televised reports about world events when the vast majority of people think local rather than global? Those who advocate the media finding new ways of creating popular interest in foreign affairs by making stories more interesting and accessible are really advocating a propaganda on behalf of informing the citizens of the global village. This indeed may well be desirable, but that is surely not the responsibility of the media, who have become so central and so successful by virtue of the fact that this is precisely what they have avoided doing so far. This is because the media, and television in particular, are primarily regarded as instruments of entertainment. Hence news bulletins, documentaries and current affairs programmes regularly command much smaller audiences than movies, sports, soaps and game shows. The fact that they do this indicates that those who are interested in such fact-based programmes are being catered for, but they are still none the less in the minority. To argue anything else is to place its advocates in the same category as those who suggest that the media should depict more of the realities of war in order to shock people into opposing war, and even alongside those military thinkers who believe that war reports should be heavily censored in order to sustain public morale.

From the deployment of public diplomacy at the strategic level to the use of PSYOPS at the tactical level, nation-states utilise communication strategies in a heavily planned way. That planning and its history has formed a significant part of this book, because of the importance of examining the question of *intent* as the principal way of defining and delineating different forms of communication from one another, especially propaganda. I trust few will now doubt that nation-states have become progressively more engaged in propaganda. But equally I hope that any doubts about the wisdom of this have not so much been eased but modified through a reconsideration of the way propaganda is actually conducted in practice. The planned attempt to make us think and act in a predetermined way is not automatically a bad thing, especially if it prevents children from walking into a minefield. Is that worse than forcing them from doing so? For propaganda is a process of persuasion and its success or otherwise depends on the degree to which it strikes a chord within the target audience. Like advertising, there are standards for its conduct, standards which have been provided not necessarily by some regulating body but by best practice in the past. The historical record is adamant about the importance of credibility, timing and empathy. The new propaganda, the battle for global public opinion, is effectively part of our Third Wave, and it is unlikely that it will be confined to the fourth dimension of foreign policy but will permeate everywhere. The trick is how to spot it, and then recognise it for what it is by measuring practice against intentions before judgements about its use can be made.

The Wars of the Yugoslav Succession in many ways provide a microcosm of the challenges of the post-Cold War information age: from traditional peacekeeping operations in Croatia to humanitarian intervention in Bosnia, and from peace enforcement in Serbia to attempts at prevention with Macedonia. Yet the dramatic shift in nature from inter-state to intra-state conflicts – twenty-nine out of the thirty of those taking place in 1992 – has meant that the post-Cold War Security Council of the UN simply has to confront a problem inherent in its own Charter, namely Article 2:7 which forbids third-party intervention in the internal affairs of another state. Yet, ultimately, how Article 2:7 is interpreted is crucial, since intervention depends on political will to find new ways of dealing with national crises by the international community demanded by the changing circumstances of the post-Cold War era. This is especially true within an international community still coming to terms with conflicts that are being determined by ethnic, religious or extreme nationalist factors defining not only their more complex origins of conflict but also their particularly nasty characteristics.

Enter the media. The very conditions which make it difficult for the blue helmets to go in are ideal for journalists. Wars, crises, famines and the like are highly conducive to television in particular. The media are next to useless in explaining how such inter-ethnic conflicts begin, but once they have begun they are at their best when providing snapshots of how they are being conducted, especially given the chaotic nature of conflicts conducted by factions who are not always in complete control of their own people and who thus allow relatively unfettered media access – at admittedly high risks to the journalists themselves. The result, if the journalists manage to stay alive, is dramatic footage of war damage to civilians, of human rights abuses, ethnic cleansing, genocide, and masses of refugees. This in turn prompts an occasional cry to 'do something' when doing something is infinitely more complicated than the media can ever convey. As such, this alone makes the media a factor which no consideration of the area of crisis management can afford to ignore.

Our contemporary international environment is characterised by the existence of instantaneous global communications systems – satellites and satphones, digital data transmission from laptop computers, information superhighways and the like – all of which were developed largely as a result of military research into command and control warfare. However, their application beyond the world of the military, thanks to the climate of deregulation in the 1980s, has been most visibly taken up by the media and commercial communication corporations. This in turn has required more proactive strategies, for C2 to become C3 planning. Whatever the New World Order might be, it is the media's capability to report on events anywhere in the world in real time, which can frequently give the appearance of having added a fourth 'C': chaos. There is thus a need to bring order to disorder in terms of information strategies by the agencies involved in resolving the crisis, not just in reality but also in terms of perception and expectations. And now there is also a fifth 'C'. The emergence of global television services such as CNN has indeed added an further dimension to the conduct of international affairs, of wars, and of military operations in 'conflicts other than war' such as peacemaking, peace promoting, peace enforcement and peace-building, as well as peace-keeping and humanitarian exercises. How to deal with this has become a matter of high-level concern.

Various ways of influencing the outside perception of a crisis is to exclude the media altogether, as in Grenada; to delay their arrival, as in Panama; to make them totally dependent upon the military for their safety, transport and communications, as in the Falklands; or a combination of all of these, as in Desert Shield/Desert Storm. But peacekeeping exercises, alas, rarely provide such ready solutions. Perhaps those involved in them should think more about doing so, although the UN has always been reluctant to go down any of these routes. UNESCO, after all, has long been committed to a 'free-flow of information' as a basic human right and deplores interference in the freedom of the press to report freely and openly. But the time has come to recognise the realities of today's international communications environment. This requires imaginative re-thinking about two activities in particular: Public, or Media, Relations and Psychological Operations.

In so far as the media are concerned, there are considerable obstacles. Sadly, neither the public nor the UN is being well served by commercial competitive media organisations, who regard news as an entertainment commodity. Here, I am of course in danger of making a massive generalisation. I recognise that there are many intelligent, informed, specialised journalists in foreign affairs and defence matters. But the massive growth of the communications industry in the past twenty years has seen them relegated to a minority. Of the 1,500 journalists in Saudi Arabia for Desert Storm, how many could be said to have stood back from the conflict and reported the war from as objective a standpoint as humanly possible, rather than become cheerleaders for the coalition? How seriously are we to take reports by an American journalist who, drinking Slimfast and wearing a t-shirt endowed with a naked woman, went looking for dramatic stories of human tragedy in Somalia? Or another who was escorted to the site of a building in Iraq hit by a coalition air strike – not the infamous 'Baby-Milk Plant' – who, on raising his light meter which displayed a reading of f-16, was beaten up by his Iraqi minders who were convinced he was calling in a

197

further air strike by American F-16 fighters? Or the journalist with one of the warring factions in Lebanon in the aftermath of the USS *New Jersey*'s shelling of the coastline who, when asked whereabouts in the US he was from, responded 'New Jersey'? Or those manning the CNN desk in Jerusalem who donned gas masks and broadcast live that the city was under attack from chemical weapons? There are far too many of these journalists reporting from trouble spots who are insensitive to local conditions, who firefight stories in search of Pulitzer prizes rather than the truth, and whose behaviour as loose cannons frequently adds confusion to the story when clarity is required. If such reporting is transmitted live to a global audience, the potential dangers are plain for all to see.

One solution is to educate the next generation of journalists to concentrate on the message rather than the tricks of the medium. This is hard work, because the technology is glamorous and mesmerising, especially to young people, and it is easier to master than the kind of intellectual rigour which is required for high-quality analytical journalism. That aside, however, because it is a long-term solution, there is an urgent need in the meantime to consider ways in which the pertinent issues of any given conflict are publicised. Because the media rarely do this, one solution would be to increase official information through public diplomacy channels – despite the inevitable charges of increased 'propaganda'. Another is to give greater prominence to the type of targeted informational activities we are now seeing pioneered in PSYOPS. As Colonel Jeffrey Jones, while commander of 4th PSYOPS group at Fort Bragg, argued:

> we cannot afford to look at the world as we once did. . . . Preventing wars, providing nation and humanitarian assistance, conducting peacekeeping and peace enforcement operations, and helping to build democracy around the globe are essential missions for our armed forces. . . . Psychological operations can make a significant difference in these endeavors as the United States meets the new challenges and takes advantage of the new opportunities that face it in the future.[6]

This requires considerable attention to detail, to *planning*. Indeed, in the *Commander's Guide to Face-to-Face Communication* issued by Fort Bragg, entitled 'Building Bridges', it is recognised that soldiers' very 'actions and communication skills will reflect directly on the image of the United States'. One culturally insensitive comment at a border post might result in the escalation of a crisis. In short, this type of attention to detail can only enhance the process of peacekeeping, especially where credibility and limited use of force are pre-requisites.

This is a weapons system resting not on the power of devastation but on the power of persuasion. And because objectivity and impartiality are also required, in peacekeeping at least (though not so in peace enforcement), so also must the operational information being deployed remain likewise. The precondition of equal trust by all the warring partners is an obstacle that will have to be overcome, and there will always be some warring faction which fears such activity. But there is always a warring faction which does not want to see the UN present anyway. Psychological operations such as broadcasting conducted from outside the crisis zone can by-pass those warring factions by targeting the people directly – and with no casualties to blue helmets. As Colonel Jones has argued:

> To the Panamanian Defense Force soldier during Operation JUST CAUSE, PSYOP was the voice of reason. . . . To the Kurdish people during PROVIDE COMFORT, PSYOP was the multi-faceted print, audio and audio visual support to the humanitarian assistance and protection efforts after the STORM. . . . To the Somali citizen during Operation RESTORE HOPE, it was a radio program and a newspaper, both called 'Rajo' or hope, providing a credible source of information to over 100,000 citizens throughout the country. . . . To US ambassadors in Central and South America and the Caribbean, PSYOP is a tool used effectively in interagency drug interdiction, eradication and education programs; medical and engineer assistance projects; public information initiatives; natural disaster relief efforts; professionalization of foreign forces; and sustainment of fragile democratic growth.[7]

Why the UN distrusts this type of organised activity so much is probably connected to the nervousness of many Third World members concerning the susceptibility of their less educated publics to outside mind manipulation and propaganda. It is perhaps a long-term legacy of colonialism and the mistrust that colonialism generated. But this fundamentally clashes with the new perceptions of PSYOPS by its leading proponents.

As for peacekeeping by the UN, the only occasion when it has tried anything like this, in Cambodia, it was an outstanding success. Radio Untac, based in Phnom Penh in 1993, was the first time the UN had invested in its own broadcasting station, with a $3 million outlay for studios and transmitters – just 0.15 per cent of the Transnational Authority's total cost of $2 billion. Broadcasting 15 hours a day, it was supplemented by a smaller television operation and guaranteed air time to each of the twenty political parties fighting the election. Untac's spokesman Eric Falt claimed that the operation 'possibly changed the lives of millions of Cambodians, and was certainly a key factor in the success of the mission'. By driving home messages about voting rights to a war-weary population starved of objective information after fourteen years of the Cambodian People's Party, it was felt to have contributed not only to the massive voter turnout of 95 per cent, but also to the defeat of the Khmer Rouge. 'In every location and in some places in nearly every house', said a

UN spokesman, 'people are listening to Radio Untac.' 'We listen', said a Khmer Rouge defector, 'because we see it's the only radio that broadcasts the truth.'[8] It is for this reason that converts such as Alvin and Heidi Toffler have started to lobby the UN: 'Clearly what is needed, not just by the United States but by the UN itself, if the UN is going to continue the pretence of peacekeeping, is a rapid reaction contingency broadcasting force that can go anywhere, set up, and beam news to those cut off from it – and not just on radio, but television as well.'[9] Nor are they alone. Keith Spicer chairman of Canada's official Radio-Television and Telecommunications Commission, has added his voice:

> The Security Council could order a new, well-equipped media section in its Department of Peacekeeping Operations to broadcast corrective news and views to places inundated with aggressive propaganda. At the heart of such an effort – call it propaganda for peace – should be a handful of experts in the use of the media for war and peace. They should be trained in politics, mass psychology and traditional and unconventional warfare . . . the emphasis should always be on freedom: on countering evil voices, not silencing them. A few journalists may be skittish about anything that seems to involve the news media in public purposes. But we are not talking about corrupting the media. We are talking about using new technology, a few volunteers and some vision – all at a pittance – to stop the ethnic bloodbaths. We are talking about using our heads to stop wars that always start, and end, in somebody's head.[10]

These are forceful arguments and suggest that informational strategies, whether labelled Psychological Operations or something else, can generally aid peacekeeping in the following ways. Within theatre itself, they can psychologically prepare the region for the introduction of foreign peace-keeping forces. They can assist in securing non-interference, if. not cooperation, with peacekeeping operations, and contribute to the safety of peacekeepers and even of regional factions and populations. They can also counter divisive or hostile propaganda and mould realistic, obtainable, local expectations, including preparing the local population for the eventual withdrawal of peacekeeping forces. And they can create a climate of opinion for the international media to report on events in a manner beneficial to the entire exercise. On an international level, they can provide insight into the cultural, historical, political, religious and other psychological factors contributing to the conflict, advertise success and mould international expectations. In humanitarian and disaster relief operations, PSYOPS can help to reduce despair and build hope, defeat rumours and forestall panic, overcome shock and motivate local populations to self-help. But if it is achieve all of this, it must be considered as an integral part of the overall planning from the earliest possible stage. Whether it works depends upon how effectively it is planned. But the dangers of not doing it are plain for all to see, especially in Bosnia and Rwanda. By not preparing the psychological environment, the entry of peacekeeping forces could be jeopardised by factions uncertain of the identity or motives of the arriving forces, or those who have something to lose as a result of the deployment of peacekeeping forces. The ground is laid open for hostile propaganda portraying peace-keeping forces as opportunistic aggressors, interfering and patronising colonisers who wish to exploit natural resources.

The upshot of all this is the creation of a situation in a military operation in which the information flowing both within and beyond the crisis zone is determined by a pre-planned psychological master plan. This can only be done by the UN re-thinking its traditional reluctance to employ such activi-ties as broadcasting across frontiers, especially when civil and ethnic conflicts are concerned. Perhaps aid organisations and other NGOs should do likewise. The American military has already demonstrated that they have re-thought the applications of PSYOPS in such civilian situations: such as in the case of Hurricane Andrew, when Special Forces teams went in to re-establish a communications infrastructure to aid disaster relief; in mine disposal exercises all over the world where leaflets and posters are used to explain how to detect unexploded munitions; and in the fight against narco-terrorism, with exhortations to farmers to grow cocoa rather than cocaine.

As for the role of democratic media organisations, more proactive measures are also required to assist them through the complexities of inter-national crises. For good or ill, the media are today a central part of the foreign-policy-making process – whether as observer, participant or catalyst. They can't any longer be ignored or dismissed as being irresponsible or a nuisance. If they are, they are likely to cause more trouble and jeopardise the operation under review. Their business is to get a story, not quite any story, but the best they can within reasonable human risks. If armed forces deny them the opportunity to go to the Falkland Islands or Grenada, they will find a way of invading the island themselves – and they'll be waiting for them on the beaches as they were in Somalia. They were again in Haiti. The media cannot always be trusted to put their safety in the hands of the mili-tary – especially if the administration has spent weeks conducting its diplomatic and military plans to invade in public rather than in private.[11] Haiti, after all, is closer than Kuwait, and Restore Democracy commanded less public support than Desert Storm.

There is a need to recognise that reporters are only part of a professional chain. They answer to editors who have a significant role in shaping the slant of a given story. It is therefore important to realise how the entire process of the news business operates from the gathering stage to publication. This is a full-time business for specialists, people who understand both the media and foreign policy. In peacekeeping operations the rules for the application of informational or psychological activities are the same as those for successful public relations, and they are really quite simple: 'Tell as much as you can and tell it fast; centralize the source of information with an effective and well-informed spokesperson, usually the chief executive; deal with rumours swiftly; make as much available to the press as possible; update information frequently; stay on the record; and never tell a lie'.[12] Bullets and bombs admittedly win wars, not words, but to be successful in the modern informa- tion environment, governments need to pay as much attention to matters of presentation and perception as they do to traditional ways of resolving disputes. They can't rely on the media to do this for them, at least not wittingly, since the media have their own agenda. Foreign policy is not normally at the top of that agenda, except in times of crisis. Moreover, now that we no longer have the Cold War to provide a prism through which to look at the world in terms of 'us versus them', West versus East, 'good guy versus bad guy', it is more difficult to establish what foreign policy issues the media will seize upon. A three-sided dispute such as Bosnia only adds to their confusion.

Domestic news is cheaper and more comprehensible than foreign; preoc- cupation with domestic financial recession is always likely to dominate. Yet if the story is dramatic, if it is an event rather than an issue, and if there are dramatic pictures to go with it, a foreign story may secure a place on the media agenda. That in turn may influence the political agenda, which is how it should be. We are, after all, witnessing the triumph of democracy, the essence of which is informed debate to achieve consensus. This is bound to please those who believe that we should be told everything, but only once they realise that never in the history of the world has there been an example of a true democracy waging a war against another democracy. In other words, giving the media the stories and pictures they want will do less harm and more good than is often suspected, because, if they use them in ways that offend public opinion, they will quickly discover that the really grue- some visual material merely serves to turn the public against them – which they literally can't afford to let happen. Turbulence will in the end produce a form of consensus. The key issue in our modern information society is to ensure that the cameras get to where the dictator is flapping his arms in the first place.

GLOSSARY

Cyberspace	The digital environment of the Internet
Demassification	The process whereby industrial institutions and practices break down to serve niche markets
Desert Shield, Operation	The coalition's military build-up to prevent an Iraqi invasion of Saudi Arabia in 1990, and the prelude to Desert Storm
Desert Storm, Operation	The coalition's military exercise to expel Iraqi forces from Kuwait in 1991
Digital superhighways	The pathways connecting Internet sites
First Wave	Agricultural societies
First World	Western – recently, all advanced – societies
Fourth Dimension	The psychological/informational dimension to international affairs
Infotainment	The packaging of news and information in a popularly entertaining manner
Infowar	Information Warfare
Internet	A global network of linked computers
Just Cause, Operation	The American intervention in Panama, 1989
Narrowcasting	Specialised broadcasting, e.g. all-news channels
New World Order	Vague description of the international environment after the end of the Cold War
Op-ed	Opinion editorials

Provide Comfort, Operation	The humanitarian intervention in Northern Iraq, 1991
Real-time reporting	Live, instantaneous reporting
Restore Hope, Operation	The humanitarian intervention in Somalia, 1991
Second Wave	Industrial societies
Second World	Communist countries
Sound-bite	A short, memorable statement designed for media consumption
Third Wave	Process of transformation from an industrial to an informational society
Third World	Underdeveloped countries or LDCs
Uphold Democracy, Operation	The American intervention in Haiti, 1994
World Wide Web	The accessible front pages of the Internet

NOTES

INTRODUCTION

1 For substantiation of this audacious claim see Nicholas Jones, *Soundbites and Spin Doctors: how politicians manipulate the media – and vice versa* (London, Cassell, 1995).
2 Bob Franklin, *Packaging Politics: Political Communications in Britain's Media Democracy* (London, Edward Arnold, 1994).
3 *Contemporary International Politics* by two American professors of Government, Walter R. Sharp and Grayson Kirk (Rinehart and Co., New York, 1940).
4 H. G. Wells, *'42 to '44: A Contemporary Memoir upon Human Behaviour during the crisis of the World Revolution* (London, Secker and Warburg, 1944).
5 Asa Briggs, *The Communications Revolution* (Leeds, Leeds University Press, 1966).
6 Hamid Mowlana, 'Toward a NWICO for the Twenty-First Century', *Journal of International Affairs*, vol. 47, Summer 1993, no. 1, p. 59.
7 J. Baudrillard, *In the Shadow of the Silent Majorities, or, The End of the Social and other essays*, trans. Paul Foss, Paul Patton and Philip Beitchman (New York, Semiotext(e), 1983) p. 95.
8 In my opinion, six of the best examples of recent work by younger scholars who have altered the way we view past events by looking at them from this perspective are Richard Cockett, *Twilight of Truth: Chamberlain, Appeasement and the Manipulation of the Press* (London, Weidenfeld and Nicolson, 1989), Nicholas J. Cull, *Selling War: The British Propaganda Campaign against American 'Neutrality' in World War II* (Oxford, Oxford University Press, 1995), Susan Carruthers, *Winning Hearts and Minds: British Governments, the Media and Counter-Insurgency* (Leicester, Leicester University Press, 1995), Sian Nicholas, *The Echo of War: Home Front Propaganda and the Wartime BBC, 1939–45* (Manchester, Manchester University Press, 1996), Gary D. Rawnsley, *Radio Diplomacy and Propaganda: the BBC and VOA in International Politics, 1956–64* (Basingstoke, Macmillan, 1996), and Tony Shaw, *Eden, Suez and the Mass Media* (London, I.B. Taurus, 1996).
9 Michael Cockerell, *Live from Number 10: The Inside Story of Prime Ministers and Television* (London, Faber and Faber, 1988); Laurence Rees, *Selling Politics* (London, BBC Books, 1992).
10 See especially Mort Rosenblum, *Who Stole the News? Why we can't keep up with what happens in the world and what we can do about it* (New York, John Wiley, 1993).
11 Most coherently articulated by American sociologist Daniel Bell, *The Coming*

of Post-Industrial Society. A Venture in Social Forecasting (Harmondsworth, Penguin, 1976 edition, first published in New York, 1973).

12 *Newsweek*, 6 July 1970, pp. 29–30.

13 For a discussion of the variety of theoretical approaches, see Frank Webster, *Theories of the Information Society* (London, Routledge, 1995).

14 Francis Fukuyama, *The End of History and the Last Man* (London, Hamish Hamilton, 1992).

15 *Ibid.*, p. 7.

16 *Ibid.*, p. 6.

17 Marion May Dilts, *The Telephone in a Changing World* (New York, Longman's Green, 1941) p. 19.

18 Cited in I. de Sola Pool, *Forecasting the Telephone: a retrospective technology assessment of the telephone* (Norwood, NJ, Ablex, 1983) p. 21.

19 Julian Hale, *Radio Power: propaganda and international broadcasting* (London, Elek, 1975) p. xiii.

20 L. White and R. D. Lee, *Peoples Speaking to Peoples*, cited in T. H. Qualter, *Opinion Control in the Democracies* (London, Macmillan, 1985) p. 219.

21 Hale, *op. cit.*, p. ix.

22 Cited in G. Mansell, *Let the Truth be Told – 50 Years of BBC External Broadcasting* (London, Weidenfeld and Nicolson, 1982) p. 2.

23 Cited in John Tusa, *Conversations with the World* (London, BBC Books, 1990) p. 4.

24 Cited in Hale, *op. cit.*, p. 2.

25 This speech was downloaded from the Internet on 18 April 1994. The address then was gopher@nywork1.undp.org.

26 Including by that distinguished perennial critic of the US media establishment, Herbert I. Schiller, *Information Inequality: the deepening social crisis in America* (New York, Routledge, 1996).

27 Richard Cockett, 'The "end of history" debate revisited', in B. Brivati, J. Buxton and A. Seldon, *The Contemporary History Handbook* (Manchester, Manchester University Press, 1996) pp. 39–40.

28 See for example the special issue on Early Non-Fiction Cinema in *The Historical Journal of Film, Radio and Television*, vol. 15 (1995) p. 4.

29 This is despite the work of Donald R. Browne and Laurien Alexandre in the United States, and of Briggs, Scannel, Rawnsley and Nicholas in the UK.

30 Philip M. Taylor, 'The case for preserving our contemporary communications heritage', in Brivati *et. al.*, *op. cit.*, pp. 280–8.

31 9 November 1996.

32 A. Toffler, *The Third Wave* (London, Collins paperback edition, 1981).

33 *Ibid.*, p. 24.

34 A rare recent exception is Herbert Schiller, *op. cit.*, p. 105, who writes that it is not necessary to endorse fully Toffler's explanation for this spreading development, but it does describe rather well the 'direction that can be detected *inside* the United States today, to say nothing of other areas and regions of the world'.

35 James Gleick, *Chaos: Making a new science* (Harmondsworth, Penguin, 1987) p. 38.

36 Rosenblum, *op. cit.*, p. 95.

37 Toffler, *Future Shock*, (London, Pan, 1970) p. 25.

38 Nod Miller and Rod Allen, *It's Live but is it Real?* (London, John Libbey, 1993).

39 gopher@nywork1.undp.org.

40 For an elaboration of this, see Philip M. Taylor, *Munitions of the Mind: a*

history of propaganda from the ancient world to the present era (Manchester, Manchester University Press, 1995).

41 Cited in Hale, *op. cit.*, p. 60.

42 E. Herman and N. Chomsky, *Manufacturing Consent* (New York, Pantheon Books, 1988).

43 The title of a recent study by two psychologists, Anthony Pratkanis and Elliot Aronson, *The Age of Propaganda: The Everyday Use and Abuse of Persuasion* (New York, W. H. Freeman and Co., 1991).

44 The literature is so rich on this that I barely need to address it, except where relevant. For the most recent discussion by a leading scholar, see Cees Hamelink, *World Communication: disempowerment and self-empowerment* (London and New Jersey, Zed Books, 1995).

45 Cited in A. A. Snyder, 'US Foreign Affairs in the Information Age' (Washington DC, The Annenberg Washington Program in Communications Policy Studies, 1995). http://www.annenberg.nwu.edu/pubs/usfal

46 Ed Turner, 'The Power and the Glory', in Christopher Young, 'The role of the media in International Conflict', a report on a two-day seminar at the Canadian Institute for International Peace and Security, December 1991.

47 H. Lasswell, 'Political and Psychological Warfare', in W. Daugherty and M. Janowitz (eds), *A Psychological Warfare Casebook* (Baltimore, Johns Hopkins Press, 1958) p. 24.

48 See Susan Strange's slightly different four-prong model in *States and Markets: an introduction to international political economy* (London, Pinter, 1988).

49 C. Hamelink, *The Politics of World Communication* (London, Sage, 1994).

50 Hamid Mowlana, *op. cit.*, p. 67.

51 Nicholas Negroponte, *Being Digital* (London, Hodder and Stoughton, 1995) p. 163.

52 James W. Carey, 'The Mass Media and Democracy: Between the Modern and the Postmodern', *Journal of International Affairs*, vol. 47, Summer 1993, no. 1, p. 19.

53 *Ibid.*, pp. 168–9.

54 Mark D. Alleyne, *International Power and International Communication* (Oxford, St. Anthony's/Macmillan, 1995) p. 4.

55 Taylor, *Munitions of the Mind*, p. 6.

56 H. Morgenthau, *Politics Amongst Nations* (New York, Knopf, 1978 edition) p. 30.

57 James W. Carey, *op. cit.*, p. 6.

58 E. Said, *Covering Islam* (New York, Random House, 1981) p. 37.

59 Cited in John Tomlinson, *Cultural Imperialism* (London, Pinter, 1991) p. 152.

1 INTERNATIONAL COMMUNICATIONS AND INTERNATIONAL POLITICS SINCE 1945

1 These and the following extracts from UN documents were downloaded from the UN's WWW service at http://www.undp.org.

2 For a further discussion see John Lewis Gaddis, *The Long Peace: Inquiries into the history of the Cold War* (New York, Oxford University Press, 1987) pp. 36ff.

3 Ronald Steele, *Walter Lippmann and the American Century* (Boston, Little Brown and Co., 1980) pp. 438–9.

4 Robert Dallek, *The American Style of Foreign Policy: Cultural Politics and Foreign Affairs* (New York, Knopf, 1983) p. 174.

5 V. Kortunov, *The Battle of Ideas in the Modern World* (Moscow, Progress, 1979).
6 V. Artemov, *Information Abused: Critical Essays* (Moscow, Progress, 1981) p. 13.
7 *Ibid.*, pp. 8–9.
8 Richard H. Shultz and Roy Godson, *Dezinformatsia: Active Measures in Soviet Strategy* (Washington, Pergamon/Brassey's, 1984).
9 *Ibid.*, p. 3.
10 A. Panfilov, *Broadcasting Pirates, or Abuse of the Microphone* (Moscow, Progress, 1981) p. 137.
11 See Gaddis, *op. cit.*, pp. 114–15.
12 John Young, *Winston Churchill's Last Campaign: Britain and the Cold War, 1951–55* (Oxford, Clarendon Press, 1996) p. 85.
13 John B. Whitton, *Propaganda and the Cold War* (Connecticut, Public Affairs Press, 1963) p. 3.
14 For further details see Stephen E. Ambrose, *Eisenhower* (New York, Simon and Schuster, 1983).
15 See Gary D. Rawnsley, *Radio Diplomacy and Propaganda: the BBC and VOA in International Politics, 1956–64* (Basingstoke, Macmillan, 1996) and James Critchlow, *Radio Hole-in-the-Head. Radio Liberty: an insider's story of Cold War broadcasting* (Washington, American University Press, 1995).
16 H. Greene, *The Third Floor Front* (London, The Bodley Head, 1969) p. 32.
17 J. C. W. Reith, *Into the Wind* (London, Hodder and Stoughton, 1949) p. 354.
18 Cited in Rawnsley, *op. cit.*, p. 81.
19 *The Times*, 13 November 1956.
20 Greene, *Third Floor Front*, pp. 29–31.
21 Quoted in T. Soronsen, *The Word War* (New York, Harper and Row, 1968) p. 44.
22 *Ibid.* It might be added that Rawnsley, *op. cit.*, takes issue with this judgement, feeling that VOA was much more cautious than Sorenson maintained.
23 Anthony Nutting, *No End of a Lesson* (London, Constable, 1967) p. 101.
24 Rawnsley, *op. cit.*, p. 46.
25 *Ibid.*
26 F. C. Barghoon, *Soviet Foreign Propaganda* (Princeton, Princeton University Press, 1964).
27 L. Schapiro, 'The International Department of the CPSU: Key to Soviet Policy', *International Journal* (Winter 1976–7) p. 44.
28 Collen Roach, 'American Textbooks vs NWICO History', in G. Gerbner, H. Mowlana and K. Nordenstreng, *The Global Media Debate: its rise, fall, and renewal* (Norwood, NJ, Ablex, 1993) p. 39.
29 Michael R. Beschloss, 'Presidents, Television and Foreign Crisis' (Washington DC, The Annenberg Washington Program in Communications Policy Studies of Northwestern University, 1993). This was downloaded from the World Wide Web. E-mail: awp@nwu.edu.
30 *Ibid.*
31 For further details see Hale, *Radio Power*, and M. Lissan, *Broadcasting to the Soviet Union: International Politics and Radio* (New York, Praeger, 1975).
32 D. Lerner, *The Passing of Traditional Society* (Glenco, Il., Free Press, 1958) p. 55.
33 W. Schramm, *Mass Media and National Development: the role of information in the developing countries* (Stanford University Press, 1964) p. ix.
34 Mort Rosenblum, *Coups and Earthquakes* (New York, Harper and Row, 1979).
35 O. Boyd-Barrett and D. Kishan Thussu, *Contra-Flow in Global News:*

International and Regional News Exchange Mechanisms (London, John Libbey, 1992) p. 35.

36 Ian Jarvie, *Hollywood's Overseas Campaign: The North Atlantic Movie Trade, 1920–50* (Cambridge, Cambridge University Press, 1992) p. 87.
37 *American Cinematographer*, March 1950.
38 K. Nordenstrung and T. Varis, *Television Traffic – A One Way Street? A Survey and Analysis of the International Flow of Television Programme Material* (Paris, UNESCO, 1974) p. 31.
39 B. Pavlic and C. Hamelink, *The New International Economic Order: Links between Economics and Communications* (Paris, UNESCO, 1985) p. 13.
40 Cited in G. Gerner, H. Mowlana and K. Nordenstreng, *The Global Media Debate: its rise, fall and renewal* (Norwood, NJ, Ablex, 1993) p. x.
41 S. MacBride, *Many Voices, One World* (Paris, UNESCO, 1980) pp. 68ff.
42 *Ibid.*, pp. 91–2.
43 D. Maitland, *The Missing Link* (Geneva, ITU, 1984) p. 13.
44 R. S. Fortner and D. A. Durham, *A Worldwide Radio Receiver Population Analysis* (Washington, Academy for Educational Development, 1986).
45 J. Fenby, *The International News Services* (New York, Schocken Books, 1986) pp. 7ff.
46 Cited in Gerbner *et. al.*, *op. cit.*, pp. x–xi.
47 'Shock Wave (Anti) Warrior': a conversation with Peter Schwartz, *Wired Magzine Online*, 1993–4, http://www.info@wired.com.
48 H. Kissinger, 'An opportunity for a breakthrough', *Washington Post*, 17 November 1985.
49 Annual Report of the US Advisory Commission on Public Diplomacy, 1986, p. 10.
50 D. S. Meta, *Mass Media in the USSR* (Moscow, Progress, 1987) pp. 60–1.
51 Ed Turner, 'The Power and the Glory', in Christopher Young, 'The role of the media in International Conflict', a report on a two-day seminar at the Canadian Institute for International Peace and Security, December 1991.
52 Robert S. Fortner, *International Communication: history, conflict and control of the global metropolis* (Belmont, Ca., Wadsworth Publishing Co., 1993) p. 208.
53 For further details see United States Department of State, *Active Measures: a report on the substance and process of anti-US Disinformation and Propaganda Campaigns* (DoS Publication 9630, August 1986); *Soviet Influence Activities: a report on active measures and propaganda, 1987–88* (DoS Publication 9720, August 1989).
54 Robert S. Fortner, *Public Diplomacy and International Politics: the symbolic constructs of summits and international radio news* (Westport, Praeger, 1994).
55 H. Dixon, 'The paranoia eases', *Financial Times*, 19 April 1990.
56 'USIA published guide to TV in Eastern Europe', *Broadcasting*, 5 March 1990.
57 Gwyn Prins (ed.), *Spring in Winter: the 1989 revolutions* (Manchester, Manchester University Press, 1990) p. 156.
58 A good survey of the changes in the Soviet media throughout this period is Linda Jensen, 'The Press and Power in the Russian Federation', *Journal of International Affairs*, vol. 47, Summer 1993, no. 1, pp. 97–126.
59 D. Hoffman, 'Global Communications Network Was Pivotal in Defeat of Junta', *Washington Post*, 23 August 1991.
60 Jonathan Yardley, 'In the Soviet Union, the Tube Test', *Washington Post*, 26 August 1991.
61 Cited in Robert J. Donovan and Ray Schere, *Unsilent Revolution: television news and American public life* (Cambridge, Cambridge University Press, 1992) p. 317.
62 Andrew Walker, *A Skyful of Freedom* (London, Broadside, 1992) p. 128.

63 Cited by Ed Turner, 'The Power and the Glory'.
64 World Broadcasting Information (BBC Monitoring Service), no. 12 (24 March 1982) A7.
65 'All available means to be used to respond to anti-Cuban TV', World Broadcasting Information (BBC Monitoring Service), no. 49 (2 December 1988) A5.
66 L. Feldmann, 'Yeltsin welcomes Radio Liberty's presence in Russia', *Christian Science Monitor*, 4 September 1991.
67 World Broadcasting Information (BBC Monitoring Service), no. 12 (24 March 1989) A7.
68 An interview with Malcolm S. Forbes, reprinted in the *Journal of International Affairs*, vol. 47, Summer 1993, no. 1, p. 75.
69 'Mouse Fever is about to strike Europe', *Business Week*, 20 March 1992.
70 Hamelink, *The Politics of World Communication*, p. 33.
71 Schiller, *Information Inequality*, pp. 72–3.

2 BRUSHFIRES AND FIREFIGHTERS

1 Sydney Fay, *The Origins of the World War* (2nd edition, New York, Macmillan, 1948), vol. 1, p. 47; Richard Cockett, *Twilight of Truth* (London, Weidenfeld and Nicolson, 1989); Philip M. Taylor, *A Call to Arms: Propaganda and Rearmament in the 1930s* (Leeds, InterUniversity History Film Consortium, 1985); Nicholas Pronay, 'Rearmament and the British Public: policy and propaganda', in J. Curran, A. Smith and P. Wingate, *Impacts and Influences* (London, Methuen, 1987).
2 Cited in Barry Rubin, *International News and the American Media* (Beverly Hills, Sage, 1977) p. 8.
3 Stephen Badsey, *Modern Military Operations and the Media*, (London, Strategic and Combat Studies Institute, Occasional Paper No. 8) p. 3.
4 *The Times*, 27 July 1866.
5 Zara Steiner, *The Foreign Office and Foreign Policy, 1898–1914* (Cambridge, Cambridge University Press, 1969) p. 172.
6 J. A. Spender, *The Public Life* (2 vols, London, Cassell, 1925) II, p. 40.
7 I am thinking here principally of the 1915 Treaty of London, by which Italy joined the allied powers in return for promises of territorial returns, particularly in what became Yugoslavia, which at war's end could not be fulfilled. It was the Bolsheviks who first released details of these secret arrangements, discrediting not only the allies but also 'secret diplomacy'. It was one of the contributing factors to the rise of Mussolini after the war.
8 Philip M. Taylor, 'The Impact of the First World War upon Foreign Office attitudes to the press', in David N. Dilks (ed.), *Retreat from Power* (London, Macmillan, 1981) vol. 1, pp. 42–63.
9 Cited in Hugh Cudlipp, *The Prerogative of the Harlot* (London, The Bodley Head, 1980) p. 82.
10 Gary Messenger, *British Propaganda and the State in the First World War* (Manchester, Manchester University Press, 1992); Peter Buitenhuis, *The Great War of Words: Literature as Propaganda 1914–18 and after* (London, Batsford, 1989).
11 With the single exception of the National Insurance Commission, established in 1911 by that publicity-conscious politician David Lloyd George who, as Prime Minister after 1916, also brought in Beaverbrook and Northcliffe to conduct national propaganda.

12 The phrase used by the anonymous author of *The History of The Times* vol. IV, Part II: *The 150th Anniversary and Beyond, 1921–48* (London, Printing House Square, 1952) p. 1027.

13 Although he did not invent it, the phrase 'the media age' has most recently been employed by Lawrence Freedman in reference to the linkage between international crises and the role of the media in prompting multinational responses to them. See *Independent*, 19 May 1993.

14 Memorandum by J. D. Gregory, 'Reconstruction of Press and News Department', 21 February 1925. Public Records Office, PRO FO 366/783.

15 New York, Macmillan, 1922.

16 Cited in De Witte C. Poole, *The Conduct of Foreign Relations under Modern Democratic Conditions* (New Haven, Yale University Press, 1924) p. 137.

17 The FO News Department was originally created in 1914 to meet wartime needs, and was retained in 1919 to serve a permanent peacetime role in dealing with the British and foreign press. Downing Street did not move down this path until 1930, relying before then on a less formalised system of private relations between ministers and newspaper proprietors. See Philip M. Taylor, 'The Projection of Britain: British Overseas Publicity and Propaganda, 1914–39, with particular reference to the work of the News Department of the Foreign Office', University of Leeds PhD thesis, 1978.

18 Harold Nicolson, *Diplomacy* (Oxford, Oxford University Press, 1963 edition) p. 97.

19 Anon., *The History of The Times*, vol. 3: *The Twentieth Century Test, 1884–1912* (London, 1947) pp. 137–8.

20 James Reston, *The Artillery of the Press: Its Influence on American Foreign Policy* (New York, Harper and Row, 1967) pp. 30–1. Reston argues that if the press had published the story in advance, it might have prompted the government to go more carefully and thus have avoided the fiasco.

21 Michael Schudson, *Discovering the News* (New York, Basic Books, 1978) ch. 4.

22 James W. Carey, 'The Mass Media and Democracy: Between the Modern and the Postmodern', *Journal of International Affairs*, vol. 47, Summer 1993, no. 1, p. 13.

23 *Ibid.*

24 Cited by R. A. Schroth in the *National Catholic Reporter*, 15 March 1991.

25 Ernest R. May, 'The News Media and Diplomacy', in Gordon A. Craig and Francis L. Loewenheim, *The Diplomats, 1939–79* (Princeton, NJ, Princeton University Press, 1994). My emphasis.

26 Leon V. Sigal, *Reporters and Officials: the organization and politics of News-making* (Lexington, Mass., 1973) p. 9. The official was William Tyrrell, later head of the British Board of Film Censors.

27 M. Fitzwater, *Call the Briefing! A decade with Presidents and the Press* (New York, Times Books, 1995) pp. 10–11.

28 Cesar Saerchinger, 'Propaganda Poisons European Air', *Broadcasting*, 15 April 1938, p. 20.

29 See Julian Hale, *Radio Power* (London, Elek, 1975).

30 Robert S. Fortner, *Public Diplomacy and International Relations: the symbolic constructs of summits and international radio news* (New York, Praeger, 1994).

31 See Philip M. Taylor, *Munitions of the Mind: a history of propaganda from the ancient world to the present era* (Manchester, Manchester University Press, 2nd edition, 1995) ch. 24.

32 See Stephen R. Mackinnon and Oris Friesen, *China Reporting: An oral history of American Journalism in the 1930s and 1940s* (Berkeley, University of California Press, 1987).

33 The level of mutual cooperation is explored in N. J. Cull, *Selling War: The British Propaganda Campaign against American Neutrality in World War II* (Oxford, Oxford University Press, 1995).

34 For example, Paris had over a dozen large circulation daily newspapers in 1947, but by the end of the 1970s this was down to only four with circulations of over half a million. In 1963 New York had twelve daily newspapers, but by the end of the 1970s it, too, was down to four. In Britain, there were eleven national newspapers in 1945 and, although there were still ten in 1979, six of these were tabloids.

35 Sources are: Mort Rosenblum, *Coups and Earthquakes: Reporting the World for America* (New York, 1979); and Oliver Boyd-Barrett, 'The Collection of Foreign News in the National Press', Part A of the Royal Commission on the Press, *Studies on the Press* (London, HMSO, 1977).

36 S. Ghorpade, 'Foreign correspondents cover Washington for the world', *Journalism Quarterly*, vol. 61 (1984) p. 667.

37 Sigal, *op. cit.*, p. 48.

38 Jack Matlock, 'The Diplomat's View of the Press and Foreign Policy', *Media Studies Journal*, Fall 1993, p. 51.

39 May, *op. cit.*, p. 669.

40 Donald Read, *The Power of News: The History of Reuters* (New York, Oxford University Press, 1992).

41 P. Hester, 'The News from Latin America via a World News Agency', *Gazette*, vol. 20 (1971) no. 2, pp. 82–98.

42 1935 and 1978. For the former, see Tom Stannage *Baldwin Thwarts the Opposition* (London, Croom Helm, 1980). On 1978, see H. Afkhami, 'Foreign News Coverage by the Media during the British General Elections of 1979, 1983, 1987 and 1992', University of Leeds PhD thesis, 1995.

43 For further details, see Philip M. Taylor, *A Call to Arms: Propaganda and Rearmament in the 1930s* (British Universities Historical Studies in Film, 1985), film and pamphlet.

44 See H. I. Schiller, *Mass Communications and American Empire* (New York, August M. Kelly, 1969) .

45 V. O. Key, *Public Opinion and American Democracy* (New York, Knopf, 1961) pp. 173–4. See also Robert W. Oldendick and Barbara A. Bardes, 'Mass and Elite Foreign Policy Opinions', *Public Opinion Quarterly*, vol. 45 (1982) 368–82.

46 Mark Pedelty, *War Stories: the culture of foreign correspondents* (London, Routledge, 1995) p. 24.

47 Edward S. Herman, 'The Media's Role in U.S. Foreign Policy', *Journal of International Affairs*, vol. 47, Summer 1993, no. 1, p. 25.

48 Robert B. Bathurst, *Intelligence and the Mirror: On Creating an Enemy* (London, Sage/PRIO, 1993).

49 Cited by Douglas Cater, *The Fourth Branch of Government* (Boston, Houghton Mifflin, 1959) pp. 129–30.

50 Preface to 'Global News after the Cold War', *Media Studies Journal*, Fall 1993, p. xiii.

51 Cited in Nicholas Hopkinson, *The Media and International Affairs After the Cold War*, Wilton Park paper 74 (London, HMSO, 1993) p. 11.

52 Johanna Neuman, 'Ambassadors: Relics of the sailing ships?' (Washington DC, The Annenberg Washington Program in Communications Policy Studies, 1995). http://www.annenberg.nwu.edu/pubs/usfal

53 'Human interest stories and trend analysis that never would have made the newscast or the front page in the past earned new currency. In that context, international news seemed old-fashioned, utterly committed to a world view

based almost always on geopolitics.' Preface to 'Global News after the Cold War', *Media Studies Journal*, Fall 1993, p. xiv.

54 Cited in Nik Gowing, 'Real Time Television Coverage of Armed Conflicts and Diplomatic Crises: Does it Pressure or Distort Foreign Policy Decisions?', Discussion Paper 94–1, J.F.K. School of Government, Harvard University, June 1994, p. 4.

55 An interview with Malcolm S. Forbes, *Journal of International Affairs*, vol. 47, Summer 1993, no. 1, p. 76.

56 For example, the British Foreign Office advised the Nigerian government to hire a media advisor during the civil war in the late 1960s while the Sandinistas (!) even retained *American* PR consultants to help in their media policies. For a fuller discussion see James E. Grunig, 'Public Relations and International Affairs: Effects, Ethics and Responsibility', in *Journal of International Affairs*, vol. 47, Summer 1993, no. 1, pp. 137–62.

57 For further discussion see Philip M. Taylor, *The Projection of Britain: British overseas publicity and propaganda, 1919–39* (Cambridge, Cambridge University Press, 1981) Ch. 3.

58 18 March 1946, Memorandum to the Secretary of State from William Benton, Assistant Secretary of State, cited in A. A. Snyder, 'US Foreign Affairs in the Information Age' (Washington DC, The Annenberg Washington Program in Communications Policy Studies,1995).http://www.annenberg.nwu.edu/pubs/usfal

59 Milton Lehman, 'We Must Sell America Abroad', *Saturday Evening Post*, 15 November 1947.

60 'Public Diplomacy for the 21st Century', Report of the United States Advisory Commission on Public Diplomacy, March 1995.

61 Erik Barnouw, *Tube of Plenty: the evolution of American television* (Oxford, Oxford University Press, 2nd edition, 1990) pp. 238–9.

62 Gary D. Rawnsley, 'Nation Unto Nation: the BBC and VOA in International Politics, 1956–64', University of Leeds PhD thesis, 1994. The US Presidential Commission on International Broadcasting was 'confident' that these stations, 'by providing information and interpretation, will continue to be of help in future negotiations and cooperation between the Soviet Union and the United States'. Cited in Hale, *Radio Power*, p.170.

63 P. Flichy, *Dynamics of Modern Communications* (London, Sage, 1995) p. 148.

64 I prefer this phrase to 'the first television war' because, strictly speaking, the Korean War really deserves this title. See Howard Smith, 'The BBC Television Newsreel and the Korean War', *The Historical Journal of Film, Radio and Television*, vol. 8 (1988) no. 3, pp. 227–53.

65 M. McLuhan, *Understanding Media: The Extensions of Man* (New York, McGraw-Hill, 1964); M. McLuhan and Q. Fiore, *War and Peace in the Global Village* (New York, Bantam Books, 1968).

66 H. Kissinger, *Diplomacy* (New York, Simon and Schuster, 1994) pp. 667–8.

67 James Larson, 'Global Television and Foreign Policy', *Foreign Policy Association Headline Series*, no. 283 (February 1988) pp. 22–3.

68 Michael R. Beschloss, 'Presidents, Television and Foreign Crisis' (Washington DC, The Annenberg Washington Program in Communications Policy Studies of Northwestern University, 1993). This was downloaded from the World Wide Web. E-mail: awp@nwu.edu.

69 Cited in Jon Vanden Heuval, 'For the Media, a Brave (and Scary) New World', *Media Studies Journal*, Fall 1993, p. 17.

70 Ellen Mickiewicz, *Split Signals: Television and Politics in the Soviet Union* (Oxford, Oxford University Press, 1988).

71 Richard Collins, *Culture, Communication and National Identity: the case of*

Canadian Television (Toronto, University of Toronto Press, 1990); Kurt R. Hesse, 'Cross-Border Mass Communication from West to East Germany', *European Journal of Communications*, vol. 5 (1990) pp. 355–71.

72 Taylor, *Munitions of the Mind*, p. 256.

73 I have set this exercise on numerous occasions for my postgraduate students, especially those from overseas, to get them to see through the lack of empirical evidence, indeed the contradictory nature of the empirical evidence once it is collected, supporting the notion of American cultural imperialism.

74 For further details, see Taleb Al-Ahmady, 'The image of Saudi Arabia in the British Press, with particular reference to Saudi Arabia's Islamic Mission', University of Leeds PhD thesis, 1995.

75 According to Richard Johns in *Financial Times*, 24 April 1980.

76 PAL (Phase Alternating Line) was adopted by most West European countries except France, which embraced SECAM (Sequential Couleur Avec Memoire), the Russian and East European preference, while the USA adopted NTSC (National Television Systems Committee). It is common for Europeans to quip that the American system stands for 'Never the Same Colour', while Americans respond that SECAM means 'Something Else Contrary to America'.

77 G. D. Ganley, *The Exploding Power of Personal Media* (Norwood, NJ, Ablex, 1992) p. 29.

78 William M. Brinton, 'The Role of the Media in a Telerevolution', in William M. Brinton and Alan Ruler (eds), *Without Force or Lies: Voices from the Revolution of Central Europe in 1989–90* (New York, Mercury House, 1990). More recently, it is becoming axiomatic that the Internet has immense potential for disrupting authoritarian societies. See Andrew Brown, 'Asia tries to censor the Net', *Independent on Sunday*, 10 March 1996.

79 Cited in Snyder, *op. cit.*

80 *Ibid.*

81 'Murdoch cut BBC to please China', *Financial Times*, 14 June 1994.

82 Heather Hudson, *Communication Satellites* (New York, Collier Macmillan, 1990).

83 Lawrence Freedman, 'The media and foreign policy', *Despatches: the journal of the Territorial Army Pool of Information Officers* (1996) p. 141.

84 Mark D. Alleyne, *International Power and International Communication* (Oxford, St. Anthony's/Macmillan, 1995).

85 This problem stems partly from the nature of news as a human and cultural 'construction', a 'peculiar form of knowledge'. For further discussion see S. Cohen and J. Young, *The Manufacture of News: deviance, social problems and the mass media* (London, Constable, 1976); Philip Schlesinger, *Putting Reality Together* (London, Routledge, 1987); and R. Willis and S. Baran, *The Known World of Broadcast News* (London, Routledge, 1990).

86 For example, the use of the 'News Bunny' on the Mirror Group's cable service 'Live TV'. For a photo of the rabbit, in fact a man inside a pink bunny outfit, see Eric Reguly, 'Cable lays out cash but fails to hone in on success', *The Times*, 6 February 1996.

87 A problematical concept described by a former 'Panorama' employee thus: 'What the editor was really doing was to make acceptable something which in reality is quite unacceptable'. Robert MacNeil, quoted in Alan Hooper, *The Military and the Media* (Aldershot, Gower, 1984) p. 119.

88 For further discussion of the Al-Amiriya incident, see Philip M. Taylor, *War and the Media: Propaganda and Persuasion in the Gulf War* (Manchester, Manchester University Press, 1992) and David E. Morrison, *Television and the Gulf War* (London, John Libbey, 1992). There is a further consideration to all

this. On 5 February 1996, the Institute of Communications Studies at the University of Leeds monitored horrendous pictures sent over the Reuters feeds of the clean-up operation following the Peruvian air crash on a village. Here the issue is not so much whether such pictures could ever be broadcast, but that the story itself – another Third World disaster – received minimal attention in the Western media, typically no more than a few lines in the 'World in Brief' section.

89 N. Hopkinson, *The Media and International Affairs after the Cold War* (HMSO, 1993) p. 18.

90 Schlesinger, *Putting Reality Together*, p. 47.

91 James F. Hoge, 'The End of Predictability', *Media Studies Journal*, Fall 1993, p. 5.

92 William A. Henry III, 'History as it Happens', *Time*, 6 January 1992.

93 Freedman, 'Media and Foreign Policy', p. 132.

94 Gowing, *op. cit.*

95 As when the *Daily Mail* accused the BBC of being the 'Baghdad Broadcasting Corporation' when it transmitted the heavily self-censored pictures of the dead at Al-Amiriya, or when Peter Arnett was accused of being an 'Iraqi sympathiser' when he stayed in Baghdad during the war to cover such stories as the notorious 'baby-milk plant' bombing. See Taylor, *War and the Media*.

96 A view held, amongst others, by journalist John Pilger, who argued that the 'video-game war' in the Gulf, orchestrated by the coalition's media managers, merely deflected attention away from its brutal realities in order to sustain public support for the war. See John Pilger, *Distant Voices* (London, Vintage, 1992).

97 All the historical research into this has exposed the myth of a hostile media. See Daniel Hallin, *The Uncensored War: The Media and Vietnam* (Oxford, Oxford University Press, 1986).

98 Frank Aukofer and William P. Lawrence, *America's Team: The Odd Couple. A report on the relationship between the media and the military* (Vanderbilt, Freedom Forum First Amendment Centre, 1995).

99 T. B. Allen, F. Clifton Berry and N. Polmar, *CNN: War in the Gulf* (New York, Maxwell International, 1991) p. 13. It should come as no surprise that different people observe the same images differently. In a study of cultural products, such as the film 'Rambo', Australian aborigines saw a quite different meaning to President Reagan. See John Fiske, *Remote Control: Television Audiences and Cultural Power* (London, Routledge, 1989).

100 Speech at the Travellers Club, London, 9 September 1993. While recognising that to ignore the media was no longer possible, Mr Hurd asserted that 'there are some foreign policy subjects where absolute secrecy is possible', and pointed to the post-Falklands negotiations with Argentina, the Middle East Peace negotiations, and the '2 plus 4' discussions over the reunification of Germany as examples. See Gillian Tett, 'Hurd hits at role of journalists in Bosnia: success of media-free negotiations gives diplomats food for thought', *Financial Times*, 10 September 1993.

101 T. McNulty, 'Television's Impact on Executive Decision-Making and Diplomacy', *The Fletcher Forum of World Affairs*, vol. 17 (Winter 1993) p. 71.

102 Likewise, Michael Leeded, an aide to a former US Secretary of State, estimated that their staff had spent 80–90 per cent of their time worrying about the media. See Simon Serfaty (ed.), *The Media and Foreign Policy* (New York, The Free Press, 1990) p. xiv.

103 Cited in Hopkinson, *The Media and International Affairs*, p. 11.

104 Edward Mortimer, 'No news is bad news: in the absence of TV cameras, victims of aggression can be left to suffer', *Financial Times*, 27 October 1993.

105 *Ibid.*
106 The media had largely left the country because it was getting too dangerous. A departing Reuters crew handed over their camcorder to the driver of their 'technical' with instructions to film anything of interest.
107 Edward Pilkington, *Guardian*, 11 October 1993.
108 Cited in P. Brock, 'Dateline Yugoslavia: the Partisan Press', *Foreign Policy*, vol. 48 (Winter 1993/4) no. 1, p. 155.
109 Maxwell E. McCombs and Donald Shaw, 'The agenda-setting function of the mass media', *Public Opinion Quarterly* (1972), pp. 176–87.
110 Gowing, 'Real Time', p. 17.
111 This assertion, derived from audience research finding, recognises that TV can have an impact on *some* people at any given time, say, in advertising or on violent behaviour or on Bob Geldhof – but that, despite thirty or more years of research, it is still not possible to determine how, and how many of, the audience will be affected. Many watch, but few act. This is as great a problem for democrats wishing to increase turn-out during elections as it is for politicians trying to get people to vote for one party as distinct from another, let alone advertisers getting people to buy one brand of soap powder rather than another.
112 This is essentially Nik Gowing's thesis in 'Real Time', although it might be noted that the author spends most of his time in this paper documenting occasions when the reverse was true.
113 Cited in Frank J. Stech, 'Winning CNN Wars', *Parameters*, Autumn 1994, p. 38.
114 Nik Gowing, 'Real Time', p. 5.
115 Lewis Friedland, *Covering the World: International Television News Services* (New York, 20th Century Fund Press, 1992) pp. 7–8.
116 Stech, op. cit., 38.
117 Hearing of the House Foreign Affairs Committee on the Impact of Television on U.S. Foreign Policy. Transcript supplied by the Federal News Service, Washington DC.
118 *Ibid.*
119 McNulty, *op. cit.*, p. 72.
120 The phrase is Ed Turner's, head of news at CNN. See Tony Downmount, *Channels of Resistance* (London, BFI, 1993) p. 1.
121 P. Harveson, 'A leader in Global TV News: aggressive expansion by CNN Television Network', *Financial Times*, 1 November 1994.
122 E. Bickham, 'Playing to the heart of the Nation', *Spectrum*, Autumn 1993, p. 3.
123 Quoted in McNulty, 'Television's Impact', p. 72.
124 See in particular John MacArthur, *Second Front: Censorship and Propaganda in the Gulf War* (Berkeley, University of California Press, 1993 edition).
125 George C. Church, 'This Time We Mean It: NATO's pull-back-or-we-bomb ultimatum to Bosnia's Serbs looks genuine, but will it help end the war?' *Time*, 21 February 1994.
126 Ted Koppel, cited in Stech, 'Winning CNN Wars', p. 42.
127 Henry, 'History as it Happens'.
128 J. Wood, *A History of International Broadcasting* (London, Peter Peregrinus, 1992) p. 235.
129 This was the celebrated 'cruel hoax' incident, described in greater detail in Philip M. Taylor, 'Back to the Future? Integrating the media into the history of international relations', *Historical Journal of Film, Radio and Television*. vol. 14 (1994) no. 3.
130 T. J. McNulty, 'Television's Impact', pp. 81–2.

131 Preface to 'Global News after the Cold War', *Media Studies Journal*, Fall 1993, p. xv.
132 Robert Kubey and Mihaly Csikszentmihalyi, *Television and the Quality of Life* (Hillsdale, NJ, Erlbaum Associates, 1990) p. 189. Cited by Schiller in *Information Inequality*, pp. 71–2.
133 James Hoge, 'The End of Predictability', p. 9.
134 Ed Turner, 'The Power and the Glory', in Christopher Young, 'The role of the media in International Conflict', a report on a two day seminar at the Canadian Institute for International Peace and Security, December 1991.
135 *Ibid.*
136 *Ibid.*
137 *Ibid.*

3 ILLUSIONS OF REALITY

1 Extracts from Martin Bell's pre-release article about his Bosnian memories, *In Harm's Way*, in the *Observer*, 17 September 1995.
2 Second World War veteran correspondent Michael Reynolds noted how reticent soldiers where when on leave but less so at the front: there, the soldier 'is desperately anxious to talk, to make you understand what he is going through and how awful and important it is. And of course it is a civilian he then wants to talk to; there is no satisfaction in unloading all this pent-up emotion on to a fellow-soldier who has gone through the same experience himself. And that is where the war correspondent cashes in; because he is the only civilian who can go to the front; he is the only civilian with access to the soldier in his most communicative mood'. Michael Reynolds, 'The War Correspondent's Job', *Army Quarterly and Defence Journal*, vol. 59, January 1950.
3 Philip Knightley, *The First Casualty: the war correspondent as hero, myth-maker and propagandist from the Crimea to Vietnam* (London, Quartet Books, 1975).
4 See Daniel Pick, *War Machine: the rationalisation of slaughter in the modern age* (New Haven, Yale University Press, 1993).
5 For further details, see M. L. Sanders and Philip M. Taylor, *British propaganda during the First World War* (Basingstoke, Macmillan, 1982).
6 P. Fussell, *The Great War and Modern Memory* (Oxford, Oxford University Press, 1975); Modris Eksteins, *Rights of Spring: the Great War and the Birth of the Modern Age* (London, Bantam Press, 1989).
7 See Cate Haste, *Keep the Home Fires Burning* (London, Lane, 1977).
8 Cited in Trevor Hoyle, *War Report: the war correspondent's view of battle from the Crimea to the Falklands* (London, Grafton Books, 1987) p. 38.
9 See Philip M. Taylor, 'Censorship in Britain in World War Two: an overview', in A. C. Duke and G. Tanse (eds), *Too mighty to be free: Censorship and the Press in Britain and Netherlands* (Zutphen, de Walburg Pers, 1987).
10 Frederick Voss, *Reporting the War: the journalistic coverage of World War II* (New York, Greenwood Press, 1989) p. 24.
11 Alfred Challener (ed.), *The Papers of Dwight David Eisenhower: vol. 4 The War Years* (Baltimore, Johns Hopkins University Press, 1970), document 1999.
12 George H. Roeder, *The Censored War: American visual experience during World War Two* (New Haven, Yale University Press, 1993).
13 See Knightley, *op. cit.*, p. 337; Michael Linfield, *Freedom under Fire: US Civil Liberties in Times of War* (Boston, Southend Press, 1990).
14 Valerie Adams, *The Media and the Falklands Campaign* (London, Macmillan, 1986) pp. 25–30.

15 For the latest evaluation see Tony Shaw, *Eden, Suez and the Mass Media: Propaganda and Persuasion during the Suez Crisis* (London, I. B. Taurus, 1996).
16 Harry G. Summers, Jr. *On Strategy: A critical analysis of the Vietnam war* (New York, Dell Publishing, 1982) p. 63.
17 Daniel Hallin, *The Uncensored War: The Media and Vietnam* (Oxford, Oxford University Press, 1986).
18 Derrik Mercer, Geoff Mungham and Kevin Williams, *The Fog of War: The Media on the Battlefield* (Heinemann, London, 1987) p. 214.
19 Quoted in Joseph Fromm, 'The Media and the Making of Defence Policy: the US example', in Christoph Betram (ed.), *Defence and Consensus: the domestic aspects of western security* (London, Macmillan/IISS, 1983) p. 34.
20 Frank Aukofer and William P. Lawrence, *America's Team: The Odd Couple. A report on the relationship between the media and the military* (Vanderbilt, Freedom Forum First Amendment Centre, 1995). p. 40.
21 Jeffrey P. Kimball, 'The Stab-in-the-Back Legend and the Vietnam War', *Armed Forces and Society*, vol. 14 (1988) no. 13.
22 William Prochnau, *Once Upon a Distant War: Reporting from Vietnam* (Edinburgh and London, Mainstream Publishing, 1996) p. 12.
23 For further details see Larry Berman, *Lyndon Johnson's War* (New York, W.W. Norton, 1989).
24 Mercer *et. al.*, *The Fog of War*, pp. 224–5.
25 Philip M. Taylor, 'Wayne's World: "The Green Berets" ', *History Today*, vol. 45 (March 1995).
26 For further details see Philip M. Taylor, *Munitions of the Mind: a history of propaganda from the ancient world to the present era* (Manchester, Manchester University Press, 2nd edition, 1995)
27 See Bruce Cumings, *War on Television* (London, Verso, 1992) p. 88.
28 Berman, *op. cit.*, p. 175.
29 Hallin, *Uncensored War*, p. 192.
30 Daniel Hallin, *We Keep America on Top of the World: Television Journalism and the Public Sphere* (London, Routledge, 1994) p. 47.
31 *Ibid.*, p. 51. My emphasis.
32 See Caroline Page, *U.S. Official Propaganda during the Vietnam War, 1965–73* (London, Leicester University Press, 1996).
33 Taylor, *Munitions of the Mind*, p. 272.
34 See Michael J. Arlen, *The Living Room War: Writings about Television* (New York, Viking, 1969).
35 Hallin, *We Keep America on Top of the World*, p. 55.
36 William M. Hammond, 'The Press in Vietnam as an Agent of Defeat: a critical examination', *Reviews in American History*, vol. 17 (1989) no. 2, p. 321.
37 'Foreign Correspondents – the view from Saigon', *Time*, 20 September 1963.
38 Braestrup, author of *Big Story* (Boulder, Co., Westview, 1977), made this statement at a conference held by the Freedom Forum Centre to commemorate Vietnam war reporting twenty years after the event. A summary of the proceedings can be found on the World Wide Web at http://www.nando/net/prof/freedom/1994/reports/Vietnam.html.
39 Harry G. Summers, Jr. *On Strategy: A critical analysis of the Vietnam War* (New York, Dell Publishing, 1982) p. 68.
40 A possibility first postulated rhetorically by Robin Day in a famous article in *Encounter* in 1970. 'Television has a built-in bias towards depicting any conflict in terms of the visible brutality. You can say, of course, that this is what war is – brutality, conflict, starvation and combat. All I am saying is that there are other issues which cause these things to come about . . . One wonders if in future a

democracy which has uninhibited television coverage in every home will ever be able to fight a war, however just.'

41 Stephen Badsey, *Modern Military Operations and the Media*, (Strategic and Combat Studies Institute, Occasional Paper No. 8) p. 13.

42 Henry Fairlie of the *Washington Post* wrote on 13 July 1980 that 'It is the nature of most important events to be dull and by nature television cannot handle the dull. . . . It is monstrously untrue that the camera cannot lie. It is the most eager and pliant of liars. Its nature is what its name says. Motion. It needs action, and of a particular kind.'

43 Cited in Mort Rosenblum, *Who Stole the News?* (New York, John Wiley and Sons, 1993) p. 1.

44 General Sir Michael Dugan, 'Generals versus Journalists', in H. Smith (ed.), *The Media and the Gulf War: the press and democracy in wartime* (Washington, Seven Locks Press, 1992) p. 60.

45 House of Commons Defence Committee, First Report 1982–3, *The Handling of the Press and Public Information During the Falklands Conflict*, vol. I and II, (London, HMSO, 1982).

46 For a slight discussion of this, see Stephen Badsey, 'Twenty things you thought you knew about the media', *Despatches,* no. 5 (Spring 1995) p. 57.

47 For a discussion of this, see Taylor, *Munitions of the Mind*, p. 279.

48 Mercer *et. al.*, *The Fog of War*, Chapter V.

49 A concept originally developed by Daniel Boorstein, *The Image* (New York, Athenaeum, 1962).

50 Baudrillard began the controversy with his article 'The Reality Gulf', published in *Guardian*, 11 January 1991, in which he argued that the Gulf War never happened as a reality for most spectators. For a criticism of this approach see Christopher Norris, *Uncritical Theory: Postmodernism, Intellectuals and the Gulf War* (London, Lawrence and Wishart, 1992). Developments with the Internet give even greater opportunities along these lines. See P. Virilio, 'Red Alert in Cyberspace', *Radical Philosophy*, no. 74 (November/December 1995) pp. 2–4.

51 Cited in Nan Levinson, 'Snazzy visuals, hard facts and obscured issues', in *Index on Censorship*, vol. 20, nos 4 and 5, April/May 1991, p. 27.

52 The phrase is Christopher Wain's of the BBC. See Alan Hooper, *The Military and the Media* (Aldershot, Gower, 1984) p. 118.

53 Cited in Trevor Hoyle, *War Report: the war correspondent's view of battle from the Crimea to the Falklands* (London, Grafton Books, 1987) p. 15.

54 Ibid., pp. 14–15.

55 John Simpson, *From the House of War*, (London, Arrow Books, 1991) pp. xv–xvi.

56 A. Aldgate, 'Creative Tensions: *Desert Victory*, the Army Film Unit and Anglo-American Rivalry, 1943–45', in Philip M. Taylor (ed.), *Britain and the Cinema in the Second World War* (Basingstoke, Macmillan, 1988).

57 Roger Smither, 'A Wonderful Idea of the Fighting: the question of fakes in *The Battle of the Somme*', *Historical Journal of Film, Radio and Television*, vol. 13 (1993) no. 2; G. Mallins, *How I Filmed the War* (London and Nashville, Imperial War Museum reprint, 1994).

58 Martin Bell, *In Harm's Way: Reflections of a War Zone Thug* (London, Hamish Hamilton, 1995) p. 30.

59 *Ibid.*, p. 31. When two British soldiers were killed in Split, the Army's Public Information team found that 'despite the speed of communications in our chain of command we still only learned of one of the deaths from SKY News before

we had been informed'. See Captain Tristan Lovering, 'Grappling with the News', *Despatches*, no. 5, Spring 1995, p. 82.

60 Colonel B. Stewart, *Broken Lives: a personal view of the Bosnian Conflict* (London, Harper Collins, 1994).

61 John Fialka, *Hotel Warriors: Covering the Gulf War* (Washington, Woodrow Wilson Center Press, 1991).

62 *Ibid.*, p. 2.

63 As told by Ed Cody, pool reporter for the *Washington Post*. See *Financial Times*, 16 March 1991.

64 G. Meade, 'Hard Groundrules in the Sand', *Index on Censorship*, vol. 20, nos. 4 and 5, April/May 1991, p. 6.

65 M. Massing, 'Debriefings: what we saw, what we learned', *Columbia Journalism Review*, May–June 1991, p. 23.

66 Cited in Fialka, *Hotel Warriors*, p. 27.

67 *Independent*, 7 February 1991.

68 Reynolds, 'The War Correspondent's Job'.

69 Colin Wills in *Reporting the War: a collection of experiences and reflections on the Gulf*, a discussion paper published by the British Executive of the International Press Institute, May 1991, p. 6.

70 *Ibid.*, p. 7.

71 *Washington Post Weekly Edition*, 18–24 February 1991.

72 Wills, *Reporting the War*, p. 6.

73 *Newsweek*, 11 February 1991.

74 Donald Mould, 'Press Pools and Military–Media Relations in the Gulf War: a case study of the Battle of Khafji, January 1991', *Historical Journal of Film, Radio and Television*, vol. 16, no. 2, June 1996.

75 As recounted by Colin Wills in *Reporting the War*, p. 6.

76 *Ibid.*, p. 1, and personal discussion.

77 *Ibid.*, p. 2.

78 These issues have been examined in greater detail in Philip M. Taylor, *War and the Media*.

79 See Philip M. Taylor, 'Film as a Weapon in the Second World War', in D. Dutton (ed.), *Statecraft and Diplomacy: Essays presented to P. M. H. Bell* (Liverpool, Liverpool University Press, 1995) p. 144.

80 Anthony Aldgate, *Cinema and History: British Newsreels and the Spanish Civil War* (London, Scolar Press, 1979) p. 158.

81 Harris to the Under Secretary of State for Air, 25 October 1943, Public Records Office, London, AIR 14/32.

82 Noble Frankland, *The Bomber Offensive Against Germany* (London, HMSO, 1965) p. 97.

83 B. Allen, F. Clinton Berry and N. Polmar, *CNN: War in the Gulf. From the Invasion of Kuwait to the Day of Victory and Beyond* (London, Maxwell-Macmillan International, 1991) p. 236.

84 These findings are to be found in David Morrison's *Television and the Gulf War* (London, John Libbey, 1992).

85 FM 100–5, Operations (Washington DC, US Government Printing Office) 14 June 1993.

86 *Ibid.*

87 Lieutenant-General H. Hugh Shelton and Lieutenant-General Timothy D. Vane, 'Winning the Information War in Haiti', *Military Review*, vol. LXXV (November–December 1995) no. 6.

88 M. Browne, 'Vietnam Reporting: three years of crisis', *Columbia Journalism Review*, Fall 1964.

89 John Fialka, cited in Frank Aukofer and William P. Lawrence, *America's Team: the Odd Couple*, p. 57.
90 *Ibid.*
91 *Ibid.*, p. 62.
92 Major-General Patrick Brady, 'United States Army public affairs', *Despatches*, no. 2, Autumn 1991, p. 81. General Brady served in Vietnam.

4 MIND GAMES

1 'We had to arrange their minds in the order of battle just as carefully and as formally as other officers would arrange their bodies. And not only our own men's minds, though naturally they came first. We must arrange the minds of the enemy, so far as we could reach them; then those other minds of the nation supporting us behind the firing line, since more than half the battle passed there in the back; then the minds of the enemy nation waiting the verdict; and the neutrals looking on; circle beyond circle.' T. E. Lawrence, *Severn Pillars of Wisdom* (London, Jonathan Cape, 1965 edition).
2 Joint Doctrine for Command and Control Warfare, Joint Publication 3–13.1, 7 February 1996 (Washington DC).
3 John Arqilla and David Ronfeldt, 'Cyberwar is Coming!', *Journal of Comparative Strategy*, vol. 12 (1993) no. 2, pp. 141–65.
4 Martin C. Libicki, *What is Information Warfare?* (Washington, D.C., National Defense University Press, 1995.).
5 David S. Alberts and Richard E. Haynes, 'The Realm of Information Dominance: Beyond Information War', First International Symposium on Command and Control Research and Technology (June 1995): pp. 560–65.
6 Daniel E. Magsig, 'Information Warfare in the Information Age', Institute for the Advanced Study of Infowar, http://www.psycom.net.
7 As stated in the 1944 Standing Directive for Psychological Warfare against members of the German Armed Forces, reprinted in D. Lerner, *Psychological Warfare Against Nazi Germany* (Cambridge, Mass., MIT Press, 1971).
8 *Ibid.*
9 Jay M. Parker and Jerold L. Hale, 'Psychological Operations in the Gulf War: Analyzing Key Themes in Battlefield Leaflets', in Thomas A. McCain and Leonard Shyles (eds), *The 1,000 Hour War: Communication in the Gulf* (Westport CT, Greenwood Press, 1994) p. 90.
10 *Ibid.*
11 *Ibid.*
12 *Ibid.*
13 US Department of the Army, *Field Manual 33–1: Psychological operations* (Washington DC, Government Printing Office, 1992) p. 12. See also US Department of Defense, Joint Chiefs of Staff, *DoD Dictionary of Military and Associated Terms and Abbreviations* (JCS Publication 1–02, republished by Greenhill Books, 1990) p. 291.
14 *Ibid.* Emphasis added.
15 'Military aspects of psychological warfare', Training circular no. 17, Department of the Army, 12 December 1950. Public Records Office, PRO WO 216/425. One can only speculate as to how this American document came to be copied to British military authorities.
16 In a note for the Prime Minister in 1941, Major Morton noted that 'the Axis enjoys great advantage over us from having recognized that diplomacy, foreign propaganda and economic warfare together form a fourth fighting arm of

modern war. We should do likewise.' 29 April 1941. See Public Records Office, PRO PREM 3/365/11.

17 Cited in James Adams, 'Dawn of the Cyber Soldiers', *Sunday Times*, 15 October 1995.

18 Copy in author's possession. The booklet consists of innocuous drawings for children to colour in. However there are two join-the-dots exercises which, when completed, show land-mines in an attempt to inform children how to learn what they look like.

19 Colonel Jeffrey B. Jones, 'The Third Wave and the Fourth Dimension', draft paper supplied by the author, 1995.

20 Alan D. Campen, (ed.) *The First Information War: The Story of Communications, Computers, and Intelligence Systems in the Persian Gulf War* (Fairfax, VA, AFCEA International Press, 1992).

21 For a history of war propaganda see Philip M. Taylor, *Munitions of the Mind: a history of propaganda from the ancient world to the present era* (Manchester, Manchester University Press, 2nd edition, 1995). The best introduction to psywar remains T. H. Qualter's *Propaganda and Psychological Warfare* (New York, Random House, 1962).

22 Sun Tzu, *The Art of War*, trans. S. B. Griffiths (Oxford, Oxford University Press, 1971) pp. 77–8.

23 This tends to explain why John Keegan's *The Face of Battle* (London, Cape, 1976) created such an impact when it was first published.

24 Susan Carruthers, *Winning Hearts and Minds: British Governments, the Media and Counter Insurgency* (Leicester, Leicester University Press, 1995).

25 Northcliffe to General Charteris, 6 August 1916, cited in R. Pound and G. Harmsworth, *Northcliffe*, (London, Cassell, 1959) p. 468.

26 E. E. Slosson, quoted in G. C. Bruntz, 'Propaganda as an Instrument of Policy', *Current History*, July 1930.

27 Sir Campbell Stuart, *Secrets of Crewe House* (London, Hodder and Stoughton, 1920).

28 Mark Cornwall, 'The Role of Allied Propaganda in the Collapse of the Austro-Hungarian Empire in 1918,' University of Leeds PhD thesis, 1988.

29 E. A. Powell, *The Army Behind the Army* (New York, 1919) pp. 347–8.

30 'Gen. Propaganda explains how he won Bosche over', *Stars and Stripes*, 3 January 1919.

31 Both these quotations were cited in a World War Two publication produced by the Ministry of Information, 'RAF against Goebbels: the story of the great truth offensive over Europe', 1941.

32 *The Times*, 31 October 1919. Even this statement must be treated with caution, given that *The Times* was owned by Lord Northcliffe who was keen to vindicate his wartime reputation as the 'Minister for the Destruction of German Confidence'.

33 J. F. C. Fuller, *Tanks in the Great War, 1914–18* (London, Murray, 1920) p. 320.

34 A. Ponsonby, *Falsehood in Wartime* (London, Allen and Unwin, 1928) p. 18.

35 S. Wallingford, 'Western Samoa Operations, 1930: Air Report', *Royal Air Force Quarterly*, vol. 1 (1930) no. 4, p. 640.

36 Ladilas Farago, *War of Wits – the anatomy of Espionage and Intelligence* (New York, Paperback Library, 1952) p. 241.

37 It is, however, worth pointing out that the official wartime history of PWE, 'Political Warfare Activities carried out by the Departments EH, and SO1 and PWE from the Munich Crisis till the surrender of Germany', written by David Garnett in 1947, was only released into the Public Record Office in the summer of 1996.

38 N. F. Newsome, 'Special Standing Directive', 1 October 1943. BBC Written Archives Centre, Caversham. E2/135 Foreign General Directives, 1940–3.
39 Supreme Headquarters Allied Powers Europe, the military HQ of NATO.
40 Lecture delivered to NATO Defence College, Paris, September 1959.
41 From the Latin *sibilare*, to whisper.
42 For a detailed discussion of the propaganda implications of the policy of unconditional surrender, see Wallace Carroll, *Persuade or Perish* (Boston, Houghton Mifflin and Co., 1948) Ch.7.
43 On British black propaganda in the Second World War, see Michael Balfour, *Propaganda in War* (London, Routledge, 1979); C. Cruickshank, *The Fourth Arm: Psychological Warfare, 1938–45* (London, Davis-Poynter, 1977); Sefton Delmer, *Black Boomerang* (London, Secker and Warburg, 1962); Ellic Howe, *The Black Game* (London, Michael Joseph, 1982).
44 D. Lerner, 'The Psychological Warfare Campaign Against Germany: D-Day to VE-Day', in Anthony Rhodes, *Propaganda – The Art Of Persuasion: World War II* (London, Angus and Robertson, 1976) .
45 Newsome, 'Special Standing Directive'.
46 Cited in Lerner, *op. cit.*
47 *Ibid.*
48 A. Panfilov, *Broadcasting Pirates, or Abuse of the Microphone* (Moscow, Progress, 1981) p. 79.
49 Martin F. Herz, 'Some Psychological Lessons from Leaflet Propaganda in World War II', *Public Opinion Quarterly*, Fall 1949, p. 472.
50 *Ibid.*
51 James P. Warburg, *Unwritten Treaty* (New York, Harcourt Brace, 1946).
52 Reprinted in W. E. Daugherty, 'Bomb warnings to friendly and enemy targets', in W. E. Daugherty and M. Janowitz (eds), *A Psychological Warfare Casebook* (Baltimore, Johns Hopkins Press, 1958) p. 360.
53 Wallace Carroll, *Persuade or Perish*, pp. 364–5.
54 Including by Sir Peter de la Billiere in his memoirs, *Storm Command: a personal account of the Gulf War* (London, Harper Collins, 1992) pp. 126–7. Deception involves the manipulation, distortion or falsification of evidence and is usually directed at decision maker(s) rather than those responsible for carrying out the decisions.
55 Howard Becker, 'The Nature and Consequences of Black Propaganda', *American Sociological Review*, vol. 14 (1949) pp. 221–34.
56 See US Department of State, *Soviet Influence Activities: a report on active measures and propaganda, 1977–8* (Publication 9720, August 1989). Also see 'Too Good To Be True' in *Newsweek*, 26 June 1995, which exposed the transplant story as false but identified it as one of those persistent rumours which travel the world rather than as a product of former Soviet black propaganda.
57 Cited in the précis of a lecture by Lieutenant-Colonel G. P. Orde, 'Propaganda and its organisation for war', which was used as an addendum to Monthly Intelligence Summary, No. 8, of 1 August 1924. Public Records Office, PRO ADM 1/8657/44.
58 Cornwall, *op. cit.*
59 Farago, *War of Wits*, p. 254.
60 See, in particular, Paul Linebarger, *Psychological Warfare* (Washington DC, Infantry Journal Press, 1948); Daniel Lerner (ed.), *Propaganda in War and Crisis* (New York, Stewart, 1950).
61 See Trevor Barnes, 'The Secret Cold War: the CIA and American Foreign Policy in Europe, 1946–56, Part 1 and Part 2', *Historical Journal*, vols 24 and 25, (1981 and 1982) pp. 399–415 and pp. 649–70 respectively.

62 For further details, see Scott Lucas, 'Campaigns of Truth: the Psychological Strategy Board and American Ideology, 1951–53', *International History Review*, vol. XVIII (May 1996) no. 2, pp. 279–302.

63 Stephen E. Pease, *Psywar: Psychological Warfare in Korea, 1950–53* (Harrisburg, Stackpole Books, 1992).

64 James I. Matray (ed.), *Historical Dictionary of the Korean War* (London, Greenwood Press, 1991): see entry for 'Operation Moolah'.

65 See S. Mickelson, *America's Other Voice: the story of Radio Free Europe and Radio Liberty* (New York, Praeger, 1982).

66 As revealed in the preface to Farago's *War of Wits*.

67 Alfred H. Paddock, *US Army Special Warfare: Its Origins* (Washington DC, National Defense University Press, 1982).

68 Carnes Lord, 'The Psychological Dimension in National Strategy', in C. Lord and F. R. Barnett (eds), *Political Warfare and Psychological Operations: Rethinking the US Approach* (Washington DC, National Defense University Press, 1989) p. 15.

69 Cited in M. E. Haas, *Air Commando! 1950–75: Twenty Five Years at the Tip of the Spear* (United States Special Operations Command, Hurlbert Field, 1994). In author's possession.

70 See Robert Chandler, *War of Ideas: The US Propaganda Campaign in Vietnam* (Boulder, Co., Westview, 1981); Thomas Sorenson, *The Word War: the story of American propaganda* (New York, Harper and Row, 1968).

71 *Ibid.*

72 Kevin Generous, *Vietnam: the secret war* (New York, Gallery Books, 1985) p. 173.

73 John Schlight, *The War in South Vietnam: The years of the Offensive, 1965–8* (Washington DC, Office of Air Force History, 1988) p. 244.

74 *Ibid.*, pp. 240ff.

75 'South Vietnam: the tube takes hold', *Time*, 30 November 1970.

76 R. S. Nathan, 'Psychological Warfare: key to success in Vietnam', *Military Review*, April 1968, p. 28.

77 JUSPAO, 'The NVA Soldier in South Vietnam as a PSYOP Target', *Psyop Policy*, 20 February 1968, no. 59, pp. 1–2.

78 DoD Psychological Operations Master Plan 1985 (Washington, 1985).

79 Fred W. Walker, 'Truth is the Best Propaganda: a study in military psychological operations', *National Guard Magazine*, October 1987, p. 28. See also A. H. Paddock, 'Psyop in the early 1980s: the way we were', *Special Warfare*, 6 (October 1993) p. 4.

80 Colonel Ronald T. Sconyers, 'The Information War', *Military Review*, February 1989.

81 Sergeant. P. Jones and Colonel J. B. Jones, 'Psychological Operations and Nation Building in Panama: Operation Promote Liberty', *Perspectives*, vol. 8 (Fall 1993) no. 3.

82 'Psychological Operations During Desert Shield/Desert Storm: A Post-Operational Analysis' (USSOC, 1993) pp. 1–5.

83 Colonel Jeffrey B. Jones, 'Psychological Operations in Desert Shield, Desert Storm and Urban Freedom', *Special Warfare*, July 1994.

84 Parker and Hale, *op. cit.*, pp. 91–2.

85 'Psychological Operations During Desert Shield/Desert Storm'.

86 Jeffrey B. Jones, 'Psychological Operations in Desert Shield, Desert Storm and Urban Freedom'.

87 Cited in Major Robert B. Adolph, Jr., 'PSYOP: Gulf War Force Multiplier', *Army*, December 1992, p. 16.

88 Much of what follows is gleaned from the post-war publication of a collection of leaflets, published by the 4th Psychological Operations Group, normally based at Fort Bragg in North Carolina.

89 See also *Chicago Tribune*, 24 January 1991 and *Sunday Telegraph*, 20 January 1991.

90 *Daily Telegraph*, 21 January 1991. This was confirmed after the war by de la Billiere, who wrote: 'The tapes were mainly of popular Arab music played by leading entertainers and so were worth listening to in their own right, but they also contained factual yet seditious messages, telling listeners how Saddam Hussein was ruining their country, how he had violated Islamic principles by his invasion of Kuwait, how Kuwait was not worth dying for and how the Allies would crush them unless they gave themselves up'. He also states that about 50,000 such tapes were smuggled in 'apparently to good effect'. See *Storm Command*, p. 126.

91 Major Jack N. Summe, 'PSYOP Support to Operation Desert Storm', *Special Warfare*, October 1992, pp. 6–9.

92 *The Times*, 13 February 1991. The director of VOA was 'promoted' soon after this incident to become ambassador to the Seychelles.

93 BBC2 'Newsnight', 8 May 1991. When the BBC Monitoring Service at Caversham first began picking up the Voice of Free Iraq, BBC TV reported that it was 'unclear' who was operating it but implied that it was run by opposition groups within Iraq, since it was clearly anti-Saddam. BBC1 17 January 1991, 11:52 GMT. University of Leeds Institute of Communications Studies Gulf War Archive [hereafter ULICS]. It was also being jammed – but this was presumably by the Iraqis.

94 According to the Voice of Free Iraq on 10 February 1991, 'the Ba'athist clique has undertaken the occupation of Kuwait thus giving a justification for foreign forces to enter our sacred land', Summary of World Broadcasts (hereafter SWB), Part 4, 13 February 1991.

95 World Broadcasting Information (hereafter WBI), 1 February 1991. Emphasis added.

96 On 12 February 1991 the Voice of Free Iraq carried a report from the Saudi news agency, SPA, quoting Ibrahim Al-Zubaydi, who was identified as 'the former director of Iraqi Radio and the director of the Voice of Free Iraq Radio'. WBI, 15 February 1991. That it was a CIA operation was hinted at by Mark Urban, who confused the station with the military's Voice of the Gulf after the war. See 'The secret war against him', *Daily Telegraph*, 8 January 1993.

97 SWB, Part 4, 1 February 1991.

98 SWB, Part 4, 31 January 1991.

99 SWB, Part 4, 13 February 1991. The broadcast was monitored on 10 February.

100 It would appear that a station identifying itself as 'This is Kuwait', the usual call sign for official Kuwaiti radio, began transmitting on 29 August 1990 from Dammam in Saudi Arabia. While the Iraqis took over the old station in Kuwait City, the Egyptian news agency stated on 29 December 1990 that this Kuwaiti government-in-exile station was established by the Egyptian Radio and Television Union. SWB, Part 4, 27 February 1991. Radio Kuwait also broadcast from Cairo.

101 Summe, *op. cit.*, p. 8.

102 SWB, Part 4, 8 February 1991.

103 C. P. Freund, 'The War on Your Mind: Psychological Warfare from Genghis Khan to PoWs to CNN', *Washington Post*, 27 January 1991.

104 *Financial Times*, 28 January 1991.

105 H. A. Friedman, 'A brief look at Iraqi propaganda leaflets', *Perspectives*, Fall 1992.

106 According to CNN, 05:35 GMT, 14 February 1991. ULICS.
107 *Sunday Telegraph*, 20 January 1991.
108 *The Times*, 7 February 1991.
109 The *Guardian*, 7 February 1991.
110 For further discussion of the leaflets, together with illustrations of some of them, see Parker and Hale, *op. cit.*
111 *The Times*, 7 February 1991.
112 *Newsweek*, 17 June 1991, put the final figure at 29 million. To put this in some kind of perspective, even in the final six weeks of the First World War only five million leaflets were dropped by the allies over German lines. M. L. Sanders and Philip M. Taylor, *British Propaganda during the First World War* (Basingstoke, Macmillan, 1982) pp. 237–8.
113 Pentagon Briefing, Riyadh (General McPeak), CNN, 15 March 1991. ULICS.
114 *International Herald Tribune*, 22 January 1991.
115 B. Brown and D. Shukman, *All Necessary Means: Inside the Gulf War* (London, BBC Books, 1991) p. 96.
116 This entire story was told in *Newsweek*, 17 June 1991. At the Saudi briefing in Riyadh on 9 February 1991, the news was announced that seven soldiers, including a Lieutenant Colonel, had defected. It seems likely that this group was the one to which the *Newsweek* story refers. The Saudi briefing was monitored on the Visnews uplink on 10 February 1991 at 05:35 GMT. ULICS.
117 Summe, *op. cit.*
118 Colonel Jeffrey B. Jones, 'Psychological Operations in Desert Shield, Desert Storm and Urban Freedom'.
119 *International Herald Tribune*, 24 January 1991.
120 *International Herald Tribune*, 28 January 1991.
121 *International Herald Tribune*, 30 January 1991.
122 Christopher Walker in *The Times*, 29 January 1991.
123 Reprinted in *Psychological Operations Support for Operation Provide Comfort* (Fort Bragg, 1994).
124 *Ibid.*
125 Preface in *Ibid.*
126 Lieutenant-Colonel Charles P. Borchini and Mari Borstelmann, 'PSYOP in Somalia: The Voice of Hope', *Special Warfare*, October 1994.
127 Ken York, 'PSYOP Personnel Put the Word Out', *Armed Forces Journal International*, December 1993.
128 Reprinted in *Psychological Operations in support of Operation Restore Hope 9 December 1992 – 4 May 1993* (Fort Bragg, 1994). Copy in author's possession.
129 York, *op. cit.*
130 Cited in Borchini and Borstelmann, 'PSYOP in Somalia'.
131 'Putting the aria into Somalia', *The Economist*, 24 April 1993, p. 72.
132 Borchini and Borstelmann, 'PSYOP in Somalia'.
133 *Ibid.*
134 4 May 1995. Reprinted in *PSYOP Support to Operation Uphold Democracy: A Psychological Victory* (Fort Bragg, 1995). Copy in author's possession.
135 *Ibid.*, p. 6.
136 Jim Pogue, 'Radio Democracy', *Monitoring Times*, vol. 13, September 1994, no. 9, p. 17.
137 Tony Capaccio, 'Commando Solo: Winning the Hearts and Minds of Haitians', *Defense Week*, 17 October 1994.
138 *PSYOP Support to Operation Uphold Democracy: A Psychological Victory*, p. 8.
139 *Ibid.*, p. 18.

140 *Ibid.*, p. 20.

141 Capaccio, *op. cit.*

142 One such example of PSYOPS to promote PSYOPS can be found in 'Psyching out the enemy', *Army Times*, 28 February 1994. Really, this should have been called 'how to win friends and influence people'.

143 Cited in *Ibid.*

144 *Ibid.*

145 *PSYOP Support to Operation Uphold Democracy: A Psychological Victory*, p. 24.

146 Cited in Z.A.B. Zeman, *Nazi Propaganda* (Oxford, Oxford University Press, 1973) p. 86.

147 US Special Operations Forces, *Posture Statement 1994*. In author's possession.

148 *Ibid.*

149 *Ibid.*

150 *Ibid.*

151 Lt. Col. D. J. A. Stone, ' "Out of the Shadows": The re-emergence of the UK's Psychological Operations capability since 1945', *British Army Review*, no. 114 (December 1996), p. 7.

152 Major R. R. Smith, 'The Use of Psychological Operations, and their Role in the Return to Normality in Bosnia-Herzegovina', *British Army Review*, no. 114 (December 1996), pp. 13–19.

153 Cited in Captain Janice M. Morrow, 'Never Seen, Always Heard', *Airman*, February 1993, p. 4.

154 4th Psychological Operations Group (A), *Psychological Operations support to Noncombatant Evacuation Operations* (Fort Bragg, 1995).

155 *The Times*, 29 May 1996.

156 Douglas Waller, 'Onward Cyber Soldiers', *Time*, 21 August 1995.

157 Cited in James Adams, 'Dawn of the Cyber Soldiers', *Sunday Times*, 15 October 1995.

158 Since its creation in 1955, the Bundeswehr has used PSYOPS units, notably the Fernmelder Battalion 950, a regular battalion of 650 personnel, capable of doubling in size by the addition of reservists. It mainly worked to counter East German propaganda during the Cold War but has since been deployed in Somalia. Italy has the Monte Grappa Battalion, about which little is known, while Turkey and Greece also have small units. The British, burned by their experience in Northern Ireland and the Colin Wallace affair, maintain a smaller capability still.

159 See Alfred H. Paddock. ' "No More Tactical Information Detachments": US Military Psychological Operations in Transition', *Low Intensity Conflict and Law Enforcement*, vol. 2 (1993) Bo. 2, pp. 195–211.

160 Brian Cloughley, 'Peace in Mind: will the UN give psyops a chance?', *Jane's International Defence Review*, no. 3, 1996, p. 59.

161 Thomas A. Timmes, 'Military Psychological Operations in the 1990s', *Special Warfare*, January 1994.

162 William Daugherty for the American Institutes for Research in the Behavioral Sciences, *The Art and Science of Psychological Operations: Case Studies of Military Applications*, vol. 1 (Department of the Army, Washington, 1976) p. 17.

163 Fred Walker, 'Truth is the Best Propaganda: a study in Military Psychological Operations', *National Guard*, October 1987, p. 27.

164 Thimmes, *op. cit.*

CONCLUSION

1 Walter R. Sharp and Grayson Kirk, *Contemporary International Politics* (New York, Rinehart and Co, 1940) p. 191.
2 Preface to *Media Studies Journal*, special issue on 'Global News after the Cold War', Fall 1993, p. xiv.
3 Michael Crichton, 'The Mediasaurus: Today's mass media is tomorrow's fossil fuel', *Wired*, 1.4, info@wired.com.
4 'Assessing the Press: The Public and the Media', in *The Media at War: the Press and the Persian Gulf Conflict*, Garnett Foundation Report (Columbia University, 1991) p. 83.
5 The US sociologist David Riesman, cited in Robert Dallek, *The American Style of Foreign Policy: Cultural Politics and Foreign Affairs* (New York, Knopf, 1983) p. 189.
6 'Psychological Operations: Combat Multiplier, Peacetime Contributor', US Army Special Operations Command, Public Affairs Office, Release No. 307–17, 22 July 1993.
7 *Ibid.*
8 'UN air waves won Cambodia's heart', *Guardian*, 24 September 1993.
9 A. and H. Toffler, *War and Anti War*, (London, Little, Brown and Co., 1993) p. 238.
10 K. Spicer, 'To Combat Hate Broadcasts, Let's Try Propaganda for Peace', *International Herald Tribune*, 12 December 1994.
11 On Haiti, see Nik Gowing, 'Real-time television wins a war', *Independent*, 27 September 1994.
12 Roy Eldon Hiebert, 'Public Relations and a Weapon of Modern Warfare', in B. Greenberg and W. Gantz (eds), *Desert Storm and the Mass Media* (Creskill, NJ, Hampton Press, 1993) p. 31.

BIBLIOGRAPHY

A NOTE ON PRIMARY SOURCES

A glance at the footnotes will indicate the eclectic range of sources used for this book. Major archives used are the Public Records Office at Kew, the BBC Written Archives at Caversham (especially the Summaries of World Broadcasting and World Broadcasting Information), the Imperial War Museum and the Library of Congress in Washington. Also, the Institute of Communications at the University of Leeds has extensive audio-visual records, essentially from the period of its foundation in 1990. Its Gulf War archive has been drawn upon extensively for this book. I have also used the library at the US Air Force Special Operations School at Hurlbert Field in Florida and have drawn upon five years of interviews and discussions with military, diplomatic and journalistic personnel. Obviously, traditional newspaper sources have been consulted, but this is now greatly facilitated by accessing them on CD-Rom, where available. New technology provides exciting opportunities for gathering information on new topics. Some useful World Wide Web sites are also listed below (correct at the time of writing). But, with a topic like communications, matters change very rapidly, and so one must undertake research literally every day if one is to keep up to date with developments.

INTERNET/WWW SITES

BBC One World Online: http://www.bbcnc.org.uk
CNN: http://www.cnn.com
Federal Communications Commission: http://www/fcc.gov
Global democracy: http://www.igc.apc.org
Global Politics home page: http://www.yorku.ca
Institute for Propaganda Analysis: http://carmen.artsci.washington.edu
Institute for the Advanced Study of Infowar: http://www.psycom.net
International Telecommunications Union: gopher://info.itu.ch
Media Watchdog: http://theory.lcs.mit.edu
The Annenburg Washington Programme: http://www.annenburg.nwu.edu
The Press Association News Centre: http://www.pa.press.net
The Resource Centre for Communication: http://www.commweb.com
UK Government departments: http://open.gov.uk
UK Media Internet directory: http://www.mcc.ac.uk
United Nations: http://www.undp.org
United States Information Agency: http://www.usia.gov
US Army home page:http://www.army.mil

229

US Department of State Foreign Affairs Network: gopher://dosfan.lib.uic.edu
US Government sources: http://iridium.nttc.edu
US House of Representatives home page: http://www.house.gov
US Senate Gopher service: gopher://gopher.senate.gov

BOOKS

Adams, Valerie, *The Media and the Falklands Campaign* (Basingstoke, Macmillan, 1986)

Aldgate, Anthony, *Cinema and History: British Newsreels and the Spanish Civil War* (London, Scolar Press, 1979)

Allen, T. B., Berry, F. Clifton, and Polmar, N., *CNN: War in the Gulf. From the Invasion of Kuwait to the Day of Victory and Beyond* (London, Maxwell International, 1991)

Alleyne, Mark D., *International Power and International Communication* (London, St. Anthony's/Macmillan, 1995)

Anderson, Robin, *Media Transformation in the Age of Persuasion* (Boulder, Co., Westview Press, 1993)

Arnett, Peter, *Live from the Battlefield. 35 Years in the World's War Zones, from Vietnam to Baghdad* (New York, Simon and Schuster, 1994)

Artemov, V., *Information Abused: Critical Essays* (Moscow, Progress, 1981)

Article XIX, *Forging War: The Media in Serbia, Croatia and Bosnia-Herzengovina* (London, Article XIX, 1984)

Balfour, Michael, *Propaganda in War, 1939–45* (London, Routledge, 1979)

Barghoon, F. C., *Soviet Foreign Propaganda* (Princeton, Princeton University Press, 1964)

Barnouw, Erik, *Tube of Plenty: the evolution of American television* (Oxford, Oxford University Press, 2nd edition, 1990)

Bathurst, Robert B., *Intelligence and the Mirror: On Creating an Enemy* (London, Sage/PRIO, 1993)

Baudrillard, J., *In the Shadow of the Silent Majorities, or, The End of the Social and other essays* (trans. P. Foss, P. Patton and P. Beitchman), (New York, Semiotext(e), 1983)

Bell, Daniel, *The Coming of Post-Industrial Society. A Venture in Social Forecasting* (New York, Basic Books, 1973)

Bell, Martin, *In Harm's Way: Reflections of a War Zone Thug* (London, Hamish Hamilton, 1995)

Berman, Larry, *Lyndon Johnson's War: the road to stalemate in Vietnam* (New York, Norton, 1989)

Boorstein, Daniel, *The Image* (New York, Athenaeum, 1962)

Boyd-Barrett, O. and Kishan Thussu, D., *Contra-Flow in Global News: International and Regional News Exchange Mechanisms* (London, John Libbey, 1992)

Braestrup, Peter, *Big Story* (Boulder, Co., Westview Press, 1977)

Brinton, William M. and Ruler, Alan (eds), *Without Force or Lies: Voices from the Revolution of Central Europe in 1989–90* (New York, Mercury House, 1990)

Brivati, B., Buxton, J. and Seldon, A., *The Contemporary History Handbook* (Manchester, Manchester University Press, 1996)

Buitenhuis, Peter, *The Great War of Words: Literature as Propaganda 1914–18 and after* (London, Batsford, 1989)

Campen, Alan D. (ed.), *The First Information War: The Story of Communications, Computers, and Intelligence Systems in the Persian Gulf War* (Fairfax, VA: AFCEA International Press, 1992)

Carruthers, Susan, *Winning Hearts and Minds: British Governments, the Media and Counter Insurgency* (Leicester, Leicester University Press, 1995)

Cater, Douglas, *The Fourth Branch of Government* (Boston, Houghton Mifflin, 1959)

Challener, Alfred (ed.), *The Papers of Dwight David Eisenhower: vol. 4 The War Years* (Baltimore, Johns Hopkins University Press, 1970)

Chandler, Robert, *War of Ideas: The US Propaganda Campaign in Vietnam* (Boulder, Westview Press, 1981)

Chomsky, Noam, *Dettering Democracy* (New York, Hill and Wang, 1991)

Cockerell, Michael, *Live from Number 10: The Inside Story of Prime Ministers and Television* (London, Faber and Faber, 1988)

Cockett, Richard, *Twilight of Truth: Chamberlain, Appeasement and the Manipulation of the Press* (London, Weidenfeld and Nicolson, 1989)

Cohen, S. and Young, J., *The Manufacture of News: deviance, social problems and the mass media* (London, Constable, 1976)

Collins, Richard, *Culture, Communication and National Identity: the case of Canadian Television* (Toronto, University of Toronto Press, 1990)

Critchlow, James, *Radio Hole-in-the-Head. Radio Libert: an insider's story of Cold War broadcasting* (Washington DC, American University Press, 1995)

Cruickshank, C., *The Fourth Arm: Psychological Warfare, 1938–45* (London, Davis-Poynter, 1977)

Cudlipp, Hugh, *The Prerogative of the Harlot* (London, The Bodley Head, 1980)

Cull, Nicholas J., *Selling War: the British propaganda campaign against American 'Neutrality' in World War II* (Oxford, Oxford University Press, 1995)

Dallek, Robert, *The American Style of Foreign Policy: Cultural Politics and Foreign Affairs* (New York, Knopf, 1983)

Daugherty, W. and Janowitz, M. (eds), *A Psychological Warfare Casebook* (Baltimore, Johns Hopkins University Press, 1958)

de la Billiere, Sir Peter, *Storm Command: a personal account of the Gulf War* (London, Harper Collins, 1992)

Delmer, Sefton, *Black Boomerang* (London, Secker and Warburg, 1962)

Denton, Robert E. (ed.), *The Media and the Persian Gulf War* (London, Praeger, 1993)

Dilts, Marion May, *The Telephone in a Changing World* (New York, Longman's Green, 1941)

Downmount, Tony, *Channels of Resistance* (London, BFI, 1993)

Eksteins, Modris, *Rights of Spring: the Great War and the Birth of the Modern Age* (London, Bantam Press, 1989)

Farago, Ladilas, *War of Wits – the anatomy of Espionage* (New York, Paperback Library, 1954)

Fay, Sidney, *The Origins of the World War* (2nd edition, New York, Macmillan, 1948)

Fenby, J., *The International News Services* (New York, Schocken Books, 1986)

Fialka, John, *Hotel Warriors: Covering the Gulf War* (Washington, Woodrow Wilson Center Press, 1991)

Fiske, John, *Remote Control: Television Audiences and Cultural Power* (London, Routledge, 1989)

Flichy, P., *Dynamics of Modern Communications* (London, Sage, 1995)

Flourney, Don, *CNN World Report: Ted Turner's International News Coup* (London, John Libbey, 1992)

Fortner, Robert S., *International Communication: history, conflict and control of the global metropolis* (Belmont, Ca., Wadsworth Publishing Co., 1993)

——, *Public Diplomacy and International Politics: the symbolic constructs of summits and international radio news* (Westport, Praeger, 1994)

Franklin, Bob, *Packaging Politics* (London, Edward Arnold, 1993)

Friedland, Lewis, *Covering the World: International Television News Services* (New York, 20th Century Fund Press, 1992)

Fukuyama, Francis, *The End of History and the Last Man* (London, Hamish Hamilton, 1992)

Fuller, J. F. C., *Tanks in the Great War, 1914–18* (London, Murray, 1920)

Fussell, Paul, *The Great War and Modern Memory* (Oxford, Oxford University Press, 1975)

Galtung, J. and Vincent, R. C., *Global Glasnost: Toward a New International Information/Communication Order?* (Cresskill, NJ, Hampton Press, 1992)

Ganley, G. D., *The Exploding Power of Personal Media* (Norwood, NJ, Ablex, 1992)

Generous, Kevin, *Vietnam: the secret war* (New York, Gallery Books, 1985)

Gerbner, G., Mowlana, H. and Nordenstreng, K. (eds), *The Global Media Debate: its rise, fall, and renewal* (Norwood, NJ, Ablex, 1993)

Giddens, Anthony, *The Consequences of Modernity* (Cambridge, Polity, 1990)

Glasgow University Media Group, *War and Peace News* (Milton Keynes, Open University Press, 1995)

Gleick, James, *Chaos: Making a New Science* (Harmondsworth, Penguin, 1987)

Greenberg, Bradley and Gantz, Walter (eds), *Desert Storm and the Mass Media* (Creskill, NJ, Hampton Press, 1993)

Greene, H., *The Third Floor Front* (London, The Bodley Head, 1969)

Hale, Julian, *Radio Power: propaganda and international broadcasting* (London, Elek, 1975)

Hallin, Daniel, *The 'Uncensored War': The Media and Vietnam* (Oxford, Oxford University Press, 1986)

——, *We Keep America on Top of the World: Television Journalism and the Public Sphere* (London, Routledge, 1994)

Hamelink, Cees, *The Politics of World Communication* (London, Sage, 1994)

——, *World Communication: disempowerment and self-empowerment* (Zed Books, London and New Jersey, 1995

Herman, Edward and Chomsky, Noam, *Manufacturing Consent* (New York, Pantheon Books, 1988)

Hooper, Alan, *The Military and the Media* (Aldershot, Gower, 1984)

Howe, Ellic, *The Black Game* (London, Michael Joseph, 1982)

Hoyle, Trevor, *War Report: the war correspondent's view of battle from the Crimea to the Falklands* (London, Grafton Books, 1987)

Hudson, Heather, *Communication Satellites* (New York, Collier Macmillan, 1990)

Jarvie, Ian, *Hollywood's Overseas Campaign: The North Atlantic Movie Trade, 1920–50* (Cambridge, Cambridge University Press, 1992)

Jones, Nicholas, *Soundbites and Spindoctors: how politicians manipulate the media – and vice versa* (London, Cassell, 1995)

Keegan, John, *The Face of Battle* (London, Cape, 1976)

Kellner, D., *The Persian Gulf TV War* (Boulder, Westview Press, 1992)

Key, V. O., *Public Opinion and American Democracy* (New York, Knopf, 1961)

Kissinger, Henry, *Diplomacy* (New York, Simon and Schuster, 1994) pp. 667–8

Knightley, Philip, *The First Casualty: the war correspondent as hero, myth-maker and propagandist from the Crimea to Vietnam* (London, Quartet Books, 1975)

Kortunov, V., *The Battle of Ideas in the Modern World* (Moscow, Progress, 1979)

Lawrence, T. E., *The Severn Pillars of Wisdom* (London, Jonathan Cape, 1965 edition)

Lerner, D. (ed.), *Propaganda in War and Crisis* (New York, Stewart, 1950)

——, *The Passing of Traditional Society* (Glenco, Il., Free Press, 1958)

——, *Psychological Warfare Against Nazi Germany* (Boston, Mass., MIT Press, 1971 edition)

Libicki, Martin C., *What is Information Warfare?* (Washington, D.C., National Defense University Press, 1995)

Linebarger, Paul, *Psychological Warfare* (Washington DC, Infantry Journal Press, 1948)

Linfield, Michael, *Freedom under Fire: US Civil Liberties in Times of War* (Boston, Southend Press, 1990)

Lissan, M., *Broadcasting to the Soviet Union: International Politics and Radio* (New York, Praeger, 1975)

Lord, C. and Barnett, F. R. (eds), *Political Warfare and Psychological Operations: Rethinking the US Approach* (Washington DC, National Defense University Press, 1989)

MacArthur, John, *Second Front: Censorship and Propaganda in the Gulf War* (Berkeley, University of California Press, 1993 paperback edition)

McNair, B., *Images of the Enemy* (London, Routledge, 1988)

McQuail, Denis, *Mass Communications Theory* (London, Sage, 1987)

——, *Media Performance* (London, Sage, 1992)

Maitland, D., *The Missing Link* (Geneva, ITU, 1984) p. 13

Mansell, G., *Let the Truth be Told – 50 Years of BBC External Broadcasting* (London, Weidenfeld and Nicolson, 1982)

Matray, James L. (ed.), *Historical Dictionary of the Korean War* (London, Greenwood, 1991)

Mercer, Derrik, Mungham, Geoff and Williams, Kevin, *The Fog of War: The Media on the Battlefield* (London, Heinemann, 1987)

Messenger, Gary, *British Propaganda and the State in the First World War* (Manchester, Manchester University Press, 1992)

Meta, D. S., *Mass Media in the USSR* (Moscow, Progress, 1987)

Mickelson, S., *America's Other Voice: the story of Radio Free Europe and Radio Liberty* (New York, Praeger, 1982)

Mickiewicz, Ellen, *Split Signals. Television and Politics in the Soviet Union* (Oxford, Oxford University Press, 1988)

Miller, Nod and Allen, Rod, *It's Live, but is it Real?* (London, John Libbey, 1993)

Morgenthau, Hans, *Politics Amongst Nations* (New York, Knopf, 1978 edition)

Morrison, David, *Television and the Gulf War* (London, John Libbey, 1992)

Morrison, David and Tumber, H., *Journalists at War: the dynamics of news journalism* (London, Sage, 1988)

Mowlana, H., *Global Information and World Communication: New Frontiers in International Relations* (White Plains, NY, Longman, 1986)

Mowlana, H., Gerbner, G. and Schiller, H. I., *Triumph of the Image: The Media's War in the Persian Gulf: a global perspective* (Boulder, Westview Press, 1992)

Negroponte, Nicholas, *Being Digital* (London, Hodder and Stoughton, 1995)

Nicholas, Sian, *The Echo of War: Home Front Propaganda and the Wartime BBC, 1939–45* (Manchester, Manchester University Press, 1996)

Nicolson, Harold, *Diplomacy* (Oxford, Oxford University Press, 1963 edition)

Nordenstrung, K. and Varis, T., *Television Traffic – A One Way Street? A Survey and Analysis of the International Flow of Television Programme Material* (Paris, UNESCO, 1974)

Norris, Christopher, *Uncritical Theory: Postmodernism, Intellectuals and the Gulf War* (London, Lawrence and Wishart, 1992)

Nutting, Anthony, *No End of a Lesson* (London, Constable, 1967)

Paddock, Alfred H., *US Army Special Warfare: Its Origins* (Washington DC, National Defense University Press, 1982)

Page, Caroline, *U.S. Official Propaganda during the Vietnam War, 1965–73* (London, Leicester University Press, 1996)

Panfilov, A., *Broadcasting Pirates, or Abuse of the Microphone* (Moscow, Progress, 1981)

Parenti, Michael, *Inventing Reality* (New York, St. Martin's Press, 1986)

Parsons, Anthony, *From Cold War to Hot Peace: UN interventions, 1947–94* (London, Michael Joseph, 1995)

Pavlic, B., and Hamelink, C., *The New International Economic Order: Links between Economics and Communications* (Paris, UNESCO, 1985)

Pease, Stephen E., *Psywar: Psychological Warfare in Korea, 1950–53* (Harrisburg, Stackpole Books, 1992)

Pedelty, Mark, *War Stories: the culture of foreign correspondents* (London, Routledge, 1995)

Pick, Daniel, *War Machine: the rationalisation of slaughter in the modern age* (New Haven, Yale University Press, 1993)

Pilger, J., *Distant Voices* (London, Vintage, 1992)

Ponsonby, A., *Falsehood in Wartime* (London, Allen and Unwin, 1928)

Pool, I. de Sola, *Forecasting the Telephone: a retrospective technology assessment of the telephone* (Norwood, NJ, Ablex, 1983)

——, *Technologies of Freedom: On free speech in an electronic age* (London, Belknap Press, 1983)

Poole, De Witte C., *The Conduct of Foreign Relations under Modern Democratic Conditions* (New Haven, Yale University Press, 1924)

Powell, E. A., *The Army Behind the Army* (New York, C. Scribner's Sons, 1919)

Pratkanis, Anthony and Aronson, Elliot, *The Age of Propaganda: The Everyday Use and Abuse of Persuasion* (New York, W. H. Freeman and Co., 1991)

Prins, Gwyn (ed.), *Spring in Winter: the 1989 revolutions* (Manchester, Manchester University Press, 1990)

Prochnau, William, *Once Upon a Distant War: Reporting from Vietnam* (Edinburgh and London, Mainstream Publishing, 1996)

Qualter, T. H., *Propaganda and Psychological Warfare* (New York, Random House, 1962)

——, *Opinion Control in the Democracies* (London, Macmillan, 1985)

Rawnsley, Gary D., *Radio Diplomacy and Propaganda: the BBC and VOA in International Politics, 1956–64* (London, Macmillan, 1996)

Rees, Laurence, *Selling Politics* (London, BBC Books, 1992)

Reith, J. C. W., *Into the Wind,* (London, Hodder and Stoughton, 1949)

Reston, James, *The Artillery of the Press: Its Influence on American Foreign Policy* (New York, Harper and Row, 1967)

Roeder, George H., *The Censored War: American visual experience during World War Two* (New Haven, Yale University Press, 1993)

Rosenblum, Mort, *Coups and Earthquakes: Reporting the World for America* (New York, Harper and Row, 1979)

——, *Who Stole the News? Why we can't keep up with what happens in the world and what we can do about it* (New York, John Wiley, 1993)

Rubin, Barry, *International News and the American Media* (Beverly Hills, Sage, 1977)

Said, Edward, *Covering Islam* (New York, Jonathan Cape, 1983)

Sanders M. L. and Taylor, Philip M., *British propaganda during the First World War* (Basingstoke, Macmillan, 1982)

Serfaty, Simon (ed.), *The Media and Foreign Policy* (New York, St. Martin's Press, 1990)

Schiller, H. I., *Mass Communications and American Empire* (New York, August M. Kelly, 1969)

——, *Information Inequality: the deepening social crisis in America* (New York, Routledge, 1996)

Schlesinger, Philip, *Putting Reality Together* (London, Routledge, 1987)

Schlight, John, *The War in South Vietnam: The years of the Offensive, 1965–8* (Washington DC, Office of Air Force History, 1988) p. 244

Schramm, W., *Mass Media and National Development: the role of information in the developing countries* (Stanford, Cal., Stanford University Press, 1964)

Sharkey, J., *Under Fire: US Military Restrictions on the Media from Grenada to the Persian Gulf* (Washington DC, The Center for Public Integrity, 1992)

Sharp, Walter R. and Kirk, Grayson, *Contemporary International Politics* (New York, Rinehart and Co., 1940)

Shaw, Martin, *Civil Society and Media in Global Crises: Representing Distant Violence* (London, Pinter, 1996)

Shaw, Tony, *Eden, Suez and the Mass Media: Propaganda and Persuasion during the Suez Crisis* (London, I. B. Taurus, 1996)

Shultz, Richard H. and Godson, Roy, *Dezinformatsia: Active Measures in Soviet Strategy* (London, Pergamon/Brassey's, 1984)

Sigal, Leon V., *Reporters and Officials: the organization and politics of News-making* (Lexington, Mass., D. C. Heath, 1973)

Simpson, John, *From the House of War* (London, Arrow Books, 1991)

Smith, Hedrick (ed.), *The Media and the Gulf War* (Washington DC, Seven Locks Press, 1992)

Smith, Perry, *How CNN Fought the War* (New York, Birch Lane Press, 1991)

Soronsen, T., *The Word War* (New York, Harper and Row, 1968)

Spender, J. A., *The Public Life* (2 vols, London, Cassell, 1925)

Steele, Ronald, *Walter Lippmann and the American Century* (Boston, Little, Brown and Co., 1980)

Steiner, Zara, *The Foreign Office and Foreign Policy, 1898–1914* (Cambridge, Cambridge University Press, 1969)

Stewart, Colonel B., *Broken Lives: a personal view of the Bosnian Conflict* (London, Harper Collins, 1994)

Strange, Susan, *States and Markets: an introduction to international political economy* (London, Pinter, 1988)

Stuart, Sir Campbell, *Secrets of Crewe House* (London, Hodder and Stoughton, 1920)

Summers, Harry G. Jr., *On Strategy: A critical analysis of the Vietnam war* (New York, Dell Publishing, 1982)

Sun Tzu, *The Art of War* (trans. S. B. Griffiths) (Oxford, Oxford University Press, 1971)

Taylor, Philip M., *The Projection of Britain: British overseas publicity and propaganda, 1919–39* (Cambridge, Cambridge University Press, 1981)

——, *War and the Media: Propaganda and Persuasion in the Gulf War* (Manchester, Manchester University Press, 1992)

——, *Munitions of the Mind: a history of propaganda from the ancient world to the present era* (2nd edition, Manchester, Manchester University Press, 1995)

The Times, The History of The Times, vol. 3: The Twentieth Century Test, 1884–1912 (London, PHS, 1947)

Toffler, Alvin, *Future Shock* (London, Pan Books, 1970)

——, *The Third Wave* (London, Collins paperback edition, 1981)

Toffler, A. and Toffler, H., *War and Anti-War: Survival at the Dawn of the 21st Century* (London, Little, Brown and Co., 1993)

Tusa, John, *Conversations with the World* (London, BBC Books, 1990)

US News and World Report, Triumph without Victory: the Unreported History of the Persian Gulf War (New York, US News and World Report, 1992)

Voss, Frederick, *Reporting the War: the journalistic coverage of World War II* (New York, Greenwood Press, 1989)

Walker, Andrew, *A Skyful of Freedom* (London, Broadside, 1992)

Wallace, Carroll *Persuade or Perish* (Boston, Houghton Mifflin and Co., 1948)

Warburg, James P., *Unwritten Treaty* (New York, Harcourt Brace, 1946)

Webster, Frank, *Theories of the Information Society* (London, Routledge, 1995)

Weiner, R., *Live from Baghdad* (New York, Doubleday, 1992)

Wells, H. G., *'42 to '44: A Contemporary Memoir upon Human Behaviour during the crisis of the World Revolution* (London, Secker and Warburg, 1944)

Whitton, John B., *Propaganda and the Cold War* (Connecticut, Public Affairs Press, 1963)

Willis R. and Baran, S., *The Known World of Broadcast News* (London, Routledge, 1990)

Wood, J., *A History of International Broadcasting* (London, Peter Peregrinus, 1992)

Young, John, *Winston Churchill's Last Campaign: Britain and the Cold War, 1951–55* (Oxford, Clarendon Press, 1996)

Zeman, Z. A. B., *Nazi Propaganda* (Oxford, Oxford University Press, 1973)

ARTICLES, PAMPHLETS AND REPORTS

Active Measures: a report on the substance and process of anti-US Disinformation and Propaganda Campaigns, United States Department of State (DoS Publication 9630, August 1986)

Adams, James, 'Dawn of the Cyber Soldiers', *Sunday Times,* 15 October 1995

Adolph, Major Robert B. Jr., 'PSYOP: Gulf War Force Multiplier', *Army,* December 1992

Alberts, David. S. and Haynes, Richard E., 'The Realm of Information Dominance: Beyond Information War', First International Symposium on Command and Control Research and Technology (June 1995), pp. 560–65

Alexandre, L., 'Television Marti: Electronic Invasion in the post-Cold War', *Media, Culture and Society*, vol. 14 (1992) no. 4

Anderson, Robin, 'USIA Propaganda as Public Diplomacy', *Covert Action*, no. 39 (Winter 1991–2)

——, 'Media, Marketing and Politics in the Age of Fragmentation', in H. I. Schiller *et al.*, *The Ideology of International Communications* (New York, Institute for Media Analysis, Inc., 1992)

Annual Reports of the US Advisory Commission on Public Diplomacy.

Arqilla, John and Ronfeldt, David, 'Cyberwar is Coming!', *Journal of Comparative Strategy*, vol. 12 (1993) no. 2, pp. 141–65

Aukofer, Frank and Lawrence, William P., *America's Team: the Odd Couple. A Report on the Relationship between the Media and the Military* (Freedom Forum First Amendment Center, Vanderbilt University, Nashville, 1995)

Badsey, Stephen, *Modern Military Operations and the Media* (London, Strategic and Combat Studies Institute, 1994)

Barnes, Trevor, 'The Secret Cold War: the CIA and American Foreign Policy in Europe, 1946–56, Part 1 and Part 2', *Historical Journal*, vols 24 and 25, (1981 and 1982), pp. 399–415 and pp. 649–70 respectively

Baudrillard, J., 'The Reality Gulf', *Guardian*, 11 January 1991

Becker, Howard, 'The Nature and Consequences of Black Propaganda', *American Sociological Review*, vol. 14 (1949) pp. 221–34

Beschloss, Michael, 'Presidents, Television and Foreign Crises', (Washington DC, Annenburg Washington Programme in Communications Policy Studies of Northwestern University, 1993)

Bickham, Edward, 'Playing to the heart of the Nation', *Spectrum*, Autumn 1993

Borchini, Lt. Col. Charles P. and Borstelmann, Mari, 'PSYOP in Somalia: The Voice of Hope', *Special Warfare*, October 1994

Boyd-Barrett, Oliver, 'The Collection of Foreign News in the National Press', Part A of the Royal Commission on the Press, *Studies on the Press* (London, HMSO, 1977)

Brady, Major General Patrick, 'United States Army public affairs', *Despatches*, no. 2 (Autumn 1991)

Briggs, Asa, *The Communications Revolution* (Leeds, Leeds University Press, 1966)

British Executive of the International Press Institute, *Reporting the War: a collection of experiences and reflections on the Gulf*, a discussion paper published May 1991

Brock, P., 'Dateline Yugoslavia: the Partisan Press', *Foreign Policy*, vol. 48 (Winter 1993/4) no. 1

Browne, M., 'Vietnam Reporting: three years of crisis', *Columbia Journalism Review*, Fall 1964

Bruntz, G. C., 'Propaganda as an Instrument of Policy', *Current History*, July 1930

Capaccio, Tony, 'Commando Solo: Winning the Hearts and Minds of Haitians', *Defense Week*, 17 October 1994

Carey, James W., 'The Mass Media and Democracy: Between the Modern and the Postmodern', *Journal of International Affairs*, vol. 47 (Summer 1993) no. 1

Chiventone, F. J., 'Ethics and Responsibility in Broadcasting', *Military Review*, vol. 71 (1991) no. 8

Church, George C., 'This Time We Mean It: NATO's pull-back-or-we-bomb ultimatum to Bosnia's Serbs looks genuine, but will it help end the war?' *Time*, 21 February 1994

Cloughley, Brian, 'Peace in Mind: will the UN give psyops a chance?', *Jane's International Defence Review*, no. 3 (1996)

Daugherty, William, *The Art and Science of Psychological Operations: Case Studies of Military Applications*, vol. 1 (American Institutes for Research in the Behavioral Sciences, Department of the Army, Washington, 1976)

DoD Dictionary of Military and Associated Terms and Abbreviations, US Department of Defense, Joint Chiefs of Staff (JCS Publication 1–02, republished by Greenhill Books, 1990)

Dugan, Gen. Sir Michael, 'Generals versus Journalists', in H. Smith (ed.), *The Media and the Gulf War: the press and democracy in wartime* (Seven Locks Press, Washington, 1992)

Feldmann, L., 'Yeltsin welcomes Radio Liberty's presence in Russia', *Christian Science Monitor*, 4 September 1991

Field Manual 33–1: Psychological operations, U.S. Department of the Army (Washington DC, Government Printing Office, 1992)

Fortner, Robert S. and Durham, D. A., *A Worldwide Radio Receiver Population Analysis* (Washington, Academy for Educational Development, 1986)

Fourth Psychological Operations Group, *Psychological Operations Support for Operation Provide Comfort* (Fort Bragg, 1994)

Fourth Psychological Operations Group (A), *Psychological Operations Support to Noncombatant Evacuation Operations* (Fort Bragg, 1995)

Freedman, Lawrence, 'The media and foreign policy', *Despatches: the journal of the Territorial Army Pool of Information Officers*, 1996

Freund, C. P., 'The War on Your Mind: Psychological Warfare from Genghis Khan to PoWs to CNN', *The Washington Post*, 27 January 1991

Friedman, H. A., 'A brief look at Iraqi propaganda leaflets', *Perspectives*, Fall 1992

Fromm, Joseph, 'The Media and the Making of Defence Policy: the US example', in Christoph Betram (ed.), *Defence and Consensus: the domestic aspects of western security* (London, Macmillan/IISS, 1983)

Galtung, J. and Ruge, H., 'The Structure of Foreign News', *Journal of Peace Research*, no. 1 (1965)

Garnett Foundation, *The Media at War: the press and the Persian Gulf War* (New York, Columbia University Press, 1991)

Gerbner, G., 'Instant History: the case of the Moscow Coup', *Political Communication*, vol. 10 (1993)

Ghorpade, S., 'Foreign correspondents cover Washington for the world', *Journalism Quarterly*, vol. 61 (1984)

Gottschalk, M., 'Operation Desert Cloud: the Media and the Gulf War', *World Policy Journal*, vol. IX (1992) no. 3

Gowing, Nik, 'Real Time Television Coverage of Armed Conflicts and Diplomatic Crises: Does it Pressure or Distort Foreign Policy Decisions?', Discussion Paper 94–1, J. F. K. School of Government, Harvard University, June 1994

Haas, M. E., 'Air Commando! 1950–75: Twenty Five Years at the Tip of the Spear' (Hurlbert Field, 1994)

Hammelink, Cees, 'The Gulf War, the media and human rights', *Media Development*, October 1991

Hammond, William M., 'The Press in Vietnam as an Agent of Defeat: a critical examination', *Reviews in American History*, vol. 17 (1989) no. 2.

Harveson, P., 'A leader in Global TV News: aggressive expansion by CNN Television Network', *Financial Times*, 1 November 1994

Henry, William A., 'History as it Happens', *Time*, 6 January 1992

Herz, Martin F., 'Some Psychological Lessons from Leaflet Propaganda in World War II', *Public Opinion Quarterly*, Fall 1949

Hesse, Kurt R., 'Cross-Border Mass Communication from West to East Germany', *European Journal of Communications*, vol. 5 (1990) pp. 355–71

Hester, F., 'The News from Latin America via a World News Agency', *Gazette*, vol. 20 (1971) no. 2

Heuval, Jon Vanden, 'For the Media, a Brave (and Scary) New World', *Media Studies Journal*, Fall 1993 p. 17

Hoge, James F., 'The End of Predictability', *Media Studies Journal*, Fall 1993

Hopkinson, Nicholas, *The Media and International Affairs After the Cold War*, Wilton Park paper 74 (London, HMSO, 1993)

House Foreign Affairs Committee on the Impact of Television on U.S. Foreign Policy. Transcript supplied by the Federal News Service, Washington DC

House of Commons Defence Committee, First Report 1982–3, *The Handling of the Press and Public Information During the Falklands Conflict*, vols I and II (London, HMSO, 1982)

Hudson, Richard, 'The Issue of the Age: Unilateralism vs. Multilateralism. The UN Must do More, but who runs the Show?', *Global Report*, no. 37 (Winter 1992–3)

Hunter, Joe, 'Sowing Disorder, Reaping Disaster', *Covert Action*, no. 37 (Summer 1991)

Jones Sgt. P. and Jones, Col. J. B., 'Psychological Operations and Nation Building in Panama: Operation Promote Liberty', *Perspectives*, vol. 8 (Fall 1993) no. 3

Jones, Col. Jeffrey B., 'Psychological Operations in Desert Shield, Desert Storm and Urban Freedom', *Special Warfare*, July 1994

JUSPAO, 'The NVA Soldier in South Vietnam as a PSYOP Target', *Psyop Policy*, 20 February 1968, no. 59

Katz, E., 'The End of Journalism? Notes on Watching the War', *Journal of Communication*, vol. 42 (1992) no. 3

Kepplinger, H. M. and Kocher, R., 'Professionalism in Media Work', *European Journal of Communication*, vol. 5 (1990)

Kimball, Jeffrey P., 'The Stab-in-the-Back Legend and the Vietnam War', *Armed Forces and Society*, vol. 14 (1988) no. 13

Kissinger, Henry, 'An opportunity for a breakthrough', *Washington Post*, 17 November 1985

Larson, James, 'Global Television and Foreign Policy', *Foreign Policy Association Headline Series*, no. 283 (February 1988)

Layne, C. and Schwarz, B., 'American Hegemony – without an enemy', *Foreign Policy*, no. 92 (Fall 1993)

Lehman, Milton, 'We Must Sell America Abroad', *Saturday Evening Post*, 15 November 1947

Lerner, D., 'The Psychological Warfare Campaign Against Germany: D-Day to VE-Day', in Anthony Rhodes, *Propaganda – The Art Of Persuasion: World War II* (New York, Chelsea House, 1976)

Levinson, Nan, 'Snazzy visuals, hard facts and obscured issues', *Index on Censorship*, vol. 20 (April/May 1991) nos 4 and 5

Lovering, Captain Tristan, 'Grappling with the News', *Despatches*, no. 5 (Spring 1995) p. 82

Lucas, Scott, 'Campaigns of Truth: the Psychological Strategy Board and American Ideology, 1951–53', *The International History Review*, vol. XVIII (May 1996) no. 2, pp. 279–302

MacBride, S., *Many Voices, One World* (Paris, UNESCO, 1980)

McCombs, Maxwell E. and Shaw, Donald, 'The agenda-setting function of the mass media', *Public Opinion Quarterly*, vol. 35 (1972)

McNulty, T., 'Television's Impact on Executive Decision-Making and Diplomacy', *The Fletcher Forum of World Affairs*, vol. 17 (Winter 1993)

Magsig, Daniel E., 'Information Warfare in the Information Age', http://www.psycom.net

Makinda, Samuel, 'Seeking Peace from Chaos: Humanitarian Intervention in Somalia', International Peace Academy, Occasional Paper series (Boulder, Lynne Reinner, 1993)

Massing, M., 'Debriefings: what we saw, what we learned', *Columbia Journalism Review*, May–June 1991

Matlock, Jack, 'The Diplomat's View of the Press and Foreign Policy', *Media Studies Journal*, Fall 1993

May, Ernest R., 'The News Media and Diplomacy', in Gordon A. Craig and Francis L. Loewenheim, *The Diplomats, 1939–79* (Princeton, Princeton University Press, 1994)

Meade, G., 'Hard Groundrules in the Sand', *Index on Censorship*, vol. 20 (April/May 1991) nos. 4 and 5

Morrow, Capt. Janice M., 'Never Seen, Always Heard', *Airman*, February 1993

Mould, Donald H., 'Press Pools and Military–Media Relations in the Gulf War: a case study of the Battle of Khafji, January 1991', *Historical Journal of Film, Radio and Television*, vol. 16 (June 1996) no. 2

Mowlana, H., 'Toward a NWICO for the Twenty First Century', *Journal of International Affairs*, vol. 47 (Summer 1993) no. 1

Nathan, R. S., 'Psychological Warfare: key to success in Vietnam', *Military Review*, April 1968, p. 28

Nohrstedt, Stig, 'Ideological News Reporting from the Third World', *European Journal of Communication*, vol. 1 (1986) no. 4

Noyes, Harry F., 'New Master Weapon – News Media', *Military Review*, August 1991

Oldendick, Robert W. and Bardes, Barbara A., 'Mass and Elite Foreign Policy Opinions', *Public Opinion Quarterly*, vol. 45 (1982) pp. 368–82

Ottosen, Rune, 'The Gulf War with the Media as Hostage', PRIO Report No. 4, October 1991

——, 'Media and War Reporting: Public Relations vs. Journalism', PRIO Report No. 5, 1992

Paddock. Alfred H., ' "No More Tactical Information Detachments": US Military Psychological Operations in Transition', *Low Intensity Conflict and Law Enforcement*, vol. 2 (1993) no. 2

——, 'Psyop in the early 1980s: the way we were', *Special Warfare*, 6 (October 1993) p. 4

Parker, Jay M. and Hale, Jerold L., 'Psychological Operations in the Gulf War: Analyzing Key Themes in Battlefield Leaflets', in Thomas A. McCain and Leonard Shyles (eds), *The 1,000 Hour War: Communication in the Gulf* (Westport, Connecticut, Greenwood Press, 1994)

Philo, Greg, 'From Buerk to Band Aid: the media and the 1984 Ethiopian Famine', in John Eldridge (ed.), *Getting the Message: News, Truth and Power* (London, Routledge, 1993)

Pogue, Jim, 'Radio Democracy', *Monitoring Times*, vol. 13 (September 1994) no. 9

'Psychological Operations During Desert Shield/Desert Storm: A Post-Operational Analysis' (USSOC, 1993)

Reynolds, M., 'The War Correspondent's Job', *Army Quarterly and Defence Journal*, vol. 59 (January 1950)

Rogers, Paul, 'The Myth of the Clean War', *Covert Action*, no. 37 (1991)

Schapiro, L., 'The International Department of the CPSU: Key to Soviet Policy', *International Journal* (Winter 1976–77)

Schlesinger, Philip, 'From Production to Propaganda', *Media, Culture and Society*, vol. 11 (1989) no. 3

Sconyers, Col. Ronald T., 'The Information War', *Military Review*, February 1989

Shelton, Lt. Gen. H. Hugh and Vane, Lt. Gen. Timothy D., 'Winning the Information War in Haiti', *Military Review*, vol. LXXV (November–December 1995) no. 6

Sidle, Winant, 'A Battle behind the Scenes: The Gulf War Reheats Military–Media Controversy', *Military Review*, no. 9 (September 1991)

Smith, Howard, 'The BBC Television Newsreel and the Korean War', *Historical Journal of Film, Radio and Television*, vol. 8 (1988) no. 3

Smith, Major R. R., 'The Use of Psychological Operations, and their Role in the Return to Normality in Bosnia-Herzegovina', *British Army Review*, no. 114 (December 1996), pp. 13–19

Soviet Influence Activities: a report on active measures and propaganda, 1987–88, United States Department of State (DoS Publication 9720, August 1989)

Stech, Frank J., 'Winning CNN Wars', *Parameters*, Autumn 1994

Stone, Lt. Col. D. J. A., ' "Out of the Shadows": The re-emergence of the UK's Psychological Operations capability since 1945', *British Army Review*, no. 114 (December 1996) pp. 3–12

Summe, Major Jack N., 'PSYOP Support to Operation Desert Storm', *Special Warfare*, October 1992

Taylor, Philip M. 'The Impact of the First World War upon Foreign Office attitudes to the press', in David N. Dilks (ed.), *Retreat from Power* vol. I (Basingstoke, Macmillan, 1981)

——, *A Call to Arms: Propaganda and Rearmament in the 1930s* (British Universities Historical Studies in Film, 1985)

——, 'Censorship in Britain in World War Two: an overview', in A. C. Duke and G. Tanse (eds), *Too mighty to be free: Censorship and the Press in Britain and Netherlands* (Zutphen, de Walburg Pers, 1987)

——, 'Back to the Future? Integrating the media into the history of international relations', *Historical Journal of Film, Radio and Television*, vol. 14 (1994) 3

——, 'Wayne's World: "The Green Berets" ', *History Today*, March 1994

——, 'Film as a Weapon in the Second World War', in D. Dutton (ed.), *Statecraft and Diplomacy: Essays presented to P. M. H. Bell* (Liverpool, Liverpool University Press, 1995)

Thimmes, Col. Thomas A., 'Military Psychological Operations in the 1990s', *Special Warfare*, January 1994

Virilio, P., 'Red Alert in Cyberspace', *Radical Philosophy*, no. 74 (November/December 1995)

Walker, Fred W., 'Truth is the Best Propaganda: a study in military psychological operations', *National Guard Magazine*, October 1987

Waller, Douglas, 'Onward Cyber Soldiers', *Time*, 21 August 1995

Wallingford, S., 'Western Samoa Operations, 1930: Air Report', *Royal Air Force Quarterly*, vol. 1 (1930) no. 4

York, Ken, 'PSYOP Personnel Put the Word Out', *Armed Forces Journal International*, December 1993

Young, Christopher, 'The role of the media in international conflict', a report on a two-day seminar at the Canadian Institute for International Peace and Security, December 1991

UNPUBLISHED THESES

Al-Ahmady, Taleb, 'The image of Saudi Arabia in the British Press, with particular reference to Saudi Arabia's Islamic Mission', University of Leeds PhD thesis, 1995

Afkhami, Hossein, 'Foreign News Coverage by the Media during the British General Elections of 1979, 1983, 1987 and 1992', University of Leeds PhD thesis, 1995

Carruthers, Susan, 'Political Violence, Propaganda and Persuasion: The Presentation of Terrorism in the Media', University of Leeds PhD thesis, 1994

Cornwall, Mark, 'The Role of Allied Propaganda in the Collapse of the Austro-Hungarian Empire in 1918', University of Leeds PhD thesis, 1988

Cull, N. J. 'The British Campaign Against American "Neutrality"; Policy and Propaganda, 1939–41', University of Leeds PhD thesis, 1992

Rawnsley, Gary D., 'Nation Unto Nation: the BBC and VOA in International Politics, 1956–64', University of Leeds PhD thesis, 1994.

INDEX